Lecture Notes of the Institute for Computer Sciences, Social Informatics and Telecommunications Engineering

282

More information about this series at http://www.springer.com/series/8197

Jiyu Jin · Peng Li · Lei Fan (Eds.)

Green Energy
and Networking

6th EAI International Conference, GreeNets 2019
Dalian, China, May 4, 2019
Proceedings

 Springer

Editors
Jiyu Jin
Dalian Polytechnic University
Dalian, China

Peng Li
Dalian Polytechnic University
Dalian, China

Lei Fan
Dalian Polytechnic University
Dalian, China

ISSN 1867-8211 ISSN 1867-822X (electronic)
Lecture Notes of the Institute for Computer Sciences, Social Informatics
and Telecommunications Engineering
ISBN 978-3-030-21729-7 ISBN 978-3-030-21730-3 (eBook)
https://doi.org/10.1007/978-3-030-21730-3

This Springer imprint is published by the registered company Springer Nature Switzerland AG
The registered company address is: Gewerbestrasse 11, 6330 Cham, Switzerland

Preface

We are delighted to present the proceedings of the sixth edition of the 2019 European Alliance for Innovation (EAI) International Conference on Green Energy and Networking (GreeNets). This conference aimed at establishing a multidisciplinary scientific meeting to discuss complex societal, technological, and economic problems of green communication and green IoT for researchers, developers, and practitioners around the world. All of the topics related to these subjects were addressed during the GreeNets 2019 conference.

The technical program of GreeNets 2019 consisted of 29 full papers in oral presentation sessions during the main conference tracks. The conference tracks were: Track 1—Green Cooperative Communication; Track 2—Green IoT; Track 3—IT Energy-Aware Technologies; and Track 4—Light and Lighting. Aside from the high-quality technical paper presentations, the technical program also featured two keynote speeches. The two keynote speeches were given by Dr. Su Hu from the University of Electronic Science and Technology of China and Dr. Fan-Yi Meng from Harbin Institute of Technology.

It was a great pleasure to work with the excellent organizing team of the EAI, which was absolutely essential for the success of the GreeNets 2019 conference. In particular, the peer-review process of papers led to a high-quality technical program compiled by the Technical Program Committee. We are also grateful to all the authors who submitted their papers to the GreeNets 2019 conference.

We strongly believe that the GreeNets 2019 conference provided a good forum for all researchers, developers, and practitioners to discuss all scientific and technological aspects of green energy and networking. We are pleased that the GreeNets 2019 conference was successful and stimulating, as indicated by the contributions presented in this volume.

May 2019

Jiyu Jin
Peng Li
Xin Liu

Organization

Steering Committee

Imrich Chlamtac   Bruno Kessler University of Trento, Italy

Organizing Committee

General Chairs

Jiyu Jin   Dalian Polytechnic University, China
Peng Li   Dalian Polytechnic University, China
Xin Liu   Dalian University of Technology, China

TPC Chairs

Peng Li   Dalian Polytechnic University, China
Zhenyu Na   Dalian Maritime University, China

Sponsorship and Exhibit Chairs

Guan Gui   Nanjing University of Posts and Telecommunications,
                               China
Jun Mou   Dalian Polytechnic University, China

Local Chairs

Zijun Gao   Dalian Polytechnic University, China
Yang Liu   Liaoning Normal University, China

Workshops Chair

Xin Liu   Dalian University of Technology, China

Publicity and Social Media Chairs

Haijun Zhang   University of Science and Technology Beijing, China
Jinpeng Wang   Dalian Polytechnic University, China

Publications Chairs

Lei Fan   Dalian Polytechnic University, China
Su Hu   University of Electronic Science and Technology
                               of China, China

Web Chair

Xinzhe Wang   Dalian Polytechnic University, China
Lisheng Fan   Guangzhou University, China

Technical Program Committee

Fanyi Meng   Harbin Institute of Technology, China
Guiyue Jin   Dalian Polytechnic University, China
Guan Gui   Nanjing University of Posts and Telecommunications,
                                China
Hong Tang   Dalian University of Technology, China
Haijun Zhang   University of Science and Technology Beijing, China
Jie Tang   South China University of Technology, China
Jun Mou   Dalian Polytechnic University, China
Lisheng Fan   Guangzhou University, China
Mingjun Li   Central South University, China
Su Hu   University of Electronic Science and Technology
                                of China, China
Xiaohong Gao   Jilin Jianzhu University, China
Xiaolin Jiang   Heilongjiang University of Science and Technology,
                                China
Xueyan Zhang   Dalian University of Technology, China
Xuemei Li   Dalian Jiaotong University, China
Yang Liu   Liaoning Normal University, China
Zheng Chang   University of Jyvaskyla, China

Contents

Green IoT

Energy-Efficient Networking

Lighting Measurements and Evaluation

Green Cooperative Communication

The Research of Non-cooperative Power Control Method Based on Fairness and User Selection Strategy in Cognitive Radio Networks

Guanglong Yang$^{(\boxtimes)}$, Xuezhi Tan, and Xiao Wang

School of Electronics Information Engineering, Harbin Institute of Technology,
Harbin 150001, People's Republic of China
yang3616@126.com, {Tanxz1957,hitwx}@hit.edu.cn

Abstract. When studying the power control problem of cognitive radio based on non-cooperative game theory, most scholars pay more attention to constraints such as interference, signal-to-noise ratio of secondary users, primary user interference threshold and so on. Optimization objectives focus on system throughput, system energy consumption, convergence rate, etc. The fairness problem caused by secondary users in order to increase system throughput is ignored, and the research on whether all the secondary users participate in the communication meets the communication conditions is in blank state. Based on the fairness problem, an automatic power control game algorithm based on cost function is proposed in this paper. When the cost function is designed, the influence of distance on channel gain is fully considered, and the penalty mechanism is introduced by adjusting the weight adaptively. The interference between users is reduced, and the near-far effect caused by different user location is effectively overcome. In order to solve the problem of whether the secondary users meet the communication conditions, a sub-user selection strategy is proposed to accurately control the secondary users who participate in the communication, thus avoiding the hidden danger to the stability of the system caused by the users who do not meet the communication conditions. The necessity and practical value of the user selection strategy are verified by simulation. At the same time, the performance of the proposed algorithm in convergence speed and energy saving is also highlighted.

Keywords: Cognitive radio · Underlay spectrum sharing ·
Distributed power control

1 Introduction

With the rapid development of communication technology and the increase of communication services, the demand for wireless spectrum resources is becoming more and more intense. For example, with the popularity of the Internet of things and the popularization of vehicle networking equipment, the number of frequency points is increasing; for example, the development of video services, the improvement of bandwidth requirements. This requires more advanced wireless systems that can

© ICST Institute for Computer Sciences, Social Informatics and Telecommunications Engineering 2019
Published by Springer Nature Switzerland AG 2019. All Rights Reserved
J. Jin et al. (Eds.): GreeNets 2019, LNICST 282, pp. 3–13, 2019.
https://doi.org/10.1007/978-3-030-21730-3_1

accommodate more users and provide higher throughput. Cognitive radio technology has effectively improved the throughput of the next generation communication terminals. Enabling cognitive users to access free spectrum at any time, anywhere, many scholars have done a lot of work on optimization of cognitive users [1–3].

In reference [4–7], the distributed power control of cognitive radio is studied based on the user model. For the cognitive radio network model of a primary user and a secondary user in a cognitive system, Srinivasa and Bansal proposed a distributed power control algorithm. However, a user scenario is a special case, and the proposed algorithm is difficult to extend to multi-user systems. Sun et al. have improved the cognitive model and increased the number of secondary users. In the underlay cognitive radio network, the distributed power control problem is studied with the minimum transmit power as the optimization objective. Jin et al. extended the cognitive model to coexistence of multiple secondary users and multiple primary users, and studied the distributed power control problem in multi-user scenarios [7]. If each cognitive user wantonly increases their transmit power in order to maximize their throughput, the cognitive system will undoubtedly interfere with the primary user and other secondary users. The inherent competition problem of distributed power control problem urges us to use game theory to solve this problem.

In the framework of game theory, utility functions are used to quantify user satisfaction. The goal of each user is to maximize utility functions. So the design of utility function is very important. K-G algorithm and SINR balance algorithm are the classical power control game algorithms. Goodman and Mandayam proposed a model of non-cooperative game power control (Non-cooperative Power Control Game) [8], and proved the existence of Nash equilibrium, but the equilibrium solution is not always optimal. Furthermore, the non-cooperative mode power control problem based on cost (Pricing) [9] is studied. It is proved that Pareto is superior to Pareto in improving (Pareto Dominance), but it affects the fairness of signal quality in the receiver to some extent. Increased computational complexity. Nadkar et al. proposed a distributed power control algorithm based on game theory, which achieves the maximum throughput per secondary user [10].

Although some good results have been achieved in some aspects, most of the literatures do not refine the multi-user interference, do not consider the fairness of the signal quality at the receiver, and ignore the discussion of different parameter selection range and energy consumption.

In reference [11], the author discusses energy efficiency in OFDM cognitive radio networks using a game theory approach. In reference [12], a new utility function based on chaos is introduced to design the power control algorithm, which fully considers the interference from the primary user and the interference threshold constraint of the primary user, and proves the existence of Nash equilibrium, which reduces the power consumption. The convergence rate is improved. In reference [13], a non-cooperative game power control scheme was proposed considering the cognitive user fairness, and the sliding model iterative algorithm was used to improve the total throughput of the system.

In the design of utility function, most scholars think more about convergence, user satisfaction, algorithm complexity, etc. There is less research on whether the convergent user satisfies the communication condition, and how to select the secondary user who meets the communication condition.

In order to solve the above problems, this paper is organized as follows: Sect. 2 establishes the system model and communication scene. Section 3 optimizes the mathematical model. In Sect. 4, a power iterative algorithm is proposed. Section 5 proposes user selection strategy. In Sect. 6, the simulation results are given. Section 7 conclusion.

2 System Model

In this paper, the underlay spectrum access mode is considered, so it is unnecessary to consider the communication situation of the primary user, and the time of sensing and judging the primary user's activity is reduced indirectly. This paper considers the underlay multi-user distributed cognitive radio scene, as shown in Fig. 1. Primary and secondary users coexist in the network, including M for secondary users, N for primary users. The secondary user is represented by the set $A = \{1, 2, \cdots, M\}$ and the primary user by the set $B = \{1, 2, \cdots, N\}$. Order $\forall i,j \in A, \forall k \in B$.

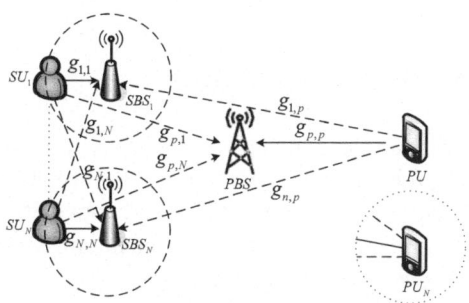

Fig. 1. Cognitive system model.

Assuming that the channel is flat fading, the average SINR of SU_i can be expressed as:

$$\bar{\gamma}_i = \frac{\bar{g}_{i,i} p_i}{N_s + N_p + \delta^2} \tag{1}$$

Which is

$$N_S = \sum_{j=1, j \neq i}^{M} \bar{g}_{i,j} p_j, \quad N_P = \bar{g}_{i,p} p_p, \quad p_i \in \left[0, p_i^{\max}\right]$$

$g_{i,i}$, Instantaneous link gain from SU_i to SBS_i; $g_{i,j}$, Instantaneous link gain from SU_i to PBS; $g_{p,i}$, Instantaneous link gain from SU_i to PBS; $g_{p,p}$, Instantaneous link gain from PU to PBS; $g_{i,p}$, Instantaneous link gain from PU to SBS_i; p_i, the i th secondary user transmit power; $p_i^{\max}$, Secondary user maximum transmit power; p^{total}, Total interference power from SU_i to primary user; p^{th}, Main user's interference threshold; N_S, Other secondary user interference; N_P, Primary user interference; δ^2, Background noise; γ_i^{th}, The SINR value for the i th secondary user when the QoS requirement is satisfied.

In order to ensure the normal communication of the primary user, the interference power cannot exceed the interference threshold of the primary user. Therefore, in order to meet the interference threshold, the total interference power of the secondary user must be met

$$p^{total} = \sum_{i=1}^{N} p_i \bar{g}_{p,i} \leq p^{th} \tag{2}$$

In a cognitive system, in order to ensure a secondary user's QoS requirements, each secondary user's receiving SINR needs to meet a certain threshold value:

$$\bar{\gamma}_i \geq \gamma_i^{th} \tag{3}$$

3   Optimization Mathematical Model

In the following chapters, we select an appropriate utility function and use the iterative algorithm to solve the problem, and prove the existence and uniqueness of Nash equilibrium. In order to ensure the non-negativity and convexity of utility function, the SINR requirement of secondary user γ_i^{th} and the maximum transmit power limit $p_i^{\max}$ should be considered in selecting utility function.

$$u_i(p_i, p_{-i}) = \alpha \log(\bar{\gamma}_i - \gamma_i^{th}) + \beta(p_i^{\max} - p_i)^{\frac{1}{2}} \tag{4}$$

Where α and β are non-negative weight factors. How to choose the weight Factor in the expression of Utility function α and β is very important. Based on the degree of interference, the high power threshold is chosen when the primary user is far from the cognitive network, and the low power threshold is chosen when the primary user is close to the cognitive network. Select the appropriate SINR threshold γ_i^{th} according to QoS requirements. If $\bar{\gamma}_i < \gamma_i^{th}$, α and β remain unchanged; if $\bar{\gamma}_i > \gamma_i^{tar}$, adaptive weight adjustment by $\beta_{i+1} = \beta_i \bar{\gamma}_i / \gamma_i^{th}$. Secondary users reduce interference with other users by punishing themselves.

4   Power Iterative Algorithm

In this section, we propose an iterative power control algorithm. The i th secondary user power iteration function can be represented as

$$p_i^{(m+1)} = \begin{cases} \dfrac{p_i^{(m)}}{\bar{\gamma}_i^{(m)}} \gamma_i^{th} + \dfrac{2\alpha_i}{\beta_i} \left(p_i^{\max} - p_i^{(m)} \right)^{\frac{1}{2}} & p_i^{(m+1)} < p_i^{\max} \\[3mm] p_i^{\max} & p_i^{(m+1)} \geq p_i^{\max} \end{cases} \tag{5}$$

Each secondary user is updated iteratively until the utility function in (4) is maximized. An automatic non-cooperative power control algorithm designed in this paper (APCGA, Automatic Power Control Game Algorithms). The process is as follows:

Step 1: Initialization power vector $p_i(0)$ and p_0, count $\gamma_i(0)$.

Step 2: If $\bar{\gamma}_i < \gamma_i^{th}$, β_i remain unchanged; otherwise automatically adjust β_i through $\beta_{i+1} = \beta_i \bar{\gamma}_i / \gamma_i^{th}$.

Step 3: Order $m = m + 1$, recalculate power $p_i^{(m+1)}$ using.

If $p_i^{(m+1)}$ meet (2), go on, otherwise the iteration stops.

Step 4: The i th secondary user, $|U_i^{(m+1)} - U_i^{(m)}| < \omega$ (precision $\omega > 0$), the iteration stops; Otherwise, return to step 2.

5 User Selection Strategy

If we do not consider whether the secondary user satisfies the communication condition, we can use the power iteration algorithm in Sect. 4 to solve the transmission power of this user. However, by carefully analyzing the utility function of expression (4), we find that the utility function only constrains the convergence of the function itself, but does not correlate with whether the actual secondary user satisfies the cognitive radio communication. As a result, some secondary users appear to converge through iterative algorithms, but they do not meet their own SINR requirements. We assume a multiple user model, in which the i th secondary user is a little far away. This scenario can cause the i th secondary user to converge to transmit power $p_i = p_i^{\max}$ after formula (4) iteration, but it cannot meet the $\bar{\gamma}_i \geq \gamma_i^{th}$ requirements, so the user is an interference source in the system. The existence of these users caused great interference to the system, and even directly affected the stability of the system. As can be seen from formula (2), the excessive number of cognitive users will lead to the failure of formula (2), that is, the cognitive system has a certain limit on the number of cognitive users, if this limit is exceeded, It is bound to interfere with the primary user. These two cases can be called cognitive user selection problem, which has been neglected in the research of cognitive radio power control. However, in practical applications, how to select cognitive users is a problem to be considered.

5.1 Cognitive User Selection

The following discusses how to screen and accept cognitive users, eliminating interference and ensuring system capacity.

(1) Primary election

Because the distance between users determines the size of the channel gain, interference constraints can be represented as

$$p_i^{\max} \bar{g}_{p,i}^{\min} \le p_i^{th(\min)} \tag{6}$$

Assume that the secondary user location can be obtained by perception. Through formula (6), cognitive primary selection can be realized, although it is slightly conservative, the primary user can be protected to the greatest extent. The remaining secondary user collection is

$$\Theta = A - \Psi \tag{7}$$

Where Ψ is the set of selected users, and $\Theta = \{1, 2, \cdots, K\}$ is the set of excluded users. Order $\forall \lambda, \rho \in \Theta$.

Cognitive user in set Ψ uses 3.5-Section iterative algorithm to solve the transmit Power of Cognitive user.

2. Admit

Formula (1) can be converted into formula

$$\frac{\bar{\gamma}_\lambda \times \left(N_\Theta + N_s + N_p + \delta^2 \right)}{\bar{g}_{\lambda,\lambda}} = p_\lambda$$
$$N_\Theta = \sum_{\rho=1,\rho\neq\lambda}^{k} \bar{g}_{\lambda,\rho} p_\rho \tag{8}$$

All satisfying $p_\lambda < p_i^{\max}$ sub-user sets are accepted by Z and merged with the original Ψ set to form a set of users that ultimately allow communication to recognize

$$\Xi = Z + \Psi \tag{9}$$

In the set Ξ, cognitive users are solved by 3. 5 iterative algorithm.

Through (1) primary selection and (2) admission operation, cognitive user selection is completed.

5.2 Cognitive User Capacity

Assuming that the number of secondary users M in the secondary user set A far exceeds the maximum number of users in the cognitive system, it is necessary to select the secondary users who participate in the communication. In order to minimize the energy consumption of the secondary user, it is necessary to solve and compare the different sub-user combinations. One method is to obtain the maximum strategy set of the sub-user combination through exhaustive method, which will greatly increase the system delay. The complexity of the algorithm is increased and the system needs to be optimized again when the secondary user launches the communication or the new secondary user joins in the communication.

Next, we adopt the sub-optimal scheme for the selection of secondary users. The selection criteria are that the set of secondary users can meet the rapid convergence, and the cognitive system can accommodate more user directions and adopt a random selection method.

$$M' \leq \frac{p^{th(\min)}}{p_i^{\max} \bar{g}_{p,i}} \tag{10}$$

where

$p^{th(\min)}$ is primary user minimum interference threshold
$p_i^{\max}$ is maximum estimated transmit power for secondary users
$\bar{g}_{p,i}$ is average channel gain

The selection process is as follows

Step 1: Preliminary definition of system capacity M' by formula (9).
Step 2: Perform the 5.1 (1) primary step, if $M' < \Psi$ element number, random extraction of M' th secondary users from a set Ψ; if $M' \geq \Psi$ element number, represents that all secondary users in the set Ψ can be accommodated by the cognitive system.
Step 3: The second user set is selected and the cognitive user transmit power is solved by 5 section iterative algorithm.
Step 4: Perform step (2) admission in 5.1 to form a set of users that ultimately allow communication cognition.

6 Simulation Results and Analysis

In this section, the performance of the algorithm is simulated. Parameters are set as follows: assumed channel gain $h_i = 0.075 \times d_i^{-3.6}$. The location of the secondary user is randomly generated in the cognitive network. The transmission power initialized is $p_i(0) = 5 \times 10^{-15}$ W. The transmission power of the primary user is $p_0 = 0.05$ W, maximum transmit power of secondary user is $p_i^{\max} = 1$ W. The SINR threshold is set to $\gamma_i^{th} = 7$ dB. The threshold for interference temperature is $p^{th} = 3 \times 10^{-3}$ mW. Background noise is $\sigma^2 = 5 \times 10^{-15}$ W, $\omega = 10^{-15}$, $2\alpha/\beta = 3 \times 10^{-4}$.

6.1 Scenario 1

Firstly, the fairness of the proposed algorithm is verified, assuming that four secondary users and one primary user share spectrum resources. After the iteration is stabilized, three new users are added, assuming that the 7 users meet the communication requirements of the cognitive system after selection.

From the above simulation, we can see that the convergence of the proposed algorithm is very obvious, which means that the proposed algorithm can adapt to the dynamic network environment and rapidly converge to the real Nash equilibrium point.

Because of the distributed control, the information exchange between users is less, so the time to converge to the stable point is faster. It can be clearly seen in Figs. 2 and 3 that secondary users converge to different transmit power with different positions, which fully proves the fairness of the proposed algorithm. By comparing Figs. 2 and 3, we can see that as the number of secondary users in the cognitive system increases, the convergent transmit power of each secondary user becomes larger, because as the number of secondary users increases, there is also an increase in inter-system inter-ference. In order to meet their own SINR requirements, secondary users are bound to enhance transmission power.

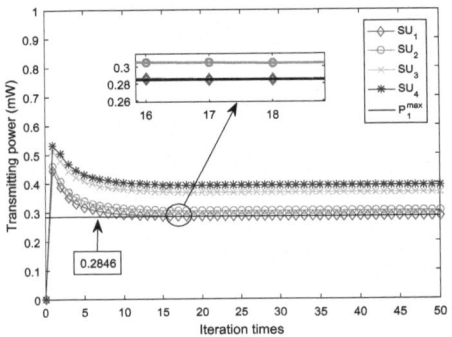

Fig. 2. User transmit power converges with iteration number (M = 7, N = 1)

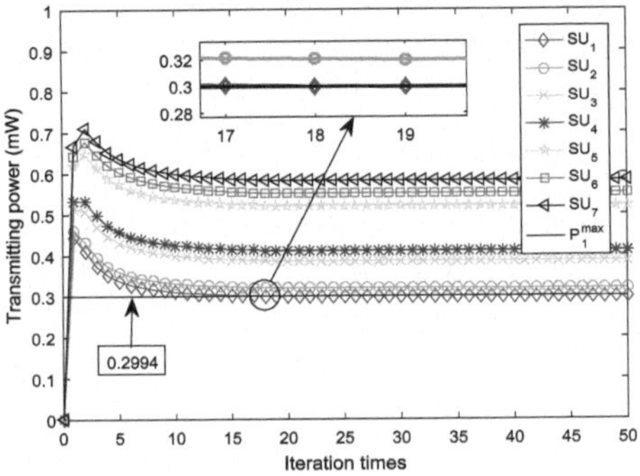

Fig. 3. User transmit power converges with iteration number (M = 4, N = 1)

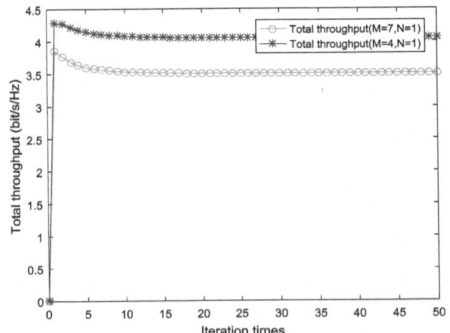

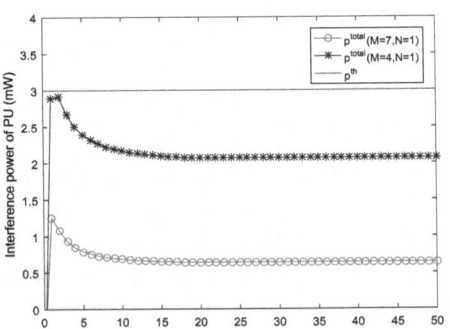

Fig. 4. Total user throughout varies with iterations

Fig. 5. Main user interference power varies with iteration number

Figure 4 shows that the total throughput of the system converges to a stable value, and the throughput increases with the increase in the number of secondary users, but the increase is not directly proportional to the increase in the number of secondary users, because as the number of secondary users increases, so does the interference of the system. The more the secondary users increase, the greater the system interference.

When the number of secondary users tends to saturation, the total throughput of the system also tends to saturation. Figure 5 shows that the primary user interference tends to be stable with the convergence of the secondary user power. The primary user receiver interference mainly comes from other primary user interference, secondary user interference, system noise and so on. This section discusses that there is only one primary user in the model, and the system noise is negligible compared with the secondary user interference, so the primary user interference can approach only from the secondary user interference. It can be seen from Fig. 5 that the increase of interference at the primary user's receiving end is higher than that of the secondary user's increase. This is because secondary users increase their transmit power in order to satisfy their own communication SINR, with the increase of secondary users in the system. It also increases the interference amplitude of the main user.

6.2   Scenario 2

Assuming that one secondary user is added on the basis of scenario 1, there are 8 secondary users and 1 primary user in the system, and one of the secondary users does not satisfy the system communication conditions. When the user selection strategy is not considered, it is known from formula 5 that when the transmission power is increased to satisfy its own communication SINR, but due to the limitation of the secondary user's maximum transmission power, when the transmission power reaches the upper limit of the secondary user's transmission power, the iteration stops (Fig. 6).

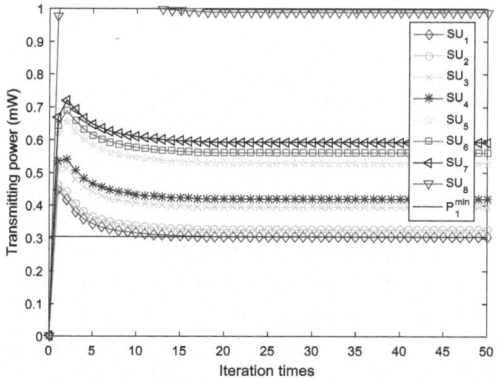

Fig. 6. User transmit power converges with iterations (close user selection strategy)

When the user selection strategy is adopted, the secondary user 8 is eliminated in the early stage, and scene 2 becomes scene 1. The simulation results of 7 users participating in communication are shown in Fig. 3. Comparing with Figs. 7 and 3, we can see that when the secondary user 8 is excluded, With the decrease of the interference in the system, the transmit power of the secondary user is also reduced, and the interference of the primary user receiver is also reduced, so the primary user communication is better protected.

6.3 Scenario 3

Assuming that there are 13 secondary users and 1 primary user in the system, the location information of the secondary user is given randomly. Figure 7 shows that 13 secondary users are included in the system to communicate without considering the user selection strategy. It can be seen that the number of secondary users involved in the communication exceeds the system capacity, resulting in the sub-user 11-13 unable to communicate normally. Other secondary users of normal communications sacrifice transmit power to ensure communication requirements. After selecting the cognitive user selection strategy, the system accommodates 10 secondary users through pre-liminary estimation of system capacity. At the same time, according to step 2, the culled secondary users are filtered. Finally, as shown in Fig. 8, the system can accommodate 12 secondary users.

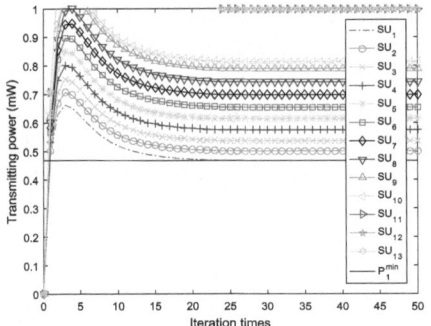

Fig. 7. Closing non-user selection policy   **Fig. 8.** Enable user selection policy

7 Conclusion

In this paper, the main user interference threshold, secondary user interference, secondary user communication SINR requirements, system convergence speed and other issues are fully summarized, and a non-cooperative power control model is established. Aiming at the problem of sub-user fairness in cognitive radio systems, an automatic power control algorithm (APCGA), based on game theory is proposed to effectively save energy consumption and overcome the near-far effect. At the same time, the communication situation of secondary users after power convergence is deeply ana-lyzed, and the conclusion that the secondary users can not meet their own communi-cation SINR requirements is concluded, and the user selection strategy is given. The secondary users involved in the system communication are screened from the two perspectives of user selection and user capacity, which effectively ensure the effec-tiveness of the secondary user communication, reduce the system interference, and improve the stability of the system. Finally, the performance of this algorithm is highlighted by simulation.

References

1. Sun, C., Alemseged, Y.D., Tran, H.N., Harada, H.: Transmit power control for cognitive radio over a Rayleigh fading channel. IEEE Trans. Veh. Technol. **59**(4), 1847–1856 (2010)
2. Liang, Y.C., Chen, H.H., Mitola, J., et al.: Guest editorial-cognitive radio: theory and application. IEEE J. Sel. Areas Commun. **26**(1), 1–4 (2008)
3. Haykin, S.: Cognitive radio: brain-empowered wireless communications. IEEE J. Sel. Areas Commun. **23**(2), 201–220 (2005)
4. Srinivasa, S., Jafar, S.A.: Soft sensing and optimal power control for cognitive radio. IEEE Trans. Wirel. Commun. **9**(12), 3638–3649 (2010)
5. Bansal, G., Hossain, J., Bhargava, V.K.: Optimal and suboptimal power allocation schemes for OFDM-based cognitive radio systems. IEEE Trans. Wirel. Commun. **7**(11), 4710–4718 (2008)
6. Sun, S.Q,. Dj, J.X,. Ni, W.M.: Distributed power control based on convex optimization in cognitive radio networks. In: International conference Wireless Communications and Signal Processing, Suzhou, pp. 21–23. IEEE Press (2010)
7. Xiao, Y., Bi, G.A., Niyato, D.: A simple distributed power control algorithm for cognitive radio networks. IEEE Trans. Wirel. Commun. **10**(11), 3594–3600 (2011)
8. Nadkar, T., Thumar, V., Tej, G.P., et al.: Distributed power allocation for secondary user in a cognitive radio scenario. IEEE Trans. Wirel. Commun. **11**(4), 1576–1586 (2012)
9. Goodman, D., Mandayam, N.: Power control for wireless data. IEEE Pers. Commun. Mag. **7**(4), 48–54 (2000)
10. Saraydar, C., Mandayam, N., Goodman, D.: Efficient power control via pricing in wireless data networks. IEEE Trans. Commun. **50**(2), 291–303 (2002)
11. Bacci, G., Sanguinetti, L., Luise, M., Poor, H.: A game-theoretic approach for energy-efficient contention-based synchronization in OFDMA systems. IEEE Trans. Signal Process. **61**(5), 1258–1271 (2013)
12. AI Talabani, A., Nallanathan, A., Nguyen, H.X.: A novel chaos based cost function for power control of cognitive radio networks. IEEE Commun. Lett. **19**(4), 657–660 (2014)
13. Xie, X., Yang, H., Vasilakos, A.V., He, L.: Fair power control using game theory with pricing scheme in cognitive radio networks. J. Commun. Netw. **16**(2), 183–192 (2014)

Cooperative NOMA-Based DCO-OFDM VLC System

Xin Liu[1]([⊠])[iD], Yuyao Wang[2][iD], and Zhenyu Na[2][iD]

[1] School of Information and Communication Engineering,
Dalian University of Technology, Dalian 116024, China
liuxinstar1984@dlut.edu.cn
[2] School of Information Science and Technology,
Dalian Maritime University, Dalian 116026, China

Abstract. In this paper, relaying technique and non-orthogonal multiple access (NOMA) are adopted to improve performance of visible light communication (VLC) system. Due to the adoption of relay terminal, the link reliability and communication coverage of VLC system are boosted. Besides, the utilization of NOMA can greatly increase spectral efficiency and support massive connectivity. So, a cooperative NOMA-based DCO-OFDM VLC system is proposed. All the optical transmission links use DCO-OFDM to accomplish information transmission. The relay terminal in the proposed system not only forwards the source signal but also sends its own signal simultaneously. The signals over the links between relay and two users are superposed based on NOMA. Under different cases, the total throughput is analyzed and the optimal power allocation factor is obtained. In addition, the OMA-based system is taken as the benchmark system. The simulation results further verify the theoretical results and the superiority that the proposed system has.

Keywords: Relay · NOMA · VLC · DCO-OFDM

1 Introduction

In recent days, the requirements for wireless communication achieve explosive growth. As a result, the available spectrum resources are getting more and more tense. Thus, communication techniques need to be innovated and improved. Visible light communication (VLC) has emerged as one of the promising solutions for indoor high-speed transmission, which can realize illumination and communication simultaneously [1]. VLC has free and wide optical spectrum, high secrecy and security, and low-cost implementation, so it has attracted significant interests. In VLC system, OFDM is one of the most commonly used technologies to decrease the bit error rate (BER). There are some typical VLC schemes based on OFDM have been put forward, such as DCO-OFDM, ACO-OFDM, PAM-DMT, PM-OFDM, U-OFDM and ADO-OFDM [2–4]. Compared with other systems,

© ICST Institute for Computer Sciences, Social Informatics and Telecommunications Engineering 2019
Published by Springer Nature Switzerland AG 2019. All Rights Reserved
J. Jin et al. (Eds.): GreeNets 2019, LNICST 282, pp. 14–24, 2019.
https://doi.org/10.1007/978-3-030-21730-3_2

DCO-OFDM is easier to achieve and has lower cost. So, DCO-OFDM is used in all the transmission links of our proposed system.

There are always some obstacles such as furniture and home appliances in the application scenes of VLC network. The existence of these obstacles may block the light. And then, the information transmission will be interrupted. Besides, the signals will suffer great attenuation when the distance between the light emitting diode (LED) and photodiode (PD) is too far. The application of relaying technique in VLC system can compensate this weakness. Cooperative VLC system has stronger link reliability and wider communication coverage than traditional VLC system [5]. Therefore, it has attracted wide attention of many scholars. [6] shows the performance improvement that amplify-and-forward (AF) and decode-and-forward (DF) relay brought to VLC system. [7] demonstrates the superiority of full-duplex (FD) relay-assisted VLC system over half-duplex (HD) relay-assisted VLC system in BER performance.

Non-orthogonal multiple access (NOMA) technique is a promising candidate for 5G multiple access techniques. Compared with orthogonal multiple access (OMA), NOMA supports more users at the same time [8]. In the power-domain NOMA method, more transmission power is allocated to the user with poorer channel condition, while less power is allocated to the user with better channel condition [9]. Then, the signals from various users are superposed together and sent to receiver side. At receiver side, the superposed signals are de-multiplexed by using serial interference cancellation (SIC) [10]. Nowadays, there are some researches on the application of NOMA to VLC system. [11] proposes a NOMA-DCO-OFDM system and shows its superiority over OMA-DCO-OFDM system. [12] and [13] also make performance evaluation of NOMA in VLC system and reveal its performance gain over OMA system.

However, there are few studies on the joint application of relaying technique and NOMA in VLC system. Therefore, we propose a cooperative NOMA-based DCO-OFDM VLC system. The system uses DF relay to forward the signal from source terminal. By using NOMA, the relay terminal not only forwards the source signal, but also transmits relay signal to corresponding destination terminal. The optimal power allocation factor is obtained by maximizing the system throughput. In addition, the superiority of NOMA-based system over OMA-based system is also verified.

2   System Model

Consider a typical office space with one main light source (S) at the ceiling, one relay terminal (R) at the desk, and two destination terminals (U and D) closer to R. The cooperative NOMA-based DCO-OFDM VLC system is shown in Fig. 1. S and R are equipped with LED units to convert electrical signals to optical signals and send them out, while R, U and D are equipped with PD to convert optical signals to electrical signals for demodulation. There are two independent time slots in the proposed system. As Fig. 1 shows, the blue line represents the first time slot, while the red lines represent the second time slot.

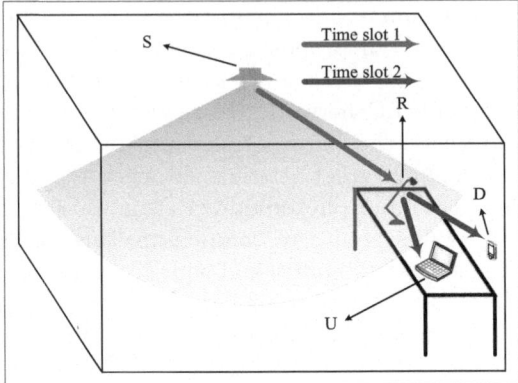

Fig. 1. System model.

During the first time slot, the bit streams are encoded and modulated at S and S sends the modulated signals to R. Then, R receives and decodes the bits that S transmits. During the second time slot, the source signals decoded at R are encoded again. The re-encoded signals are sent out by R with the relay signals together. These two kinds of signals are superposed in power domain according to NOMA and they use the same frequency band at the same time. U and D receive the superposed signals and decode the signals to obtain the transmission bit streams of S and R, respectively.

A cooperative OMA-based DCO-OFDM VLC system is taken as the benchmark system in this paper. Different from the transmission based on NOMA, the re-encoded signals and relay signals in the benchmark system share the frequency band and each of them uses half the bandwidth. The sub-bands they used are orthogonal to each other. The comparison of throughput between these two systems are discussed in the following sections.

3 Model Analysis

In the proposed system, the total transmission power of S and R is constrained to P_t and the transmission power of S and R are set to be the same, i.e. $P_S = P_R = \frac{1}{2}P_t$. Because of the adoption of DCO-OFDM scheme in the four links, we use the model of non-linear clipping operation in [11]. The signal sent from transmitter to receiver is double-sided clipped. Then, DC bias is added to the clipped signal to make the signal be positive signal. Supposing that the signal transmitted by S is x, while the signal after non-linear clipping process is x_{clip}. x is a Gaussian random signal whose mean $\mu_x = 0$ and variance $\sigma_x^2 = P_S$. In this section, we first introduce the clipping model of S-to-R link. Then, the total throughput of the signals received by U and D during the second time slot is deduced. Finally, the comparison of the total throughput of U and D between the NOMA-based and OMA-based systems is given.

3.1   Clipping Model

The non-linear double-sided clipping operation of DCO-OFDM scheme is defined as

$$C_1(x) = \begin{cases} \lambda_t^S - B_{dc}^S & x > \lambda_t^S - B_{dc}^S \\ x & \lambda_b^S < x < \lambda_t^S \\ \lambda_b^S - B_{dc}^S & x < \lambda_b^S - B_{dc}^S \end{cases} \tag{1}$$

where λ_t^S and λ_b^S are the upper and lower boundaries of the clipping operation at S, respectively. B_{dc}^S is the DC bias of the non-linear clipping operation at S. According to Bussgang Theorem, x_{clip} can be divided into two parts as follows [11].

$$x_{clip} = a_S x + d_S \tag{2}$$

where a_S and d_S are the attenuation factor and clipping noise caused by the non-linear clipping operation at S. According to Bussgang Theorem, a_S can be calculated by

$$a_S = \frac{1}{2}\text{erf}\left(\frac{l_S}{\sqrt{2}}\right) - \frac{1}{2}\text{erf}\left(\frac{m_S}{\sqrt{2}}\right) \tag{3}$$

where $l_S = \frac{\lambda_t^S - B_{dc}^S}{\sigma_x}$ and $m_S = \frac{\lambda_b^S - B_{dc}^S}{\sigma_x}$. d_S is usually a Gaussian random noise with non-zero mean and it can be divided into two separate parts as

$$d_S = \mu_S + \mathbb{E}[d_S] \tag{4}$$

where $\mathbb{E}[d_S]$ means the operation to get the mean value of d_S. μ_S is a zero-mean random variable uncorrelated with x. According to (4), the power of clipping noise $P_{clip}^S = \mathbb{D}[d_S] = \mathbb{E}[\mu_S^2]$, where $\mathbb{D}[d_S]$ is the operation to get the variance of d_S. By substituting (4) into (2), P_{clip}^S is obtained as

$$P_{clip}^S = \mathbb{E}[x_{clip}^2] - a_S^2\mathbb{E}[x^2] - \mathbb{E}[d_S]^2 \tag{5}$$

Therefore, the calculation of P_{clip}^S is converted to be the calculation processes of $\mathbb{E}[x_{clip}^2]$ and $\mathbb{E}[d_S]$. According to (1), the probability density function of x_{clip} can be obtained. So, the expressions of $\mathbb{E}[x_{clip}^2]$ and $\mathbb{E}[d_S]$ can be obtained as follows.

$$\begin{aligned} \mathbb{E}[x_{clip}^2] = \frac{\sigma_x^2}{2}\Big[&l_S^2 + m_S^2 - (l_S^2 - 1)\,\text{erf}\left(\frac{l_S}{\sqrt{2}}\right) \\ &+ (m_S^2 - 1)\,\text{erf}\left(\frac{m_S}{\sqrt{2}}\right) + 2m_S g\,(m_S) - 2l_S g\,(l_S)\Big] \end{aligned} \tag{6}$$

$$\mathbb{E}[d_S] = \frac{\sigma_x}{2}\left[l_S + m_S - l_S\text{erf}\left(\frac{l_S}{\sqrt{2}}\right) + m_S\text{erf}\left(\frac{m_S}{\sqrt{2}}\right) + 2g\,(m_S) - 2g\,(l_S)\right] \tag{7}$$

And $\mathbb{E}[x^2] = \sigma_x^2$, according to (3), (6) and (7), P_{clip}^S can be rewritten as

$$
\begin{aligned}
P_{clip}^S \\
&= \frac{\sigma_x^2}{2}\left[m_S^2 + 2m_Sg(m_S) + (m_S^2 - 1)\mathrm{erf}(\frac{m_S}{\sqrt{2}}) + l_S^2 - (l_S^2 - 1)\mathrm{erf}(\frac{l_S}{\sqrt{2}}) - 2l_Sg(l_S)\right] \\
&\quad - \left\{\frac{\sigma_x}{2}\left[l_S + m_S - l_S\mathrm{erf}(\frac{l_S}{\sqrt{2}}) + m_S\mathrm{erf}(\frac{m_S}{\sqrt{2}}) + 2g(m_S) - 2g(l_S)\right]\right\}^2 - a_S^2\sigma_x^2
\end{aligned}
\tag{8}
$$

3.2   Throughput Analysis

The signal received by R during the first time slot is expressed as

$$
z_1 = h_1 * (x_{clip} + B_{dc}^S) + n_1 \tag{9}
$$

According to DCO-OFDM, B_{dc}^S only affects the DC signal, not the power of useful signal. So, substituting (2) into (9), the signal-to-noise ratio (SNR) of z_1 is expressed by

$$
\gamma_1 = \frac{|h_1|^2 a_S^2\sigma_x^2}{|h_1|^2 P_{clip}^S + \sigma_n^2} \tag{10}
$$

where σ_n^2 is variance of channel noise n_1. In this paper, all channel noises are seen as Gaussian random signals with zero-mean and variance σ_n^2. So, the throughput of the signals transmitted from S to R during the first time slot is

$$
T_1 = \frac{1}{2}\log_2(1 + \gamma_1) = \frac{1}{2}\log_2\left(1 + \frac{|h_1|^2 a_S^2\sigma_x^2}{|h_1|^2 P_{clip}^S + \sigma_n^2}\right) \tag{11}
$$

To simplify the discussion, the relay terminal R is assumed to decode the signal transmitted from S successfully. During the second time slot, the decoded source signal and relay signal are superposed together in the power domain based on NOMA. The signals transmitted by R to both D and U are consisted of two independent parts: the decoded source signal y_1 and relay signal y_2. y_1 and y_2 are both Gaussian random signals whose mean values are zero and variances are 1. So, the transmitted superposed signal in R-to-U and R-to-D links is expressed as follows

$$
y = \sqrt{(1 - \beta)P_R}y_1 + \sqrt{\beta P_R}y_2 \tag{12}
$$

where β is the power allocation factor between R-to-U and R-to-D links during the second time slot. Denoting that the superposed signal transmitted by R after clipping operation is y_{clip}, the non-linear double-sided clipping operation at R is given by

$$
C_2(y) = \begin{cases} \lambda_t^R - B_{dc}^R & y > \lambda_t^R - B_{dc}^R \\ y & \lambda_b^R < y < \lambda_t^R \\ \lambda_b^R - B_{dc}^R & y < \lambda_b^R - B_{dc}^R \end{cases} \tag{13}
$$

where λ_t^R and λ_b^R are the upper and lower boundaries of the double-sided clipping operation at R, respectively. B_{dc}^R is the DC bias of the clipping operation at R. According to Bussgang Theorem, y_{clip} can be modeled as

$$y_{clip} = a_R y + d_R \tag{14}$$

where a_R and d_R are the attenuation factor and clipping noise caused by the non-linear clipping operation, respectively. Correspondingly, a_R can be calculated by

$$a_R = \frac{1}{2}\mathrm{erf}\left(\frac{l_R}{\sqrt{2}}\right) - \frac{1}{2}\mathrm{erf}\left(\frac{m_R}{\sqrt{2}}\right) \tag{15}$$

where $l_R = \frac{\lambda_t^R - B_{dc}^R}{\sigma_y}$ and $m_R = \frac{\lambda_b^R - B_{dc}^R}{\sigma_y}$, $\sigma_y^2 = P_R$ is the variance of y. Similar to d_S, d_R is a Gaussian random noise with non-zero mean and it can be divided into two separate parts as

$$d_R = \mu_R + \mathbb{E}[d_R] \tag{16}$$

where $\mathbb{E}[d_R]$ is the mean value of d_R, μ_R is a zero mean random variable uncorrelated with y. Thus, the power of the clipping noise y_{clip} is $P_{clip}^R = \mathbb{D}[d_R] = \mathbb{E}[\mu_R^2]$. By substituting (16) into (14), P_{clip}^R can be rewritten as

$$P_{clip}^R = \mathbb{E}[\mu_R^2] = \mathbb{E}[y_{clip}^2] - a_R^2\mathbb{E}[y^2] - \mathbb{E}[d_R]^2 - 2a_R\mathbb{E}[y]\mathbb{E}[d_R] \tag{17}$$

Similar to the calculation of P_{clip}^S, the result of (17) can be obtained as

$$
\begin{aligned}
P_{clip}^R \\
= \frac{\sigma_y^2}{2}\left[m_R^2 + 2m_R g(m_R) + (m_R^2 - 1)\mathrm{erf}(\frac{m_R}{\sqrt{2}}) + l_R^2 - (l_R^2 - 1)\mathrm{erf}(\frac{l_R}{\sqrt{2}}) - 2l_R g(l_R)\right] \\
- \left\{\frac{\sigma_y}{2}\left[l_R + m_R - l_R\mathrm{erf}(\frac{l_R}{\sqrt{2}}) + m_R\mathrm{erf}(\frac{m_R}{\sqrt{2}}) + 2g(m_R) - 2g(l_R)\right]\right\}^2 - a_R^2\sigma_y^2
\end{aligned} \tag{18}
$$

The signals received by U and D during the second time slot are respectively expressed as follows

$$
\begin{aligned}
z_2 &= h_2 * (y_{clip} + B_{dc}^R) + n_2 \\
z_3 &= h_3 * (y_{clip} + B_{dc}^R) + n_3
\end{aligned} \tag{19}
$$

where h_2 and h_3 mean the channel gains of R-to-U and R-to-D links, respectively. y_{clip} is the clipping signal transmitted from R to both U and D. n_2 and n_3 are the channel noises of R-to-U link and R-to-D link, respectively.

Supposing that $h_2 > h_3$, based on the demodulation principle of NOMA, the SNR of U and D are respectively calculated as

$$\gamma_2 = \frac{|h_2|^2 a_R^2 (1 - \beta) P_R}{|h_2|^2 P_{clip}^R + \sigma_n^2} \tag{20}$$

$$\gamma_3 = \frac{|h_3|^2 a_R^2 \beta P_R}{|h_3|^2 P_{clip}^R + |h_3|^2 a_R^2 (1 - \beta) P_R + \sigma_n^2} \tag{21}$$

The throughput of the signals transmitted from R to U during the second time slot is expressed by

$$T_2 = \frac{1}{2}\log_2\left(1 + \gamma_2\right) = \frac{1}{2}\log_2\left(1 + \frac{|h_2|^2 a_R^2\left(1-\beta\right)P_R}{|h_2|^2 P_{clip}^R + \sigma_n^2}\right) \tag{22}$$

Since DF relay is adopted in this system, the total throughput of the source signal is

$$T_S = \min\left(T_1, T_2\right) \tag{23}$$

In addition, the throughput of signal transmitted from R to D during the second time slot is

$$T_R = \frac{1}{2}\log_2\left(1 + \gamma_3\right) = \frac{1}{2}\log_2\left(1 + \frac{|h_3|^2 a_R^2\beta P_R}{|h_3|^2 P_{clip}^R + |h_3|^2 a_R^2\left(1-\beta\right)P_R + \sigma_n^2}\right) \tag{24}$$

Moreover, as a benchmark, the SNR of the signals received by U and D during the second time slot in the OMA-based system are expressed as

$$\widetilde{\gamma}_2 = \frac{|h_2|^2 a_R^2\left(1-\beta\right)P_R}{|h_2|^2 P_{clip}^R + \sigma_n^2} \tag{25}$$

$$\widetilde{\gamma}_3 = \frac{|h_3|^2 a_R^2\beta P_R}{|h_3|^2 P_{clip}^R + \sigma_n^2} \tag{26}$$

Then, the total throughput of source signal in the benchmark system is given as follows

$$\widetilde{T}_S = \min\left(\frac{1}{2}\log_2\left(1 + \gamma_1\right), \frac{1}{4}\log_2\left(1 + \widetilde{\gamma}_2\right)\right) \tag{27}$$

The throughput of signal transmitted from R to D during the second time slot is

$$\widetilde{T}_R = \frac{1}{4}\log_2\left(1 + \widetilde{\gamma}_3\right) = \frac{1}{4}\log_2\left(1 + \frac{|h_3|^2 a_R^2\beta P_R}{|h_3|^2 P_{clip}^R + \sigma_n^2}\right) \tag{28}$$

4   Simulations and Discussions

In the previous sections, the throughput performance of the system have been theoretically analyzed. According to the theoretical deduction, we analyze the throughput with different parameters by simulation in this section. Some parameters used in the simulation are set as follows, the total power of S and R $P_t = 26\,\mathrm{W}$, the transmission power of S and R $P_S = P_R = 13\,\mathrm{W}$, $\lambda_t^S = 7\,\mathrm{V}$, $\lambda_t^R = 5\,\mathrm{V}$, $\lambda_b^S = \lambda_b^R = 0\,\mathrm{V}$ and power of noise $P_n = \sigma_n^2 = 1\,\mathrm{W}$.

Figure 2 shows the total throughput of signals transmitted to both U and D during the second time slot with varying power allocation factor β. It is seen that $T_S + T_R$ first increases and then decreases with the increase of β. When B_{dc}^R is too small, the clipping noise is too big. So $T_S + T_R$ is small at the beginning and increases with B_{dc}^R. However, when B_{dc}^R reaches to a certain value, it will waste many power. Correspondingly, the useful power will get smaller, so $T_S + T_R$ stops increasing and begins to decrease with the increase of B_{dc}^R. There is an optimal B_{dc}^R to maximize $T_S + T_R$ no matter what β is. Figure 2 also shows that the performance is the same when the sum of two β equals to 1. In this section, we set $h_2 = 0.9, h_3 = 0.6$ when $h_2 > h_3$ and $h_2 = 0.6, h_3 = 0.9$ when $h_2 < h_3$. Therefore, the theoretical expressions are symmetric and the throughput results are the same when the sum of two β equals to 1.

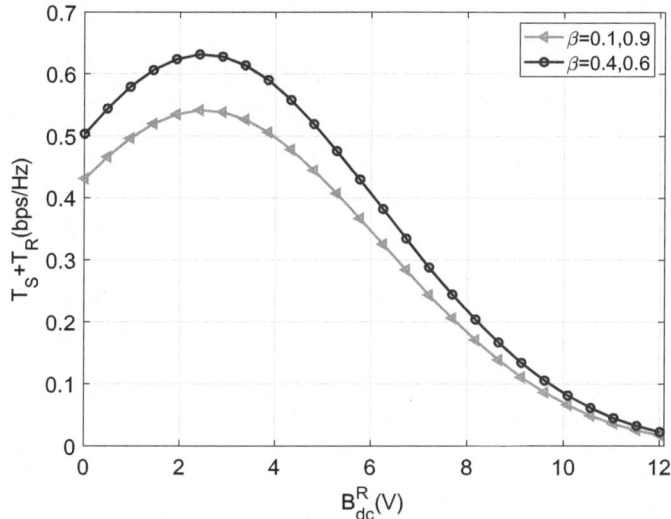

Fig. 2. The total throughput of U and D during the second time slot with varying B_{dc}^R.

Figure 3 shows the throughput performance with varying β. It can be seen that $T_S + T_R$ first increases and then decreases, and it reaches its maximum at $\beta = 0.5$. When $\beta < 0.5$, the increase of β means the increase of power allocated to D with better channel condition. As well, when $\beta > 0.5$, the increase of β means the decrease of power allocated to U with better channel condition. Therefore, $T_S + T_R$ increases with the increase of β when $\beta < 0.5$. On the other hand, $T_S + T_R$ decreases with the increase of β when $\beta > 0.5$, i.e., when the power allocated to the user with better channel condition increases, the throughput performance gets better. So, when $\beta = 0.5$, the power allocated to the user with better channel gets its maximum value and the throughput performance reaches its maximum value.

Figure 4 shows the comparison of the throughput performance between the proposed NOMA-based system and the benchmark system based on OMA. It can be seen that with the increase of β, the trend of the throughput curve of OMA-based system is the same as the one of NOMA-based system. Furthermore, the

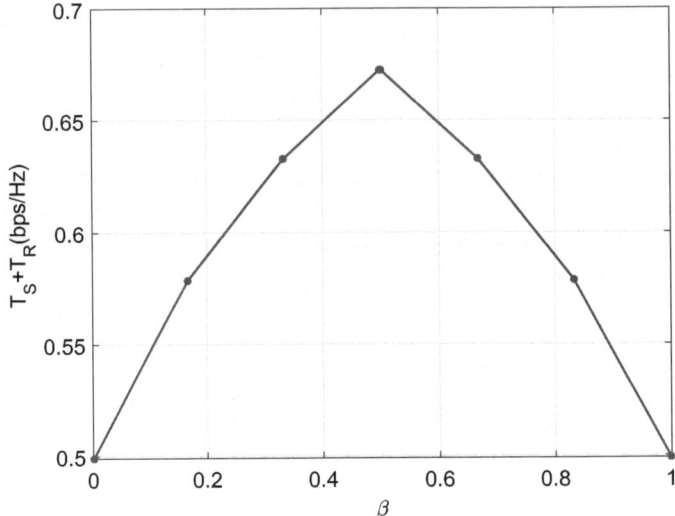

Fig. 3. The throughput performance with varying β during the second time slot.

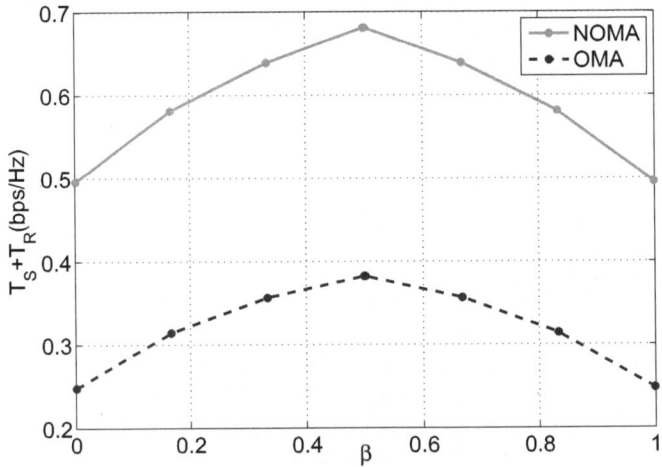

Fig. 4. The comparison of throughput performance with varying β between NOMA-based and OMA-based system.

introduction of NOMA improves the system throughput performance in general. Because the spectrum efficiency of OMA-based system is almost half of that in NOMA-based system. The total throughput of NOMA-based system is almost twice the throughput of the benchmark system based on OMA.

5   Conclusion

In this paper, a cooperative NOMA-based DCO-OFDM VLC system is proposed and analyzed. In the proposed system, all the transmission links use DCO-OFDM scheme to transmit signal. The DF relay terminal forwards the source signal and transmits relay signal to corresponding destination terminals at the same time. These two kinds of signals are superposed in the power domain based on NOMA. The clipping noise and total throughput are modeled and analyzed. The simulation results show that when the power allocated to the user with better channel condition increases during the second time slot, the total throughput increases. So, the selection of appropriate value of the power allocation factor is necessary for the system performance. Besides, the comparison between the proposed system based on NOMA and the benchmark system based on OMA reveals the performance gain that NOMA brings to the system.

Acknowledgements. This work was supported by the National Natural Science Foundations of China under Grant 61601221, the Joint Foundations of the National Natural Science Foundations of China and the Civil Aviation of China under Grant U1833102, and the China Postdoctoral Science Foundations under Grants 2015M580425 and 2018T110496.

References

1. Grobe, L., et al.: High-speed visible light communication systems. IEEE Commun. Mag. **51**(12), 60–66 (2013)
2. Elgala, H., Mesleh, R., Haas, H.: Indoor broadcasting via white LEDs and OFDM. IEEE Trans. Consum. Electron. **55**(3), 1127–1134 (2009)
3. Armstrong, J., Lowery, A.J.: Power efficient optical OFDM. Electron. Lett. **42**(6), 370–372 (2006)
4. Dissanayake, S.D., Panta, K., Armstrong, J.: A novel technique to simultaneously transmit ACO-OFDM and DCO-OFDM in IM/DD systems. In: 2011 IEEE GLOBECOM Workshops (GC Wkshps), pp. 782–786, December 2011
5. Kizilirmak, R.C., Uysal, M.: Relay-assisted OFDM transmission for indoor visible light communication. In: 2014 IEEE International Black Sea Conference on Communications and Networking (BlackSeaCom), pp. 11–15, May 2014
6. Yang, H., Pandharipande, A.: Full-duplex relay VLC in LED lighting linear system topology. In: IECON 2013 - 39th Annual Conference of the IEEE Industrial Electronics Society, pp. 6075–6080, November 2013
7. Narmanlioglu, O., Kizilirmak, R.C., Miramirkhani, F., Uysal, M.: Cooperative visible light communications with full-duplex relaying. IEEE Photonics J. **9**(3), 1–11 (2017)
8. Dai, L., Wang, B., Ding, Z., Wang, Z., Chen, S., Hanzo, L.: A Survey of non-orthogonal multiple access for 5G. IEEE Commun. Surv. Tutor. **20**, 2294–2323 (2018)
9. Ding, Z., Fan, P., Poor, H.V.: Impact of user pairing on 5G nonorthogonal multiple-access downlink transmissions. IEEE Trans. Veh. Technol. **65**(8), 6010–6023 (2016)
10. Ding, Z., Lei, X., Karagiannidis, G.K., Schober, R., Yuan, J., Bhargava, V.K.: A survey on non-orthogonal multiple access for 5G networks: research challenges and future trends. IEEE J. Sel. Areas Commun. **35**(10), 2181–2195 (2017)

11. Chu, W., Dang, J., Zhang, Z., Wu, L.: Effect of clipping on the achievable rate of non-orthogonal multiple access with DCO-OFDM. In: 2017 9th International Conference on Wireless Communications and Signal Processing (WCSP), pp. 1–6. IEEE (2017)
12. Yin, L., Wu, X., Haas, H.: On the performance of non-orthogonal multiple access in visible light communication. In: 2015 IEEE 26th Annual International Symposium on Personal, Indoor, and Mobile Radio Communications (PIMRC), pp. 1354–1359, August 2015
13. Yin, L., Popoola, W.O., Wu, X., Haas, H.: Performance evaluation of non-orthogonal multiple access in visible light communication. IEEE Trans. Commun. **64**(12), 5162–5175 (2016)

Robust Power Control Algorithm Based on Probabilistic Constraints in Cognitive Radio Networks

Guanglong Yang$^{(\boxtimes)}$, Xuezhi Tan, and Xiao Wang

School of Electronics Information Engineering, Harbin Institute of Technology,
Harbin 150001, People's Republic of China
yang3616@126.com, {Tanxz1957,hitwx}@hit.edu.cn

Abstract. When the channel fading is assumed to be fast fading and the transient variation of the channel gain is considered, the signal-to-interference noise ratio (SINR, Signal to Interference plus Noise Ratio) of the secondary user changes with the channel gain. This will cause some secondary users to fail to get the SINR, required for normal communication if the secondary user transmit power is enhanced, although it meets the secondary user communication requirements, at the same time, the interference to the primary user exceeds the interference threshold. Affects the normal communication of the primary user. In order to solve this problem, a robust power control algorithm based on probabilistic constraints is proposed. In this paper, the average SINR model is transformed into the uncertain distribution model by introducing the uncertain parameters satisfying the exponential distribution. In this paper, the SINR probability density functions of primary and secondary users are given, and the probabilistic constraints are transformed into deterministic constraints. In order to solve the secondary user transmit power, the interference temperature of the primary user is taken as the constraint condition, and the complete iterative algorithm is used to realize the fast convergence of the secondary user transmit power. Since the protection of the primary user will lead to the damage of the interests of some secondary users, this chapter introduces the admission control, according to the highest degree of dissatisfaction first eliminate the mode of the sub-users who do not meet the requirements of communication to implement admission control. The number of secondary users meeting the communication condition in the system is increased. The simulation results show that the algorithm can quickly identify the secondary users who do not meet the communication conditions, and avoid the excessive elimination of the secondary users, increase the number of secondary users who can communicate normally, and increase the total throughput of the system.

Keywords: Cognitive radio · Underlay spectrum sharing ·
Distributed power control · Probabilistic constraints · Robust power control

J. Jin et al. (Eds.): GreeNets 2019, LNICST 282, pp. 25–35, 2019.
https://doi.org/10.1007/978-3-030-21730-3_3

1 Introduction

There are many factors affecting the wireless channel, and the channel state is also time-varying and stochastic. At present, most researches only consider the accurate known channel state and ignore the influence of channel uncertainty, which leads to the failure to guarantee the communication quality of each user [1]. The instability of the wireless signal is caused by the variability of the wireless channel, so the channel gain from the signal transmitter to the signal receiver is also variable. Wireless signals are generally divided into three kinds of fading: free space fading, shadow slow fading and multipath fast fading.

The uncertainty of channel parameters is an important problem in wireless communication. Some scholars consider the influence of the transient change of channel gain on the system, and adopt remedial measures to reduce the influence of the system. This method can be regarded as a "compensation method" [2]. In reference [3], the problem of distributed robust transmission scheduling and power control in cognitive space-time division multiple access (STDMA) networks is studied. By considering the uncertainty of channel gain, the QoS conflict caused by the transient channel gain is avoided, and a distributed two-level algorithm for distributed column generation is proposed. At the same time, the bound of signal-to-noise ratio (SINR) constraint violation probability and the expected number of additional time slots needed to meet the needs of the user's link traffic are derived. Reference [4] considers cognitive radio networks where a single primary user and multiple secondary users coexist. According to the channel conditions, the SNR is dynamically adjusted under the given BER requirement, and the admission control is adopted to eliminate the SINR secondary users. In reference [5], a robust ergodic resource allocation scheme (ERA, Ergodic Resource Allocation),) is proposed under the framework of underlying heterogeneous networks based on orthogonal frequency division multiple access (OFDMA). This scheme not only guarantees the interference requirement of macro network, but also improves the average and speed of the network. The previously proposed ERA schemes are assumed to satisfy the average constraint value, but in heterogeneous networks, the instantaneous interference threshold for macro users is not guaranteed [6]. In this paper, the scheme can solve the above problems very well. In the cognitive radio environment, SU and PU share the same spectrum. Since PU has higher channel access priority than SU, it is necessary to study more SU access systems when all primary users satisfy their own SINR. Each primary user tracks its target SINR. by adopting a traditional TPC algorithm. As long as the total reception power at the main receiver is lower than the given threshold, each transmit SU adopts TPC, otherwise, it reduces its transmission power according to the ratio of the given threshold to the total received power at the main receiver. The algorithm proposed in this paper can increase the number of SU in the access system under the condition that all PU's SINR are guaranteed.

2   System Model

In this paper, the underlay spectrum access mode is considered, so it is unnecessary to consider the communication situation of the primary user, and the time of sensing and judging the primary user's activity is reduced indirectly. This paper considers the underlay multi-user distributed cognitive radio scene, as shown in Fig. 1. Primary and secondary users coexist in the network, including M for secondary users, N for primary users. The secondary user is represented by the set $A = \{1, 2, \cdots, M\}$ and the primary user by the set $B = \{1, 2, \cdots, N\}$. Order $\forall i, j \in A$, $\forall k \in B$.

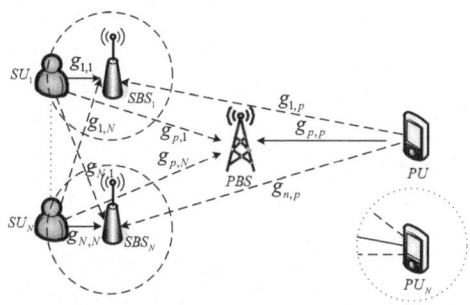

Fig. 1. Cognitive system model

Assuming that the channel is flat fading, the average SINR of SU_i can be expressed as:

$$\bar{\gamma}_i = \frac{\bar{g}_{i,i} p_i}{N_s + N_p + \delta^2} \tag{1}$$

Which is

$$N_S = \sum_{j=1, j \neq i}^{M} \bar{g}_{i,j} p_j, N_P = \bar{g}_{i,p} p_p, p_i \in \left[0, p_i^{\max}\right]$$

$g_{i,i}$, Instantaneous link gain from SU_i to SBS_i; $g_{i,j}$, Instantaneous link gain from SU_i to PBS; $g_{p,i}$, Instantaneous link gain from SU_i to PBS; $g_{p,p}$, Instantaneous link gain from PU to PBS; $g_{i,p}$, Instantaneous link gain from PU to SBS_i; p_i, the ith secondary user transmit power; $p_i^{\max}$, Secondary user maximum transmit power; p^{total}, Total interference power from SU_i to primary user; p^{th}, Main user's interference threshold; N_S, Other secondary user interference; N_P, Primary user interference; δ^2, Background noise; γ_i^{th}, The SINR value for the ith secondary user when the QoS requirement is satisfied.

In order to ensure the normal communication of the primary user, the interference power cannot exceed the interference threshold of the primary user. Therefore, in order to meet the interference threshold, the total interference power of the secondary user must be met

$$p^{total} = \sum_{i=1}^{N} p_i \bar{g}_{p,i} \leq p^{th} \tag{2}$$

In a cognitive system, in order to ensure a secondary user's QoS requirements, each secondary user's receiving SINR needs to meet a certain threshold value:

$$\bar{\gamma}_i \geq \gamma_i^{th} \tag{3}$$

3 Mathematical Model

The average SINR can not reflect the instantaneous performance, so this paper mainly studies the instantaneous SINR of the secondary users. The receiver SINR has the characteristics of fast fading with channel fading. In order to reflect the instantaneous characteristics of SINR, we transform the average SINR model into the instantaneous characteristic model:

$$\gamma_i = E\bar{\gamma}_i = E\left(\frac{\bar{g}_{i,i}p_i}{\sum_{j=1,j\neq i}^{N} \bar{g}_{i,j}p_j + \bar{g}_{i,p}p_p + \delta^2} \right) \tag{4}$$

Among them, the E clothing is exponentially distributed with a mean value of 1, and the probability density equation is $f_E(\chi) = e^{-\chi}$.

By using the method of [7] transformation, the robust optimization problem is transformed into:

$$\min \sum_{i=1}^{N} p_i$$

$$\text{s.t} \begin{cases} \bar{\gamma}_i \geq \frac{1}{-\ln(1-\varepsilon)} \breve{\gamma}_i \\ \bar{I}_p \leq -\frac{\bar{g}_{p,p}p_p \ln(1-\varphi)}{\breve{\gamma}_p} - \delta^2 \\ 0 \leq p_i \leq p_i^{max} \end{cases} \tag{5}$$

4 Robust Optimal Control Algorithm

For the robust optimization problem of formula (5), a power control algorithm is proposed in this section, which not only realizes the power allocation to secondary users, but also ensures that the primary users are not disturbed. Due to the interference threshold of the primary user and the minimum communication SINR requirement of the secondary user, some SU SINR can not meet the communication requirements in the actual process. Therefore, this section introduces admission control to realize the optimal utilization of network resources.

4.1 Robust Power Iterative Mathematical Model

For the robust optimization problem (5), considering the Qos constraint of SU, we can obtain,

$$p_i \geq \frac{\breve{\gamma}_i}{-\ln(1-\varepsilon)} \times \frac{\bar{N}_i + \bar{g}_{i,p} p_p + \delta^2}{\bar{g}_{i,i}} \tag{6}$$

Which, $\bar{N}_i = \sum\limits_{j=1, j \neq i}^{N} \bar{g}_{i,j} p_j$.

Considering the threshold constraint $0 \leq p_i \leq p_{i,\max}$ of SU_i transmission power, the following power iterations can be obtained:

$$p_i(t+1) = \min \left\{ \left[\frac{\breve{\gamma}_i}{-\ln(1-\varepsilon)} \times \frac{\bar{N}_i(t) + \bar{g}_{i,p} p_p + \delta^2}{\bar{g}_{i,i}} \right]^+ , p_i^{\max} \right\} \tag{7}$$

which, $[\chi]^+ = \max[\chi, 0]$.

According to the power iteration formula in formula (7), when the maximum power threshold $p_i^{\max} \gg p_i^{opt}$, the $p_i^{\max}$ has little constraint on the transmitting power of SU_i, whereas the maximum power threshold $p_i^{\max}$ has a very strong constraint on the transmission power of SU_i. It can avoid the interference of SU_i transmit power to PU.

4.2 Complete Iterative Robust Power Control Algorithm

Formula (7) mainly uses $p_i^{\max}$ to constrain the power of the secondary user in the iteration process, and does not protect against the interference threshold of the primary user. Next, we give the protection strategy of the PU.

All SU interference with PU is $\bar{I}_p$. Its size directly affects the communication quality of PU. With the decrease of $\bar{I}_p$, the communication quality of PU becomes better and better. When the limit condition is $\bar{I}_p = 0$, the communication quality of PU is the best, which becomes a non-cognitive radio model. The reason for the decrease of $\bar{I}_p$ is, on the one hand, the decrease in the transmitting power of SU, on the other hand, the decrease in the number of SU. In order to improve the communication quality of PU, the number of SU will decrease. To take into account both the quality of PU communication and the number of SU, we select the following interference thresholds:

$$I_{th} = -\frac{\bar{g}_{p,p}p_p \ln(1-\varphi)}{\breve{\gamma}_p} - \delta^2 \tag{8}$$

I_{th} is the largest interference PU can tolerate. In order to limit the transmission power of SU and guarantee the Qos of PU, we give the following formula:

$$\hat{I}_p = \sum_{i=1}^{N} \hat{p}_i \bar{g}_{p,i} \leq I_{th} \tag{9}$$

$\hat{p}_i$ is the transmission power of SU_i after stabilization $\hat{p}_i = \min\{p_i^{opt}, p_i^{max}\}$. $\hat{I}_p$ indicates the interference to PU caused by the final transmit power of SU_i.

Since p_i^{max} can limit the transmission power of SU_i, we propose a robust power control algorithm for maximum power regulation.

First set the minimum transmit power of the SU is $p^{(1)min} = \{p_1^{(1)min},$ $p_2^{(1)min}, \cdots, p_N^{(1)min}\}$, then, adequate evaluation of interference threshold I_{th} by SU. Estimate the maximum transmit Power $p^{(1)max} = \{p_1^{(1)max}, p_2^{(1)max}, \cdots, p_N^{(1)max}\}$ of all SU based on I_{th}. Determination of power renewal step size $\Delta p^{(n)} = \frac{p^{(1)max} - p^{(n)min}}{2}$ by dichotomy, which $\Delta p^{(1)} = \frac{p^{(1)max} - p^{(1)min}}{2}$. Since all SU have the same transmit priority, all SU iterate simultaneously according to the minimum transmit power. The following flow steps of the minimum power regulation algorithm are given.

1. Initialization: the number of adjustments is $n = 1$, The number of iterations per adjustment is $t = 1$, The initial minimum transmit power is $p^{(1)min} = \rho$.
2. For $i = 1, 2, \cdots, N$, Iterative formula based on power of SU

$$p_i(t+1) = \min\left\{\left[\frac{\breve{\gamma}_i}{-\ln(1-\varepsilon)} \times \frac{\bar{N}_i(t) + \bar{g}_{i,p}p_p + \delta^2}{\bar{g}_{i,i}}\right]^+, p_i^{(n)max}\right\}$$

Repeat 2 steps to update power, order $t = t + 1$, power eventually converges to $\hat{p}_i^{(n)}$.

3. Using $\hat{p}_i^{(n)}$, to calculate the interference $\hat{I}_p^{(n)}$ of PU, which $\hat{I}_p^{(n)} = \sum_{i=1}^{N} \hat{p}_i^{(n)} \bar{g}_{p,i}$.

4. $\hat{I}_p^{(n)}$ was compared with I_{th}. If $\hat{I}_p^{(n)} < I_{th}$, order $n = n + 1$, synchronously increase the transmit power of SU, $p^{(n+1)min} = p^{(n)min} + \Delta p^{(n)}$, start over from step 2. If $I_{th} - \hat{I}_p^{(n)} < \omega(\omega > 0)$, then $\hat{p}_i = \hat{p}_i^{(n)}$.

According to the above iterative algorithm, the communication quality of SU is guaranteed by limiting the maximum transmit power of PU. However, it is likely that some SU_i transmit power can not meet its own SINR requirements. If these cognitive users continue to communicate, it will only cause a waste of resources and cause more interference. Therefore, in order to optimize resource utilization, admission control is introduced. The implementation process is as follows.

4.3 Admission Control Algorithms

1. SU calculation average SINR $\hat{\gamma}_i$ based on the formula $\hat{\gamma}_i = \dfrac{\bar{g}_{i,i}\hat{p}_i}{\sum\limits_{j=1,j\neq i}^{N} \bar{g}_{i,j}\hat{p}_j + \bar{g}_{i,p}p_p + \delta^2}$, the $\hat{\gamma}_i$
   is compared with the optimal average SINR $\bar{\gamma}_i$, which $\bar{\gamma}_i = \dfrac{1}{-\ln(1-\varepsilon)}\breve{\gamma}_i$. If $\hat{\gamma}_i < \bar{\gamma}_i$, the SU_i enters the queue to be removed.
2. In the removal queue, the SU_i corresponding to the smallest $\hat{\gamma}_i$ is removed from the communication cognitive user by ordering the $\hat{\gamma}_i$ according to the size.
3. The remaining SU is updated according to the iterative algorithm. If all SU meets $\bar{\gamma}_i > \hat{\gamma}_i$, admission control ends, otherwise, step 1 is returned.

$$
p_i^{(m+1)} = \begin{cases} \dfrac{p_i^{(m)}}{\bar{\gamma}_i^{(m)}}\gamma_i^{th} + \dfrac{2\alpha_i}{\beta_i}\left(p_i^{\max} - p_i^{(m)}\right)^{\frac{1}{2}} & p_i^{(m+1)} < p_i^{\max} \\ p_i^{\max} & p_i^{(m+1)} \geq p_i^{\max} \end{cases} \tag{10}
$$

Each secondary user is updated iteratively until the utility function in (4) is maximized. An automatic non-cooperative power control algorithm designed in this paper (APCGA, Automatic Power Control Game Algorithms) The process is as follows:

Step 1: Initialization power vector $p_i(0)$ and p_0, count $\gamma_i(0)$.

Step 2: If $\bar{\gamma}_i < \gamma_i^{th}$, β_i remain unchanged; otherwise automatically adjust β_i through $\beta_{i+1} = \beta_i \bar{\gamma}_i / \gamma_i^{th}$.

Step 3: Order $m = m+1$, recalculate power $p_i^{(m+1)}$ using.

If $p_i^{(m+1)}$ meet (2), go on, otherwise the iteration stops.

Step 4: The ith secondary user, $|U_i^{(m+1)} - U_i^{(m)}| < \omega$ (precision $\omega > 0$), the iteration stops; Otherwise, return to step 2.

5 Simulation Results and Analysis

In this section, the proposed power control algorithm and admission control algorithm are simulated and verified, and the network performance under these two algorithms is evaluated. The following are some of the simulation parameters in this chapter: $R_p = 450\,\text{m}$, $\delta^2 = 10^{-10}$, $p^{\max} = 50\,\text{mW}$, $p_p = 100\,\text{mW}$; which $i = 1, 2, \cdots, N$, $\breve{\gamma}_p = 5\,\text{dB}$, $\breve{\gamma}_i = 15\,\text{dB}$; $\rho = 5 \times 10^{-15}\,\text{w}$, $\omega = 10^{-15}$. Assuming 30 SU users, we randomly selected 20 cognitive system ($N = 20$) to verify the algorithm. Probability threshold $\varepsilon = \varphi = 0.1$.

5.1   Algorithm Convergence

Figure 2 shows the power iteration process of SU. The convergence of the complete iterative algorithm can be clearly seen in the diagram. At the same time, all SU have completed convergence within 15 steps, and most SU have completed convergence in 10 steps.

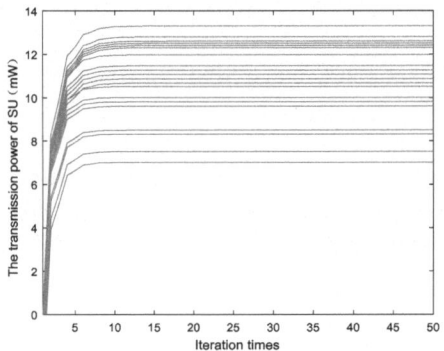

Fig. 2. Iterative convergence of transmit power in SU

5.2   Admission Control Algorithm

According to the final transmission power of SU, the average SINR $\hat{\gamma}_i$, of SU_i can be obtained as shown in Fig. 3(a). The average SINR of four SU is lower than the target SNR, so the four SU users can not meet their own communication SINR requirements. In addition, the figure shows that the average SINR of SU_{20} is the lowest. According to the execution process of admission control, the SU_{20} is removed from the network, and the power of the remaining 19 SU is recalculated using the complete iterative algorithm.

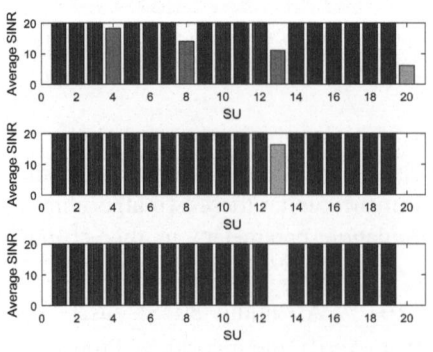

Fig. 3. Average SINR of SU

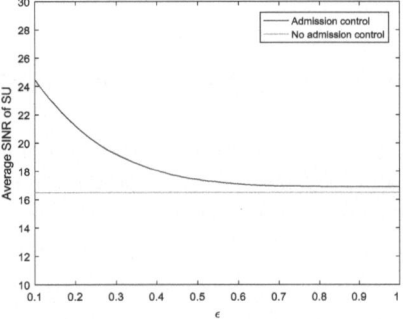

Fig. 4. Relationship between SU mean signal-to-noise ratio and ε

As shown in Fig. 3(b), after SU_{20} is eliminated, the average SINR of both SU_4 and SU_8 meets the communication requirements, and the SNR of the remaining cognitive users exceeds the target SNR requirement, and the performance is significantly improved than that before admission control. This is because the function of admission control is to eliminate the secondary users whose performance is poor and can not meet the requirements of communication, which indirectly reduces the interference of the remaining users, so the signal-to-noise ratio is increased. Figure 3(b) shows that the average SINR of SU_{13} still cannot meet the communication requirements and needs to be eliminated.

As shown in Fig. 3(c), the average SINR of the remaining 18 SU meets the requirements after SU_{13} is removed. The purpose of adopting admission control is to find the users farthest from the average SINR in the system and eliminate the unnecessary interference from other users, and to make it possible for the users with small average SINR deviation to realize the communication requirements. If the simulation results mentioned above, there are 4 SU users who can not meet the normal communication requirements. After adopting admission control, two SU users are eliminated, and the normal communication of the other 2 SU users is realized. The number of normal communication SU has changed from 16 to 18. At the same time, the system interference is reduced. This also fully reflects the effect of the admission control algorithm proposed in this chapter.

It can be seen from Fig. 4 that the average SINR of cognitive users is larger under admission control than without admission control in the case of fixed channel gain and fixed interrupt probability. Because a part of the secondary users who can not complete the communication normally is eliminated under the admission control algorithm, the total interference of the primary users is reduced, which indirectly improves the signal-to-noise ratio of the primary users. As can be seen from Figs. 3(c) and 4, the introduction of admission control can improve the overall performance of cognitive systems. However, with the increase of uncertain parameter ε, the average SINR of secondary users decreases. This is because the normal communication of the secondary users is affected with the increase of the bad channel environment, resulting in the decrease of the average SINR of the secondary users.

5.3 Complete Iterative Algorithm

Figure 5 shows the curve of cognitive user interrupt probability when the target SNR is different. The probability of outage is defined as the ratio of the number of users to the total number of users. It can be seen from Fig. 5 that the outage probability increases with the increase of SINR.

In this paper, the power control algorithm (the complete iterative algorithm) is used to determine how to eliminate the cognitive users who can not communicate normally when each power iteration converges to a stable value, which will result in a high overall interruption probability. This is because cognitive users who can not communicate normally have been in the system for a long time as interference sources. This method is used to filter out the secondary users' nonconformance caused by transient,

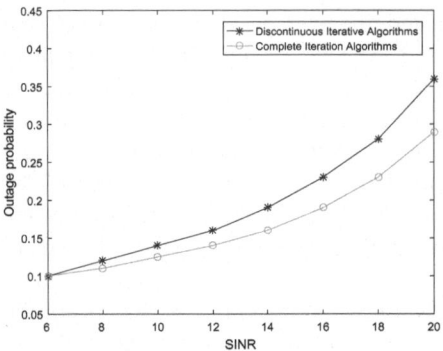

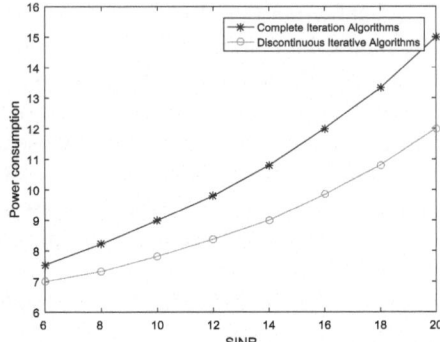

Fig. 5. Relationship between SU outage probability and signal-to-noise ratio

Fig. 6. Relationship between SU power consumption and PU signal-to-noise ratio

although the outage probability is increased, the total number of secondary users who can communicate normally is also increased, and the total throughput of cognitive system is improved. The increase in the number of secondary users that can communicate normally, as shown in Fig. 6, also increases system energy consumption. If the interference temperature is detected at all times in the iterative process and the algorithm (discontinuous iteration algorithm) is used to verify the Qos requirement of the cognitive user, it is found that the dissatisfied cognitive user can be eliminated in order to reduce the outage probability. However, this method will amplify the transient state, cause excessive elimination of secondary users, reduce the number of secondary users who can communicate normally, and reduce the throughput of cognitive systems.

6 Conclusion

In this chapter, the objective of the instantaneous SINR, is to minimize the energy consumption, and the robust power allocation of SU is realized by the interference management of PU. First, assuming the exponential distribution of the user's instantaneous SINR service, the probabilistic constraint equations of SU and PU are given respectively. The probabilistic constraints are solved by the distribution function of SINR, and the optimal SINR and PU interference constraint expressions of SU are obtained. Based on the interference constraints of PU, a robust power control algorithm based on complete iteration is proposed. The algorithm can effectively ensure the fast convergence of SU power in the range of PU interference constraints. Therefore, this paper adopts admission control to eliminate these SU and make rational use of network resources. The simulation results show the effectiveness of the algorithm and the practicability of the overall solution.

References

1. Han, S., Liang, Y.-C., Soong, B.-H.: Robust joint resource allocation for OFDMA-CDMA spectrum refarming system. IEEE Trans. Commun. **64**(3), 1291–1302 (2016)
2. Bao, Y., Chen, H.: Design of robust broadband beamformers using worst-case performance optimization: a semidefinite programming approach. IEEE/ACM Trans. AudioSpeech Lang. Process. **25**(4), 895–907 (2017)
3. Phunchongharm, P., Hossain, E.: Distributed robust scheduling and power control for cognitive spatial-reuse TDMA networks. IEEE J. Sel. Areas Commun. **30**(10), 1934–1946 (2012)
4. Du, H., Ratnarajah, T.: Robust utility maximization and admission control for a MIMO cognitive radio network. IEEE Trans. Veh. Technol. **62**(4), 1707–1718 (2013)
5. Mokari, N., Saeedi, H., Azmi, P.: Quantized ergodic radio resource allocation in cognitive femto networks with controlled collision and power outage probabilities. IEEE J. Sel. Areas Commun. **32**(11), 2090–2104 (2014)
6. Rasti, M., Hasan, M., Le, L.B., Hossain, E.: Distributed uplink power control for multi-cell cognitive radio networks. IEEE Trans. Commun. **63**(3), 628–642 (2015)
7. Xu, Y.J., Zhao, X.H.: Robust probabilistic distributed power control algorithm for underlay cognitive radio networks under channel uncertainties. Wirel. Pers. Commun. **78**(2), 1297–1312 (2014)

Dual Optimal Robust Power Control Algorithm Based on Channel Uncertainty

Guanglong Yang[(✉)], Xuezhi Tan, and Xiao Wang

School of Electronics Information Engineering, Harbin Institute of Technology,
Harbin 150001, People's Republic of China
yang3616@126.com, {Tanxz1957,hitwx}@hit.edu.cn

Abstract. In order to improve the fault-tolerant ability under parameter perturbation, the robust power control problem based on channel uncertainty is studied. In this paper, the robust optimization theory and stochastic optimization theory commonly used to deal with uncertain parameters are deeply analyzed, and the mathematical significance, application scenarios, advantages and disadvantages of the two optimization theories are summarized. A comprehensive solution for bounded uncertainty and probabilistic constraints is proposed. On the one hand, the scheme guarantees the rights and interests of the primary user under the worst error, on the other hand, the secondary user is satisfied with a certain interrupt probability under the condition of system robustness. In this paper, the main user interference temperature and the secondary user probability SINR are taken as the constraint conditions, the maximum throughput of the system is transformed into a convex optimization form, and the Lagrange dual (LD, Lagrange Duality) principle is used to solve the problem. The results show that the double optimization solution is a compromise between probabilistic constraint algorithm, Worst-case algorithm and non-robust algorithm, which not only fully protects the rights and interests of the primary user, but also takes into account the robustness. At the same time, the conservatism of the bounded uncertain design method is avoided.

Keywords: Cognitive radio · Underlay spectrum sharing ·
Distributed power control

1 Introduction

The uncertainty of channel parameters can be described by a variety of uncertain models. For example, the additive uncertainty model describes the uncertainty of channel parameters as the sum of estimated values and estimated errors, that is, the channel parameters vary in a bounded range [1]. In dealing with uncertain parameters, robust optimization theory [2] and stochastic optimization theory [3] are usually used. The robust optimization theory describes the parameter uncertainty as an appropriate closed-loop set of uncertainties, which contains all uncertain estimates, and transforms the robust uncertainty constraints by the worst-case principle (Worst-case). Becomes a deterministic solvable problem. The stochastic optimization theory considers that it is difficult to obtain the upper bound of the error of uncertain parameters, but its statistical

© ICST Institute for Computer Sciences, Social Informatics and Telecommunications Engineering 2019
Published by Springer Nature Switzerland AG 2019. All Rights Reserved
J. Jin et al. (Eds.): GreeNets 2019, LNICST 282, pp. 36–46, 2019.
https://doi.org/10.1007/978-3-030-21730-3_4

model can be obtained by training or other means, and the optimization mathematical model can be described by means of probabilistic constraint. The non-deterministic optimization problem is transformed into a deterministic solvable form by certain mathematical means.

In reference [4], the methods of robust optimization are described in detail, and the different methods of robust optimization in practical application are discussed, including mathematical programming, deterministic nonlinear optimization, direct search, etc. The advantages and disadvantages of different methods are discussed, which provides the basis for adopting the most suitable robust method. In reference [5], the channel gain is defined by the bounded distance between the estimated value and the exact value. Considering the conservatism of worst-case interference, a compromise between robust worst-case interference control and secondary user throughput is proposed. The interference probability of the secondary user to the primary user is controlled under the given threshold. A distributed uplink robust power control algorithm was proposed in reference [6]. Each uncertain parameter is modeled by the bounded distance between the estimated value and the exact value of each uncertain parameter, and the robust power allocation problem is described by the constraint protection value. Lagrange duality decomposition is used to solve the problem by distributed algorithm. SU needs to estimate the worst-case total interference at the PU receiver to ensure that PU is not interfered with.

To sum up, the power control problem of cognitive radio in Underlay mode is studied in the perfect channel and imperfect channel respectively.

2 System Model

In this paper, the underlying spectrum access mode is considered, so it is unnecessary to consider the communication situation of the primary user, and the time of sensing and judging the primary user's activity is reduced indirectly. This paper considers the underlying multi-user distributed cognitive radio scene, as shown in Fig. 1. Primary and secondary users coexist in the network, including M for secondary users, N for primary users. The secondary user is represented by the set $\mathrm{A} = \{1, 2, \cdots, M\}$ and the primary user by the set $\mathrm{B} = \{1, 2, \cdots, N\}$.

Order $\forall i, j \in \mathrm{A}$, $\forall k \in \mathrm{B}$.

In this paper, the interference temperature model in reference [7] is used to describe the interference size of the primary user receiver. In order to achieve the maximum throughput of secondary users, achieve optimal power control, and ensure the stability of primary user communication, the optimization problems considered in this chapter need to satisfy the following three conditions simultaneously:

$$\max \sum_i \log(1 + \gamma_i)$$
$$\text{s.t.} \begin{cases} c_1 : 0 \leq p_i \leq p_i^{\max} \\ c_2 : \sum_i p_i h_{i \leftrightarrow k} \leq I_k^{th} \\ c_3 : \gamma_i \geq \gamma_i^d \end{cases} \tag{1}$$

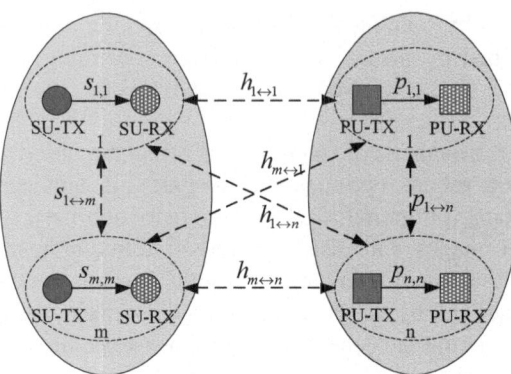

Fig. 1. Multi-user cognitive radio system

Formula (1) is a non-robust optimization problem. There are many uncertain parameters in the formula. The real value is difficult to obtain and can only be obtained by the method of estimation. At the same time, there is a certain error between the formula and the real value.

It can be seen from the constraint c_2 that there is uncertainty in channel gain $h_{i \rightarrow k}$, which may lead to the primary user receiving more interference power, thus leading to the deterioration of the primary user's communication quality and even the interruption of the communication. Constrained c_3 shows that there are uncertainties between channel gain $s_{i \rightarrow j}$ and primary interference I_{ip} between secondary users. This uncertainty may result in the secondary user communication γ_i not reaching the target value, thus the secondary user QoS.

3   Mathematical Model

For the mathematical model of (1), it is necessary to use appropriate methods to describe the uncertain parameters and perform robust control. The methods used to deal with parameter uncertainty are robust optimization and stochastic optimization. In the cognitive radio communication scenario, the communication quality requirement of the primary user is the highest, and any secondary user activities that affect the communication quality of the primary user are not allowed, so the most important prerequisite of this chapter is to ensure the communication quality of the primary user. Because there is no information feedback between primary and secondary users, the estimation error probability distribution of channel gain uncertainty between primary and secondary users is not easy to obtain. The robust optimization will adopt Worst-case method according to the uncertain set. The secondary user transmit power is sacrificed to guarantee the communication quality of the primary user. For cognitive users, a variety of means can be used to obtain a certain amount of information effectively. At the same time, the communication of cognitive users also allows the existence of a certain interruption probability of user equipment. Therefore, stochastic optimization based on probabilistic constraints among cognitive users can keep the overall performance of the system at a stable average.

3.1 Robust Optimization Mathematical Model

The channel gain uncertainty between secondary and primary users can be described using additive uncertainty [8], as follows:

$$\wp = \left\{ h_{i \leftrightarrow k} \middle| \bar{h}_{i \leftrightarrow k} + \Delta h_{i \leftrightarrow k} : |\Delta h_{i \leftrightarrow k}| \leq \kappa_{ik} \bar{h}_{i \leftrightarrow k} \right\} \tag{2}$$

Which, $|\bullet|$ represents an absolute operator. (2) the formula can be described as $h_{i \leftrightarrow k} = \bar{h}_{i \leftrightarrow k} + \Delta h_{i \leftrightarrow k}$, where $\bar{h}_{i \leftrightarrow k}$ represents the estimated value of channel gain, $\Delta h_{i \leftrightarrow k}$ denotes the corresponding estimation error, and $\kappa_{ik} \in [0, 1)$ denotes the uncertainty factor, which can describe the magnitude of uncertainty as well as the accuracy of parameter estimation. When the κ_{ik} is small, the estimation error is small, and the estimated channel gain is close to the real physical channel, that is, $\bar{h}_{i \leftrightarrow k} \to h_{i \leftrightarrow k}$. In special cases, when $\kappa_{ik} = 0$, the equivalent exact channel parameter optimization model based on (2) description of robust optimization problem is presented. When the κ_{ik} is very large, the representative parameter estimation is very large, and the estimation accuracy is not high. Therefore, the magnitude of κ_{ik} value is closely related to the robustness and optimality of the system. In general, the value of κ_{ik} can be determined by estimating the accuracy of the algorithm and the channel state model.

Similarly, considering the uncertainty of secondary users being interfered by primary users, the problem of robust resource allocation can be written as

$$\max \sum_i \log(1 + \gamma_i)$$
$$\text{s.t.} \begin{cases} c_1 : 0 \leq p_i \leq p_i^{\max} \\ c_2'' : \sum_i p_i \bar{h}_{i \leftrightarrow k} (1 + \kappa_{ik}) \leq I_k^{th} \\ c_3 : \gamma_i \geq \gamma_i^d \end{cases} \tag{3}$$

From the constraint c_2'', we can see that the upper limit of secondary user transmit power is smaller than that of accurate channel parameter model (such as $\kappa_{ik} = 0$) because of the introduction of κ_{ik}. Therefore, theoretically speaking, the throughput of the robust optimization problem of cognitive radio system is smaller than that of the non-robust optimization problem. In the uncertain mode, in order to prevent the secondary user's transmit power from affecting the primary user, the secondary user increases the protection of the primary user by transmitting lower power. The purpose of constrained c_3 is to prevent the parameter estimation error from causing the sub-user receiver to actually receive less γ_i than the target value. Next we discuss the uncertainty of c_3 by means of stochastic optimization.

3.2 Stochastic Optimization Mathematical Model

In the previous section, the uncertainty of channel gain between secondary user and primary user is solved by using robust optimization theory. In this section, the stochastic optimization theory is used to solve the uncertainty of channel gain between secondary user and primary user. In order to ensure that the constraint c_3 is true in most communication scenarios in the case of parameter perturbation, the service probability of the secondary user is as follows:

$$\max \sum_i \log(1 + \gamma_i)$$
$$\text{s.t.} \begin{cases} c_1 : 0 \le p_i \le p_i^{\max} \\ c_2'' : \sum_i p_i \bar{h}_{ik}(1 + \kappa_{ik}) \le I_k^{th} \\ c_3' : \Pr\{\gamma_i \ge \gamma_i^d\} \ge \beta_i \end{cases} \tag{4}$$

Which, $\beta_i \in [0, 1]$ is the satisfaction probability of the secondary user set in advance, representing the degree of the actual signal-to-noise ratio higher than the target γ_i^d. The larger the value of β_i is, the less interference between secondary users is required, that is, the lower the transmitting power is, the lower the mutual interference between primary users is to avoid interruptions.

Similar to the traditional stochastic optimization problem [11], problem (4) is not easy to solve, and it needs to be transformed into a deterministic form to obtain an analytical solution.

The stochastic optimization problem is formulated as:

$$\min \sum_i p_i$$
$$\text{s.t.} \begin{cases} c_1 : 0 \le p_i \le p_i^{\max} \\ c_2'' : \sum_i p_i \bar{h}_{ik}(1 + \kappa_{ik}) \le I_k^{th} \\ c_3'' : \gamma_i^d / \bar{\gamma}_i \le \hat{\beta}_i \end{cases} \tag{5}$$

which $\hat{\beta}_i = \ln \frac{1}{\beta_i}$.

4   Double Optimal Robust Power Control

Since problem (5) is a convex optimization problem, the following Lagrangian function can be constructed to solve the problem.

$$J(\{p_i\}, \{\varpi_{i \leftrightarrow k}\}, \{\psi_i\}) = \sum_i p_i$$
$$+ \sum_k \varpi_{i \leftrightarrow k} \left(\sum_i p_i \bar{h}_{i \leftrightarrow k}(1 + \kappa_{ik}) - I_k^{th} \right) \tag{6}$$
$$+ \sum_i \psi_i \left(\frac{\gamma_i^d}{\bar{\gamma}_i} - \hat{\beta}_i \right)$$

Where $\varpi_{i \leftrightarrow k} \geq 0$ and $\psi_i \geq 0$ are the Lagrangian multipliers corresponding to the constraint conditions of problem (5) c_2'' and c_3''. Dual variables can be obtained by updating the following algorithm:

$$\varpi_{i \leftrightarrow k}(t+1) = \left[\varpi_{i \leftrightarrow k}(t) + \lambda\left(p_i \bar{h}_{i \leftrightarrow k}(1 + \kappa_{ik}) - I_k^{th}\right)\right]^+ \tag{7}$$

$$\psi_i(t+1) = \left[\psi_i(t) + \theta\left(\gamma_i^d/\bar{\gamma}_i(t) - \hat{\beta}_i\right)\right]^+ \tag{8}$$

Where λ and θ are non-negative step-size factors.

5   Simulation Results and Analysis

In this section, the effectiveness of the algorithm is verified by simulation results. Firstly, the influence of channel uncertainty between primary and secondary users and the probability of secondary user satisfaction on system performance is analyzed. Then compared with Worst-case robust algorithm [9], probabilistic constraint algorithm [10] and non-robust algorithm, the superiority of the proposed algorithm is illustrated. Suppose there are three secondary users and two primary users in the network model. Channel interference gain $\bar{h}_{i \leftrightarrow k} \in [0, 0.1]$. between secondary and primary users Satisfaction probability $\beta = 0.9$ of secondary users Background noise $\sigma_i \in [0, 0.1]$. Assume that the primary user interferes with the secondary user sum is $I_{ip} = 2\sigma_i$. Assume the minimum SINR $\gamma_i^d \in [2\,\text{dB}, 6\,\text{dB}]$, maximum transmit power $p_i^{\max} = 1\,\text{mW}$ for each secondary user in the network model.

Figure 2 illustrates the relationship between channel gain uncertainty and total throughput between primary and secondary users at different interference temperatures.

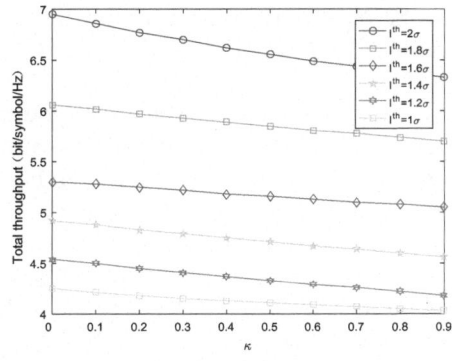

Fig. 2. Effect curve with the change of uncertainty κ in interference channel for the total throughput.

When the disturbance uncertainty is $\kappa = 0$, the uncertainty estimation error of the system is 0. The larger the uncertain parameter κ is, the greater the estimation error is, and the bigger the deviation between the estimated channel gain and the real value is. From Fig. 2, assume that each secondary user has the same SINR, that is, $\gamma_1^d = 2$ dB. It can be seen that the total throughput of the secondary users decreases with the increase of the channel gain uncertainty parameter κ between the primary and secondary users for the fixed interference temperature I^{th}. Due to the uncertainty of the estimation error increasing, the secondary user can only reduce the transmit power in order to satisfy the constraint condition of the primary user interference. In the case of the same parameter κ, the larger the interference temperature I^{th} of the primary user is, the larger the total throughput of the secondary user is. This is because as the primary user I^{th} increases, the secondary user transmit power range is more relaxed, secondary users can use higher transmission power. However, due to p_i^{max} constraints, secondary users have the maximum transmit power limit.

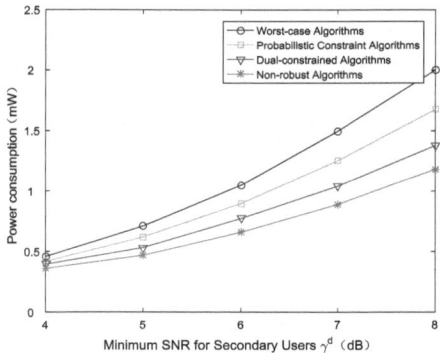

Fig. 3. Contrast curve of power dissipation for different algorithms

Figures 3 and 4 show the superiority of the algorithm by comparing it with Worst-case algorithm, probabilistic constraint algorithm and non-robust algorithm respectively.

Figure 3 describes the relationship between the total power consumption of secondary users and the target SINR. Assume that the interference temperature threshold in the network model is $I_{th} = 0.01$ mW. It can be seen from Fig. 3 that the total power consumption of secondary users increases with the increase of secondary user target SINR. Secondary users need to meet service probabilities, while secondary users also need to gradually increase transmission power to achieve higher SINR. It can be seen from the figure that the non-robust algorithm consumes the least power and the Worst-case algorithm consumes the maximum power. The Worst-case algorithm needs to transmit higher power to suppress the SINR drop caused by the worst parameter uncertainty in the system. The non-robust algorithm assumes that the system parameters are known accurately and does not need to adjust the transmission power to suppress the influence of uncertain parameters such as the Worst-case algorithm, so the power consumption is the minimum, but the robustness is the worst. The energy consumed by the probabilistic constraint algorithm lies between the above two algorithms. The power consumption of the proposed double constraint algorithm is between probabilistic constraint algorithm and non-robust algorithm.

The dual constraint algorithm takes full account of the uncertainty of channel gain between primary and secondary users, and reduces the use of the method between secondary users.

Figure 4 shows the actual SINR performance curve received by sub-users of different algorithms. The perturbed range of channel parameters is determined in $\Delta s \in [-0.05, 0.05]$. In a cognitive radio network where 2 primary users coexist with 3 secondary users, the interrupt probability of secondary users is The target SINR is $\gamma_i^d = 2\,\text{dB}$.

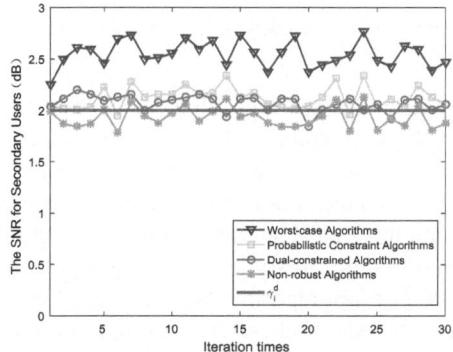

Fig. 4. Contrast curve of robustness for different algorithms

As can be seen from Fig. 4, there is no direct mathematical relationship between the non-robust algorithm and the variation of channel gain, so the variation of channel parameters will not affect the transmission power, so that although the power consumption is the minimum, it is the best protection for the primary user. However, the robustness is the worst, which can not satisfy the service probability of the secondary users well, and the robustness is the worst compared with other algorithms. In imperfect channels, as shown in Fig. 4, the non-robust algorithm leads to higher outage probability for secondary users. In order to realize the normal communication for all secondary users, Worst-case adjusts the transmission power based on the worst uncertain parameters, and the probability of the secondary user satisfaction is equal to 100. The probabilistic constraint algorithm uses the service probability of different users as the constraint condition, as shown in Fig. 4, this algorithm leads to 6.7% outage probability of the secondary user, which is greatly improved compared with the non-robust algorithm. In this paper, the probability of service between secondary users is used as the constraint condition, and the worst-case uncertain set of channel gain is fully considered between primary and secondary users. In order to suppress the uncertainty of gain, the transmit power of secondary users will be reduced. Indirectly, the probability of secondary user service is reduced.

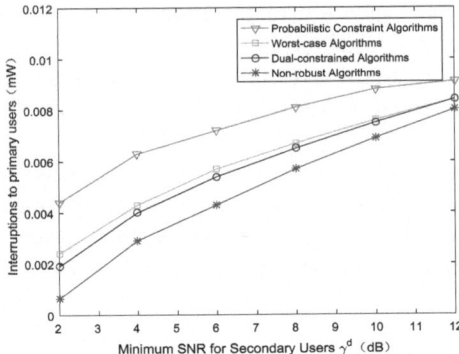

Fig. 5. Interference curve caused by different algorithms for primary users

It can be seen from Fig. 5 that the non-robust algorithm with minimal interference to the primary user and the probabilistic constraint algorithm with the greatest interference on the primary user. The non-robust channel is based on the excellent channel state. With the increase of channel information accuracy, the probabilistic constraint algorithm can more accurately control the interference to the primary user, and it is also the closest control method to the primary user interference. Compared with the Worst-case algorithm, the dual constraint algorithm has less interference to the primary user. In order to suppress the influence of channel uncertainty on the secondary user SINR, the secondary user in the Worst-case algorithm is bound to increase the power more, while the dual constraint algorithm adopts the method of satisfying the service probability among the secondary users, which provides more protection to the primary user.

The non-robust algorithm does not need to overcome the uncertain influence to increase the power consumption, the power consumption is minimum, the primary user protection is the best, but the robustness is the worst. The Worst-case algorithm considers all the worst uncertain sets. The transmission power is used to ensure that the user can communicate normally under the uncertainty of the worst-case parameters.

For cognitive systems, the Worst-case algorithm is applied to the power control between secondary users, and the algorithm will consider increasing the transmission power to meet the higher SINR requirements of the secondary users, resulting in the maximum power consumption.

Probabilistic constraint algorithm mainly makes primary user and secondary user satisfy certain interrupt probability constraint. It is a compromise method based on Worst-case algorithm and non-robust algorithm. However, the above method assumes that the cognitive system knows the distribution of uncertain parameters. However, for the diversity and time-varying of the communication environment between primary and secondary users, it is difficult to obtain a statistical model with uncertain parameters, which has the greatest interference to primary users.

It can be seen from the above results that it is important to ensure that the primary users in cognitive radio systems are not interfered with, taking into account the power consumption of the algorithm and the robust performance of the secondary users. The double optimization algorithm proposed in this paper is a compromise method between several algorithms, which not only fully protects the primary user, but also takes into account some robustness, and at the same time is not as conservative as the bounded uncertainty design method.

6 Conclusion

In this chapter, the existing uncertain parameters in cognitive radio systems are fully listed, and the reasons for these uncertainties are analyzed in depth, and the significance of considering these uncertain parameters in practical applications is clarified. The channel parameters between primary and secondary users are cross-system parameters. In non-cooperative mode, the channel parameters are difficult to obtain, while the channel parameters between secondary users are intra-system parameters, and channel parameters are easier to obtain. On the one hand, the channel gain uncertainty between primary and secondary users is described by additive uncertainty method, and the existence of worst-case estimation error is considered. Worst-case algorithm is used in power optimization. On the other hand, the probability distribution function is assumed to be known among secondary users, and probabilistic constraint algorithm is used in power optimization. In this chapter, two optimization methods, bounded uncertainty and probabilistic constraints, are organically combined, and a double optimization algorithm is proposed, which solves the problem of the interruption probability of primary users caused by the probabilistic constraint algorithm. At the same time, the problem of Worst-case algorithm is improved too conservatively. The simulation results show that the double constraint algorithm proposed in this paper has more practical value.

References

1. Setoodeh, P., Haykin, S.: Robust transmit power control for cognitive radio. Proc. IEEE **97** (5), 915–939 (2009)
2. Han, S., Liang, Y.-C., Soong, B.-H.: Robust joint resource allocation for OFDMA-CDMA spectrum refarming system. IEEE Trans. Commun. **64**(3), 1291–1302 (2016)
3. Dantzig, G.B.: Linear programming under uncertainty. Manage. Sci. **1**(3–4), 197–206 (1955)
4. Beyer, H.G., Sendhoff, B.: Robust optimization-a comprehensive survey. Comput. Methods Appl. Mech. Eng. **196**(33), 3190–3218 (2007)
5. Parsaeefard, S., Sharafat, A.R.: Robust worst-case interference control in underlay cognitive radio networks. IEEE Trans. Veh. Technol. **61**(8), 3731–3745 (2012)
6. Parsaeefard, S., Sharafat, A.R.: Robust distributed power control in cognitive radio networks. IEEE Trans. Mob. Comput. **12**(4), 609–620 (2013)
7. Akyildiz, I.F., Lee, W., Vuran, M.C., et al.: Next generation/dynamic spectrum access/cognitive radio wireless networks: a survey. Comput. Netw. **50**(13), 2127–2159 (2006)
8. Xu, Y., Zhao, X., Liang, Y.-C.: Robust power control and beamforming in cognitive radio networks: a survey. IEEE Commun. Surv. Tutorials **17**(4), 1834–1857 (2015)

9. Xu, Y.J., Zhao, X.H.: Robust probabilistic distributed power control algorithm for underlay cognitive radio networks under channel uncertainties. Wireless Pers. Commun. **78**(2), 1297–1312 (2014)
10. Xu, Y.J., Zhao, X.H.: Robust power control for underlay cognitive radio networks under probabilistic quality of service and interference constraints. IET Commun. **8**(18), 3333–3340 (2014)
11. Soltani, N.Y., Kim, S., Glannakis, G.B.: Chance-constrained optimization of OFDMA cognitive radio uplinks. IEEE Trans. Wireless Commun. **12**(3), 1098–1107 (2013)

Lighting Design and Energy Saving

High-Performance LED Light Source Mixed Optical System Design

Yijing Wei[1], Xinpeng Zhang[1], and Yuncui Zhang[2(✉)]

[1] Graduate School, Dalian Polytechnic University, Dalian 116034, China
[2] Polytechnic University Dalian, Dalian 116034, China
Zhang_yc@dlpu.edu.cn

Abstract. Due to the increased quality requirements of lighting environment, high-performance LED mixed-light lighting research has become a trend. According to the principle of imaging optics, an optical system design method with dual optical path mixing with long mixing distance is proposed. The optical path includes nine lenses, the semi-reverse half lens is placed at the aperture stop, and the double optical path corresponds to different performance LED integrated chips. The optical system has a longitudinal magnification of −1, a curvature of field of 0.5 mm, and a distortion of less than 0.2%, and achieves light mixing of a high uniformity and high color rendering LED.

Keywords: Optical design · Double light path · LED · Uniformity · Color rendering

1 Introduction

With the expansion of applications and deep people, users have further demand for LED lighting. The main points of these requirements are: high enough uniformity to meet the demand for lighting environment brightness; further improve the color rendering of lighting sources Sex to meet the needs of high color rendering occasions, as well as special occasions to achieve high uniformity illumination and high color rendering of LED lighting [1]. The LED mixed light can be divided into two colors, three colors and four colors according to the color of the light source. The calculation method of the mixed light is slightly different, but the light mixing ratio is determined according to the target color temperature, thereby obtaining the spectral power distribution of the white light, and then Calculate other colorimetric parameters. Hsun-Ching Hsu abroad proposed a new method for designing reflectors that provide high unidirectional illumination and good directionality. The strategy is based primarily on the law of reflection in geometric optics and the illuminance and luminous flux in photometry. And some basic terms, by dividing the luminous flux and assigning each of them to the calculated area, high illumination uniformity and good directivity can be obtained [2]. Huang Ruibin et al. analyzed the Fourier transform of the lens, and the spatial transmission of the near-field to the far-field, the influence on the color distribution of the light, the Fourier transform of the lens, and the spatial transmission of the near-field to the far-field, resulting in the color distribution of the light. The impact [3]. In this paper, two different monochromatic optical paths are proposed. By using a red

J. Jin et al. (Eds.): GreeNets 2019, LNICST 282, pp. 49–56, 2019.
https://doi.org/10.1007/978-3-030-21730-3_5

LED and other different monochromatic LEDs, the half-reverse lens is mixed to extend the mixed working distance to enhance the existing LED lighting. The optical index is mainly to improve the uniformity and color rendering of the light source. It is of great significance for the research of LED lighting and the improvement of LED lighting quality. It is the hot spot of LED lighting research and the direction of green health lighting in the future.

2 Design Principle

The research goal of high-performance LED mixed-light illumination is to use high-efficiency LEDs with other different monochromatic lights to form new types of illumination through scientific mixing to achieve high-performance LEDs with high uniformity and high color rendering. Lighting [4].

The traditional light mixing method mostly uses two different monochromatic light LEDs to mix the working area. The intersection point of the two optical paths is the working area, so the working area distance is very short, resulting in uneven mixing, short working distance, etc. The optical path performance is affected, as shown in Fig. 1. The traditional mixed light mode; therefore, in order to improve the uniformity of LED light mixing, this paper improves the traditional LED's light mixing mode, as shown in Fig. 2, using two monochromatic LED light paths, with red light. Adding other different monochromatic lights, using a half-reflex lens at the aperture stop, the two optical paths are combined into one optical path.

The difference between Figs. 1 and 2 is that the two light sources in Fig. 1 are in the same plane and only have an intersection point in a certain area, so there are disadvantages such as uneven light mixing; and the two light sources in Fig. 2 are in different plane dimensions. By synthesizing a light beam by the action of the semi-reverse half lens, it acts on the plane, which increases the working distance of the light

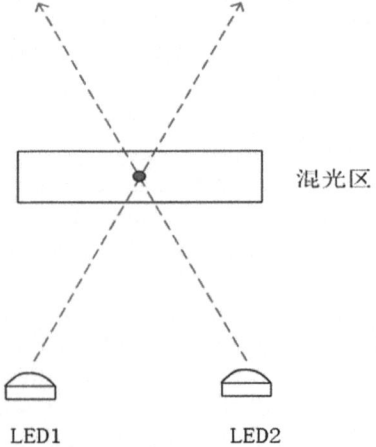

混光区

LED1   LED2

Fig. 1. Traditional LED light mixing mode

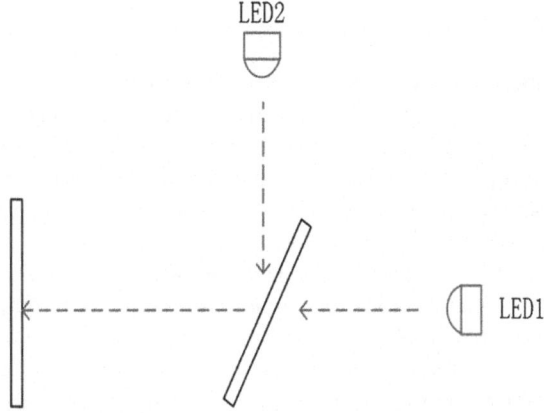

Fig. 2. Improved LED mixing mode

mixing, so that the light mixing is more uniform, thereby improving the performance of the mixed light output.

In this paper, an optical system is designed. As shown in Fig. 3, a red LED is placed at the rear lens. A half-reflex lens is placed at the aperture stop of the front focal plane of the lens of the front lens, and an LED light path is added at the top. The group of lenses has different monochromatic light LEDs, which form the basic frame of the optical system, and then the position of the half-reflex lens relative to the rear group lens is variable to balance the aberration, and the optical path lens parameters and position are adjusted, and finally the two optical paths are made. Uniform light mixing and synthesis of a light path, and greatly improve the performance of the original LED light path, embodied in uniformity and color rendering performance.

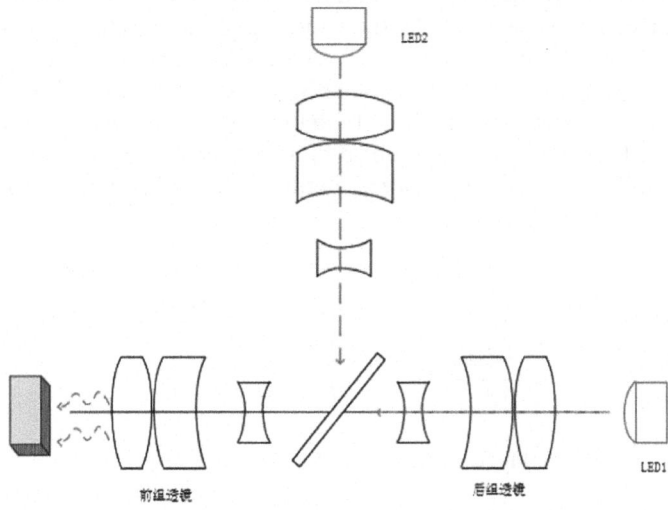

Fig. 3. LED light mixing optical system frame (Color figure online)

3 Design Goals

The uniformity of the light source is one of the important criteria for the light source. Single LED as a near-Lambert light emitting light energy output is low, and the divergence angle is large, it is difficult to directly use. In LED lighting applications, a beam with a smaller angle than the actual demand is usually designed, and then passed through a matte, microlens. Or the material is scattered and mixed [5]. In this paper, two monochromatic LED optical paths are used as the light source for mixed color light. The two optical paths are synthesized through a semi-reverse half-lens. By extending the working distance, the color light is fully mixed and output to improve the uniformity of the light source [6].

The color rendering of a light source is one of the important criteria for a light source. For high-color rendering places requiring a color rendering index Ra of 90 or more, such as printing, textile, printing and dyeing, movies, etc., we need to conduct research on high color rendering illumination on the basis of the original, and the research methods are mainly It is divided into improvements and reconstructions on the basis of the original. In this paper, by combining two different monochromatic optical paths to complement each other, Ra is improved by adding red light to improve color rendering [7].

The design of the optical system is to combine the original two different monochromatic LED optical paths, red LEDs and other different color LED optical paths, and uniformly mix the light through the semi-reverse half lens to form a complementary optical path to perform uniformity and color rendering. A holistic improvement.

4 Design Results and Analysis

Through the above theoretical analysis and parameter setting, the lens structure of the optimized 6-piece lens is selected. As shown in Fig. 4, the LED1 is placed behind the direct optical system structure, and then a semi-reverse lens is placed at the aperture stop to refract the optical path [8]. In another light path, as shown in Fig. 5, the LED 2 is placed behind the lens structure 2, and the two LED light paths are used as a light source for mixed output, and finally mixed into an optical path, as shown in Fig. 6 to obtain a high uniformity and high color rendering. Sexual high performance LED light path [9].

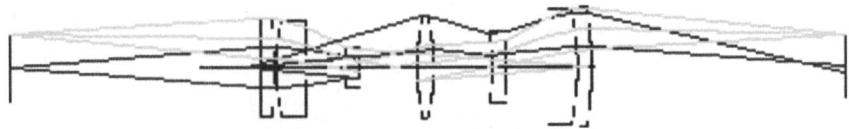

Fig. 4. Direct optical system structure

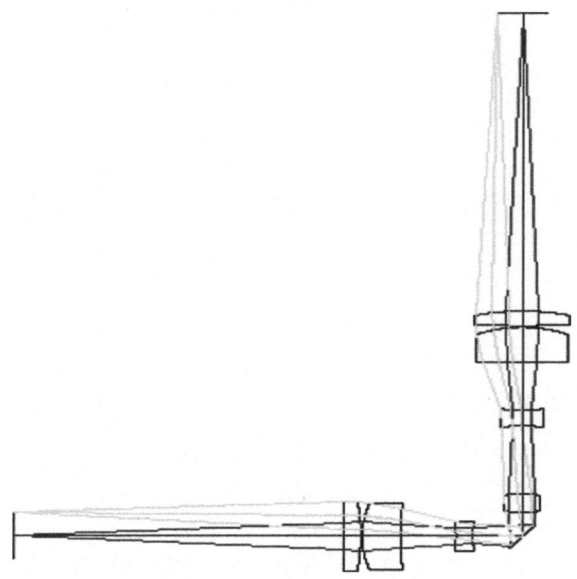

Fig. 5. Reflective optical system structure

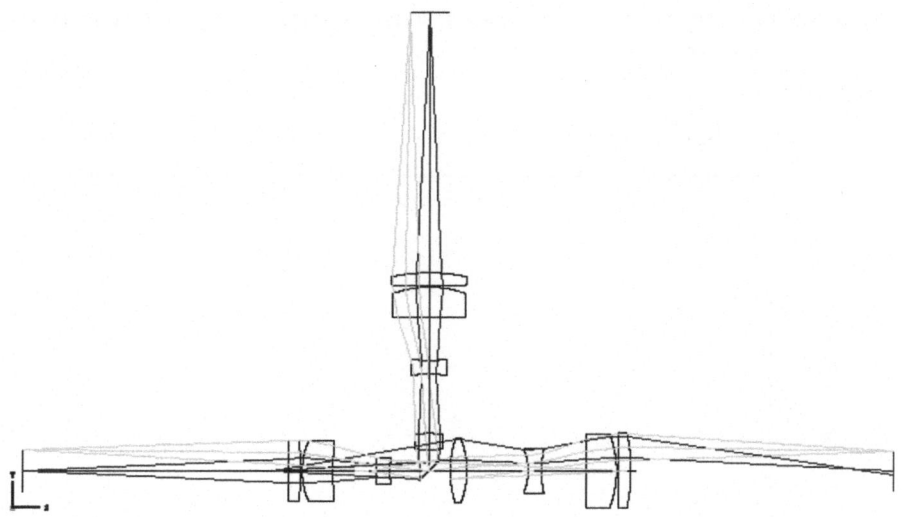

Fig. 6. Total lens structure

As shown in the figure below, after optimization, the satisfactory MTF function and small chromatic aberration can be obtained under the premise that the point map meets the requirements. The optimization result is shown in Fig. 7.

This Spot Diagrams is used to study the imaging quality of the system by achieving the convergence of the image surface light and the size of the imaged dots. As shown in the Spot Diagrams of Fig. 3, the optical system has a certain astigmatism, but no coma

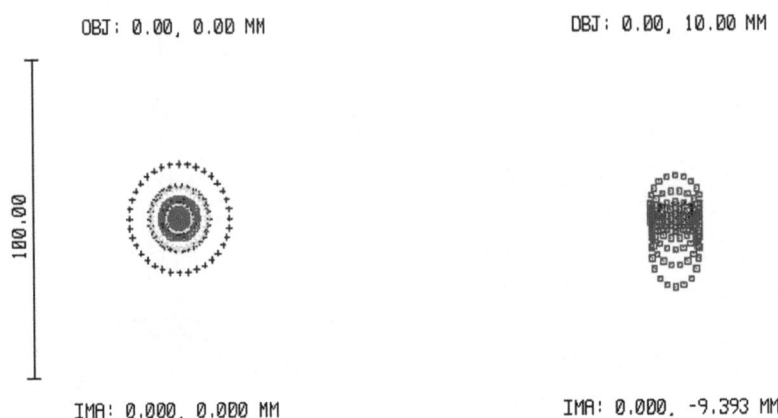

Fig. 7. Spot Diagrams

is generated. The size of the spot reaching the image plane is not perfect, but it is similar to the size of the Airy spot, and in the two fields of view. The maximum root mean square radius is 7.236 μm, which means that the design meets the requirements.

It can be seen from the MTF function curve of Fig. 8. When the cutoff frequency is below 100, the MTF value of the field of view is greater than 0.3, that is, the image reaching the image plane can be clearly seen, so the imaging quality of the lens satisfies the design requirements.

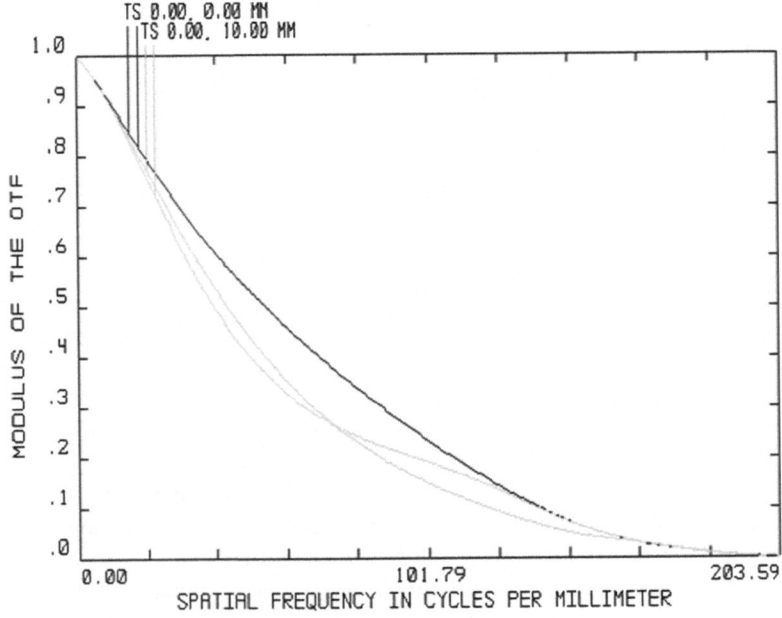

Fig. 8. MTF function

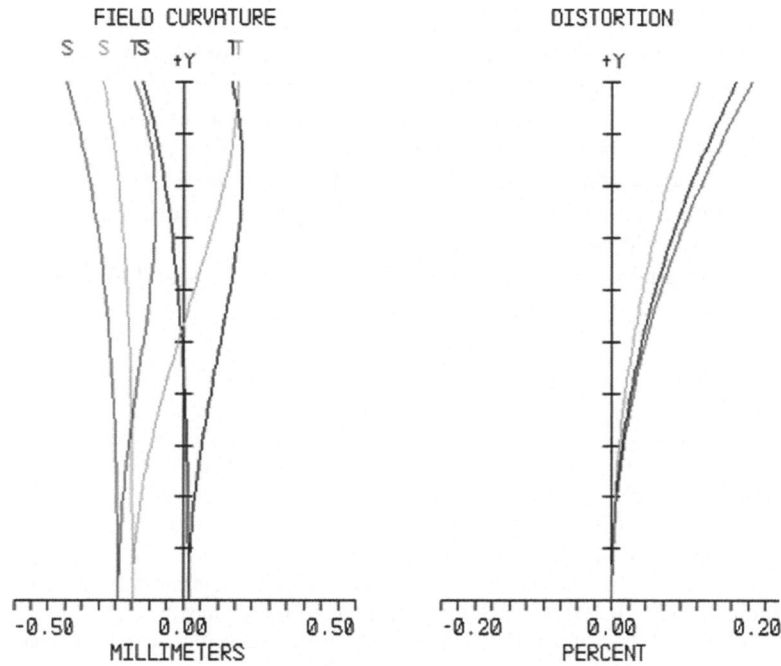

Fig. 9. Field curvature and distortion map

The field curve is an important parameter reflecting the quality of the image, which reflects the degree of surface curvature of the image [5]. As shown in Fig. 9, the field curve is in the range of 0.5 mm, which satisfies the requirements. Although the distortion does not affect the imaging quality, the distortion size affects the accuracy of the imaging, and the distortion of the system is corrected to about 0.2% by design requirements, which meets the design requirements.

5   Conclusion

In order to improve the uniformity and color rendering of the optical system, the design uses two different monochromatic LEDs as the light source to lengthen the working distance and synthesize the complementary output light source through the semi-reverse half lens to improve the uniformity of the system imaging. And color rendering, research and design of high-performance LED light source hybrid optical system.

The optical system design uses Zemax as the main design tool to design two optical path structures, one basic 6-piece lens optical structure, and the other optical structure is to add a half at a 45-degree angle to the aperture stop of the original basic optical structure. The anti-half lens makes the optical path of the rear group lens refract at 90 degrees, and then combines the two optical paths into one optical system by using multiple structures, and adds two light sources of LED1 and LED2 respectively after the two optical systems, and the two optical paths are fully synthesized and complemented. The output of the light source is improved in uniformity and color rendering. Finally, the optical quality of the optical system is analyzed by simulating the optical system. The designed optical system has a certain astigmatism, but no coma is generated. The MTF meets certain imaging standards and field curvature. The optical system with distortion control within 0.5 mm and 0.2% improves the traditional mixed light illumination mode and greatly improves the light source performance such as the uniformity of the light source.

Thank to the Shenzhen Qianbaihui Lighting Engineering Co., Ltd. Research Fund (Project No. 2017-228195).

References

1. Yuhua, Z., Youbin, P., Shen Jimei, F.: LED lighting color effect on health. China Lighting Appl. (1), 5–8 (2015)
2. Hsu, H.-C., Han, P.: High uniformity and directivity of a reflective device with optical flux partition method. J. Disp. Technol. 11(12) (2015)
3. Ruibin, H., Niansong, G., Jiandong, L.: The application of Fourier transform principle in LED lighting mixed light. In: 2014 China Lighting Forum Proceedings (2014)
4. Guang, Y.: Research on high-performance LED mixed light illumination. China Lighting Appl. 6, 11–14 (2016)
5. Wang, P., Jin, Z., Xiong, D.: Optimal optical design of UV-LED curing system with high illumination and luminance uniformity. In: 15th China International Forum on Solid State Lighting: International Forum on Wide Bandgap Semiconductors China (SSL China: IFWS), 23–25 October 2018
6. Zhu, G., Sun, J., Gan, Z.: A novel approach to calculate the deposition uniformity of multi-target sputtering system. In: 19th International Conference on Electronic Packaging Technology (ICEPT), 8–11 August 2018
7. Wu, R., Zheng, Z., Li, H., et al.: Optimization design of irradiance array for LED uniform rectangular illumination. Appl. Opt. 51(13), 2257 (2012)
8. Hsu, H.C., Han, P.: Optical flux partition method for high uniformity illumination of a refractive lens. Appl. Opt. 53, H14–H19 (2014)
9. Yingjie, S., Wenbin, B.: Study on Uniformity of Illumination in LED lighting. J. Nat. Sci. Harbin Normal University 124(3) (2008)

A Framework for Classification of Data Stream Application in Vehicular Network Computing

Ling Yu[1], Yang Gao[2], Yu Zhang[2], and Li Guo[2(✉)]

[1] Network Information Center, Dalian Polytechnic University,
Dalian 116000, Liaoning, China
[2] School of Information Science and Engineering,
Dalian Polytechnic University, Dalian 116000, Liaoning, China
guoli@dlpu.edu.cn

Abstract. Due to the fast developing of intelligent vehicles and the dynamic sensor network, a huge amount of data streams are generated continuously. How to manage these data stream will play a very important role in the development of next-generation intelligent vehicular networks. Data stream classification problem poses many new challenges to the data mining area. One of the most basic challenges is how to make a tradeoff between data stream generating and classifying process. In this paper, we address this problem using a new framework and a new classification method, namely Extreme Support Vector Machine (ESVM), for large-scale data stream classification for specialty vehicle network. Moreover, a new forgetting strategy is designed for the proposed TFS-PESVM model, which employs the residual weight matrix to optimal residual value and improves the effectiveness of new data samples. The experimental results show that the proposed data stream classification model can improve the speed of classification process and less affected by noise interference.

Keywords: Data stream classification · ESVM · Incremental learning · MapReduce · Vehicular network

1 Introduction

The specialty vehicles industry has recently shifted from developing advanced vehicles to concentrating on safety and functionality, which stimulates the development of new intelligent vehicles with advanced assistance systems and even autonomous driving. However, the current technology development is still far from the practical require-ments of intelligent vehicles. This is because the existing control approaches are mainly based on traditional sensors and cameras employed in the specialty vehicle that hinder the development of intelligent vehicles. Thanks to wireless communication networks, vehicles can be connected and can communicate with each other. Thus, the control of vehicles will become more reliable with the communication between vehicles. Therefore, managing the data stream obtained from the sensor network of vehicles has become one of the key research issues in the field of specialty vehicle control.

Currently, data stream mining has become a new research topic in the data mining community. The large-scale and real-time classification nature of data streams require

© ICST Institute for Computer Sciences, Social Informatics and Telecommunications Engineering 2019
Published by Springer Nature Switzerland AG 2019. All Rights Reserved
J. Jin et al. (Eds.): GreeNets 2019, LNICST 282, pp. 57–67, 2019.
https://doi.org/10.1007/978-3-030-21730-3_6

an efficient and effective method that is significantly different from the traditional static data mining methods [1]. However, a data stream is a fast and continuous phenomenon, which can be assumed to have infinite length. Therefore, it is impractical to store and use all the historical data for classifier training [2].

For the problem presented in the area of data stream mining for a specialty vehicle network, the most obvious alternative is the incremental learning method. Several incremental learning based data stream classification technologies have been proposed to address this problem. Also, concept drift occurs in the stream when the underlying concepts of the stream change over time, which means that the classifier needs to be updated in real time [3]. However, the existing data stream classification methods are still weak for some practical applications.

Currently, several frameworks have been introduced into the data stream classification area, e.g., MapReduce. For the parallel nature of MapReduce, most researchers are studying how to modify the traditional classification method into a MapReduce style [4, 5], and now some related methods have been proposed. A MapReduce framework based on the K-NN algorithm was proposed [6], which decreases the running time of the K-NN algorithm significantly and improves the ability of multi-classification. However, its inner problems, such as choosing a suitable distance function and related parameters, are still unsolved. An analogous method was proposed [7] that combines a decision tree with the MapReduce framework for classification. To employ the Support Vector Machine (SVM) model in MapReduce, a new minimal sequence optimization method [8] was proposed to improve the speed of computing quadratic programming problems. A parallel method [9] was proposed to compute hyperplane bias, which would accelerate the best hyperplane selection process. Based on these methods, for the concept drift problem, Zhao et al. proposed an incremental learning based SVM model [10], but in a parallel environment, the performance of this method is a little weak. Although the methods above are trying to modify the traditional classification methods in parallel, their performance still has much potential for some real applications [11].

In this paper, a new data stream classification method, called TFS-PESVM, is proposed which employs extreme support vector machine (ESVM) as a classifier [12], MapReduce as a parallel framework, an incremental learning method to track concept drift and classifier updates, and a forgetting strategy to improve the effectiveness of new data. We apply our method to some synthetic data streams for specialty vehicle networks, which includes four data sets. Also, the proposed model is also compared with two distinct data stream models. The experiment on big stream data is used to test the proposed method and the framework.

2   Framework of Data Stream Classification

Due to the high mobility of vehicles and the dynamic change of the network topology, it is difficult to provide satisfying data analysis services for vehicles through a single network. Hence, providing heterogeneous vehicular networks may support the communication, control and computation requirements of intelligent vehicles well. However, there are multiple critical challenges in designing efficient and flexible data stream mining methods since this requires the joint design and optimization of both analysis, computing and data mining model.

In this paper, we develop a MapReduce based framework, shown in Fig. 1. Suppose there are several vehicles in the vehicular network. The data stream is generated from the sensors mounted on the vehicle. There are two basic structures for analyzing the data stream named "Key" and "Value", which are correlative. The basic process contains two steps. Firstly, in the Map step, the mission is divided into some Map missions. Each map mission relies on a sensor. In the mapping step, the process is distributed to distinct computers. Secondly, in the Reduce step, the mission is grouped with a vehicle according to the "Key" and "Value" of the data stream. Distinct groups are distributed to different Reduce missions, and finally, the result is collected and outputted according to "Key" and "Value". Then, we can obtain the overview of the whole vehicle network.

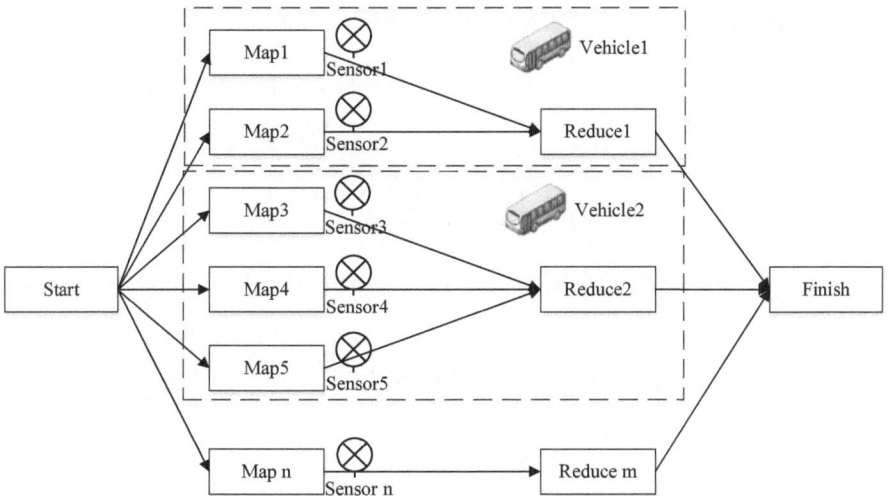

Fig. 1. 2 Framework of data stream classification.

3   The Enhanced ESVM Method

In this paper, we proposed a novel method based on the ESVM model. The ESVM model is a classification model in data mining [13], which is inspired by the Extreme learning machine (ELM) model [14]. The ESVM model employs random value and matrix computing methods to solve model parameters. Since the computation does not require iteration, ESVM is faster in the training process than the traditional SVM model.

Let $S = \{X, Y\}$ be the training sample, let $X = [x_1, x_2, \ldots, x_N]^T \in R^{N \times d}$ be training data, let $Y = [y_1, y_2, \ldots, y_N]^T \in R^{N \times 1}$ be the class label, let $y_i \in [-1, 1]$, let N denote the size of the training sample, and let d denotes the feature size. The ESVM can be formulated by the following optimal condition:

$$
\begin{cases}
min \frac{v}{2}\|\varepsilon\|^2 + \frac{1}{2}\left\|\begin{bmatrix} w \\ b \end{bmatrix}\right\|^2 \\
s.t. Y(w\varphi(X) - be) = e - \varepsilon
\end{cases}
\tag{1}
$$

where $\varepsilon = [\varepsilon_1, \varepsilon_2, \ldots, \varepsilon_N]^T$ is the ESVM model error vector, v denotes the error punish parameter, w and b denote weight vector and threshold, respectively, e denotes a unit vector, and $\varphi(x)$ denotes the kernel function of the ELM model, which can be formulated as

$$
\varphi(x) = G(Ax) = \left(g\left(\sum_{j=1}^n A_{1j}x_j + A_{1(n+1)}\right), \ldots, g\left(\sum_{j=1}^n A_{nj}x_j + A_{n(n+1)}\right)\right)
\tag{2}
$$

where the matrix $A \in R^{d \times (d+1)}$ denotes the input bias and threshold matrix, which is randomly generated.

For ESVM incremental learning, given a dataset $S_1 = \{X_1, Y_1\}$, the trained ESVM model can be formulated as

$$
\begin{bmatrix} w \\ b \end{bmatrix} = \left(\frac{1}{v} + E_{\varphi 1}^T E_{\varphi 1}\right)^{-1} E_{\varphi 1}^T Y_1
\tag{3}
$$

Given a new dataset $S_2 = \{X_2, Y_2\}$, the ESVM incremental learning is formulated as

$$
\begin{aligned}
\begin{bmatrix} w \\ b \end{bmatrix} &= \left(\frac{1}{v} + \begin{bmatrix} E_{\varphi 1}^T & E_{\varphi 2}^T \end{bmatrix}\begin{bmatrix} E_{\varphi 1} \\ E_{\varphi 2} \end{bmatrix}\right)^{-1}\begin{bmatrix} E_{\varphi 1}^T & E_{\varphi 2}^T \end{bmatrix}\begin{bmatrix} Y_1 \\ Y_2 \end{bmatrix} \\
&= \left(\frac{1}{v} + E_{\varphi 1}^T E_{\varphi 1} + E_{\varphi 2}^T E_{\varphi 2}\right)^{-1}\left(E_{\varphi 1}^T Y_1 + E_{\varphi 2}^T Y_2\right)
\end{aligned}
\tag{4}
$$

where $E_{\varphi 1}^T E_{\varphi 1}$ and $E_{\varphi 1}^T Y_1$ is same as in Eq. (3) and does not need to be recomputed. Therefore, we only need to compute $E_{\varphi 2}^T E_{\varphi 2}$ and $E_{\varphi 2}^T Y_2$ in the incremental learning process.

3.1   Parallel ESVM Model

The kernel idea of the parallel ESVM (PESVM) model can be formulated as

$$
E_\varphi^T Y = [a_1, \ldots, a_N][y_1, \ldots, y_N]^T = \sum_{i=1}^N y_i a_i \in \mathbb{R}^{(d+1) \times 1}
\tag{5.1}
$$

$$
E_\varphi^T Y = [a_1, \ldots, a_N][y_1, \ldots, y_N]^T = \sum_{i=1}^N y_i a_i \in \mathbb{R}^{(d+1) \times 1}
\tag{5.2}
$$

Where $E_\varphi^T E_\varphi$ and $E_\varphi^T Y$ are the same as in Eq. (4).

In most practical applications, the sample size is usually larger than the feature size so that the main computing process can focus on $E_\varphi^T E_\varphi$ and $E_\varphi^T Y$. According to Eqs. (5.1 and 5.2), the computing process of $E_\varphi^T E_\varphi$ and $E_\varphi^T Y$ is equivalent to the sum of a small-scale matrix, which is suitable for applying in the MapReduce framework. Therefore, the PESVM model can be illustrated as shown in Table 1.

Table 1. PESVM model algorithm.

Algorithm 1 PESVM model
Step 1 Input weighted matrix A
Step 2 Samples in the dataset are inputted into the Map process, compute $\varphi(x_i)$ using Eq. (2), and then construct $a_i = [\varphi(x_i), -1]^T$ as
$\qquad$ local_aa$^T = \sum a_i a_i^T$, local_ya $= \sum y_i a_i \qquad\qquad\qquad\qquad$ (6)
Step 3 In the Reduce step, compute
$\qquad$ global_aa$^T = global\_aa^T + \sum local_{a_i a_i}^T$, Global_ya$^T = global\_ya^T +$
$\sum local\_ya_i^T \qquad\qquad\qquad\qquad\qquad\qquad\qquad\qquad\qquad\qquad\qquad$ (7)
$\qquad$**Step 4** According to Eq. (4), parallel ESVM obtains the values of the parameters w and r .

3.2   Time-Forgetting Strategy PESVM Model

Although the PESVM model employs an incremental learning method and the MapReduce framework to accelerate the data stream classification process, there are still two basic problems. First, the parameter of the kernel function is randomly selected, which would highly affect the final classification result and make the output of classification unstable. Second, although the PESVM model updates itself by an incremental learning method, the training samples in incremental learning are not distinguished, i.e., all of them have the same learning weight.

Therefore, for the above two problems, in this paper, we propose a time-forgetting strategy PESVM model (TFS-PESVM). TFS-PESVM mainly contains two steps: firstly, it employs a kernel density method to evaluate the residual probability distribution of the training data; and secondly, it uses a weight matrix to correct the residual values and improve reliability. Also, the proposed forgetting strategy decreases the effect of old samples and increases the effect of the new samples at the same time.

3.3   TFS-PESVM Modeling

TFS-PESVM model training process can be formulated as

$$\varphi(X)^T w - be = [\varphi(X) \quad -e]\begin{bmatrix} w \\ b \end{bmatrix} = E_\varphi \begin{bmatrix} w \\ b \end{bmatrix} = Y + \varepsilon \qquad (8)$$

where the error ε is computed using the Least Square method in the original PESVM model. To correct the error, we use the residual matrix method. Let the residual matrix is P, the objective function is formulated as

$$\min \frac{v}{2} \varepsilon^T P \varepsilon + \frac{1}{2} \left\| \begin{bmatrix} w \\ b \end{bmatrix} \right\|^2 \tag{9}$$

Combining Eqs. (9) with (8), the final TFS-PESVM is

$$\begin{bmatrix} w \\ b \end{bmatrix} = \left(I + v E_\varphi^T P E_\varphi \right)^{-1} E_\varphi^T P Y \tag{10}$$

where $P = diag\{p(\varepsilon_1), p(\varepsilon_2), \cdots, p(\varepsilon_N)\}$ and $p(\varepsilon)$ is probability distribution function of the residual ε. However, in some practical situations, the residual ε cannot be obtained in advance, so we compute estimates of $\varepsilon(\widetilde{\varepsilon})$ using Eq. (8), and then use kernel density estimation to obtain $p(\varepsilon)$,

$$p(\varepsilon) = \frac{1}{N} \sum_{i=1}^{N} f\left(\frac{\varepsilon - \widetilde{\varepsilon}_i}{h_N} \right) \tag{11}$$

where N is the sample size, $h_N = h/\sqrt{N}$ is the size of the sliding window, and $f(x)$ is the window function, which is employed to obtain a smooth probability density estimation and formulated as

$$f(x) = \frac{1}{\sqrt{2\pi}} exp\left(-\frac{1}{2} x^2 \right) \tag{12}$$

According to the Eq. (10), the incremental learning of the TFS-PESVM can be formulated as

$$\begin{bmatrix} w \\ b \end{bmatrix} = \left(I + v \begin{bmatrix} E_{\varphi 1}^T & E_{\varphi 2}^T \end{bmatrix} \begin{bmatrix} P_1 & 0 \\ 0 & P_2 \end{bmatrix} \begin{bmatrix} E_{\varphi 1} \\ E_{\varphi 2} \end{bmatrix} \right)^{-1} \begin{bmatrix} E_{\varphi 1}^T & E_{\varphi 2}^T \end{bmatrix} \begin{bmatrix} P_1 & 0 \\ 0 & P_2 \end{bmatrix} \begin{bmatrix} Y_1 \\ Y_2 \end{bmatrix}$$
$$= \left(I + v E_{\varphi 1}^T P_1 E_{\varphi 1} + v E_{\varphi 2}^T P_2 E_{\varphi 2} \right)^{-1} \left(E_{\varphi 1}^T P_1 Y_1 + E_{\varphi 2}^T P_2 Y_2 \right) \tag{13}$$

In Eq. (13), the old and new samples have the same weight in the learning process. However, as we know, the new sample has more current information than the old samples. Therefore, we employ a time-forgetting parameter θ to improve the efficiency of the new sample.

Then $E_{\varphi 1}$ in Eq. (13) can be changed to

$$E_{\varphi 1}' = \theta E_{\varphi 1} \tag{14}$$

where $0 \leq \theta \leq 1$. The modified Eq. (13) is

$$\begin{bmatrix} w \\ b \end{bmatrix} = \left(I + v\theta^2 E_{\varphi 1}^T P_1 E_{\varphi 1} + v E_{\varphi 2}^T P_2 E_{\varphi 2} \right)^{-1} \left(\theta E_{\varphi 1}^T P_1 Y_1 + E_{\varphi 2}^T P_2 Y_2 \right) \qquad (15)$$

The expressions for $E_\varphi^T PE_\varphi$ and $E_\varphi^T PY$ in Eq. (15) are

$$E_\varphi^T PE_\varphi = [a_1, \ldots, a_N] \begin{bmatrix} p_1 & \cdots & 0 \\ \vdots & \ddots & \vdots \\ 0 & \cdots & p_n \end{bmatrix} [a_1, \ldots, a_N]^T = \sum\nolimits_{i=1}^{N} p_i a_i a_i^T \in \mathbb{R}^{(d+1)\times(d+1)}$$

$$E_\varphi^T PY = [a_1, \ldots, a_N] \begin{bmatrix} p_1 & \cdots & 0 \\ \vdots & \ddots & \vdots \\ 0 & \cdots & p_n \end{bmatrix} [y_1, \ldots, y_N]^T = \sum\nolimits_{i=1}^{N} y_i p_i a_i \in \mathbb{R}^{(d+1)\times 1} \qquad (16)$$

As in the PESVM model, the proposed TFS-PESVM model can also compute local $\sum_{i=1}^{\tilde{n}} p_i a_i a_i^T$ and $\sum_{i=1}^{\tilde{n}} y_i p_i a_i$ in the Map step, and collect the result of $\sum_{i=1}^{N} a_i a_i^T$ and $\sum_{i=1}^{N} y_i a_i$ in the Reduce step (Table 2).

Table 2. TFS-PESVM model algorithm.

Algorithm 2 TFS-PESVM model

Step 1 Input weighted matrix A

Step 2 Use Algorithm 1 to estimate the residual $\tilde{\varepsilon}$

Step 3 Use Eq. (11) to estimate p(ε) and compute weight matrix P

Step 4 Samples in the dataset are inputted into Map process, compute φ(xi) using Eq. (2), and then construct $a_i=[\varphi(x_i),-1]^T$ by:

local_paa$^T = \sum p_i a_i a_i^T$, local_ypa $= \sum y_i p_i a_i$

(17)

Step 5 In Reduce step, compute:

global_paa$^T = \theta^2 global$_paa$^T + \sum local$_paa^T, lobal_ypa$^T = \theta global$_ypa $+ \sum local$_ypa (18)

Step 6 According to Eq. (15), TFS-PESVM obtains the values of parameters w and r.

3.4   Complexity

The model of this paper is based on ESVM, which could reduce the complexity greatly. For ESVM model, it's a Compared with the original ESVM, we remove the unnecessary process for better data stream computing. The complexity of SVM is from o (m^2n) to o(n^3), according to the size of simples (n) and number of features (m). The proposed complexity of no more than that of SVM.

4   Experimental Result

To test the validity of the proposed model, we simulate a specialty vehicle network and generate a data stream with this network. For the application, the scene of this study is some specialty vehicle, such as a tank. Thus, it is hard to obtain a real-world data stream. In the experiment, we employ four large-scale synthetic data sets, which are generated with the tools of concept drift. The whole dataset contains 100,000,000 samples and approximately 7.43 GB of data. The environment of the experiment contains 27 computing nodes, including one main node, one scheduling node, one backup node, and 24 data nodes. Each node is running on a 2.5 GHz Dual-core Intel CPU, 8 GB Memory, Ubuntu 12.04 OS and Hadoop 0.23.0.

4.1   TFS-PESVM Performance Experiment

In this experiment, the main objective is to demonstrate the performance of the proposed model. Therefore, we employ three types of measurement, i.e., speed up, scalability and scale-growth. The speedup denotes the efficiency of acceleration with increasing number of computing nodes. The scalability shows the effect of the data set for the proposed model. The scale-growth shows the complexity of the proposed model. The experimental results are shown in Fig. 2, which contains three sub-figures.

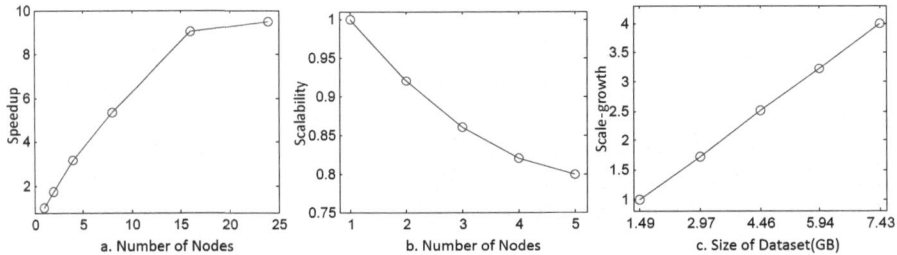

Fig. 2. Speedup, scalability and scale-growth of TFS-PESVM model.

$$Speedup\ (m) = \frac{time\ -\ cost\ of\ 1\ node\ for\ 1\ data\ set}{time\ -\ cost\ of\ m\ node\ for\ 1\ data\ set}$$

$$Scalability\ (m) = \frac{time\ -\ cost\ of\ 1\ node\ for\ 1\ data\ set}{time\ -\ cost\ of\ m\ node\ for\ m\ data\ set}$$

$$ScaleGrowth\ (m) = \frac{time\ -\ cost\ of\ 1\ node\ for\ m\ data\ set}{time\ -\ cost\ of\ m\ node\ for\ 1\ data\ set}$$

From Fig. 2a, the speedup value is increasing with the number of computing nodes in an almost linear fashion. That means in the MapReduce framework, we can employ more computing nodes to accelerate the model's running speed. Therefore, for this natural feature of the MapReduce framework, the Fig. 2a shows that the proposed model has a good speedup ability. For the Fig. 2b, the scalability decreases with an increased number of computing nodes. The reason is that in the MapReduce framework, the time cost depends on the number of nodes and the data set, so when different computing nodes work for different data sets, the whole time-cost equals to the sum of the costs of each node, which is more than one node for one data set. Finally, for the Fig. 2c, when increasing the data size, the scale-growth also increases linearly, which means the proposed model can handle a "Big Data" problem.

4.2   Comparing Experiment

In this experiment, the proposed model is compared with two distinct models, namely the forgetting factor incremental ELM (FF-IELM) and the forgetting factor incremental ESVM (FF-IESVM). The experimental results are shown in Fig. 3.

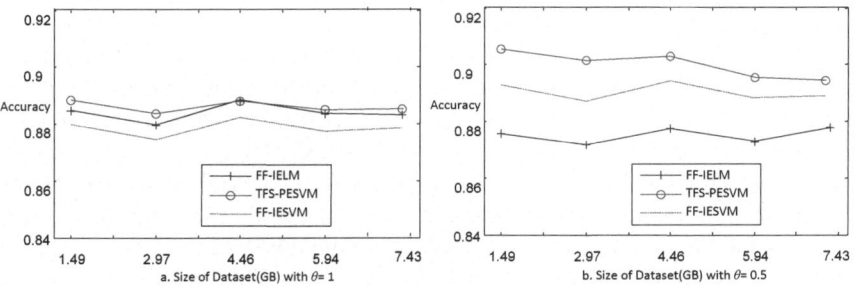

Fig. 3. Accuracy of FF-IELM, FF-IESVM and TFS-PESVM.

In Fig. 3, for $\theta = 1$, the three models have nearly the same classification accuracy, the best one is the TFS-PESVM model and the worst one is the FF-IESVM model. However, for $\theta = 0.5$, the accuracy of the proposed model TFS-PESVM is significantly better, and the worst is FF-IELM. After the analysis, two conclusions can be drawn:

After comparing with two different classification models, it can be seen that the proposed TFS-PESVM model can improve the accuracy of data stream classification significantly;

The forgetting strategy can improve the accuracy of data stream classification, which validates the new samples as more useful than the old ones.

For $\theta = 0.5$, we also repeat this experiment five times to test the stability of the proposed model, which is shown in Table 1. In Table 3, there are two new measurements, namely sensitive and specificity, which can be formulated as

$$\text{Sensitive} = \frac{pp}{pp+pn}$$

$$\text{Specificity} = \frac{nn}{pp+np}$$

Table 3. Comparing of FF-IELM, FF-IESVM and TFS-PESVM model.

Model	Measurement	Data set 1	Data set 2	Data set 3	Data set 4
FF-IELM	Accuracy	87.58 ± 1.23%	87.18 ± 1.22%	87.74 ± 1.20%	87.3 ± 1.15%
	Sensitive	82.38 ± 1.63%	82.2 ± 1.39%	88.76 ± 1.39%	90.62 ± 1.45%
	Specificity	91.98 ± 0.96%	92.14 ± 1.13%	86.9 ± 1.23%	84.84 ± 1.11%
FF-IESVM	Accuracy	89.3 ± 1.33%	88.7 ± 1.23%	89.44 ± 1.3%	88.92 ± 1.23%
	Sensitive	84.86 ± 2%	83.3 ± 1.8%	88.76 ± 1.7%	91.58 ± 1.72%
	Specificity	**93.14 ± 1.22%**	**94.06 ± 1.13%**	**90.02 ± 1.25%**	86.94 ± 1.19%
TFS-PESVM	Accuracy	**90.56 ± 1.64%**	**90.14 ± 1.77%**	**90.3 ± 1.19%**	**89.54 ± 0.89%**
	Sensitive	**87.6 ± 4.01%**	**86.32 ± 3.38%**	**91.94 ± 2.28%**	**91.96 ± 4.77%**
	Specificity	93.12 ± 1.27%	94 ± 0.98%	88.92 ± 0.9%	**87.02 ± 1.88%**

where *pp* and *nn* denote the number of correctly classified samples with positive or negative label. Additionally, *pn* and *np* denote the number of wrongly classified samples with positive or negative label.

In Table 1, for data set 1 to data set 3, the best accuracy and sensitive measurements are found with the proposed model TFS-PESVM, which means the proposed model is more stable and efficient than the others. However, for specificity, the best is the FF-IESVM model. The reason is that the FF-IESVM model is more suitable for negative label samples. For data set 4, the proposed TFS-PESVM model obtains the best classification results. Overall, the experimental results show that the forgetting strategy and the MapReduce framework used in original ESVM model can improve the accuracy of classification and model stability, which is more suitable for data stream classification in real time.

5   Conclusion

Data stream classification is a new research topic in the data mining community. The application of data stream classification on specialty vehicle network is also a novel idea. However, due to the basic features of a specialty vehicle network, the data stream classifier needs to not only improve accuracy but also improve the running speed of the classification process. Therefore, in this paper, a new data stream classification model, namely TFS-PESVM, is proposed, which employs a residual weight matrix to correct the residual matrix in ESVM model and designs a new forgetting factor to control the effect of samples and decrease the effect of noise in the data stream. The experimental results on a vehicle network simulation show that the proposed model can improve the accuracy of classification. Compared with two other models, namely FF-IELM and FF-IESVM, the proposed method is also more stable in accuracy than the others.

References

1. O'Connor, P., Neil, D., Liu, S.C., Delbruck, T., Pfeiffer, M.: Real-time classification and sensor fusion with a spiking deep belief network. Neuromorphic Eng. Syst. Appl. 61(2015)
2. Gao, Z., Cecati, C., Ding, S.X.: A survey of fault diagnosis and fault-tolerant techniques—part II: fault diagnosis with knowledge-based and hybrid/active approaches. IEEE Trans. Ind. Electron. 62(6), 3768–3774 (2015)
3. Haque, A., Khan, L., Baron, M., Thuraisingham, B., Aggarwal, C.: Efficient handling of concept drift and concept evolution over stream data. In: 2016 IEEE 32nd International Conference on Data Engineering (ICDE), pp. 481–492. IEEE, May 2016
4. Triguero, I., Peralta, D., Bacardit, J., García, S., Herrera, F.: MRPR: a MapReduce solution for prototype reduction in big data classification. Neurocomputing 150, 331–345 (2015)
5. Zhai, J., Zhang, S., Wang, C.: The classification of imbalanced large data sets based on MapReduce and ensemble of ELM classifiers. Int. J. Mach. Learn. Cybern. 1–9 (2016)
6. Zhang, C., Li, F., Jestes, J.: Efficient parallel kNN joins for large data in MapReduce. In: Proceedings of the 15th International Conference on Extending Database Technology, pp. 38–49. ACM, March 2012
7. Lee, T., Im, D.H., Kim, H., Kim, H.J.: Application of filters to multiway joins in MapReduce. Math. Probl. Eng. (2014)
8. Alham, N.K., Li, M., Hammoud, S., Liu, Y., Ponraj, M.: A distributed SVM for image annotation. In: 2010 Seventh International Conference on Fuzzy Systems and Knowledge Discovery (FSKD), vol. 6, pp. 2983–2987. IEEE, August 2010
9. Feng, W., Zhang, Q., Hu, G., Huang, J.X.: Mining network data for intrusion detection through combining SVMs with ant colony networks. Future Gener. Comput. Syst. 37, 127–140 (2014)
10. Zhao, J., Liang, Z., Yang, Y.: Parallelized incremental support vector machines based on MapReduce and bagging technique. In: 2012 IEEE International Conference on Information Science and Technology, pp. 297–301. IEEE, March 2012
11. Dean, J., Ghemawat, S.: MapReduce: simplified data processing on large clusters. Commun. ACM 51(1), 107–113 (2008)
12. Doulkeridis, C., Nørvåg, K.: A survey of large-scale analytical query processing in MapReduce. VLDB J. 23(3), 355–380 (2014)
13. Zhu, W., Miao, J., Qing, L.: Extreme support vector regression. In: Sun, F., Toh, K.-A., Romay, M.G., Mao, K. (eds.) Extreme Learning Machines 2013: Algorithms and Applications. ALO, vol. 16, pp. 25–34. Springer, Cham (2014). https://doi.org/10.1007/978-3-319-04741-6_3
14. Teo, T.T., Logenthiran, T., Woo, W.L.: Forecasting of photovoltaic power using extreme learning machine. In: 2015 IEEE Innovative Smart Grid Technologies-Asia (ISGT ASIA), pp. 1–6. IEEE, November 2015

Key Techniques Applied for Lighting Design on Chinese Historical Sites—Taking the Great Wall Resort in Kelan County as an Example

Zaizhou Li, Wen Gao, Jiayuan Lin, Xiaoyang He, Fan Cao,
and Nianyu Zou$^{(\boxtimes)}$

Research Institute of Photonics, Dalian Polytechnic University,
Dalian 116034, China
n_y_zou@dlpu.edu.cn

Abstract. As treasure of Chinese cultural heritage, Chinese historical sites are expected to display their unique historical and architectural charm at day and night. Taking the lighting project of the Great Wall Resort of Song dynasty at Kelan county as an example, this paper explores how to set off the cultural atmosphere of Chinese ancient buildings through the design of night scenery lighting and at the same time conform to the concept of green lighting. Key techniques applied in lighting design are discussed, and through which the resort atmosphere and theme corresponding to different festivals are created.

Keywords: Historical site · Lighting design · LED

1 Introduction

Night lighting is at a stage of rapid development, and it is becoming more and more common in people's daily life [1]. Architecture is no longer a dark face at night. Under this ever-changing change, Chinese ancient buildings with unique architectural features must "wear" the "new clothes" of the lights, and they are high-quality, green and environmentally-friendly "new clothes", so as to reflect the charm of ancient buildings at night [2].

With regard to ancient architecture, people gradually realized its preciousness and paid more attention to it. The structural features of Chinese ancient buildings are that the roof wing angles are lifted; the top to bottom layers is distinct, and the left and right symmetrical layouts [3]. At present, there are many problems in lighting of ancient buildings. First of all, the cultural value of ancient buildings is greater than the value of lighting design, so we should respect history and not cause damage to buildings [4]. Secondly, the installation position of lamps is too obvious, and the daytime effect is very unattractive [5]. In addition, some ancient architectural lighting cannot express the structural characteristics of the buildings, and the lighting effect loses the historical value of the ancient buildings [6].

J. Jin et al. (Eds.): GreeNets 2019, LNICST 282, pp. 68–75, 2019.
https://doi.org/10.1007/978-3-030-21730-3_7

2   The Song Dynasty Great Wall Resort Project

The Great Wall of Song Dynasty is located in Kelan county, Shanxi Province which starts from Qingcheng Mountain in Kelan County and east to Heyeping Mountain in Wuzhai County. The existing wall of the Song Great Wall, which is more than 20 km in the county and made up of pieces of stone. The preservation is about 4.2 m high and the top width is about 2.1 m. The implementation of the project can revitalize the countryside, integrate with the tourism industry to achieve a win-win situation in which the poor rural areas are beautiful and the industry is prosperous.

The project includes the architectural landscape lighting and Road lighting design of the Song Great Wall and surrounding Xikouzi Village, Koujia Village, Loufangdi Village, Xinjiawan Village, Wangjiacha Village, Ningjiacha Village, Qiannangou Village, Huangtupo Village and Wujiagou Village.

The Great Wall Resort in Song Dynasty is mostly built around local villages. Each village forms part of the historic block of the resort. Meanwhile, the ancient buildings inside the village have become landmarks. Therefore, the lighting of the block and the lighting of the building have become the focus of the whole project. In addition, good green planting lighting can also enhance the natural vitality of the scenic spot (Fig. 1).

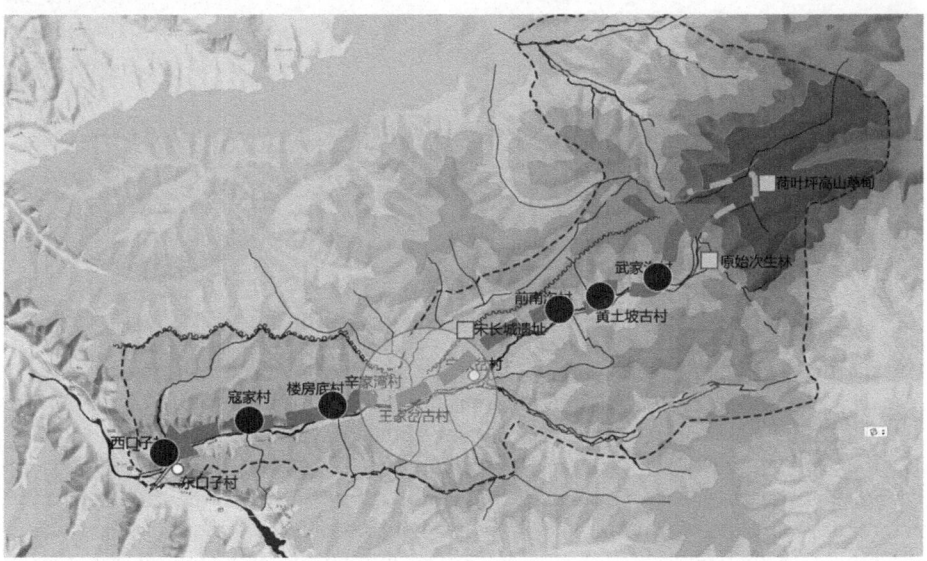

Fig. 1. The song great wall resort planning map

3   Lighting Design Concept of Ancient Architecture

3.1   Lighting of Ancient Building Streets

The opening and closing of the street are one of the artistic features of street landscape design. The opening and closing of the street start from the landscape requirements and can form a space with an open landscape. From the night landscape, it is reflected in the light and shadow changes of the street lighting. The opening and closing of the street landscape lighting brings rich light and shadow changes to the street night scene. (see Fig. 2). The turning and opening of the street lighting bring a rich contrast of light and dark, and also enhances the sense of space throughout the night scene.

Fig. 2. Ancient building street lighting.

3.2   Lighting Layer of the Facade of an Ancient Building

The facade of traditional ancient buildings is usually composed of three levels. The eaves and the edge of the foundation plus the contour of the walls on both sides constitute the first level, the column array constitutes the second level of the building, and the wall and Windows behind the column constitute the third level. To some extent, these three levels reflect the aesthetic characteristics of Chinese ancient architecture: axis, symmetry, rhythm and proportion. Therefore, for the unique facade form of Chinese ancient buildings, it is necessary to outline the architectural structure by using facade lighting. Three levels are respectively strengthened by lamps to create the independence of each level, and "dark areas" are left between floors, which will make the architectural levels highlight through lighting techniques (see Fig. 3).

Fig. 3. Lighting effect of ancient building facade.

3.3   Green Plant Lighting in Ancient Buildings Areas

Some long-standing green plants often witness the historical origins of ancient buildings, and there are some emerging green plants in these ancient buildings, which often add some vitality to ancient buildings. Therefore, in the lighting design of ancient buildings, lighting design should also be carried out on green plants. Green plants are a spatial extension of the entire landscape and can also enhance the individualization of individual lighting space. For example, the illumination of the green plants in front of the building will make the whole space three-dimensional (see Fig. 4), which not only enhances the visual beauty of the soft scenery, but also increases the natural vitality, complementing each other and setting off each other.

Fig. 4. Green plant lighting in ancient building areas. (Color figure online)

4 Key Lighting Techniques Applied on the Project

4.1 Color Controlling

The choice of lighting color in modern lighting art can be roughly divided into two types [7]. The first one is the night-time reproduction and restoration of the original color of the subject; the second is to give it a new color to express a certain subject and mood.

The historical block where the ancient buildings are located should show the details and original color of the building, and reproduce the historical charm by restoring the color of the building itself. Therefore, most of the light sources select a warm yellow light source of about 3000 K as the main color temperature, and white light and warm white light are used appropriately to distinguish the architectural level according to the specific situation.

In 1965, CIE developed a method for evaluating the color rendering of light sources. CIE stipulates that the color rendering index can be divided into special color rendering index R_i and general color rendering index Ra. In view of the color characteristics of Chinese ancient buildings, lamps only with high general color rendering index cannot fully show the color characteristics of Chinese ancient buildings. Considering the special color rendering index of the lamps, the problem of insufficient color saturation can be solved. Red is the main theme of Chinese ancient buildings, and the special color rendering index R9 is the quality index to evaluate the reproduction of red by LED. The R9 value is required at a high level, and the "Chinese Red" characteristic of the building itself is truly restored by increasing the color rendering ability of the light source to red.

4.2 Selection and Installation of Lamps

Considering the fire prevention of buildings, the light source cannot be a heat radiation source, and the lamps inside the building should fully consider the heat dissipation. In combination with the current lighting market, LEDs have been widely used in various scenes of lighting design [8].

Solve glare problems and reduce light pollution through reasonable installation. The project is based on the transformation of the village, so the lighting renovation should be carried out on the basis of not affecting the local people. For example, if the installation of the buried lamp is required, the angle of illumination should be adjusted to the wall surface, and the wall should be illuminated by the way of washing the wall. The column lamp should be illuminated from top to bottom to prevent the light from directly illuminating the human eye and causing discomfort.

The installation method cannot damage the original building structure, and more adopts the buckle and adsorption installation method. The currently popular corrugated lamp design shown in Fig. 5 avoids architectural damage caused by the mounting method by clamping the tiles or by snapping them onto the tiles.

The mechanical structure of modern lamps and the style of ancient buildings have a strong visual impact, and this visual impact is not aesthetic. In the lighting design, it is necessary to combine most of the lamps with the architectural features of the building,

Fig. 5. Corrugated lamp installation diagram

or to match the paint color of the lamp with the building to achieve the effect of "seeing the light without seeing the lamps".

4.3   Energy Saving Modes

Green lighting is a concept put forward by the US Environmental Protection Agency in the early 1990s. The complete green lighting connotation includes four indicators of high efficiency, environmental protection, safety and comfort, which are indispensable. Energy-saving means that you can get enough lighting by consuming less electric energy, which can significantly reduce the emission of air pollutants from power plants and achieve environmental protection. Ancient buildings should also follow a certain green lighting concept as part of the night lighting.

According to the structure and function analysis of the scene, reasonable lighting brightness control should be carried out. The main street building is the most crowded area. The most prominent linear space, and the luminance control level of the main building top is $15 \sim 20$ cd/m^2. The important nodes and ancient buildings on the periphery should be controlled to the next level of luminance, about $5 \sim 10$ cd/m^2.

In the overall planning of scenic spots. The Energy-saving modes are divided into weekdays, general festival lighting and festival lighting to achieve energy saving and environmental protection. Figures 6, 7 and 8 shows the different lighting modes for the entire scenic area.

Figure 6 is the lighting effect of significant festivals. The lights in the whole scene are activated, especially the laser lamp with the logo of the Great Wall of the Song Dynasty, which reflects the prosperous festival atmosphere. Figure 7 is the lighting mode of general festivals or holidays, which mainly guarantees the lighting of some commercial areas and important functional lighting. This mode stops the roof lighting

Fig. 6. Lighting effect of significant festivals.

Fig. 7. Lighting effect of general festivals.

Fig. 8. Lighting effect of ordinary days.

of villagers' residential areas and the Great Wall District area; Fig. 8 is the normal lighting mode, but also the most common lighting mode, only retained the commercial district lighting and functional lighting, 80% of the landscape lighting stopped. Through the switching of various modes, the lighting concept of environmental protection and energy saving can be achieved.

5 Summary

In summary, the paper explores the design concept of lighting and green environmental protection for ancient buildings in today's landscape lighting through the analysis and design of the Song Great Wall lighting program in Kelan County. The lighting research of Chinese ancient buildings also needs to sum up a design style that conforms to the essence of Chinese culture, popular aesthetics and energy saving and environmental protection. Through the way of light, our ancient buildings and ancient cultures can exude their unique charm even at night.

Acknowledgement. Many thanks are given to Beijing Zhongxu Design Company, which offered me internship opportunities. Special acknowledgement is to. Mr. Cai Xiaoyu and Mr. Zhang Shurun, who were my business mentors and gave much advice for this work.

References

1. Yang, T.: Landscape lighting design in historical street. Light Lighting **38**(1), 15–18 (2014)
2. Sun, B., Li, Y.: Preliminary study on the night view lighting design of chinese traditional culture block-taking the ancient culture street of Tianjin as an example. Light Lighting **39**(4), 46–48 (2015)
3. Ogando-Martínez, A., López-Gómez, J., Febrero-Garrido, L.: Maintenance factor identification in outdoor lighting installations using simulation and optimization techniques. Energies **11**, 2169 (2018)
4. Bullough, J.D., Brons, J.A., Qi, R., Rea, M.S.: Predicting discomfort glare from outdoor lighting installations. Lighting Res. Technol. **40**, 225–242 (2008)
5. Wang, Y., Yang, C.: The conceptual design of the lighting in ancient building about the Dou Gong. Light Lighting **41**(2), 42–45 (2017)
6. Zhang, X.: A brief analysis of the night lighting design of ancient buildings. Architectural Eng. Technol. Des. **12**, 5518 (2017)
7. Wang, W., Zhang, M., Sun, W.: Research on evaluation method of color rendering property of light sources used in colored drawing of Chinese classical architecture lighting. Light Lighting **28**(1), 52–56 (2017)
8. Deng, Y.: Studying the lighting design and technical application of Chinese ancient buildings at night. Architectural Eng. Technol. Des. **33**, 362 (2018)

Research on Illumination Estimation Based on Data Fitting

Yuanqi Li, Yingming Gao, Ling Yu, Bao Liu, Long Huang,
Yingjie Zhang, Juqian Li, and Xiaoyang He[✉]

Dalian Polytechnic University, Dalian 116000, China
yuling@dlpu.edu.cn

Abstract. In order to solve the illuminance sensor placed on the work surface, it is easily shielded by office objects, human activities, cannot get an accurate work surface illumination an in the indoor lighting control system. In turn, will make dimming system inaccurate and the illumination of the work surface cannot meet the needs of the human eye. Based on the theory of radio energy transmission, Discussed the distribution of sunlight in indoor space, A prediction method for replacing the illuminance sensor of the work surface with an illuminance sensor provided on the wall and the ceiling is proposed. The influence of the orientation relationship between the daylight and the sensor on the illumination of the desk was investigated by simulation.

Keywords: Illumination estimation · Data fitting · Energy saving

1 Introduction

According to the survey, indoor closed-loop control of dimming system metrics usually uses a single point calibration. This single point calibration will work as long as the operating conditions are not different from the conditions at the time of calibration. However, only certain parts of the building can meet these conditions. Most of the space that is significantly affected by sunlight is due to direct sunlight, and reflections from blind corners or the height of the window create variable solar reflection conditions. This change does not apply to single point calibration techniques. Although placing the photosensor on the work surface is an ideal location to monitor the illumination of the internal working plane, the work plane sensor is susceptible to interference from passengers or accidentally covered by paper.

Therefore, light sensors for closed loop lighting control are typically mounted on the ceiling to reduce the likelihood of being disturbed. This paper presents an effective strategy for estimating the illumination of the working plane.

Supported by Science Foundation for Goldlamp Co., Ltd (2017-228195).

J. Jin et al. (Eds.): GreeNets 2019, LNICST 282, pp. 76–82, 2019.
https://doi.org/10.1007/978-3-030-21730-3_8

2 Illumination Collection

Building address: Dalian (longitude: 121.62° latitude: 28.92°).

Volume: 5.4 m*3.6 m*2.8 m.

Building type: one floor. Orientation: South. The height of the lighting window is 0.8 m, the area is 1 m*1 m, and the wall-to-window ratio is 25.5%.

External Illumination Sensor 1- (2.0, 3.6, 1.8) Ceiling Near Window Sensor 2- (2.7, 2.4, 2.8) Ceiling Far Window Sensor 3- (2.7, 1.2, 2.8) Level Illumination Sensor 4- (1.3, 1.7, 0.85) (Figs. 1 and 2).

Fig. 1. Dialux model diagram

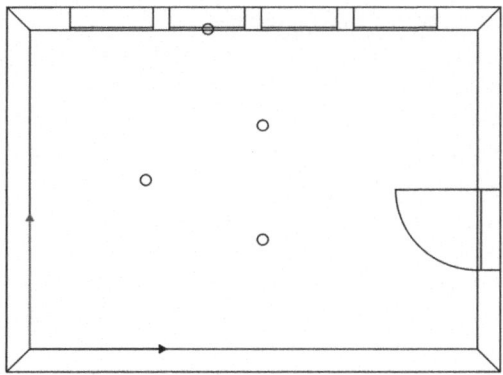

Fig. 2. Sensor position diagram

In this paper, the illuminance values of 2018.3.21-3.22 were collected as the benchmark, and the illuminance is shown in the following table.:

Table 1. illuminance value collection Table (2018.3.21)

Sensor type	Illuminance value					
Sensor 1	1896	2690	3472	4026	4667	5230
Sensor 2	48	69	91	108	128	144
Sensor 3	59	78	112	140	158	182
Sensor 4	101	143	184	213	247	277
Sensor type	Illuminance value					
Sensor 1	5705	6063	6363	6063	6595	6063
Senso 2	156	169	174	177	181	178
Sensor 3	193	209	216	220	224	220
Sensor 4	303	322	337	332	350	322
Sensor type	Illuminance value					
Sensor 1	6386	6089	5622	5284	4730	4096
Sensor 2	175	166	157	140	129	118
Sensor 3	216	206	195	170	160	143
Sensor 4	339	328	305	280	251	217

Table 2. illuminance value collection Table (2018.3.22)

Sensor type	Illuminance value					
Sensor 1	6420	6152	5781	5314	4759	4125
Sensor 2	176	168	158	143	130	114
Sensor 3	218	210	196	178	161	144
Sensor 4	340	326	307	282	252	219
Sensor type	Illuminance value					
Sensor 1	1796	2599	3361	4069	4709	5271
Sensor 2	49	79	92	108	129	144
Sensor 3	61	89	114	139	160	177
Sensor 4	95	138	178	216	250	280
Sensor type	Illuminance value					
Sensor 1	5746	6102	6363	6402	6631	6102
Sensor 2	157	169	176	178	182	179
Sensor 3	195	209	218	223	225	221
Sensor 4	305	324	337	327	352	324

3   Work Surface Illumination Estimation

Based on the theory of light energy, the working plane illuminance can be described as a linear combination of other internal sensor illuminances. Therefore, the working surface illumination can be described as:

$$I_{task} = I_S^T f(n) \tag{1}$$

Where I_{task} is the estimated working plane illuminance, I_S is the illuminance vector measured by the ceiling mounted sensor, and f(n) is the coefficient vector of condition n.

The work plane is estimated to have two steps. The first step is to classify the training data into different categories based on blind height, plate angle or external illumination. The second step is to optimally estimate the coefficient f(n) of each group by minimizing the mean square error between the measured and estimated working plane illuminance. For each clustering condition, use the corresponding estimated coefficient to estimate the work plane illumination.

3.1 Cluster Analysis

There are many factors influencing the factor f, for example: the geometry of the room is different, and the change of the weather will produce different distributions of daylight flux through the window from the external environment. Therefore, the coefficient f should be estimated for different situations. The system may consider collecting blind blind heights, slit angles, dimming levels of lights, external illumination measured by window mounted sensors, and internal illumination of ceiling mounted sensors.

In this paper, the factors affecting the external illuminance are considered and clustered. According to the measured outdoor illuminance, considering that there is no other light source in the room, the indoor illuminance is very poor according to the lighting conditions, the lighting conditions are general, and the lighting conditions are well divided into three categories. Therefore, using K-means clustering algorithm, take K = 3 (Fig. 3).

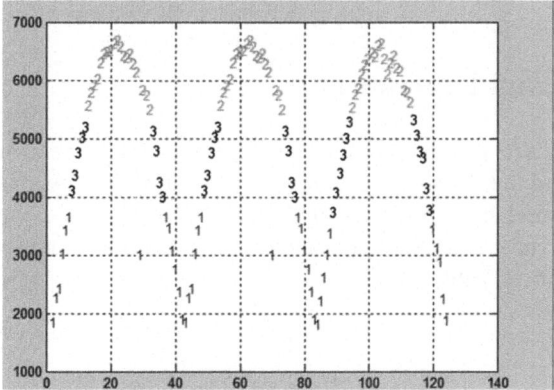

Fig. 3. Clustering result diagram

The resulting external illumination is classified as follows: the first type of boundary ans = (1796,3640); The second type of boundary ans = (3723,5314); The third type of boundary ans = (5483, 6667).

3.2   Coefficient Estimation

After data clustering, we now focus on the data fit of any condition n, i.e. the coefficient f(n) of each cluster, which represents the coefficients of a particular environmental condition. In data measurements, the illuminance of the light sensor and the illumination of the working plane are usually expressed as discrete time series.

$$I_{task} = \begin{bmatrix} I_1[1] & I_2[1] & \cdots & I_Q[1] \\ I_1[2] & I_1[2] & \cdots & I_Q[2] \\ \vdots & \vdots & \ddots & \vdots \\ I_1[M] & I_2[M] & \cdots & I_Q[M] \end{bmatrix} \begin{bmatrix} f_1 \\ f_2 \\ \vdots \\ f_Q \end{bmatrix} = \mathbf{H}f, \tag{2}$$

Where H is the discrete time measurement data of the Q internal sensor. By the least squares method, the sum of the squares of the estimation errors between the Itask of the measured value and its estimate is minimized, thereby providing a closed form solution of the optimal coefficient f. The best factor is:

$$\hat{f} = \left(H^T H\right)^{-1} H^T I_{task} \tag{3}$$

Since the system is aggregated into different conditions, the same linear estimation structure is used for different conditions, and the estimated coefficient f is a discrete function under different conditions. Therefore, the general expression of the illuminance estimation is:

$$\hat{I}_{task}[n] = H[n]\hat{f}[n] \tag{4}$$

4   Simulation and Experiment

Based on the three sets of data measured in Tables 1 and 2, the estimated coefficients are constructed, and the illuminance of the working surface is estimated for the ceiling illuminance measured by the model of 2018.4.1-2018.4.2, and the normalized root mean square error value is used to represent Estimate the error between illuminance and measured illuminance (Table 3).

$$NRMSE = \frac{\sqrt{E\left[\left(\hat{I}_{task} - I_{task}\right)^2\right]}}{\max(I_{task}) - \min(I_{task})}. \tag{5}$$

Table 3. Partial illuminance value (2018.4.1-2018.4.2)

Sensor type	Illuminance value					
Sensor 1	15	61	104	140	168	185
Sensor 2	19	76	128	173	208	229
Actual value	37	146	247	337	400	442
Estimated value	35	112	221	294	362	405
Sensor type	Illuminance value					
Sensor 1	191	157	138	101	55	28
Sensor 2	236	195	171	125	69	37
Actual value	445	375	329	245	133	68
Estimated value	412	336	289	210	115	52
Sensor type	Illuminance value					
Sensor 1	17	62	105	169	186	192
Sensor 2	21	77	130	209	230	237
Actual value	40	149	250	403	444	457
Estimated value	26	123	219	365	410	421
Sensor type	Illuminance value					
Sensor 1	185	167	139	102	52	33
Sensor 2	229	207	172	126	69	47
Actual value	442	399	331	243	120	82
Estimated value	423	356	303	216	92	59

NRMSE = 0.1432

5   Conclusion

This paper presents a strategy to estimate the working plane illumination from other internal sensors (usually mounted on the ceiling). The system first classifies the data into various categories and calculates the estimated coefficients for each category. These estimated coefficients are later used to estimate the working plane illuminance by combining the illuminance levels measured by other photosensors, The algorithm proposed in this paper performs well in the experiment.

References

1. Lee, E.S., DiBartolomeo, D.L., Selkowitz, S.E.: Thermal and daylighting performance of an automated venetian blind and lighting system in a full-scale private office. Energy Build. **29**, 47–63 (1998)
2. Athienitis, A.K., Tzempelikos, A.: A methodology for simulation of daylight room illuminance distribution and light dimming for a room with a controlled shading device. J. Sol. Energy **72**(4), 271–281 (2002). Suo Jingling, Discussion about Lighting Design for the Museum Exhibition
3. Koo, S.Y., Yeo, M.S., Kim, K.W.: Automated blind control to maximize the benefits of daylight in buildings. Build. Environ. **45**(6), 1508–1520 (2010)

4. Zhang, S., Birru, D.: An open-loop venetian blind control to avoid direct sunlight and enhance daylight utilization. Sol. Energy **86**, 860–866 (2012)
5. Lah, M.T., Zupancic, B., Peternelj, J., et al.: Daylight illuminance control with fuzzy logic. Sol. Energy **80**, 307–321 (2006)
6. Guillemin, A., Molteni, S.: An energy-efficient controller for shading devices self-adapting to the user wishes. Build. Environ. **37**, 1091–1097 (2002)
7. Kristl, Z., et al.: Fuzzy control system for thermal and visual comfort in building. Renewable Energy **33**, 694–702 (2008)
8. Courret, G., Paule, B., Scartezzini, J.L.: Anidolic zenithal openings. In: Proceedings of the European Conference on Energy Performance and Indoor Climate in Buildings, Lyon, France, pp. 569–574 (1994)
9. Galasiu, A.D., Atif, M.R.: Project to improve understanding of daylight-linked lighting systems. In: CABA Home & Building Quarterly, NRCC-44279. IRC, Ottawa, Canada (2000)
10. Guillemin, A., Morel, N.: An innovative lighting controller integrated in a self-adaptive building control system. J. Energy Build. **33**(5), 477–487 (2001)
11. Siegel, R., Howell, J.R.: Thermal Radiation Heat Transfer, 2nd edn. McGraw-Hill, New York (1981)

Green Communication and Networking

Antenna Selection Based on Energy Efficiency of Uplink in Massive MIMO Systems

Chaoyue Zhao, Zhuyun Fan, Meng Zhang, Guiyue Jin$^{(\boxtimes)}$, and Jiyu Jin

School of Information Science and Engineering,
Dalian Polytechnic University, Dalian, China
guiyue.jin@dlpu.edu.cn

Abstract. Massive multiple-input multiple-output (MIMO) system installs a large number of antennas on the base station (BS), which requires one radio frequency (RF) chain for each antenna. When the number of antennas is small, the power consumption of the RF chains is negligible compared with the transmitting power. However, with the increase of antennas and RF chains, the ratio of the RF chains power consumption to the total transmitting power is gradually increasing. Therefore, the energy efficiency (EE) of the system tends to be saturated gradually and decreases with the further increase of antennas. To improve EE in massive MIMO systems, an antenna selection method by switching antenna dynamically with channel state information (CSI) is proposed in this paper, and trade-off between EE and spectral efficiency of the system is addressed.

Keywords: Massive MIMO · Energy efficiency · Antenna selection · Spectral efficiency

1 Introduction

As one of the key technologies of 5G, massive multiple-input multiple-output (MIMO) technology [1–3] can greatly improve the spectral efficiency (SE) of the system by installing a large number of antennas on the base station (BS), this is because the data rates of the system will grow with the increased number of antennas. In communication systems, maximizing system energy efficiency (EE) is expected while improving system SE. However, considering the power consumption of the radio frequency (RF) chains, the EE of the massive MIMO system rises firstly and falls afterwards with the increase of antennas on the BS [4–6]. Therefore, improving EE is a key issue that needs to be addressed urgently in massive MIMO technologies.

Under the ideal power consumption model, [7] and [8] discussed the trade-off between SE and EE and the relationship among the number of BS antennas, users and the transmitting power in massive MIMO systems. The adverseness of using low-cost transceivers in large-scale antennas when adopting non-ideal devices is discussed in [9], the relationship between the number of BS antennas and the system EE is also analyzed. However, most of these studies are not take the power consumption of the RF chains into account in the actual system. Under the actual power consumption model,

J. Jin et al. (Eds.): GreeNets 2019, LNICST 282, pp. 85–91, 2019.
https://doi.org/10.1007/978-3-030-21730-3_9

a system energy consumption function of the number of BS antennas and users is obtained in [10], and the optimal number of RF chains was provided according to this energy consumption function to optimize the EE of the system. But the EE of the system can be further improved by antenna selection.

In this paper, an improved antenna selection method is proposed based on EE of massive MIMO systems, the antennas of optimal channel state information (CSI) are selected to reduce energy loss, and the trade-off between EE and SE of the system is illustrated. Finally, the bit error rate (BER) of the system is simulated and analyzed.

2 Energy Consumption Model of the System

This paper considers the uplink of massive MIMO systems in a single cell multi-user scenario. The bandwidth of the system is B, and M antennas are installed on the BS to serve K single-antenna users. In a flat fading channel, the channel is quasi-static within the U symbols of the time-frequency coherent block. It is assumed that the BS and the user are fully synchronized in time division duplex (TDD) protocol.

The EE of the uplink with zero-forcing (ZF) processing under perfect CSI in single cell can be modeled as

$$
\max_{M \in Z_+, K \in Z_+, \rho \geq 0, M \geq K+1} \left(\text{EE}^{(ZF)} \right) = \frac{\sum_{k=1}^{K} \left(E\left\{ R_k^{(\text{ul})} \right\} \right)}{P_{TX}^{(\text{ul})} + P_{CP}^{(ZF)}}
$$
$$
= \frac{K \zeta^{(\text{ul})} \left(1 - \frac{\tau^{(\text{ul})} K}{U \zeta^{(\text{ul})}} \right) B \log_2 (1 + \rho(M - K))}{P_{TX}^{(\text{ul}-ZF)} + P_{CP}^{(ZF)}}
$$

, (1)

where $R_k^{(\text{ul})}$ is the data rate of the kth user that the pilot overhead is not included, $P_{TX}^{(\text{ul})}$ represents the total transmitted power, circuit power consumption $P_{CP}^{(ZF)}$ is the sum of the power consumed by different analog components and digital signal processing using ZF detection. The proportions of the uplink and downlink transmissions are $\zeta^{(\text{ul})}$ and $\zeta^{(\text{dl})}$, and $\zeta^{(\text{ul})} + \zeta^{(\text{dl})} = 1$. In the uplink transmission, $U \zeta^{(\text{ul})}$ symbols are included, the user needs to transmit a pilot signal for channel estimation when the CSI is unknown, and the pilot occupies $\tau^{(\text{ul})} K$ symbols, where $\tau^{(\text{ul})} \geq 1$ to ensure the pilots among users are mutually orthogonal. ρ is the design parameter proportional to the received signal-to interference-and-noise ratio (SINR) [11].

3 Antenna Selection Based on Energy Efficiency

Figure 1 is a block diagram of the antenna selection. It is proposed in [5] when the number of RF chains on the BS is F ($F = M/2$), the EE is optimal considering the overall power consumption on both the transmitter and the receiver.

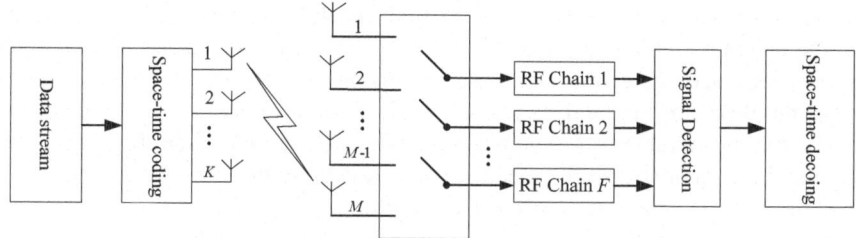

Fig. 1. Antenna selection block diagram $(F < M)$

Based on [5], an improved antenna selection scheme is described in this paper in the following steps.

3.1 Acquisition of CSI

Initialization $i = 1$, the RF chain is switched to the 1st to the Fth antenna, assume $\mathbf{H}_i$ represents the channel matrix between the BS and the users, $\mathbf{H}_i$ is an $F \times K$-dimensional matrix and estimated by the pilot signal. Then, the channel matrix $\mathbf{H}_i$ is subjected to ZF equalization, the ZF equalization matrix is

$$\mathbf{W}_i = \left(\mathbf{H}_i^H \mathbf{H}_i\right)^{-1} \mathbf{H}_i^H, \tag{2}$$

and the corresponding weight matrix $\mathbf{W}_i$ is obtained, $(\cdot)^H$ and $(\cdot)^{-1}$ stand for the conjugate transpose and matrix inversion, respectively. The two-norm of each column of the matrix $\mathbf{W}_i$ can be calculated as

$$\mathbf{k}_i = \underset{l \in \{1,2,\ldots F\}}{\arg} \left\| (\mathbf{W}_i)_l \right\|^2, \tag{3}$$

where $\mathbf{k}_i$ is the row vector of the F columns, l is the row of $\mathbf{W}_i$. Switch the RF chain to the $(F + 1)$th to Mth antenna, and then repeat channel estimation and equalization. Combine $\mathbf{k}_i$ and $\mathbf{k}_{i+1}$ by row to get $\mathbf{k}$ ($\mathbf{k} = [\mathbf{k}_i, \mathbf{k}_{i+1}]$), $\mathbf{k}$ is the row vector of M columns.

3.2 Evaluation of CSI

We sort the $\mathbf{k}$ in ascending order, then select F antennas with better CSI (the SINR is large when the two-norm is small). The F best CSI of all M antennas are selected to form a new channel matrix $\mathbf{H}_{i'}$, these selected antennas are used for the transmission and reception of next frame. And the mean value of $\mathbf{k}$ is calculated as a threshold for measuring CSI during antenna switching.

3.3 Dynamic Antenna Selection

Similarly, $\mathbf{H}_{i'}$ is subjected to ZF equalization to obtain the corresponding weight matrix $\mathbf{W}_{i'}$, the two-norm of each column of $\mathbf{W}_{i'}$ is calculated to obtain $\mathbf{k}_{i'}$, and all the elements in $\mathbf{k}_{i'}$ are compared with the threshold to find an element larger than the threshold, which the antenna CSI is smaller than the mean value, and the corresponding antenna number is recorded. After the signal detection, the RF chains of the antennas with recorded numbers are randomly switched to the idle antennas. As CSI changes continuously, the mean value of M antenna CSI will fluctuate with time. In general, when the number in $\mathbf{k}_{i'}$ greater than the mean value of $\mathbf{k}$ is more than $M/4$ (more than the half number of used antennas), let $i = i + 1$ to restart.

With the algorithm above, we consider the channel frequency domain response of each user comprehensively, reduce the number of RF chains (reduce the power consumption) to improve the EE of the system.

4   Simulation Results

4.1   Energy Efficiency and Spectral Efficiency

According to the actual power consumption parameters in [11], the exhaustive search method is adopted of the uplink in a single cell, while the number of antennas on the BS is M (340 or 384) and the number of users is K (from 1 to 150). Each combination of M and K is simulated, and the relationships between the EE and K, the SE and K of the uplink are obtained. The curve of $M = 170$ and $M = 192$ indicate that the proposed antenna selection method is used. Point A, B, D and E in Fig. 2 correspond to the point A, B, D and E in Fig. 3, respectively.

As can be seen from Fig. 2, with the same number of users, the EE of the system can be improved with antenna selection as compare to the system without antenna selection.

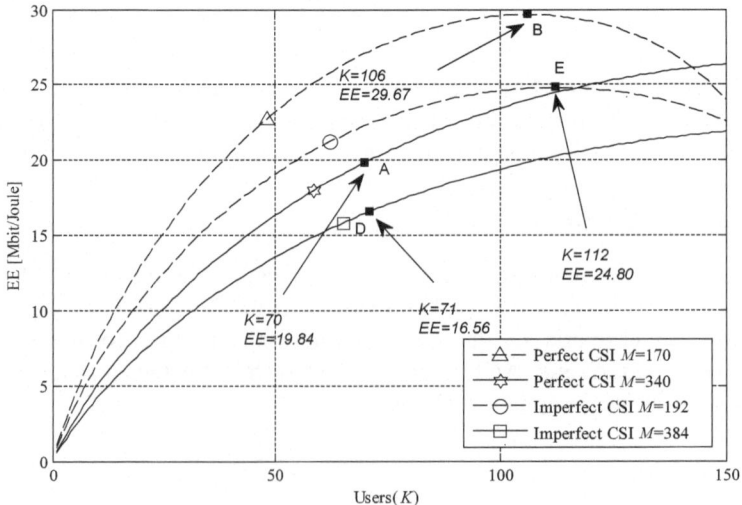

Fig. 2. Relationship of system energy efficiency and K with and without antenna selection

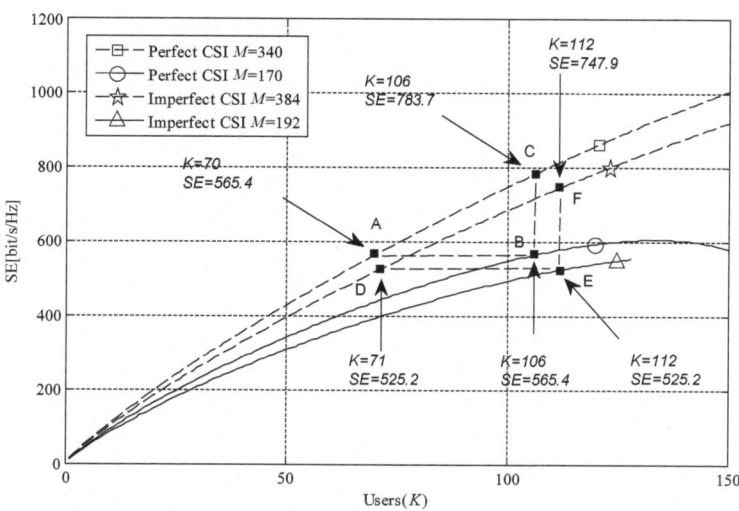

Fig. 3. Relationship of system spectral efficiency and K with and without antenna selection

It is shown in Fig. 3 that the system SE of point A and point B is 565.4 bit/s/Hz, while in Fig. 2 the system EE are 19.84 Mbits/J and 29.67 Mbits/J respectively under perfect CSI. Under imperfect CSI, the system SE of point D and point E is 525.2 bit/s/Hz, while the system EE are 16.56 Mbits/J and 24.80 Mbits/J, respectively. From results above, comparing A with B (as well as D with E), the EE of the system can be improved using antenna selection when the SE is equal.

As can be seen from Fig. 3, the SE of the system at point B is 565.4bit/s/Hz, the SE of the system at point C is 783.7 bit/s/Hz. The SE of point B is lower than point C under perfect CSI. The similar as E (SE = 525.2 bit/s/Hz) and F (SE = 747.9 bit/s/Hz), the SE of point E is lower than point F under imperfect CSI. That is because with the same number of users, the SE of the system will be reduced when the number of BS antennas decreases.

Although the SE of the system with antenna selection at point B or E is lower than that of the system without antenna selection at point C or F as shown in Fig. 3, the EE of the system with antenna selection at point B or E is higher than that of the system without antenna selection when the number of users is same.

4.2   System Error Rate

Figure 4 shows the relationship of BER and SNR under imperfect CSI in a single cell. There are 2 users when the BS antennas are 64, 128 and 256, respectively. System bandwidth B is 20 MHz, and sampling interval is $1/B$ with 16 quadrature amplitude modulation (QAM), ZF processing is adopted in multipath fading channels, and the selected antennas are half of the BS antennas (the number of configured RF chains is $M/2$).

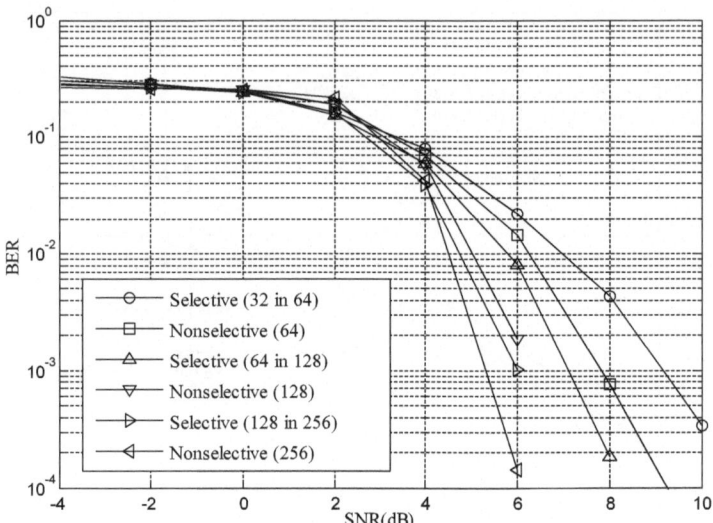

Fig. 4. The BER performance under imperfect CSI

It is shown in Fig. 4, when the antennas on BS are 64, 128 or 256, half antennas are selected in antenna selection system, the BER of system with antenna selection is higher than that of the system without antenna selection. That is because the lower diversity gain of antenna selection system leads to an increase in BER. Although the BER of the system with antenna selection is higher than that of the corresponding system without antenna selection, the EE of the antenna selection system is higher. When the diversity gain is consistent, the BER of the system with 64 or 128 selected antennas is lower than that of the system with 64 or 128 unselected antennas.

5   Conclusion

This paper has analyzed the relationship between EE and SE of the massive MIMO system. Antenna selection is performed to improve EE of the system by reducing the number of RF chains. The simulation results show that when the SE is equal, the EE of the system can be improved with antenna selection. Furthermore, the BER performance of the system with antenna selection is better than that of the system without antenna selection when the RF chains are equal.

Acknowledgment. This research is supported by the Natural Science Foundation of Liaoning Province of China (Grant No. 20180550239).

References

1. Rusek, F., Larsson, E.G., Marzetta, T.L.: Scaling up MIMO: opportunities and challenges with very large arrays. IEEE Signal Process. Mag. **30**(1), 40–60 (2013)
2. Larsson, E.G., Edfors, O., Tufvesson, F.: Massive MIMO for next generation wireless systems. IEEE Commun. Mag. **52**(2), 186–195 (2014)
3. Marzetta, T.L.: Massive MIMO: an introduction. Bell Labs Tech. J. **20**, 11–22 (2015)
4. Ha, D., Lee, K., Kang, J.: Energy efficiency analysis with circuit power consumption in massive MIMO systems. In: 2013 IEEE 24th Annual International Symposium on Personal, Indoor, and Mobile Radio Communications, London, United Kingdom, pp. 938–942 (2013)
5. Pei, Y., Pham, T.-H., Liang, Y.-C.: How many RF chains are optimal for large-scale MIMO systems when circuit power is considered? In: 2012 IEEE Global Communications Conference (GLOBECOM), Anaheim, California, USA, pp. 3868–3873 (2012)
6. Li, G.Y., Xu, Z., Xiong, C., Yang, C., Chen, Y.: Energy-efficient wireless communications: tutorial, survey, and open issues. IEEE Wirel. Commun. **18**, 28–35 (2011)
7. Muaayed, A.L.-R.: Massive MIMO system: an overview. Int. J. Open Inf. Technol. **5**(2), 5–8 (2017)
8. Ngo, H.Q., Larsson, E.G., Marzetta, T.L.: Energy and spectral efficiency of very large multiuser MIMO systems. IEEE Trans. Commun. **61**(4), 1436–1449 (2013)
9. Björnson, E., Hoydis, J., Kountouris, M., Debbah, M.: Massive MIMO systems with non-ideal hardware: energy efficiency, estimation, and capacity limits. IEEE Trans. Inf. Theory **60**(11), 7112–7139 (2014)
10. Hoydis, J., ten Brink, S., Debbah, M.: Massive MIMO in the UL/DL of cellular networks: how many antennas do we need? IEEE J. Sel. Areas Commun. **31**(2), 160–171 (2013)
11. Björnson, E., Sanguinetti, L., Hoydis, J., Debbah, M.: Optimal design of energy-efficient multi-user MIMO systems: is massive MIMO the answer? IEEE Trans. Wireless Commun. **14**(6), 3059–3075 (2015)

Dimension Selection and Compression Reconstruction Algorithm of Measurement Matrix Based on Edge Density

Jiayin Yu and Erfu Wang[(⊠)]

Electronic Engineering College, Heilongjiang University, Harbin, China
efwang_612@163.com

Abstract. This paper is based on the sparse representation of signals in orthogonal space. Data collection and compressed are combined by compressed sensing theory. The image signal can be reconstructed by fewer observations which we obtained it under the measurement matrix. Compressive sensing theory breaks through the limitation of data sampling. In the theory of compressed sensing, the selection of measurement matrix plays a key role in whether the compressed signal can be reconstructed or not. In this paper, different measurement matrices are selected to achieve the compressive sensing and their similarity coefficient matrices are analyzed to compare the different performance. This paper focus on the coefficient selection of random measurement matrix. To find the relationship between the image structure similarity coefficient and the other characteristic indexes. An algorithm for dimension design of measurement matrix is proposed. A high performance algorithm for image compression perception and image restoration is implemented.

Keywords: Compressive sensing · Sparse representation ·
Measurement matrix · Similarity coefficient

1 Introduction

Nyquist sampling theorem, also known as Shannon sampling theorem [1]. In this theorem, two processes of signal sampling and reconstruction are described: Firstly, the continuous time signal is converted to the discrete time signal, and then the discrete signal is restored. The key theory in the sampling theorem is that the sampling frequency must be higher than twice the maximum signal frequency [2]. Otherwise, the signal will be aliased. However, in practical application, this method requires a lot of computing resources.

Therefore, it is assumed that if a way can be found to realize the compression process while sampling and retain the effective information of the original signal [3], Moreover, it does not need to meet Nyquist's limit on sampling frequency to complete signal reconstruction, which can reduce the complexity of signal processing and the cost of calculation. Compressed sensing theory provides a new idea for signal processing [4]. Compressive sensing theory is to design a compression sampling algorithm

© ICST Institute for Computer Sciences, Social Informatics and Telecommunications Engineering 2019
Published by Springer Nature Switzerland AG 2019. All Rights Reserved
J. Jin et al. (Eds.): GreeNets 2019, LNICST 282, pp. 92–100, 2019.
https://doi.org/10.1007/978-3-030-21730-3_10

aiming at the sparse nature of most signals in real life. Due to the sparse nature of signals, only a small number of observation values can be used for signal reconstruction during recovery.

Compressed sensing theory was proposed by Donoho et al. as a practical signal sampling coding theory [5, 6], it has been widely applied. Mallat and Zhang proposed the matching tracking algorithm (MP&OMP) in 1993, which was the first time to use the super-complete dictionary for sparse decomposition of the original signal [7]. Tropp proved that if select gaussian matrix or Bernoulli matrix [8], we can use the greedy algorithm to reconstruct the signal [9, 10]. Candes proved that the measurement matrix which is selected in compression observation should meet the property of finite equidistant, so several common measurement matrices have been widely used in compressive perception theory. Such as gaussian random matrix, Bernoulli measurement matrix, partial hada code matrix and so on. The above research results are the important foundation of CS theory. Based on OMP reconstruction algorithm [11], this paper analyzes the influence of different measurement matrices on image compression effect. Combined with the image feature information, we analyze the influence of parameters on the reconstruction effect under the same measurement matrix [12]. In this paper, a method for calculating the parameters of measurement matrix is proposed, which can better take account of the sharpness of image and the complexity of calculation.

2 Compressive Sensing Theory

If there are few non-zero elements in a signal, or the majority of signals in this signal are zero, the signal can be considered as sparse. In practice, the signals we come into contact with are generally not absolutely sparse, but they can be approximately sparse in a certain transformation domain. In other words, as long as the sparse space that meets the conditions is found, the data can be effectively compressed and sampled.

We set the length of the signal X is N, in the transformation domain, if there are K coefficients is not zero or much greater than the other coefficients, and $K \ll N$. Then, the signal is said to be K-sparse in the corresponding transformation domain. When we obtain M observations $(K < M \ll N)$. We can compress the signal. And this M observation can reconstruct the original signal X. Because the loss is some smaller coefficient, so we can get an approximation of X. Set the orthonormal basis of the transformation domain is $\psi_i = \{\psi_1, \ldots \psi_n\}$, X can be represented linearly by $\{\theta_1, \ldots \theta_n\}$:

$$X = \sum_{i=1}^{N} \theta_i \psi_i = \psi s \tag{1}$$

Where ψ is a $N \times N$ matrix, θ is $N \times 1$ matrix. s is sparse coefficient. Domain selection is the basis of signal sparse representation. At present, classical algorithms include discrete cosine (DCT) algorithm, Fourier transform (FFT) algorithm, wavelet transform (DWT) algorithm, etc. DWT algorithm is used in this paper.

The measurement $M \times N$ matrix is used to transform the original signal of N dimension into the Y observation vector of M dimension. Then the signal information can be restored as much as possible through reconstruction algorithm. It's essentially the projection of the original signal X onto the measurement matrix that we set up to get the projection value Y. The purpose of the observation matrix design is to better realize the reconstruction of the original signal or obtain the sparse coefficient vector. In order to achieve this, the observation matrix must satisfy the RIP characteristics. The one-to-one correspondence between the original space and the sparse space is guaranteed [13]. To meet the RIP characteristics, the measurement matrix ϕ is required to be unrelated to sparse basis ψ. In this way, two different K-sparse signals will not be mapped to the same set. The expression of measured value is:

$$Y = \phi X \tag{2}$$

Where ϕ is $M \times N$ order matrix. According to formula (1), it can be obtained:

$$Y = \phi X = \phi \psi_S \tag{3}$$

In the above formula, the number of equations is far less than the number of unknowns, and the system should have infinite solutions. However, since the original signal has been sparse transformed, there are only non-zero values and we know their positions. So we can get the solutions when $M > K$. Then the original signal is recovered by nonlinear reconstruction algorithm. In this paper, several measurement matrices are compared and their parameters are further verified.

When the measurement matrix meets the RIP characteristics, we can decode the projected value according to the method of solving the norm. Thus, the signal reconstruction process is transformed into the process of solving the optimization of norm, and the process of solving the minimization of norm is a linear process. At present, reconstruction algorithms can be roughly divided into two categories. One is greedy algorithm, including matching tracking algorithm and orthogonal matching tracking algorithm. The second is convex optimization algorithm, which includes gradient projection method, base tracking method, minimum Angle regression method and so on. In this paper, we use the orthogonal matching tracking algorithm.

3   Measurement Matrix and Reconstruction

In the realization of compressed sensing, measurement matrix, as a very important part, directly affects the accuracy of image restoration [14]. When selecting the measurement matrix, in addition to meeting RIP principle [15], as the key to encrypt the information to be processed, the measurement matrix also needs to have good randomness.

Different measurement matrices with different randomness have different measurement effects on different information sources. Therefore, when the image is projected by the measurement matrix, some parameters will have a certain impact on the recovery effect in the reconstruction process.

In this paper, random matrix, gaussian matrix and Parthadamard matrix are used as measurement matrix. The elements in the random channel matrix are generated randomly and have great uncertainty, so the confidentiality is also strong. In this experiment, the dimension of semi-determined random channel is adopted. Gaussian matrix is unrelated to the sparse basis of most signals. Besides these two matrices, it is also widely used in the process of compressed sensing. In this paper, part of the hadamar matrix is selected for comparative analysis with the above two matrices.

Lena grayscale map in the image standard database is selected as the information source, and the implementation process is shown in Fig. 1.

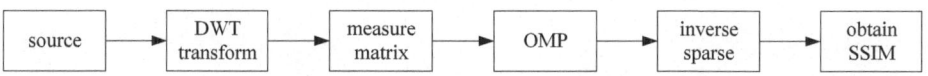

Fig. 1. The principle diagram

The observation signal can be expressed as:

$$Y = X * R \tag{4}$$

Where X is the sparse signal after DWT transformation, R is the measurement matrix. Y is reconstructed by using OMP algorithm. The reconstructed signal is transformed by inverse wavelet transform to get the restored image. In Fig. 2, (a) is the original Lena diagram, (b), (c) and (d) are respectively recovered images obtained when random matrix, gaussian random matrix and part of hadamar matrix are used as measurement matrix. Judging from the visual observation effect, images are compressed and reconstructed under all three measurement matrices, and some hadamar matrices used in (d) have better effect. In order to quantitatively evaluate the reconstruction effect of compressive perception, SSIM, the structural similarity coefficient, was used as the index to compare the similarity coefficient between the reconstructed signal and the original signal under different measurement matrices and observation values, and to obtain the performance curve. Since the value of M is too small, the restored picture is seriously distorted. Therefore, in this paper, the SSIM of the reconstructed image and the original image was calculated from $M = 128$. The simulation results are shown in Fig. 2.

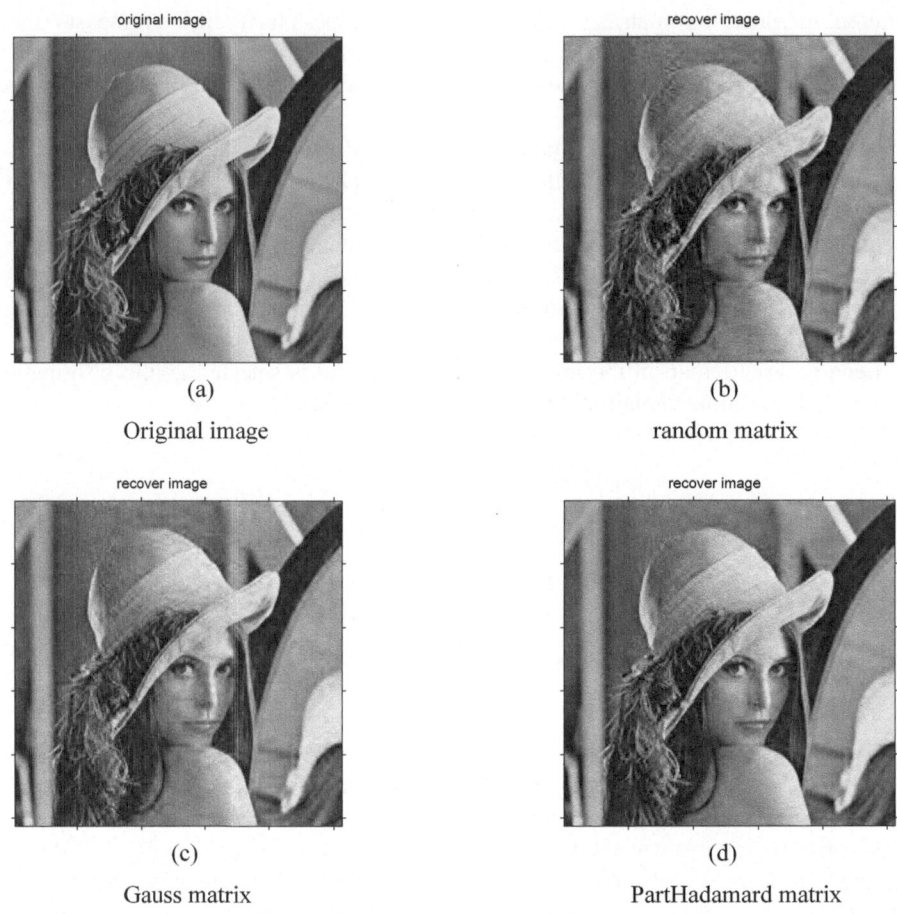

(a)

Original image

(b)

random matrix

(c)

Gauss matrix

(d)

PartHadamard matrix

Fig. 2. Image recovery under three matrices

As can be seen from the graph, the similarity coefficient between the reconstructed image and the original image under the measurement of PartHadamard matrix is larger than the other two overall, so the performance of some hadamard matrices in processing one-dimensional image information is better than that of other two random measurement matrices. In addition, due to the absence of noise, the simulation results of random gaussian channel and random channel are not different, and the performance of the two channels is similar under the conditions set in this paper. Combined with the reconstructed images above, we can more intuitively see that when some hadamard matrices are used as measurement matrices, the restored Lena graphs have clearer contour and clearer picture quality.

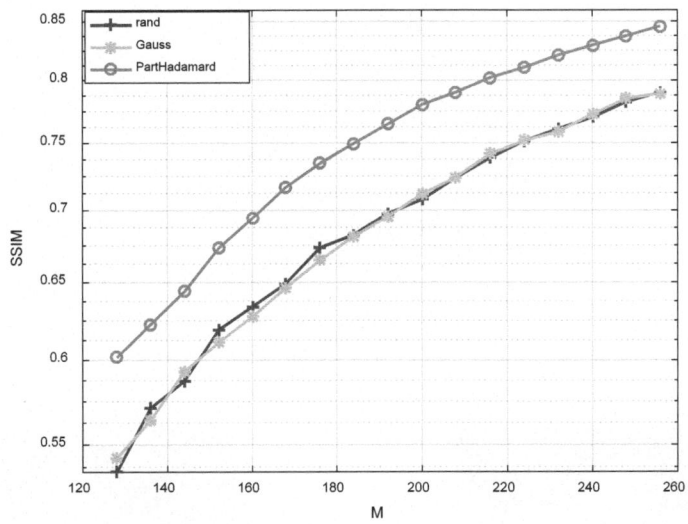

Fig. 3. SSIM of the three matrices is compared with the line graph

4   Dimension Selection Algorithm of Measurement Matrix Based on Edge Density

In compressive sensing theory, the selection of observation matrix has an important impact on reconstruction performance [13]. In the previous simulation, the observation matrix is a semi-random matrix of parameters, where is an adjustable parameter. The larger the size, the better the recovery, but the longer the program takes to run. Lena diagram and Lake diagram in the standard grayscale image library were still selected for experiment. PartHadamard matrix was selected as the measurement matrix, parameters were adjusted, and structural similarity coefficient data of two images were simulated and analyzed, as shown in Table 1.

Table 1. Structural similarity coefficient

SSIM	Lena	Lake
M = 128	0.6007	0.4542
M = 136	0.6207	0.4886
M = 144	0.6522	0.507
M = 152	0.6766	0.5346
M = 160	0.6974	0.5572
M = 164	0.7063	0.5739
M = 168	0.7169	0.5884
M = 176	0.7352	0.6057
M = 184	0.751	0.6302

(continued)

Table 1. (*continued*)

SSIM	Lena	Lake
M = 192	0.766	0.6466
M = 200	0.7779	0.6645
M = 208	0.7898	0.6821
M = 216	0.7997	0.6961
M = 220	0.8043	0.7025
M = 224	0.8095	0.7131
M = 232	0.8214	0.7238

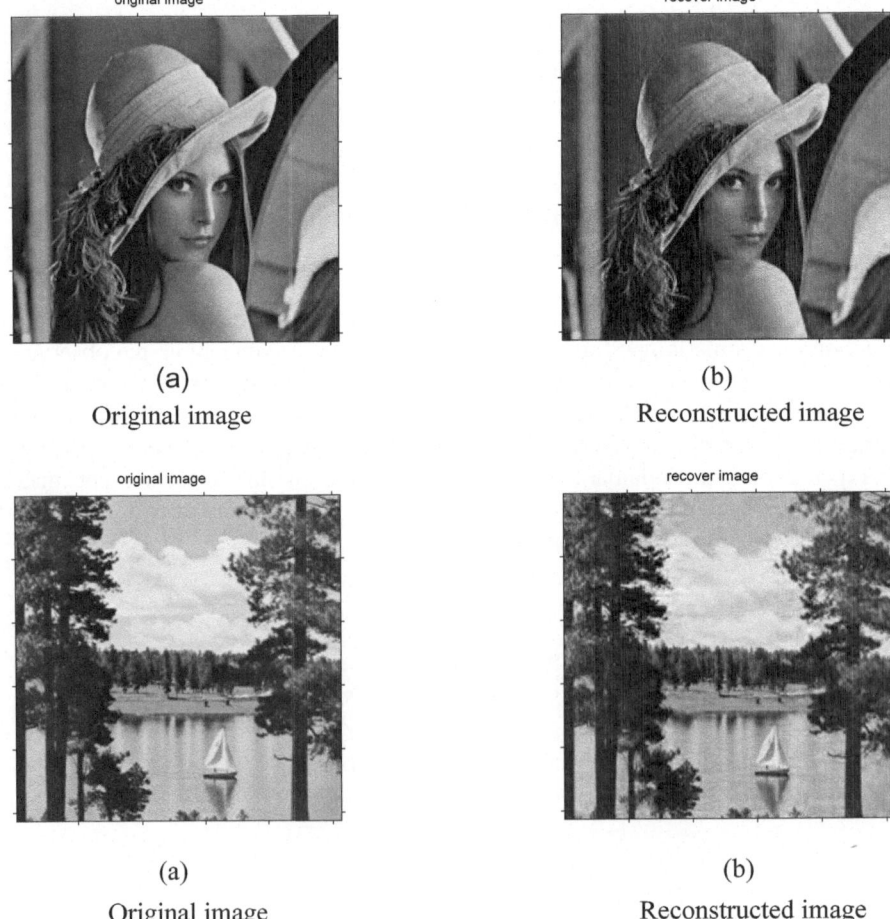

(a)   (b)

Original image   Reconstructed image

(a)   (b)

Original image   Reconstructed image

Fig. 4. The comparison between the two images under the m-value

It can be seen that, with the increase of M, the structural similarity coefficient between images also increases, which is reflected in the clearer image after reconstruction. Usually, the value of M is selected empirically. Among the edge information, edge density is an important method to evaluate the edge information. Therefore, this paper designs a dimension selection method of measurement matrix based on edge density. Define the function f(x):

$$f(x) = \lambda X + q \tag{5}$$

For different images, there is always M value range suitable for them to achieve a certain recognizable effect in reconstruction. Different images have different M value range.

Lena diagram used in this experiment has an edge density of 72.6808, and 164 is taken according to the formula M. The edge density of the Lake graph is 99.6158. According to the formula, when M is equal to 220. Lena and Lake were compressed and reconstructed with the designed M value. As can be seen from the comparison in Fig. 4, the picture quality of the reconstructed signal is clear, which can fully reflect the information of each part of the image for clear identification. The validity of the dimension selection algorithm of measurement matrix based on edge density is verified in this paper.

5 Conclusion

In recent years, compressive sensing theory has been studied and improved, great progress has been made in practical application. By introducing the analysis of measurement matrix, this paper finds that when processing one-dimensional image information, PartHadamard matrix have better performance than others. Under the same matrix dimension, the original image can be recovered better by the measurement matrix. This paper studies the problem that the dimension value of random matrix can only be determined empirically. We designs the dimension selection principle of measurement matrix based on edge density and determines the M value through the integer of defined linear function. Simulation experiments show that each part of the image can be clearly identified under the dimension of the measurement matrix designed under this criterion, so we can extend the application of compressed sensing in image processing.

References

1. Strawn, G.: Claude Shannon: Mastermind of Information Theory. IT Prof. **16**(6), 70–72 (2014)
2. Vaidya, M., Walia, E.S., Gupta, A.: Data compression using Shannon-fano algorithm implemented by VHDL. In: 2014 International Conference on Advances in Engineering & Technology Research (ICAETR - 2014), Unnao, pp. 1–5 (2014)

3. Zhang, Q., Chen, Y., Chen, Y., Chi, L., Wu, Y.: A cognitive signals reconstruction algorithm based on compressed sensing. In: 2015 IEEE 5th Asia-Pacific Conference on Synthetic Aperture Radar (APSAR), Singapore, pp. 724–727 (2015)
4. Chen, Y.-J., Zhang, Q., Luo, Y., Chen, Y.-A.: Measurement matrix optimization for ISAR sparse imaging based on genetic algorithm. Geosci. Remote Sens. Lett. IEEE **13**(12), 1875–1879 (2016)
5. Song, J., Liao, Z.: A new fast and parallel MRI framework based on contourlet and compressed sensing sensitivity encoding (CS-SENSE). In: 2016 International Conference on Machine Learning and Cybernetics (ICMLC), Jeju, pp. 750–755 (2016)
6. Hao, W., Han, M., Hao, W.: Compressed sensing remote sensing image reconstruction based on wavelet tree and nonlocal total variation. In: 2016 International Conference on Network and Information Systems for Computers (ICNISC), Wuhan, pp. 317–322 (2016)
7. Wang, L., Lu, K., Liu, P.: Compressed sensing of a remote sensing image based on the priors of the reference image. IEEE Geosci. Remote Sens. Lett. **12**(4), 736–740 (2015)
8. Stöger, D., Mathematik, Z., Jung, P., Krahmer, F., Mathematik, Z.: Blind deconvolution and compressed sensing. In: 2016 4th International Workshop on Compressed Sensing Theory and its Applications to Radar, Sonar and Remote Sensing (CoSeRa), Aachen, pp. 24–27 (2016)
9. Cambareri, V., Moshtaghpour, A., Jacques, L.: A greedy blind calibration method for compressed sensing with unknown sensor gains. In: 2017 IEEE International Symposium on Information Theory (ISIT), pp. 1132–1136 (2017)
10. Flinth, A.: Sparse blind deconvolution and demixing through ℓ 12-minimization. Adv. Comput. Math. **44**, 1–21 (2018)
11. Wei, J., Huang, Y., Lu, K., Wang, L.: Nonlocal low-rank-based compressed sensing for remote sensing image reconstruction. IEEE Geosci. Remote Sens. Lett. **13**(10), 1557–1561 (2016)
12. Huang, F., Lan, B., Tao, J., Chen, Y., Tan, X., Feng, J., Ma, Y.: A parallel nonlocal means algorithm for remote sensing image denoising on an Intel Xeon Phi platform. Access IEEE **5**, 8559–8567 (2017)
13. Rouabah, S., Ouarzeddine, M., Souissi, B.: SAR images compressed sensing based on recovery algorithms. In: IGARSS 2018 - 2018 IEEE International Geoscience and Remote Sensing Symposium, Valencia, pp. 8897–8900 (2018)
14. Wei, S., Zhang, X., Shi, J.: Compressed sensing Linear array SAR 3-D imaging via sparse locations prediction. In: 2014 IEEE Geoscience and Remote Sensing Symposium, Quebec City, QC, pp. 1887–1890 (2014)
15. Lv, W., Yang, J., Xu, W., Bao, X., Yang, X., Wu, L.: A scheme of feature analysis in SAR imaging based on compressed sensing. In: 2016 IEEE International Geoscience and Remote Sensing Symposium (IGARSS), Beijing, pp. 2901–2904 (2016)

A Multi-local World Network Model

Yunbo Zhang and Peng Li[✉]

School of Information Science and Engineering, Dalian Polytechnic University,
Dalian, China
lipeng@dlpu.edu.cn

Abstract. Although people have the characteristics of group movement in their daily life, they are not distributed in a single local-world. People from different regions are connected with each other for many reasons, such as work and study. Therefore, on the basis of a local-world evolving network model, we propose and study a network model with the concept of multi-local world connectivity, which simulates Human Daily multi-workspace and multi-residential areas. In addition, the statistical characteristics of its complex networks are analyzed by simulation experiments.

Keywords: Local-world · Multi-local · Complex networks

1 Introduction

Since the 1990s, the information technology represented by the Internet has developed rapidly. With the rapid development of continuous progress of human society, we have already stepped into the Internet era [1]. From Internet to WWW [2], power system to global transportation network, biological brain to metabolic network, scientific research cooperation network to various economic, political and social relations, people are living in a world full of complicated networks [3].

Network is like a "double-edged sword", which not only brings convenience to people's work and life, but also improves production efficiency and quality of life [4]. However, it leads to negative effects such as computer viruses. The increasing networked human society requires people to have a better under-standing of various artificial and natural complex network behaviors. To study the structural properties of various complex networks [5], a unified tool for describing networks is needed. This tool is a kind of network model or graph in mathematics [6]. All networks can be viewed as a system of nodes connected together in some way. When designing and evaluating the network system or protocol, it is very important to choose a model which is consistent with the real situation [7]. Although there are many kinds of models have been proposed, such as, the RWP model [8] and the GMM model [9]. They still can't simulate the real-life networks very well.

In this article, we construct a multi-local world network model which is better consistent with the law of human's daily behavior according to the local-world characteristics of networks [10]. It simulates the relationships among people which have multiple work and living areas [11] and analyses the connectivity, scale-free characteristics and network degree distribution of the models.

© ICST Institute for Computer Sciences, Social Informatics and Telecommunications Engineering 2019
Published by Springer Nature Switzerland AG 2019. All Rights Reserved
J. Jin et al. (Eds.): GreeNets 2019, LNICST 282, pp. 101–105, 2019.
https://doi.org/10.1007/978-3-030-21730-3_11

2   The BA Scale-Free Network Model

Barabási and Albert proposed a scale-free network model in order to explain the mechanism of a power-law degree distribution [12, 13]. According to the equation

$$\Pi_i = \frac{k_i}{\sum_j k_j} \tag{1}$$

The preferential attachment probability of each node is calculated. $P(k)$ is the probability that the degree of node i is exactly k. The degree distribution function of BA network is obtained that $P(k) \sim 2\ m^2/k^3$. All indicate that the probability $P(k)$ satisfies a power law with an exponent 3. All indicate that the probability $P(k)$ satisfies a power law with an exponent 3. The scaling exponent is independent of m, the only parameter in the model, as shown by Fig. 1(a).

3   The Multi-local World Network Model

The BA scale-free network model calculates all nodes' preferential attachment probability by using Eq. (1), and then, generating the holistic network's average degree value. Because of the local-world was proposed, we have known that each node has its local connections in the real-life networks [14]. But just like people who work in different places. Wherever we go, we always return to our residences. As a result, most of human's movements are concentrated in typical areas like dwellings or work location [15]. Therefore we proposed a multi-local world network model. The generation algorithm of the multi-local world network model is as follows:

1. Randomly set up M regions and each region has m_0 nodes.
2. When choosing the regions to which the new node connects, assume that the probability Π_{local} that a new node is connected to region M_i depends on the node number of M_i at every time step t, in such a way that

$$\Pi_{local} = \frac{t + m_0}{t + M * m_0} \tag{2}$$

3. The new node was connected to m nodes with m edges when the region has been selected. We assume the probability $\Pi_i (i \in \text{multi-local})$ that the new node is connected to node i depends on the degree k_i.
4. According to step2 and step3, using a double preferential attachment $\Pi_{local}(i)$ defined at every time step t by

$$\Pi_{local}(i) = \Pi_{local} * \Pi_i = \frac{t + m_0}{t + M * m_0} * \frac{k_i}{\sum_j k_j} \ (i, j \in multi - local) \tag{3}$$

Using Eq. (3), the newly coming node linked to the network at every time step t, which are chosen with double preferential attachment. The new node selects the region and then connects the nodes from one of the multi-local world, but does not connect to the whole system as in the BA scale-free network model. Typically, we select several living areas for growth and preferential attachment. By the same way, the workspaces would be chosen.

4 Simulations and Discussions

In this paper, we construct a multi-living area, multi-working area model and analyze its connectivity, scale-free characteristics and degree distribution. The parameters of simulation are shown as the Table 1.

Table 1. The multi-local world network model's parameter

Parameter	Value
The number of living area M *and* working area M'	3, 10
The initial number of nodes in a single region m_0	3, 10, 30
The number of edges connected m	1, 2, 3
The network size N	10000

By Matlab simulation, we built a multi-local world network model with living and working areas. As can be seen from the Fig. 1(b), this model has scale-free characteristics and the network diagram is connected.

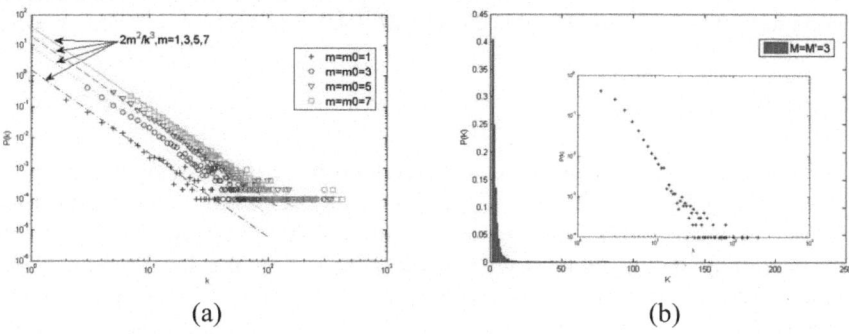

(a)	(b)

Fig. 1. (**a**). Degree distribution $P(k)$ of the BA scale-free network model, with $N = 10000$ and $m = m_0 = 1, 3, 5, 7$, where the straight lines are the theoretical power-law scaling factors, $2\ m^2/k^3$, $m = m_0 = 1, 3, 5, 7$, respectively; (**b**). Degree distribution $P(k)$ of the multi-local world network model, with $N = 10000$ and $M = M' = 3$. The initial number of nodes in a single region $m0 = 3$ and $m = 1$.

The initial number of nodes will change the network distribution. We found that the degree distribution of the multi-local world network model will varies from exponential to power-law distribution because different m0. The greater m0 is, the larger proportion it takes in the local-world after growth, the more homogeneous the evolving network. In contrast, the smaller m0 is, the smaller proportion of initial nodes in the evolutionary network will be. With the continuous growth of the number of network nodes, the final network model will become more and more uneven, as shown as Fig. 2(a).

In the real life, you will meet many people at one time when you come to a new place. So it is the same to the real-life network. The Fig. 2(b) demonstrates us that a new node adds in the multi-local world with not only one edge. The degree distribution characteristics of the multi-local world network will vary greatly. With the growing of m in the local-world, the more nodes are connected from one time to the next. The degree distribution curve becomes more and more curved. It means that the connections between nodes are closer and the networks of multiple LANS are getting evenly distributed.

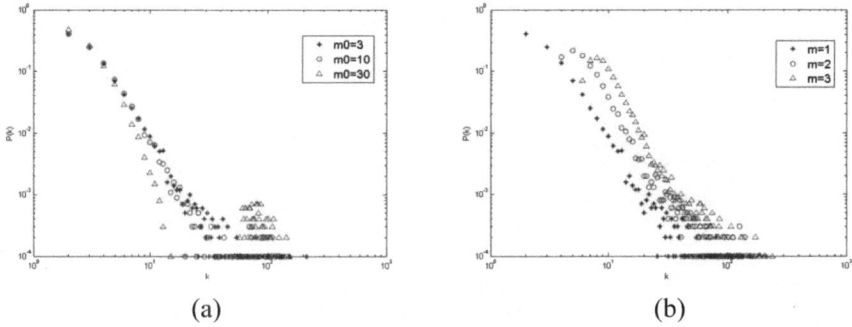

(a)   (b)

Fig. 2. (a). Degree distribution comparison in the log-log scale of the multi-local world networks. $M = M' = 3, m = 1, m_0 = 3, 10, 30, N = 10000$; (b). Degree distribution comparison in the log-log scale of the multi-local world networks. $M = M' = 3, m_0 = 3, m = 1, 2, 3, N = 10000$.

5   Conclusions

In this paper, the multi-local world network model is more in line with human behavior in real society. In the real-life network, nodes usually selected the local area network which takes up a larger proportion in the overall network, and then choose the second priority according to the node degree distribution within the local-world. Through simulation tests, we get the multi-local world network model have exponential and power law changes due to different degree distributions of parameters. Furthermore, with growth it comes more connectivity.

References

1. Duncan, J.: Watts: the new science of networks. Ann. Rev. Sociol. **30**, 243–270 (2004)
2. Dorogovtsev, S.N., Mendes, J.F.: Evolution of Networks (2003)
3. Strogatz, S.H.: Exploring complex networks. Nature **410**, 268–276 (2001)
4. Barabási, A.-L.: The new science of networks. Phys. Today **6**(5), 243–270 (2003)

5. Albert, R., Barabási, A.L.: Statistical mechanics of complex networks. Rev. Mod. Phys. **26**(1), xii (2002)
6. Erdos, P.: On the evolution of random graphs. Trans. Am. Math. Soc. **286**(1), 257–274 (2011)
7. Bandyopadhyay, S., Coyle, E., Falck, T.: Stochastic properties of mobility models in mobile ad hoc networks. IEEE Trans. Mob. Comput. **6**(11), 1218–1229 (2007)
8. Johnson, D.B., Maltz, D.A.: Dynamic source routing in ad hoc wireless networks. Mob. Comput. **353**(1), 153–181 (1999)
9. Campos, C.A.V., Otero, D.C., De Moraes, L.F.M.: Realistic individual mobility Markovian models for mobile ad hoc networks. In: IEEE WCNC 2004, pp. 1980–1985 (2004)
10. Dan, X., Xiang, L., Xiaofan, W.: Virus transmission and immune control in local complex networks. Control Decis.- Making **21**(7), 817–820 (2006)
11. Si, T., Huijia, L., Yue, Z.: Analysis of a new multi-local world network model. Comput. Appl. Res. **30**(3), 869–872 (2013)
12. Barabási, A.L., Albert, R.: Emergence of scaling in random networks. Science **286**(5439), 509–512 (1999)
13. Barabási, A.L., Bonabeau, E.: Scale-free networks. Sci. Am. **288**(5), 60 (2003)
14. Li, X., Chen, G.: A local-world evolving network model. Phys. A **328**(1–2), 274–286 (2003)
15. Pal, R., Prakash, A., Tripathi, R., et al.: Analytical model for clustered vehicular ad hoc network analysis. ICT Express **4**, 160–164 (2018). S2405959517302503

Channel Estimation in Massive MIMO TDD Systems

Zhuyun Fan, Chaoyue Zhao, Jiyu Jin$^{(\boxtimes)}$, Guiyue Jin, and Lihui Wang

School of Information Science and Engineering, Dalian Polytechnic University,
Dalian, China
jiyu.jin@dlpu.edu.cn

Abstract. Massive multiple-input multiple-output (MIMO) significantly improves the spectral efficiency and energy efficiency of the systems. In this paper, a channel estimation based on pilot method is proposed for multi-cell massive MIMO time division duplex (TDD) systems. The proposed estimator designs an orthogonal pilot structure to mitigate pilot contamination. Additionally, the receiver estimates the channel state information (CSI) at the pilot tone, and combines the interpolation algorithm to obtain the desired signal. The proposed method increases the accuracy of channel estimation with the lower computational complexity. Simulations results verify the effectiveness of the proposed method.

Keywords: Massive MIMO system · Channel estimation · Pilot contamination

1 Introduction

As one of the key technologies of the fifth generation (5G) wireless networks, massive multiple-input multiple-output (MIMO) system has been extensively studied. Massive MIMO significantly improves energy efficiency and spectral efficiency by configuring a large number of antenna arrays on the base station (BS) and spatial multiplexing technology [1]. However, the pilot of target cell will be interfered by other cells while non-orthogonal pilot is used for channel estimation, which is a primary bottleneck restricting the development of massive MIMO called pilot contamination [2, 3].

Compared with frequency division duplex (FDD) mode, the important distinguish of time division duplex (TDD) is channel reciprocity [1, 4], the channel state information (CSI) in the uplink can be reused in the downlink, which greatly reduces the time-domain resource overhead and brings higher energy efficiency. The cyclic shift of Zadoff-Chu (ZC) sequence is used to maintain the orthogonality of intra-cell, but the same pilot sequences are used in inter-cell, which causes serious pilot contamination [5]. Based on the multi-cell massive MIMO system, a pilot design criterion aiming at minimizing pilot contamination is deduced [6]. A semi-orthogonal pilot design method is proposed, the authors make the best of the asymptotic orthogonality of the channel to mitigate the interference by successive interference cancellation. But it requires slow time-varying characteristics of channel [7]. In a countless number of works, large-scale

© ICST Institute for Computer Sciences, Social Informatics and Telecommunications Engineering 2019
Published by Springer Nature Switzerland AG 2019. All Rights Reserved
J. Jin et al. (Eds.): GreeNets 2019, LNICST 282, pp. 106–113, 2019.
https://doi.org/10.1007/978-3-030-21730-3_12

fading coefficients are assumed to be known at the BS [8, 9]. Moreover, the desired signal can be obtain by zero forcing (ZF) or minimum mean square error (MMSE).

In this paper, a pilot-based channel estimation method is proposed in multi-cell massive MIMO TDD system. Considering pilot contamination, an orthogonal pilot structure is designed by using ZC sequence whatever inter-cell or intra-cell. Additionally, the receiver estimates the CSI at the pilot tone, and combines the interpolation algorithm to obtain the desired signal. As a result, simulations show the better performance of the proposed method.

2 System Model

2.1 Multi-cell Massive MIMO System Model

A multiuser multi-cell massive MIMO TDD system is shown in Fig. 1. The system consists of L hexagonal cells, which share the same time/frequency resource. In each cell, one BS with M antennas in the center serves K single-antenna users simultaneously. The users are distributed randomly, it is required that receiving antennas M are much larger than the number of users K.

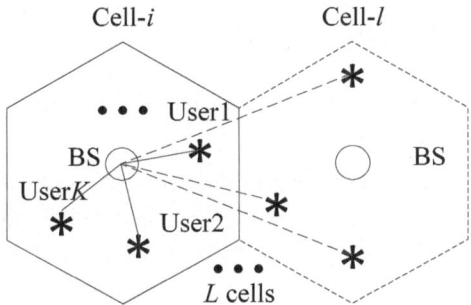

Fig. 1. Multi-cell system model.

We assume wireless channel is composed of large-scale fading and small-scale fading. The large-scale fading represents path loss and shadow fading, while the small-scale fading refers to the changes of amplitude and phase in small regions [10]. The channel response from the kth user in the ith cell to the mth antenna of the BS in the lth cell is

$$g_{ilkm} = h_{ilkm} \beta_{ilk}^{1/2},\qquad(1)$$

Where β_{ilk} is the large-scale fading coefficient and assumed constant since the path loss and shadow fading change slowly [10–12], h_{ilkm} is the small-scale fading coefficient, it is assumed to be independent and identically distributed (i.i.d), which follows a circularly symmetric complex normal distribution. The channel matrix from ith cell to the BS in lth cell is

$$\mathbf{G}_{il} = \mathbf{H}_{il}\mathbf{D}_{il} \in \mathbb{C}^{M \times K}, \tag{2}$$

Where $\mathbf{H}_{il} \in \mathbb{C}^{M \times K}$ and $[\mathbf{H}_{il}]_{m,k} = h_{ilkm}, \mathbf{D}_{il} \in \mathbb{C}^{K \times K}$ is a diagonal matrix and $[\mathbf{D}_{il}]_{k,k} = \beta_{ilk}^{1/2}$.

2.2 Uplink Frame Structure

Suppose the channel is quasi-static within the coherent time, and the inter-cell frequency reuse factor is one. The pilot sequence utilizes ZC sequence because of its constant envelope, ideal periodic autocorrelation and good cross correlation [13]. On the other hand, it still has the properties mentioned after Fourier transforms. The conventional frame structure in one coherent time can be shown in Fig. 2. By adding cyclic prefix (CP) which is intercepted from the tail of data, the cyclic convolution characteristic of signal and channel can be formed. The length of the CP is larger than the maximum multipath delay P.

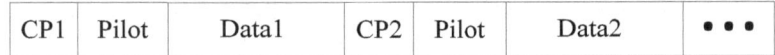

Fig. 2. The conventional frame structure.

ZC sequences are used for pilot due to their properties, the kth user's pilot can be represented by $\mathbf{s}_k = [s_k(0), s_k(1) \ldots s_k(N-1)]^T$, where $(\bullet)^T$ is the transpose, N is the length of pilot and $N > KP$. The cyclic convolution matrix as show

$$\mathbf{S}_k = \begin{bmatrix} s_k(0) & s_k(N-1) & \cdots & s_k(N-P+1) \\ s_k(1) & s_k(0) & \cdots & s_k(N-P+2) \\ \vdots & \vdots & \ddots & \\ s_k(N-1) & s_k(N-2) & \cdots & s_k(N-P+N) \end{bmatrix}, \tag{3}$$

$\mathbf{S}_k$ is a $N \times P$ cyclic shift version of $\mathbf{s}_k$ with property $\mathbf{S}_k^H \mathbf{S}_k = N\mathbf{I}_P$.

3 The Proposed Pilot Design and Channel Estimation

In order to mitigate the pilot contamination and obtain more accurate CSI, a pilot design method in frequency domain is proposed, which makes the pilot inter-cell or intra-cell be orthogonal. This paper selects ZC sequence of L-size that makes the pilot signals non-interfere among cells. After Fourier transform, the pilot signals of different users in the same cell are placed on orthogonal carriers, there is localized or distributed [14, 15].

As shown in Fig. 3, there are P carriers for each user. The pilot of 1st user is $\mathbf{a}_1 = [s_1, s_2 \ldots s_P]^T$. Fast Fourier Transform (FFT) of P points is applied to $\mathbf{a}_1$, and then mapped to $K \times P$ carriers in frequency domain. The figure shows distributed method, and remain carriers are empty. Then the frequency domain signal is converted into time domain by inverse FFT (IFFT).

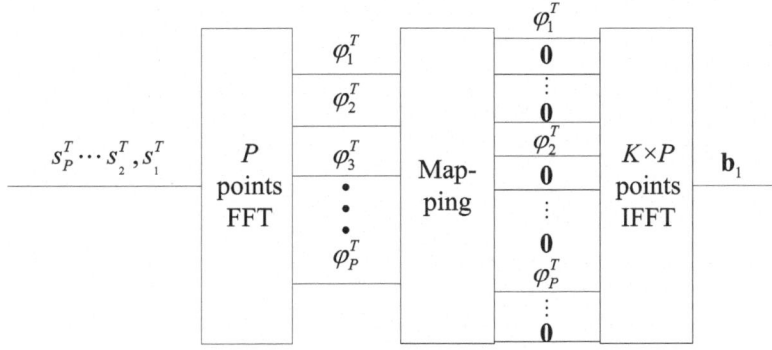

Fig. 3. Pilot design diagram.

The frame structure as shown in Fig. 4, unlike Sect. 2.2, the CP is tail of pilot that both pilot and data can form a circular matrix. The channel estimation algorithm is designed by using the properties of cyclic convolution and Fourier transform, this

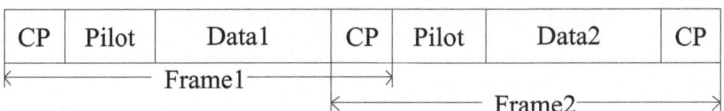

Fig. 4. Proposed frame structure.

reduces computational complexity.

The received pilot signal can be expressed as

$$r_{i-pilot} = \sqrt{q_{pilot}} \sum_{l=1}^{L} \mathbf{G}_{il}\mathbf{A} + \mathbf{N}_i, \qquad (4)$$

where $(\cdot)^H$ is the conjugate transpose. $\mathbf{A} = [\mathbf{A}_1, \mathbf{A}_2, \ldots \mathbf{A}_K]$ is the cyclic matrix of $\mathbf{a}$, $r_{i-pilot}$ is a $M \times N$ matrix. $q_{i-pilot}$ is the transmit signal to noise ratio (Tx-SNR), $\mathbf{N}_i$ is a $M \times N$ additive white Gaussian noise matrix. $\mathbf{W}_1$ is the FFT transformation matrix, and $\mathbf{W}_1^H$ is the IFFT transformation matrix. The received pilot signal in frequency domain is

$$R_{i-pilot} = \mathbf{W}_1 r_{i-pilot}. \qquad (5)$$

According to the Fig. 5, the received signal in frequency domain of kth user is obtained by

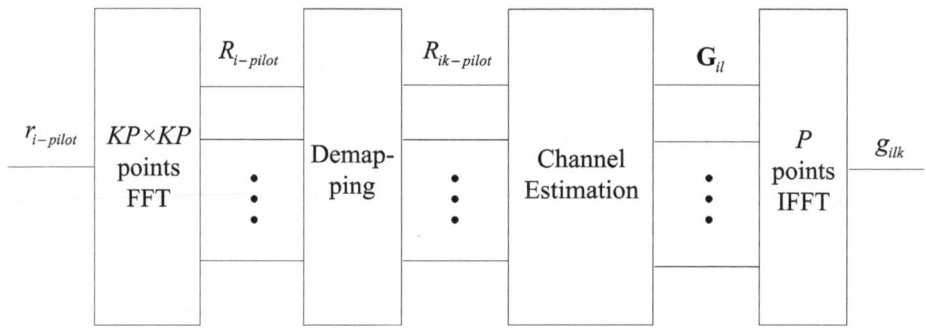

Fig. 5. Block diagram of channel estimation.

$$R_{ik-pilot} = \mathbf{V}R_{i-pilot} = \mathbf{V}\mathbf{W}_1 r_{i-pilot}, \qquad (6)$$

where $\mathbf{V}$ is the demapping matrix. The channel coefficient of pilot tone is

$$\mathbf{G}_{il} = diag\left(R_{ik-pilot}\mathbf{F}_k\right), \qquad (7)$$

$diag(\bullet)$ is the diagonal matrix, $\mathbf{F}_k$ is the pilot signal of kth user in frequency domain. The time domain impulse response of the channel is obtained by

$$g_{ilk} = \left(\mathbf{W}_2^k\right)^H \mathbf{G}_{il}, \qquad (8)$$

Where $\mathbf{W}_2$ is intercepted from $\mathbf{W}_1$.

$$\mathbf{W}_2^k = \begin{bmatrix} \mathbf{W}_1^{1,k} & \cdots & \mathbf{W}_1^{1,k+(K-1)P} \\ \vdots & \ddots & \vdots \\ \mathbf{W}_1^{K,k} & \cdots & \mathbf{W}_1^{K,k+(K-1)P} \end{bmatrix} \qquad (9)$$

The channel estimator is shown in Fig. 5.

After channel estimation of pilot tone, the CSI is estimated by DFT interpolation algorithm. It padding zeros on the time domain of g_{ilk} so that keeping consistent with the length of the data. Finally, the desired signal can be equalized in the frequency domain. The simulation results show this method can accurately obtain the time domain impulse response of the channel when the noise is ignored. The algorithm is more accurate and flexible, it utilizes the characteristics of cyclic convolution and fourier transform to design pilot.

4 Numerical Result

The parameters involved in the simulations as Table 1. Consider the frequency reuse factor is one, the large-scale coefficient is assumed constant, $\beta_{ilk} = 1$ and $\beta_{ilk} = 0.05$, $\forall l \neq i$.

Table 1. Simulation parameter.

Parameter	Description	Value
L	The number of cells	7
K	The number of users per cell	10
P	The number of paths per channel	20
M	The number of antenna per BS	30
β	The large-scale coefficient	0.05

Figure 6 depicts the mean square error (MSE) performance comparison between the proposed method in this paper and method in [5]. It can be seen the channel estimation MSE versus the signal to noise ratio at the transmitter (Tx-SNR), and the MSE of all channel estimators decreases with the increase of Tx-SNR. The MSE of proposed method is much better than [5] due to less pilot contamination. However, the system overhead will be raise by the increase of pilot length.

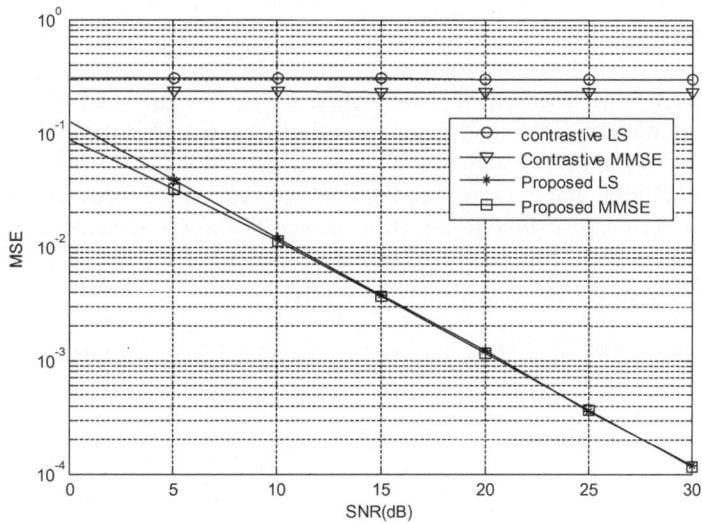

Fig. 6. The MSE of comparison for two methods.

Figure 7 shows the bit error rate (BER) performance of the proposed method. It can be noticed that the better BER performance with the increase of the number of receiving antenna M. This is because the diversity gain of the receiver increases and the better resistant to noise in this case. ZF is considered here. The BER performance in [5] is poor because of pilot contamination.

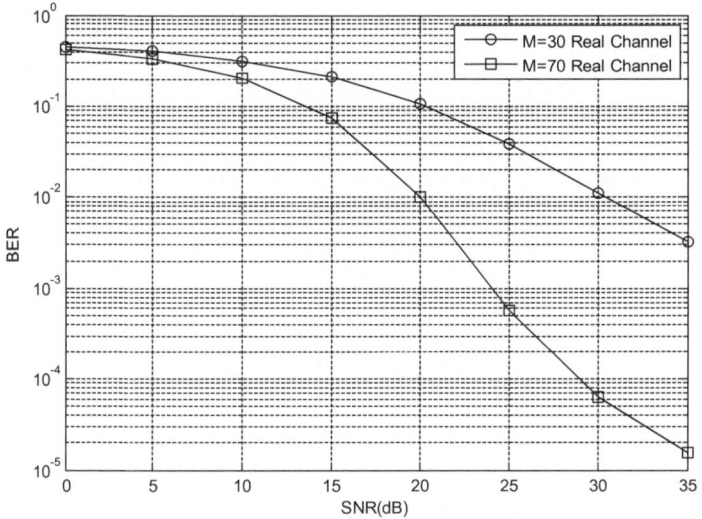

Fig. 7. The BER of proposed method.

5   Conclusion

In this paper, a pilot-based channel estimation method is proposed which takes into account pilot contamination, and guarantees the orthogonality of pilot inter-cell and intra-cells by using the characteristics of ZC sequence. At the same time, the properties of cyclic convolution and Fourier transform are utilized. At the receiver, the CSI at the pilot position is obtained firstly, and then deduce the whole channel information by using DFT interpolation algorithm. The simulation results show that the proposed method has better performance in channel estimation.

Acknowledgment. This research is supported by the Natural Science Foundation of Liaoning Province of China (Grant No. 20180550239).

References

1. Larsson, E.G., Edfors, O., Tufvesson, F., Marzetta, T.L.: Massive MIMO for next generation wireless systems. IEEE Commun. Mag. **52**, 186 (2014)
2. Jose, J., Ashikhmin, A., Marzetta, T.L., Vishwanath, S.: Pilot contamination and precoding in multi-cell TDD systems. IEEE Trans. Wirel. Commun. **10**, 2640 (2011)

3. Ngo, H.Q., Marzetta, T.L., Larsson, E.G.: Analysis of the pilot contamination effect in very large multicell multiuser MIMO systems for physical channel models. In: IEEE International Conference on Acoustics, Speech and Signal Processing, vol. 3464 (2011)
4. Lu, L., Li, G.Y., Swindlehurst, A.L., Ashikhmin, A., Zhang, R.: An overview of massive MIMO: benefits and challenges. IEEE J. Sel. Top. Signal Process. **8**, 742 (2014)
5. Figueiredo, F.A.P.D., Cardoso, F.A.C.M., Moerman, I., Fraidenraich, G.: Channel estimation for massive MIMO TDD systems assuming pilot contamination and frequency selective fading. IEEE Access **5**, 17733 (2018)
6. Hu, A., Lv, T., Gao, H., Lu, Y., Liu, E.: Pilot design for large-scale multi-cell multiuser MIMO systems. In: IEEE International Conference on Communications, vol. 5381 (2013)
7. Zheng, X., Zhang, H., Xu, W., You, X.: Semi-orthogonal pilot design for massive MIMO systems using successive interference cancellation. In: Global Communications Conference, vol. 3719 (2014)
8. Li, L., Ashikhmin, A., Marzetta, T.: Interference reduction in multi-cell massive MIMO systems II: downlink analysis for a finite number of antennas. Mathematics (2014)
9. Hoydis, J., Brink, S.T., Debbah, M.: Massive MIMO in the UL/DL of cellular networks: how many antennas do we need? IEEE J. Sel. Areas Commun. **31**, 160 (2013)
10. Sklar, B.: Rayleigh fading channels in mobile digital communication systems. I. Characterization. IEEE Commun. Mag. **35**, 136 (1997)
11. Tranter, W.H.: Principles of communication systems simulation with wireless applications (2004)
12. Marzetta, T.L.: Noncooperative cellular wireless with unlimited numbers of base station antennas. IEEE Trans. Wirel. Commun. **9**, 3590 (2010)
13. Chu, D.: Polyphase codes with good periodic correlation properties (Corresp.). IEEE Trans. Inf. Theory **18**, 531 (2003)
14. Myung, H.G., Lim, J., Goodman, D.J.: Single carrier FDMA for uplink wireless transmission. IEEE Veh. Technol. Mag. **1**, 30 (2007)
15. Kim, H.M., Kim, D., Kim, T.K., Im, G.H.: Frequency domain channel estimation for MIMO SC-FDMA systems with CDM pilots. J. Commun. Netw. **16**, 447 (2014)

A Improved AOMDV Routing Protocol Based on Load Balancing with Energy Constraining for Ad Hoc Network

Lu Guo and Peng Li[✉]

School of Information Science and Engineering,
Dalian Polytechnic University, Dalian, China
lipeng@dlpu.edu.cn

Abstract. With the development of mobile technology and the increasing demand for free communication, Ad Hoc network has developed rapidly in the field of wireless communication. Due to the dynamic change of the system network topology, there are some shortcomings in the accuracy of routing selection. Therefore, this paper designs a routing protocol based on load balancing with energy constraining, which selects nodes with lower queue capacity of MAC layer and higher residual energy to forward packets. The simulation results show that the improved protocol has been effectively improved in terms of the number of energy exhausted nodes, end-to-end delay and routing discovery frequency.

Keywords: Ad hoc network · Queue capacity · Residual energy · Load balancing

1 Introduction

In recent years, Ad Hoc network has developed rapidly in the field of wireless communication due to its characteristics of no center and self-organization [1–3]. It is considered as an important complementary form of 5G [4]. However, due to the randomness of the moving speed and mode of each node in the network [5], the network topology may change at any time, which makes some nodes over-loaded, while others are under-loaded, and failing to make full use of resources [6]. Therefore, finding a reliable data transmission path is the key to the research.

Literature [7] proposes an MSR protocol, which takes delay as the measure of path specification, and achieves load balancing, but the overhead of sending packets increases significantly. The SMR protocol proposed in literature [8] improves the load balancing capability of the whole network by using the shunting method, but causes the problems of packet sorting. The AOMDV protocol proposed in [9, 10] selects the transmission path with the RREP arrival time, which reduces the delay but makes the packet delivery rate worse. The LBMMRE-AOMDV protocol proposed in [11] has greatly improved in terms of packet delivery rate, average energy consumption and routing overhead, but increased the delay.

© ICST Institute for Computer Sciences, Social Informatics and Telecommunications Engineering 2019
Published by Springer Nature Switzerland AG 2019. All Rights Reserved
J. Jin et al. (Eds.): GreeNets 2019, LNICST 282, pp. 114–119, 2019.
https://doi.org/10.1007/978-3-030-21730-3_13

In order to overcome the above problems, this paper designs a routing protocol based on load balancing with energy constraining.

2 The Improved Routing Protocol

Since the classical routing protocol does not consider the residual energy and load of the nodes, the improved routing protocol selects nodes with lower queue capacity of MAC layer and higher residual energy to forward packets.

2.1 The Queue Capacity of MAC Layer

Queue capacity refers to the number of packets waiting to be forwarded in the interface queue. Nodes compare their current queue capacity qoc with threshold thr. If the threshold thr is greater than qoc, the node will respond to RREQ packets. Otherwise, RREQ packets are discarded directly.

The average queue capacity of nodes is calculated as shown in Eq. (1),

$$avg = \frac{qoc + \sum\limits_{i=1}^{n} nb\_qoc_i}{n+1} \tag{1}$$

The threshold value of nodes is calculated as shown in Eqs. (2) and (3),

$$\overline{d} = \frac{|qoc - avg| + \sum\limits_{i=1}^{n} |nb\_qoc_i - avg|}{n+1} \tag{2}$$

$$thr = \overline{d} + avg \tag{3}$$

Where, qoc represent the queue capacity of the node, nb_qoc_i represents the queue capacity of the neighbor node, and n represents the number of the neighbor node.

2.2 The Residual Energy of Nodes

The improved protocol uses the path with lower load to transfer packets, which effectively avoids the situation that some nodes are over-loaded while others are under-loaded. However, the residual energy of nodes is not taken into account, so the average residual energy of the nodes is introduced.

The average residual energy of nodes is calculated as shown in Eq. (4),

$$E_{avg} = \frac{E_r^i + \sum\limits_{k=1}^{n} E_r^k}{n+1} \tag{4}$$

Where, E_{avg} is the average residual energy of the neighbor node, E_r^i is the residual energy of the node n_i, n is the number of neighbor nodes of the node n_i, E_r^k is the k-th ($k = 1,2,...,n$) residual energy of adjacent nodes.

In order to determine the relationship between average queue capacity of MAC layer and the residual energy of nodes, the path selection function T is introduced,

$$T = avg_{\max} \times (1/E_{\min}) = avg_{\max} \times \left[\frac{1}{(E_r^i + E_{avg})/(n+1)} \right] \tag{5}$$

Where, $E_{\min}$ represents the minimum residual energy of all nodes, and $avg_{\max}$ represents the maximum queue capacity of all nodes on a path.

3   Simulation Results

In order to further test the network performance of the improved routing protocol, simulation is carried out using NS2 network simulation platform. In the simulation, a rectangular scene with a network range of 1000 m × 1000 m is used. A total of 100 mobile nodes are move randomly in the scene at a maximum speed of 20 m/s, and the simulation time is 300 s, the performance simulation analysis at different simulation times are as follows.

From Fig. 1, we can see that with the increase of simulation time, the energy consumption of nodes also increases, so the number of energy-exhausted nodes increases gradually. Since the improved protocol chooses the nodes with higher average residual energy to forward packets, which avoids exit the network when the energy of the intermediate nodes are exhausted, so the number of nodes exhausted in the improved protocol is relatively reduced.

Figure 2 shows that the improved protocol uses nodes with lighter load to forward packets, which reduces packet forwarding time, and then the delay is reduced. In addition, the improved protocol chooses nodes with large residual energy to forward packets. In addition, the improved protocol chooses nodes with large residual energy to forward packets, which reduces the disconnection of nodes due to energy exhausted, and the multi-path routing reduces the number of route discoveries compared with single-path routing, thus reduces the end-to-end delay.

From Fig. 3 we can see that multiple independent routes can be found in a route discovery process, the number of routing messages used for route discovery and maintenance is reduced, thus greatly reducing the number of route discovery. In addition, the improved routing protocol uses the path with lighter load to transmit the packets, and the residual energy of nodes is high, which improves the stability of the link and reduces the number of packets for routing maintenance. Therefore, the discovery frequency of the improved routing protocol is lower.

Figure 4 shows that multi-path routing protocol can find multiple independent paths of links in the process of route discovery, which greatly reduces the number of route discovery and the number of control packets are greatly reduced, so the routing overhead is lower than that of single path routing. The improved routing protocol is similar to AOMDV multipath routing protocol in routing overhead.

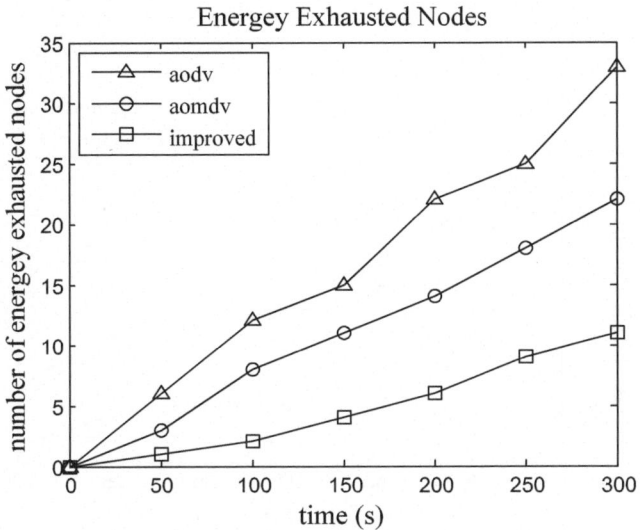

Fig. 1. The number of energy exhausted nodes

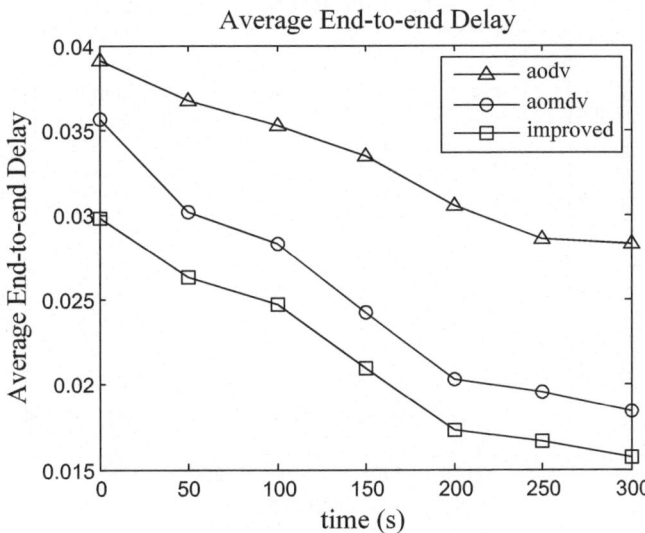

Fig. 2. Average end-to-end delay

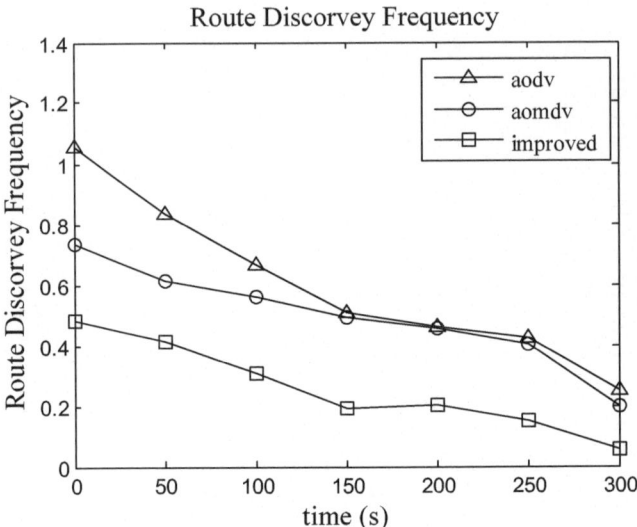

Fig. 3. Routing discovery frequency

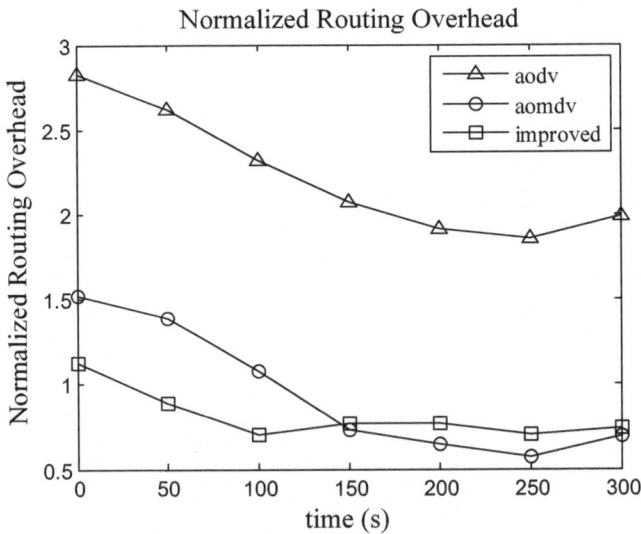

Fig. 4. The routing overhead

4   Conclusion

Aiming at the shortcomings of classical routing protocols, this paper comprehensively considers the queue capacity of MAC layer and the residual energy of the nodes. The simulation results show that to a certain extent, the improved routing protocol improves the network performance in terms of the number of energy exhausted nodes, end-to-end delay and routing discovery frequency.

References

1. Kaliappan, M., Augustine, S., Paramasivan, B.: Enhancing energy efficiency and load balancing in mobile ad hoc network using dynamic genetic algorithms. J. Network Comput. Appl. **73**, 35–43 (2016)
2. Mallapur, S.V., Patil, S.R., Agarkhed, J.V.: Multipath load balancing technique for congestion control in mobile ad hoc networks. In: Fifth International Conference on Advances in Computing & Communications (2016)
3. Allahham, A.: Performance evaluation of DSR, AODV, and OLSR routing protocols in MANET. In: The International Conference on Computer Science & Computational Mathematics, pp. 1–8 (2016)
4. Farris, I., Orsino, A., Militano, L., et al.: Federated IoT services leveraging 5G technologies at the edge. Ad Hoc Netw. **68**, 58–69 (2018)
5. Kuo, Y., Geng, C., Chen, J.: Energy optimization and load balancing QoS on-demand routing protocol. J. Appl. Sci. **30**, 25–30 (2012)
6. Zheng, S., Zhang, P., Zhang, Q.Y.: A routing protocol based on energy aware in ad hoc networks. J. Commun. **33**, 9–16 (2012)
7. Wang, L., Zhang, L., Shu, Y., et al.: Multipath source routing in wireless ad hoc networks. In: Conference on Electrical & Computer Engineering, vol. 1(1), pp. 479–483 (2000)
8. Lee, S.J.: Split multipath routing with maximally disjoint paths in ad hoc networks. In: IEEE International Conference on Communications, vol. 10(17), pp. 3201–3205 (2001)
9. Marina, M., Das, S.: On-demand multi path distance vector routing in ad hoc networks. In: International Conference on Network Protocols, pp. 14–23 (2001)
10. Singh, J., Rai, C.S.: An efficient load balancing method for ad hoc networks. Int. J. Commun. Syst. **31**(5), e3503 (2018)
11. Alghamdi, S.A.: Load balancing maximal minimal nodal residual energy ad hoc on-demand multipath distance vector routing protocol. Wireless Netw. **22**(4), 1355–1363 (2016)

Green IoT

Automatic Parking Guidance System Based on Ultraviolet Communication

Zhengpeng Ye, Jinpeng Wang$^{(\boxtimes)}$, Nianyu Zou, and Ailing Zou

School of Information Science and Engineering, Dalian Polytechnic University,
Dalian 116034, China
wangjp@dlpu.edu.cn

Abstract. In view of the existing parking guidance system in the process of vehicle guide dynamic programming efficiency is not high, poor compatibility in different parking environment, thus give negative influence large parking guidance system reliability problems, compatible with a variety of parking environment was designed based on the "blind" technology of ultraviolet communication parking guidance system, adopts the path planning algorithm in the preprocessing module, promote efficiency of dynamic programming, using the "blind" ultraviolet communication technology on the environment compatibility strong, less susceptible to environmental characteristics, improve the compatibility of the parking guidance system. Experiments show that the system can effectively reduce the dynamic path planning time, ensure the effective communication distance of single node of 4 m in a variety of parking environments, and meet the basic requirements of parking guidance system.

Keywords: Ultraviolet communication · Piloted parking · Solar blind

1 Introduction

Due to the continuous improvement of residents' economic strength in recent years, China has become the largest automobile market in the world, with the sales volume of over 28.88 million vehicles in 2017. With the continuous surge of the number of vehicles, the scale of the parking lot is increasing, and the environment is increasingly diversified. How to park vehicles orderly and efficiently in the parking lot has become a hot issue for managers and drivers [1]. At present, the commonly used parking assistance system usually marks whether the parking space is guided passively by the different colors of the lights above the parking space. When the parking area is too large and there are too many vehicles, it is difficult for the driver to directly find the available parking space through visual inspection. Existing active guidance system research of popular technology is to use visible light communication guide [2], but when parking in the underground space, cannot ensure that normally on visible light and outdoor light background noise is serious, at the same time, the path planning algorithm of active guidance system is used more A* algorithm or ant colony algorithm, the algorithm for dynamic heavy planning efficiency is low, when parking inside information change, can't fast response, which would influence the efficiency of the guidance system of [3].

J. Jin et al. (Eds.): GreeNets 2019, LNICST 282, pp. 123–132, 2019.
https://doi.org/10.1007/978-3-030-21730-3_14

In order to solve the parking guidance system, poor adaptability of heavy dynamic planning efficiency is low, this paper puts forward a "solar blind" [4–6] ultraviolet communication technology of automatic parking guidance system, with the aid of D*-lite [7, 8] algorithm for dynamic heavy planning excellent adaptability to enhance the guidance system efficiency, using the "solar blind" minimal ultraviolet communication technology background light noise disturbance and itself does not have the function of lighting, not affected by the characteristics of other functional disturbance [9–11], improve the compatibility and reliability of the guidance system. The experimental results show that the parking guidance system based on sunblind UV communication technology is feasible, which effectively improves the efficiency of the guidance system and enhances the adaptability in different environments, providing a feasible idea for the application of sunblind UV communication technology.

2   System Overview

The system is mainly composed of real-time information collection module, path planning module and ultraviolet communication module. Figure 1 is a schematic diagram of the automatic parking guidance system.

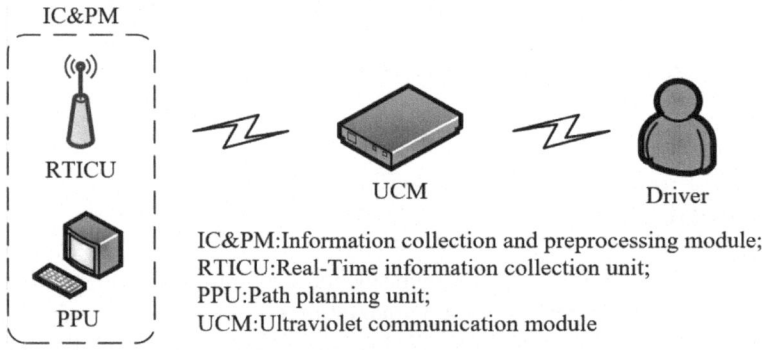

Fig. 1. Schematic diagram of the automatic parking guidance system

The real-time information collection module is responsible for collecting parking space information in the parking lot and transmitting it to the path planning module. The path planning module USES the D*-lite algorithm to plan the vehicle's travel path. Meanwhile, the path information is transmitted to the driver via the ultraviolet light communication module through the wireless channel to complete the automatic parking guidance.

The design of this system requires the effective communication within 4 m of a single ultraviolet LED node. By increasing the power and number of ultraviolet LED, the effective communication distance can be increased. If nodal network is adopted, large areas can be effectively covered and large areas of indoor and outdoor parking can be guided automatically.

For the biological security of the ultraviolet communication system, the "solar blind" ultraviolet light with a wavelength of 265 nm belongs to the photochemical ultraviolet range. According to IEC/EN 62471, when the emission limit is less than 0.003 W/m², ultraviolet light will not have a negative impact on human body. In this paper, the modulation method of ultraviolet light signal USES 4-PPM modulation, only 1/4 of the time of light emission per unit time. In the process of parking, drivers are all inside the vehicle, and the ultraviolet light irradiation during parking will not harm human body.

3 Information Collection and Preprocessing Module

3.1 Real-Time Information Collection Unit

Parking information real-time monitoring by geomagnetic parking sensor module, compared to the traditional optical and ultrasonic parking sensors, magnetic parking sensor technology better adaptability, photosensitive parking sensor is difficult to play a role in the above the surface of the parking lot, the use of ultrasonic sensor in the reversing radar makes the ultrasonic parking sensors are susceptible to interference.

The working principle of geomagnetic parking sensor is that the vehicle's iron wheel hub, engine, transmission shaft, frame and other components have disturbance effect on the geomagnetic field. The geomagnetic parking space sensor detects whether the geomagnetic field is disturbed, so as to judge whether there are vehicles parked in the parking space, and thus judge the usage of the parking space.

3.2 Path Planning Unit

D*-lite algorithm is based on the ideas of A* algorithm [12] and Dynamic SWSF-FP [13] algorithm. It is more efficient than other algorithms to search the optimal path for starting point (real-time position of vehicle) changes while ending point (parking space) is fixed.

The D*-lite algorithm requires 2D planar cell modeling for parking lots, where each cell is a cell with environmental information. The driver and the vehicle are located in the center of the cell, abstracted as a point in the center of the cell, which is also the basic unit of operation and movement. Figure 2 shows the two-dimensional plane cell model of the parking lot, in which gray shadow is the obstacle cell and white is the free cell.

A* algorithm introduces the heuristic function on the basis of Dijkstra algorithm, and the most critical one in A* algorithm is the evaluation function [12]:

$$f(v) = g(v) + h(v) \tag{1}$$

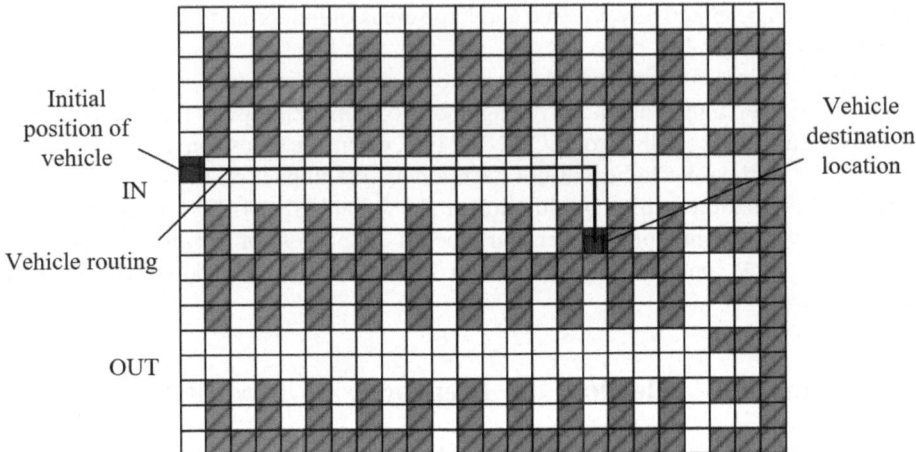

Fig. 2. Parking lot 2D planar cell model

Formula (1) $f(v)$ is the evaluation function of A* algorithm. Since the direction of D*-lite algorithm is to search from the end point to the starting point, $g(v)$ is the actual path cost from the destination cell to the current vehicle location cell v, and $h(v)$ represents the estimated path cost from the current vehicle location cell v to the vehicle destination location cell.

This paper selects the Euclidean distance. The formula (2) is the Euclidean distance calculation formula between point and point:

$$\rho = \sqrt{(x_i - x_j)^2 + (y_i - y_j)^2} \tag{2}$$

The D*-lite algorithm introduces the concept of $rhs(v)$ in the LPA* algorithm, where $rhs(v)$ represents the minimum generation value of the current node v to the target node, equal to the cost value $g(v')$ of the parent node v of the current node v plus the edge generation value $c(v, v')$. When expanding the surrounding 8 adjacent cells, $g(v)$ will be recalculated to find the smallest surrogate value $g(v)$ in the extended cell, and the $g(v)$ value of the parent v' with v will get the minimum cost of the current point v to the target point. $rhs(v)$ is defined as shown in Eqs. (3) and (4).

$$h(v) = \begin{cases} 0 & ; \quad v = v_{start} \\ \sqrt{(x_{start} - x_v)^2 + (y_{start} - y_v)^2}; & otherwise \end{cases} \tag{3}$$

$$rhs(v) = \begin{cases} 0 & ; \quad v = v_{goal} \\ \min(g(v') + c(v, v')); & otherwise \end{cases} \tag{4}$$

Where $c(v, v')$ represents the edge generation value of the current node v to its parent node v'. The priority queue for storing the points to be expanded is denoted as U, and the nodes are sorted by U according to the k value, denoted as $k(v)$, and the node with the smallest k value is selected as the new extension base point. Equation (5) is a calculation formula of the k value.

$$k(v) = min(g(v), rhs(v)) + h(v) \qquad (5)$$

The D*-lite algorithm initializes the $g(v)$ and $rhs(v)$ values of all cells to infinity, and then calculates the $g(v)$, $rhs(v)$, $h(v)$, and k values of the adjacent 8 cells according to formulas (2)–(5) from the target node. The value of $g(v)$ is greater than the value of $rhs(v)$. The value of $rhs(v)$ is assigned to $g(v)$, and then the candidate with the smallest value of K is selected as the next extended node, and the expansion process is repeated. When the new extended base point v and the initial node v_{start} are the same point, the planning is completed; From the current position, the cell with the least path cost is moved to form a driving path to the target point. When the environmental information changes, the k value of the cell is updated, and then the calculation searches for a new driving path. By using the D*-lite algorithm, the driver and the vehicle can be mapped out and the parking can be guided automatically.

The advantage of D*-lite over A* is that A* is A static path planning algorithm. When the environmental information changes, the planned path information will be invalid and must be re-planned. The D*-lite algorithm is a dynamic path planning algorithm that takes less time to plan a path using previously computed cell information when environmental information changes. In parking lots where parking information can change at any time, the D*-lite algorithm is obviously more applicable.

4   Ultraviolet Communication Module

In this paper, MCU is used as the core component of the solar blind ultraviolet communication system. Automatic parking guidance system based on real-time collected the information such as the parking lot vehicle location, the parking problem, the D*-lite path planning algorithms to calculate and get the path of the guide information by MCU modulated by ultraviolet light signals to the communication channel LED driver circuit to transfer, ultraviolet light signal is UVC sensor is converted to electrical signals, after amplification by amplifying circuit demodulation by MCU route guidance

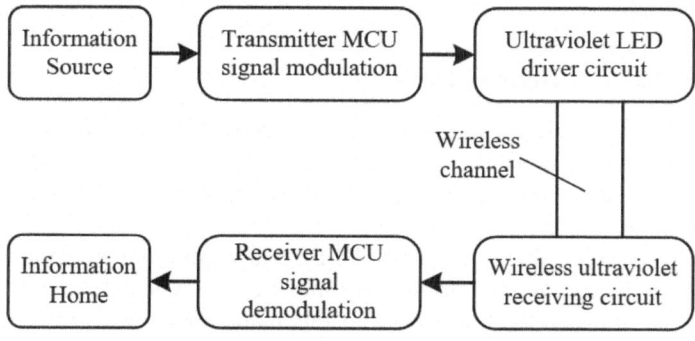

Fig. 3. Structure of ultraviolet communication module

information, finally passed to the vehicles and drivers. Figure 3 is the structure diagram of the ultraviolet communication module.

4.1 Ultraviolet Light Signal PPM Modulation

Compared with the traditional open critical control (OOK) mode, pulse position modulation (PPM) has smaller average power requirements of light radiation and stronger anti-interference ability [14]. The essence of pulse position modulation (PPM) is to control the relative position of each pulse in the transmitted pulse sequence. An n bit data are $M = (m_1, m_2, \cdots, m_n)$, and the time slot position is I, then the mapping relation of PPM modulation is as follows:

$$I = m_1 + 2m_2 + \cdots + (2n - 1)m_n, m \in \{0, 1, 2, \cdots, 2n - 1\} \tag{6}$$

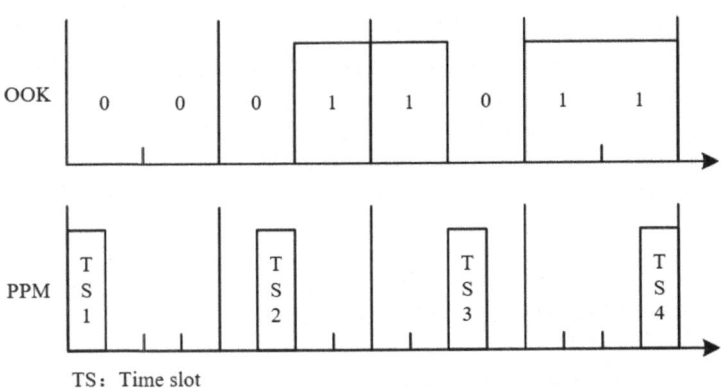

TS: Time slot

Fig. 4. PPM modulation and OOK modulation mapping comparison chart

Text is composed of 2-bit binary data, corresponding to 4-PPM modulation as an example. It coding mapping relationship and OOK comparison is shown in Fig. 4. In this paper, 4-PPM modulation is used for ultraviolet signal modulation to enhance the anti-interference ability and stability of the communication system in the communication channel.

4.2 Ultraviolet LED Driver Circuit

There are two ways of signal modulation: analog modulation and digital modulation. Compared with traditional analog modulation, digital modulation has better reliability, better anti-interference ability and longer transmission distance, so this paper chooses digital modulation for signal modulation.

The ultra-violet LED drive circuit first USES a high-precision operational amplifier to form a voltage comparator, so as to solve the "trailing" phenomenon when a single triode drives the LED and the triode is switched on and off. Capacitor C2 improves the switching rate of the drive circuit, thus improving the high-frequency performance of the drive circuit [15]. R4 is the bias resistor and R5 is the variable resistor used to regulate the current through the UV-LED. Digital modulation circuit is the use of coded signal INPUT from the INPUT end, control transistor Q1 on and off, so as to control the UV-LED on and off, so as to achieve the modulation of optical signals. Figure 5 is a schematic diagram of ultraviolet LED drive circuit.

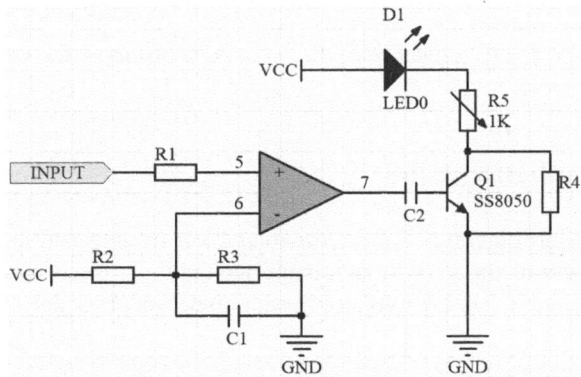

Fig. 5. Ultraviolet LED driver circuit principle that block diagram

4.3   Wireless Ultraviolet Receiving Circuit

The vehicle-mounted receiving terminal is composed of UVC ultraviolet sensor and preamplifier circuit, and the signal demodulation is completed by MCU. The UVC sensor [4, 5] converts optical signals into photoelectric signals, which are amplified by the preamplifier circuit into voltage signals that can be processed by MCU, and then demodulated by MCU. The navigation information of vehicle path after demodulation is finally transmitted to the driver through screen display. Thus, the basic function of the vehicle-mounted wireless ultraviolet receiving module in the automatic parking guidance system is realized. Figure 6 is a schematic diagram of the ultraviolet receiving circuit.

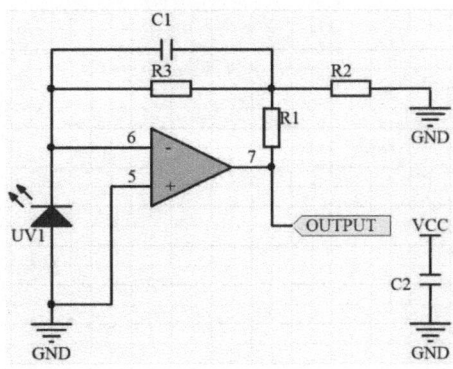

Fig. 6. Principle diagram of wireless ultraviolet receiving circuit

Among them, UV1 is the UVC sensor, R1, R2 and R3 are the feedback resistors, MCP6241 is selected as the operational amplifier, C1 is used to reduce the input noise, and C2 is used to stabilize the power supply. Formula (7) is the gain formula of the amplifier module.

$$A = R_3 \left(1 + \frac{R_1}{R_2} \right) \tag{7}$$

Adjust the appropriate resistance of R_1, R_2, and R_3 to meet the needs of the actual circuit.

5   Analysis and Discussion

Figure 7 is the detail diagram of the ultraviolet LED driving end and wireless ultraviolet receiving end of the parking automatic navigation system based on ultraviolet communication. Figure 8 is the overall physical experiment model of the system.

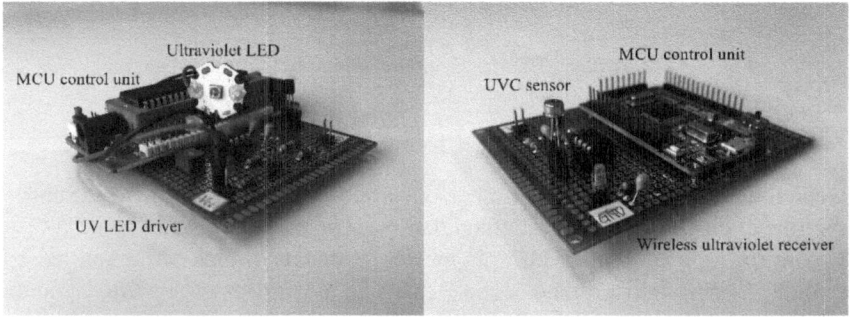

Fig. 7. Ultraviolet LED driver and wireless ultraviolet receiver

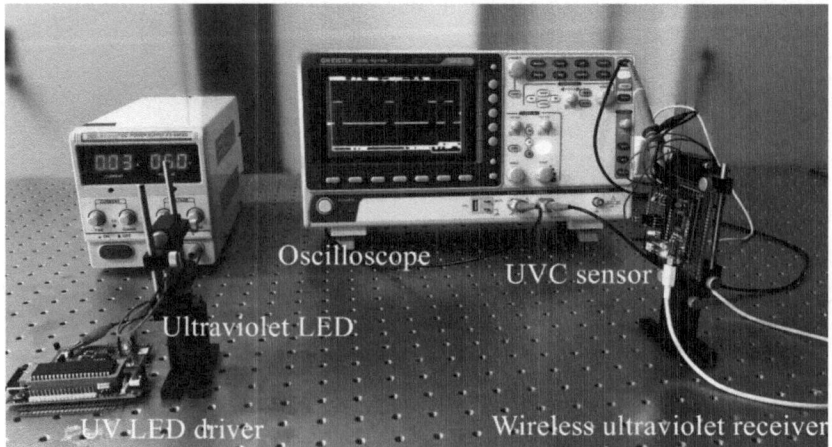

Fig. 8. Physical experiment model

This system adopts the UV-LED light source and UVC sensor's field of view Angle of 60°, the NLOS not look straight communication link model, send and receive of elevation Angle less than 90°. A single node is composed of multiple UV-LED, and each UV-LED is responsible for communication within a certain sector area. During the experiment, the Angle of the drive end and the receiver end bracket was adjusted to simulate the NLOS mode.

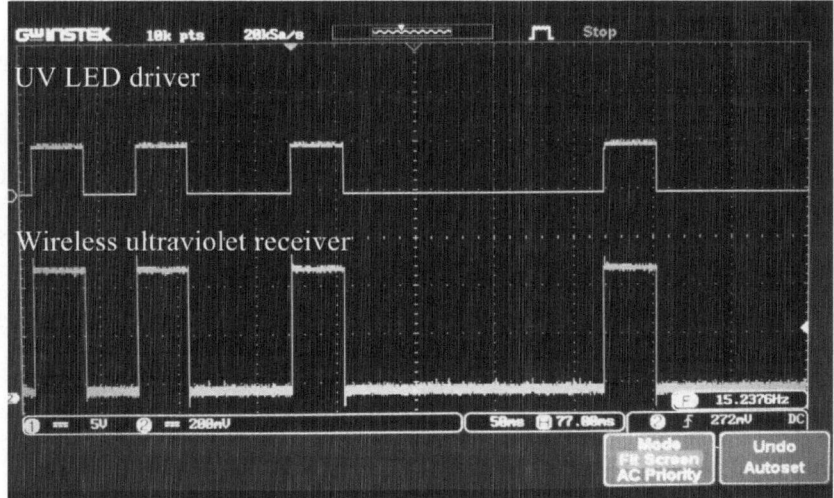

Fig. 9. Experimental waveform

The parking navigation information is modulated by MCU and sent through the ultraviolet LED2 drive circuit. The UVC sensor at the wireless ultraviolet receiver is responsible for receiving. After being processed by the amplification circuit, the information is demodulated by MCU and transmitted to the vehicle and driver. Figure 9 shows the waveform displayed on the oscilloscope by the ultraviolet LED driver and the wireless ultraviolet receiver.

Experiments have shown that UV-LED driver side and ultraviolet wireless receiver are 4 m, high level of UV-LED drive on the amplitude of 5 V, wireless receiver of ultraviolet high level after receiving signal amplified by amplifying circuit amplitude is 400 mV, transmitting and receiving signal waveform are basically the same, still can guarantee that the system within 4 m has the good communication performance, can meet the demand of communication.

6   Conclusion

This article in view of the existing parking guidance system in poor compatibility and high efficiency is not high question, designed a set of "solar blind" technology of ultraviolet communication based automatic parking guidance system, the D*-lite algorithm improve the efficiency of path planning, the use of "solar blind" ultraviolet communication technologies to promote the compatibility of the parking guidance system, attempt to provide a kind of technology of ultraviolet communication application direction in daily life. The system can still be optimized and the modulation mode can be changed to increase the transmission reliability and stability of the UV communication system.

References

1. Gao, Y., Liu, S.: Design of parking lot guidance system based on wireless communication. China Sci. Technol. Inf. **14**, 63–64 (2018)
2. Yu, Y., Xue, X., Zou, N., Wang, J.: Route navigation system in underground garage based on visible light communication. Opt. Commun. Technol. **42**(4), 51–54 (2018)
3. Zhang, Y., Sun, F., Shi, X.: Path planning of mobile robot based on fast D*Lite algorithms. Data Commun. **152**(1), 46–51 (2018)
4. Tang, G., Song, X.: Application and development of solar blind ultraviolet image intensifier. Optoelectron. Technol. **36**(3), 164–167 (2016)
5. Yang, J., Zhang, X., Zhao, W.: Solar blindness performance analysis of vacuum photoelectric detection module for ultraviolet communication. Optoelectron. Technol. **34**(3), 154–157 (2014)
6. Song, P., Zhou, X., Zhao, T.: Node design and communication performance analysis of ultraviolet mobile ad hoc networks. Acta Opt. Sin. **38**(3), 290–297 (2018)
7. Koenig, S., Likhachev, M.: D* Lite. In: AAAI/IAAI, pp. 476–483 (2002)
8. Koenig, S., Likhachev, M.: Fast replanning for unknown terrain. IEEE Trans. Robot. **21**(3), 354–363 (2005)
9. Li, C., Cui, X.: Summary of research on optical electric power sensors. Acta Opt. Sin. **38**(3), 153–164 (2018)
10. Liu, A., Yin, H., Wu, B., Liu, C.: Study on phase shift characteristics of radio frequency signals in optical wireless communication system. Acta Opt. Sin. **38**(5), 81–85 (2018)
11. Liang, J., Ju, H., Zhang, W.: Review of optical polarimetric dehazing technique. Acta Opt. Sin. **38**(4), 9–21 (2017)
12. Hart, P.E., Nilsson, N.J., Raphael, B.: A formal basis for the heuristic determination of minimum cost paths. IEEE Trans. Syst. Sci. Cybern. **4**(2), 100–107 (1968)
13. Ramalincam, G., Reps, T.: An incremental algorithm for a generalization of the shortest-path problem. J. Algorithms **21**(2), 267–305 (1996)
14. Fu, Y.: Research on dimming coding for visible communication. J. Optoelectron. Laser **29**(5), 492–498 (2018)
15. Shang, J.: Design of drive circuit based on visible light communication system. Opt. Commun. Technol. **39**(7), 24–25 (2015)

A Novel Spectral Matching Algorithm to Application Environment Fitness Evaluation Method

Fan Cao[✉], Jinpeng Wang, Zhipeng Wang, Wei Huang, and Nianyu Zou

Dalian Polytechnic University, Dalian 116034, People's Republic of China
caoqianfan@163.com

Abstract. The performance of the spectral matching algorithm of the solar simulator is affected by many factors, such as software performance, hardware performance, application environment and so on. The evaluation of spectral matching algorithm to application environment fitness is the premise of selecting the most suitable algorithm. The analytic hierarchy process (AHP) - fuzzy comprehensive evaluation method is used to evaluate the fitness. Firstly, the evaluation index system is established; secondly, the weight of each index is determined by AHP; finally, the fitness evaluation result is obtained by fuzzy comprehensive evaluation method. According to the comparison between the evaluation method of this paper and the experimental results of expert evaluation, it can be seen that the accuracy of the evaluation method in this paper is high, and the evaluation rules basically meet the requirements.

Keywords: Solar simulator · Spectral matching algorithm · Application environment fitness · Analytic hierarchy process · Fuzzy comprehensive evaluation

1 Introduction

Solar simulator as an important experiment and test equipment has been widely used in the field of space and solar energy utilization. At present, the solar simulator has been studied at home and abroad [1–4]. With the advantages of high efficiency energy saving, environmental protection, long life, strong controllability and mature spectrum matching technology, LED has been gradually applied to the research and development of new type solar simulator. The research of LED solar simulator has become the mainstream in the field of solar simulator [5–7].

The light source of the LED solar simulator is usually composed of many different monochromatic bands LED. The solar spectrum is combines with a superposition power, which is calculated by spectral matching algorithm [8–10]. There are many spectral matching algorithms, their requirements for computing resources are different, and performances are also different. In the practical application, they are limited by the application environment, such as the performance of computing resources, storage

J. Jin et al. (Eds.): GreeNets 2019, LNICST 282, pp. 133–142, 2019.
https://doi.org/10.1007/978-3-030-21730-3_15

space and so on. How to select the appropriate spectral matching algorithm for the specified application environment is a question with practical significance.

In order to sort the adaptability of different algorithms conveniently, the most suitable algorithm is selected, and the adaptation of spectral matching algorithm to the application environment is represented by "fitness". The evaluation of algorithm fitness is essentially a comprehensive evaluation influenced by multiple indexes. At present, the main methods of multi-index comprehensive evaluation are AHP, principal component analysis, artificial neural network, fuzzy comprehensive evaluation and so on [11–14]. This paper adopts the combination of subjective and objective AHP - Fuzzy comprehensive evaluation method, which provides a reasonable, scientific and reliable selection standard for the selection of the most suitable algorithm.

AHP - Fuzzy comprehensive evaluation method is the combination of analytic hierarchy process and fuzzy comprehensive evaluation method. Firstly, the hierarchical structure model of algorithm performance index is constructed by AHP [15, 16]. The weights of each evaluation index are calculated, and then the fuzzy comprehensive evaluation method is used to evaluate each index synthetically, and the comprehensive evaluation results are obtained [17–19]. Thus, set up an AHP - Fuzzy synthesis algorithm fitness evaluation model.

2 Evaluation Method

2.1 Analytic Hierarchy Process

The analytic hierarchy process is proposed by Thomas L. Saaty in the mid-1970s, who is an American operations researcher [15, 16]. This method is a qualitative and quantitative, hierarchical analysis method, which can deal with complex multi-criteria decision making problems, and can effectively analyze the non-sequential relationships between levels of the target criteria system. Enable the decision maker to make a reliable analysis and judgment. In this paper, the function of AHP is to calculate the weight of different factors in decision-making. The steps are lists as follows.

(1) Build the hierarchical model: The problem is analyzed by different constituent factors and the subordinate relation among factors, which is based on the nature of the problem and the inherent relationships between sub problems. The evaluation index system and the grade standard are formed.

(2) The construction of paired comparison matrix: For each layer of elements under specified criteria, indices on the same layer have different weights. Experts compare different influencing factors and use scaling method to decide the judgment matrix A.

(3) Calculating index weight: The hierarchical ranking of the influencing factors is to calculate the relative weights required by each factor of each judgment matrix. Then the weight vector W is calculated.

(4) Check the weight consistency: Because of the inconsistency of the pairwise comparison matrix, the consistency index (CI) is used to test the consistency, and the random consistency index (RI) is introduced because of the difference in the consistency measurement of the judgment matrix of different order. The

consistency judgment is corrected according to different orders. The weight distribution of the matrix is relatively reasonable by consistent ratio (CR). If the parameters are within the range of acceptance, the weight distribution is reasonable, and the expert needs to readjust the judgment matrix beyond the range of acceptance.

2.2 Fuzzy Comprehensive Evaluation Method

The fuzzy comprehensive evaluation method is an evaluation method which is made by multiple factors together. According to the principle of fuzzy set theory, it makes an effective and comprehensive grade evaluation of many influencing factors [17–19]. The steps of fuzzy comprehensive evaluation are as follows:

(1) According to the evaluation index system, the weight set B is established. The influence degree of each influencing factor on the evaluation object is represented by its weight value, the evaluation factor set U and the evaluation set V.
(2) Experts score the algorithm of need evaluation according to the evaluation index system and get the initial data of fuzzy evaluation.
(3) Based on the initial data, each element of the fuzzy relation matrix R is calculated as the membership value of the evaluation set V by a certain influence factor of the evaluated algorithm.
(4) The comprehensive evaluation vector B is used to describe the classification degree of the comprehensive condition of each evaluated object, and the grade judgment is made according to the comprehensive scoring method [21].

3   Algorithm Fitness Evaluation Model

The construction of algorithm fitness evaluation model is divided into two parts. The first part is to construct the algorithm fitness evaluation model by analytic hierarchy process. The second part is to use the fuzzy comprehensive evaluation method to establish an index evaluation system. The evaluation model analyzes the data collected according to the evaluation system and draws the final conclusion.

3.1   Construction of Index Evaluation System

Build Hierarchical Model. In order to select the right evaluation index, the spectral matching algorithm must be correctly analyzed, and the selected index should be able to reflect the influence of various factors as much as possible. Generally follow three principles: scientific objectivity; testability and comparability; conciseness and comprehensiveness [15]. The relationship between the factors affecting the adaptability of the algorithm is intricate. The adaptability of evaluation algorithm is a multi-index and multi-attribute problem. Therefore, the hierarchical analysis of system engineering is applied to form an orderly hierarchical structure, that is, the index evaluation system, as shown in Tables 1, 2.

Table 1. Hierarchical structure of evaluation index system

Main factor		Sub factors	
U_1	Algorithm performance	U_{11}	Average Time complexity
		U_{12}	Average Space complexity
		U_{13}	Stability
		U_{14}	Algorithmic Hidden Parallel
U_2	Computing equipment performance	U_{21}	Performance of central processor floating-point units
		U_{22}	Memory read and write speed
		U_{23}	Memory capacity
		U_{24}	Adoption parallel computing Acceleration ratio
U_3	Application environment	U_{31}	Computing equipment Electromagnetic protection capability
		U_{32}	Installation space for computing equipment
		U_{33}	Power supply for computing equipment Continuation Ability
		U_{34}	Application The severity of the environment

Table 2. Range of grading index

Main factor	Sub factor	Unit	a	b	c	d	e	f
U_1	U_{11}	——	$O(n^3)$	$O(n^2)$	$O(nlogn)$	$O(n)$	$O(logn)$	$O(1)$
	U_{12}	——	$O(n^3)$	$O(n^2)$	$O(nlogn)$	$O(n)$	$O(logn)$	$O(1)$
	U_{13}	——	None	Extremely low	Low	Middle	High	Extremely high
	U_{14}	——	None	Extremely low	Low	Middle	High	Extremely high
U_2	U_{21}	FLOPS	0	1M	100G	300G	500G	1T
	U_{22}	Byte/s	0	1M	1G	3G	5G	10G
	U_{23}	Byte	0	1M	1G	4G	8G	16G
	U_{24}	——	0	1	10	30	50	100
U_3	U_{31}	——	None	Extremely low	Low	Middle	High	Extremely high
	U_{32}	cm^3	0	10	30	50	70	100
	U_{33}	day	0	1	3	5	7	Persistent
	U_{34}	——	Extremely high	High	Middle	Low	Extremely low	None

Construction Judgment Matrix and Calculate the Index Weight. By using 1–9 scale method [15], the relative comparison between each element is carried out, the judgment matrix is constructed and the eigenvalue of the judgment matrix is solved.

The corresponding eigenvector W is obtained by calculating the maximum eigenvalue λ_{max}, which is not only the ranking weight of the relative importance of each influencing factor in the same layer as that of a certain factor in the previous layer, and then the consistency test is carried out, and the calculated results are shown in Tables 3, 4, 5 6.

Table 3. Judging matrix U and the weight of each factor

U	U_1	U_2	U_3	Weight	Consistency
U_1	1	2	1/5	0.182	λ_{max} = 3.054, CI = 0.027
U_2	1/2	1	1/5	0.115	CR = 0.046 < 0.1
U_3	5	5	1	0.703	Meet the requirements

3.2 Establishment of Fuzzy Comprehensive Evaluation Model

Determination of Grading Index. The level of adaptability of the algorithm is divided into 5 levels, that is, the evaluation set V = (V_1, V_2, V_3, V_4, V_5) = (very low, low, medium, high, very high). In order to be easy to evaluate, different ranges are assigned to the corresponding grading indexes of different adaptability levels. The range of different grades of quantitative index is the upper and lower limit value when the index is divided into 5 grades. The representative ranges of different grades of grading indexes are: grade 1 [a, b), grade 2 [b, c), grade 3 [c, d), grade 4 [d, e), Grade 5 [e, f]. Establish different rating ranges for each index, as shown in Table 2.

Determining Membership Function. By using the knowledge of fuzzy mathematics, the membership function of the fuzzy set of each ability level is established, and the degree of each parameter belonging to the ability level is expressed by the membership degree (the value between 0–1). The fuzzy value of single factor judgment matrix (R_i) can be determined after determining the numerical value of each index. The membership function is shown in formula (1), where r_{ij} represents an element in R_i.

$$R_{i1}(x_i) = \begin{cases} 0, & x_i \in [f, +\infty) \\ \frac{f-x_i}{f-e}, & x_i \in [e, f) \\ \frac{x_i-d}{e-d}, & x_i \in [d, e) \\ 0, & x_i \in [-\infty, d) \end{cases} \qquad r_{i2}(x_i) = \begin{cases} 0, & x_i \in [e, +\infty) \\ \frac{e-x_i}{e-d}, & x_i \in [d, e) \\ \frac{x_i-c}{d-c}, & x_i \in [c, d) \\ 0, & x_i \in [-\infty, c) \end{cases}$$

$$r_{i3}(x_i) = \begin{cases} 0, & x_i \in [d, +\infty) \\ \frac{d-x_i}{d-c}, & x_i \in [c, d) \\ \frac{x_i-b}{c-b}, & x_i \in [b, c) \\ 0, & x_i \in [-\infty, b) \end{cases}$$

Table 4. Judging matrix U_1 and the weight of each factor

U_1	U_{11}	U_{12}	U_{13}	U_{14}	Weight	Consistency
U_{11}	1	1	3	5	0.399	$\lambda_{max} = 4.059$
U_{12}	1	1	3	5	0.399	CI = 0.020
U_{13}	1/3	1/3	1	3	0.133	CR = 0.020 < 0.1
U_{14}	1/5	1/5	1/3	1	0.068	Meet the requirements

Table 5. Judging matrix U_2 and the weight of each factor

U_2	U_{21}	U_{22}	U_{23}	U_{24}	Weight	Consistency
U_{21}	1	3	3	5	0.535	$\lambda_{max} = 4.218$
U_{22}	1/3	1	3	5	0.267	CI = 0.073
U_{23}	1/3	1/3	1	3	0.131	CR = 0.076 < 0.1
U_{24}	1/5	1/5	1/3	1	0.067	Meet the requirements

Table 6. Judging matrix U_3 and the weight of each factor

U_3	U_{31}	U_{32}	U_{33}	U_{34}	Weight	Consistency
U_{31}	1	1	3	1/5	0.161	$\lambda_{max} = 4.222$
U_{32}	1	1	3	1/5	0.161	CI = 0.074
U_{33}	1/3	1/3	1	1/5	0.054	CR = 0.077 < 0.1
U_{34}	5	5	5	1	0.625	Meet the requirements

$$r_{i4}(x_i) = \begin{cases} 0, & x_i \in [c, +\infty) \\ \frac{c-x_i}{c-b}, & x_i \in [b, c) \\ \frac{x_i-a}{b-a}, & x_i \in [a, b) \\ 0, & x_i \in [-\infty, a) \end{cases} \qquad r_{i5}(x_i) = \begin{cases} 0, & x_i \in [b, +\infty) \\ \frac{b-x_i}{b-a}, & x_i \in [a, b) \\ \frac{x_i}{\cdot a}, & x_i \in [-\infty, a) \end{cases} \qquad (1)$$

4   Evaluation Application and Result Analysis

4.1   Evaluation Case

In order to verify the feasibility and accuracy of the adaptive classification model of the AHP -fuzzy comprehensive evaluation algorithm, the simple genetic algorithm (SGA) [20] is selected to test the fitness of an application environment. The application environment is the plant factory with variable spectral plant lighting source, the spectral matching of the light source is performed by embedded system attached to the light source, and the plant growth environment is high temperature and high humidity. The indexes are shown in Table 7.

Table 7. SGA performance and application environment index

Main factor		Subfactor		Unit	Value	Grade
U_1	Algorithm performance	U_{11}	Average time complexity	——	$O(n^2)$	2
		U_{12}	Average space complexity	——	$O(n^2)$	2
		U_{13}	Stability	——	Middle	4
		U_{14}	Implicit parallelism of algorithm	——	High	5
U_2	Computing equipment performance	U_{21}	Performance of CPU floating-point unit	FLOPS	1.5 M	2
		U_{22}	Memory read/write speed	Byte/s	512M	2
		U_{23}	Memory capacity	Byte	32M	2
		U_{24}	Parallel computing acceleration ratio	——	1	2
U_3	Application environment	U_{31}	Electromagnetic protection capability of computing equipment	——	Middle	4
		U_{32}	Installation space of computing equipment	cm^3	15	2
		U_{33}	Power supply life ability of computing equipment	day	Persistent	5
		U_{34}	The severity of the natural environment	——	Middle	2

From the application environment parameters in Table 7, it can be concluded that the application environment is in a high temperature and high humidity environment and requires high reliability of computing equipment. Therefore, an embedded system with high reliability is adopted to provide high reliability. The performance of embedded system is low, and it has no parallel computing ability, so it cannot play the advantage of implicit parallelism of simple genetic algorithm. Because of the above two contradictions, it is difficult to judge the adaptability of the simple genetic algorithm. The calculation process according to this method is as follows.

First, the single factor evaluation matrix is established, and the single factor evaluation matrix R_i, is determined by using the selected membership function. From the hierarchical index value and formula (1), we have:

$$R_1 = \begin{bmatrix} 0 & 1 & 0 & 0 & 0 \\ 0 & 1 & 0 & 0 & 0 \\ 0 & 0 & 0 & 1 & 0 \\ 0 & 0 & 1 & 0 & 0 \end{bmatrix} R_2 = \begin{bmatrix} 0 & 0 & 0 & 1 & 0 \\ 0 & 1 & 0 & 0 & 0 \\ 0 & 1 & 0 & 0 & 0 \\ 0 & 1 & 0 & 0 & 0 \end{bmatrix} R_3 = \begin{bmatrix} 0 & 0 & 0 & 1 & 0 \\ 0 & 1 & 0 & 0 & 0 \\ 0 & 0 & 0 & 0 & 1 \\ 0 & 1 & 0 & 0 & 0 \end{bmatrix}$$

According to the Analytic hierarchy process, the index weights of the first and second levels are as follows:

$$A = (0.182 \quad 0.115 \quad 0.703)$$

$$A_1 = (0.399 \quad 0.399 \quad 0.133 \quad 0.068)$$

$$A_2 = (0.535 \quad 0.267 \quad 0.131 \quad 0.066)$$

$$A_3 = (0.161 \quad 0.161 \quad 0.054 \quad 0.625)$$

The synthetic decision vector ($B_i = A_i \cdot R_i$) is used for hierarchical evaluation. A_i is the weight set on U_i and R_i is the single factor evaluation matrix of U_i.

$$B_1 = (0 \quad 0.799 \quad 0.068 \quad 0.133 \quad 0)$$

$$B_2 = (0 \quad 0.465 \quad 0 \quad 0.535 \quad 0)$$

$$B_3 = (0 \quad 0.786 \quad 0 \quad 0.161 \quad 0.536)$$

The evaluation matrix is as follows:

$$R = \begin{bmatrix} B_1 \\ B_2 \\ B_3 \end{bmatrix} = \begin{bmatrix} 0 & 0.799 & 0.068 & 0.133 & 0 \\ 0 & 0.465 & 0 & 0.535 & 0 \\ 0 & 0.786 & 0 & 0.161 & 0.536 \end{bmatrix}$$

From comprehensive scoring method [20], we have:

$$B = A \cdot R = (b_1 \quad \cdots \quad b_5) = (0 \quad 0.751 \quad 0.012 \quad 0.199 \quad 0.038)$$

$$H = \sum_{i=1}^{5} i \cdot b_i = 2.523$$

The fitness of the algorithm is level 3, which is consistent with the result of expert evaluation.

4.2 Evaluation Result Analysis

The AHP-fuzzy comprehensive evaluation method is used to classify the ability, and the accuracy of the method needs to be verified. In the experiment, 50 groups of application environment data were used, and the adaptability of the expert judgment algorithm was compared with the model system proposed in this paper. The following are the results of expert and system testing for 50 groups of different algorithms and application environment fitness levels, as shown in Table 8. It can be seen that the accuracy of the evaluation grade is high, the accuracy of 5 classifications are all above 80%, and the evaluation rules basically meet the requirements.

Table 8. Comparison of fitness grading

Evaluation results	Extremely low	Low	Middle	High	Extremely high
Expert evaluation	12	15	16	4	3
System evaluation	13	13	15	5	4

5 Conclusion

There are many kinds of spectral matching algorithms, which have their own merits and demerits in different application environments. It is of great practical value to quantify the judgment problems with many influencing factors without the influence of subjective factors. This paper integrates qualitative and quantitative aspects and puts forward a method of environmental adaptability evaluation based on AHP- comprehensive evaluation method, which solves the problem of different evaluation results caused by subjective factors in the process of application of the algorithm. It provides a more objective, quantitative and perfect evaluation method for evaluating the adaptability of spectral matching algorithm to the application environment.

Acknowledgment. The authors acknowledge the support provided by Qianbaihui Foundation (No. 2017-228195) for their visit during which this work was initiated.

References

1. Michel, D., Agnès, A.: Solar simulator. Sol. Energy **25**(4), 381–383 (1997)
2. César, D., Ignacio, A., Sala, G.: Solar simulator for concentrator photovoltaic systems. Opt. Express **16**(19), 14894–14901 (2008)
3. Sun, G., Zhang, G., Liu, S., et al.: Design of optical system for multifunctional solar simulator. Acta Photonica Sin. **44**(10), 115–119 (2015)
4. Gaël, L., Roman, B., Wojciech, L., et al.: Experimental and numerical characterization of a new 45kWel multisource high-flux solar simulator. Opt. Express **24**(22), A1360 (2016)
5. Shogo, K., Kurokawa, K.: A fundamental experiment for discrete-wavelength LED solar simulator. Sol. Energy Mater. Sol. Cells **90**(18), 3364–3370 (2006)
6. Michael, S., Brice, P., Maximilien, B., et al.: Class AAA LED-based solar simulator for steady-state measurements and light soaking. IEEE J. Photovolt. **4**(5), 1282–1287 (2017)
7. Scherff, M.L.D., Nutter, J., Fuss-Kailuweit, P., et al.: Spectral mismatch and solar simulator quality factor in advanced LED solar simulators. Jpn. J. Appl. Phys. **56**(8S2), 08MB24 (2017)
8. Yu, H., Cao, G., Zhang, J., et al.: Solar spectrum matching with white OLED and monochromatic LEDs. Appl. Opt. **57**(10), 2659–2662 (2018)
9. Zhang, Y., Dong, L., Zhang, G.: Simulation of high power monochromatic LED solar spectrum based on effective set algorithm. Chin. J. Lumin. **39**(6), 862–869 (2018)
10. Xu, G., Zhang, J., Cao, G., et al.: Simulation of solar spectrum with high-power monochromatic light emitting diodes. Chin. J. Vac. Sci. Technol. **36**, 1–5 (2016)
11. Saaty, T.L.: How to make a decision: the analytic hierarchy process. Eur. J. Oper. Res. **24**(6), 19–43 (1994)
12. Svante, W.: Principal component analysis. Chemom. Intell. Lab. Syst. **2**(1), 37–52 (1987)

13. Park, D.C., El-Sharkawi, M.A., Marks, R.J., et al.: "Electric load forecasting using an artificial neural network. IEEE Trans. Power Syst. **6**(2), 442–449 (1991)
14. Zhang, M., Yang, W.: Fuzzy comprehensive evaluation method applied in the real estate investment risks research. Phys. Procedia **24**, 1815–1821 (2012)
15. Saaty, T.L., Vargas, L.G.: Models, Methods, Concepts & Applications of the Analytic Hierarchy Process. International, vol. 7, no. 2, pp. 159–172 (2017)
16. Hadi, V., Houman, L., Ali, A.: Developing an ethics-based approach to indicators of sustainable agriculture using analytic hierarchy process (AHP). Ecol. Indic. **60**, 644–654 (2016)
17. Jiao, J., Ren, H., Sun, S.: Assessment of surface ship environment adaptability in seaways: a fuzzy comprehensive evaluation method. Int. J. Nav. Arch. Ocean. Eng. **8**(4), 344–359 (2016)
18. Liu, Y., Huang, X., Duan, J., et al.: The assessment of traffic accident risk based on grey relational analysis and fuzzy comprehensive evaluation method. Nat. Hazards **88**(3), 1409–1422 (2017)
19. Yang, W., Xu, K., Lian, J., et al.: Multiple flood vulnerability assessment approach based on fuzzy comprehensive evaluation method and coordinated development degree model. J. Environ. Manag. **213**, 440–445 (2018)
20. Liang, J., Jiang, W., Li, X.: An improvement on fuzzy comprehensive evaluation method and its use in urban traffic planning. J. Traffic Transp. Eng. **31**(2), 173–202 (2002)
21. Vose, M.D.: The Simple Genetic Algorithm. Mit Press, Cambridge, vol. 1 (1999). 31–57

Performance Analysis of 40 GB/s DWDM School LAN Modulation Mode

Rimiao Li, Shishun Liu, and Ping Li[(✉)]

School of Information Science and Engineering,
Dalian Polytechnic University, Dalian 116034, China
liping@dlpu.edu.cn

Abstract. With the development of optical fiber communication in the direction of large capacity and ultra-high speed, the needs of teachers and students in schools are increasingly requiring high-speed network support, therefore, DWDM with 40 GB/s is developing towards campus LAN. 40 GB/s DWDM technologies were used for the performance analysis of the school LAN modulation.

Keywords: Campus LAN · 40 GB/s dense wavelength division multiplexing · Modulation style

1 Introduction

Since 1995, with the increasing number of information transmission, large-capacity, high-speed, and other transmission problems have plagued people. In order to solve this problem, DWDM (Dense Wavelength Division Multiplexing) has become a focal research object by scientists from various countries [1]. DWDM communication technology greatly increases the transmission capacity of the optical fiber, and the bandwidth to the maximum extent, effectively solving the biggest problem of the communication network.

In today's schools, teachers and students are equally increasingly demanding information. They are necessary to large-capacity information transmission fibers, and high-rate information transmission rate fibers. DWDM technology that people gradually adopt can also enter inside the campus [2].

2 Application Analysis of School LAN and Its 40 GB/s System

With the advent of the era of optical transmission information represented by DWDM dense wavelength division multiplexing technology, DWDM can use it in the School-LAN. With the continuous development and improvement of DWDM technology. Compared with the backbone network in the city center, the special application environment of the campus LAN has new requirements for DWDM technology [3]. The first is the cost, cannot be too high to ask for the cost of the campus. The DWDM

J. Jin et al. (Eds.): GreeNets 2019, LNICST 282, pp. 143–149, 2019.
https://doi.org/10.1007/978-3-030-21730-3_16

on campus should have a lower cost. Secondly, information transmission in the campus has complex and varied characteristics, and it also requires the flexibility and randomness of the campus LAN DWDM. School LAN DWDM can be applied to many levels, including the core layer, aggregation layer and access, layer. According to the different network topology of DWDM, it can be divided into several basic application types. System blocks diagram show in Fig. 1.

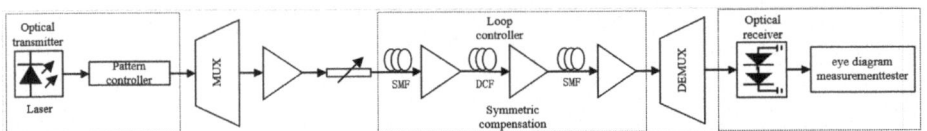

Fig. 1. System block diagram

In order to study the transmission performance of DWDM school LAN, this paper builds a simulation system. The transmitting end is constructed by a CW laser, a code pattern modulator and an optical multiplexer. The entire system is symmetrically compensated style and consists of SSMF (single mode fiber), EDFA (doped fiber amplifier), DCF (dispersion compensation fiber), EDFA, SSMF, EDFA. Because this way is better in the compensation method. The transmission part is by each distance is the same, and the number of spans is supervised by the loop controller [4]. The optical receiver is composed of a demultiplexer, a photoelectric detector, a low pass filter and an observer.

The WDM signal transmitter is sent from a continuous laser array and also requires data modulation and optical multiplexers. A continuous laser array with 32 output ports, each transmit port with the same transmit frequency spacing. The transmitted signal spacing frequency is the same, and the transmitted frequency range is between 193.1 and 194.7 Hz. And the adjacent channel frequency interval is 50 Hz.

3   40 GB/s Campus LAN DWDM Transmission Technology Research

CSRZ is carrier-suppression and is generated by modulation of two MZ modulators and one phase modulator. In the CSRZ transmitter, the electrical signal first generates an NRZ optical signal through the MZ modulator, and the generated optical signal passes through a sine wave generator having a frequency of 40 Hz and a phase of $-90°$, and through the phase modulator generates an RZ optical signal. The spectrum is changed by a phase modulator with a phase difference of 180. DRZ is a dual binary line code that can improve the dispersion tolerance. Since the bandwidth is narrower than the normal channel, the DWDM channel spacing can be lowered.

He performs preceding, pulse amplitude modulation, pattern transformation, sampling, etc. from an ordinary binary signal, and finally becomes a double binary pulse signal. MDRZ is to further suppress the inter-symbol interference between signals, called carrier-suppression duodenal return-to-zero code. First, a delay subtraction circuit is generated to drive the first MZM, and then cascaded with an MZM having a frequency of 40 Hz and a phase of −90. In a binary signal, the phase of the signal changes only when the "1" bit after the "0" bit occurs, and in the modified binary signal the phase of the "1" bit alternates between 0 and π, all The phase of the "0" bit is kept constant, and the "1" bit is added with a phase change of 180°, which makes the MDRZ have greater dispersion tolerance. I mainly use the OptiSystem simulation software, which can conveniently change the parameters of the components of the system, thus providing a good reference for the campus LAN construction [5]. For a 40 GB/s system, the specific modulation method and simulation diagram are as follows (Figs. 2, 3, 4, 5, 6 and 7):

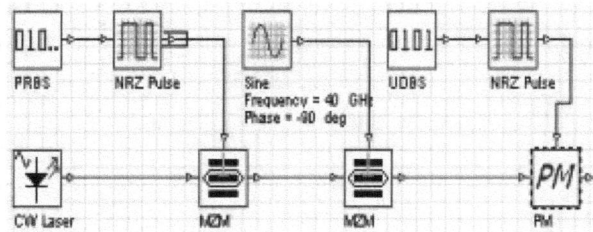

Fig. 2. CSRZ carrier suppression transmitter structure diagram

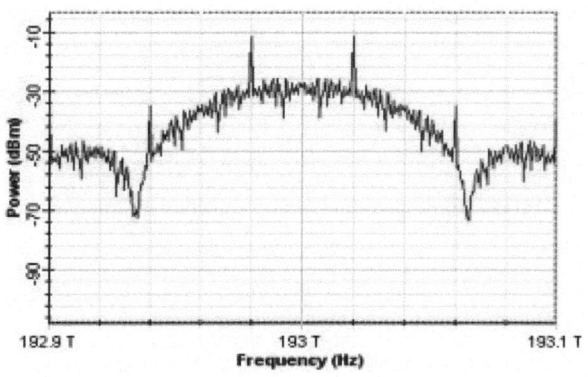

Fig. 3. CSRZ simulation diagram

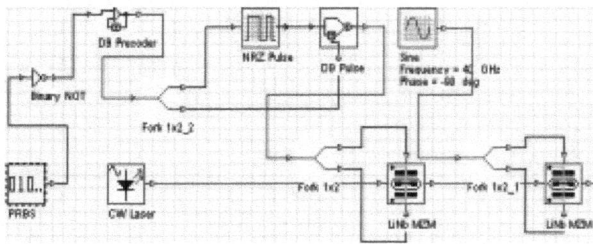

Fig. 4. DRZ dual binary transmitter structure diagrams

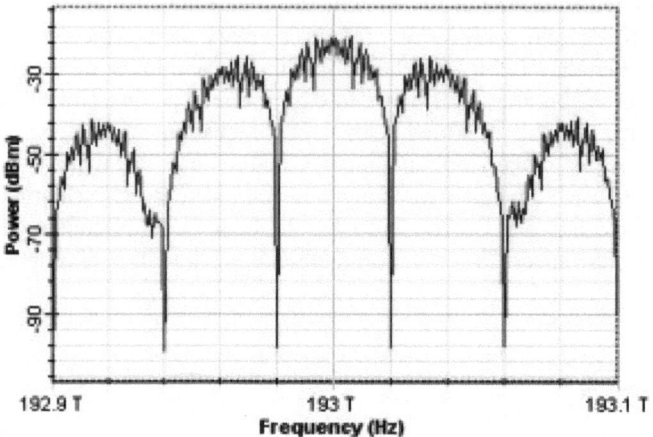

Fig. 5. DRZ simulation diagram

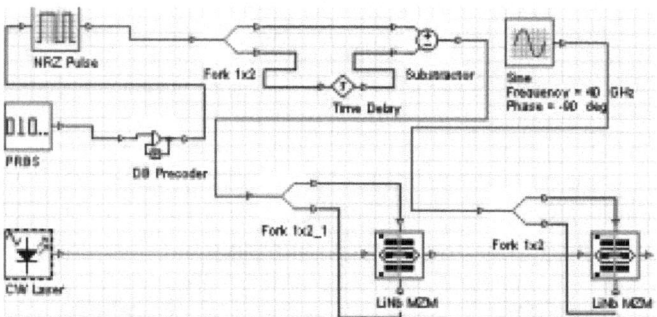

Fig. 6. MDRZ improved dual binary transmitter structure diagram

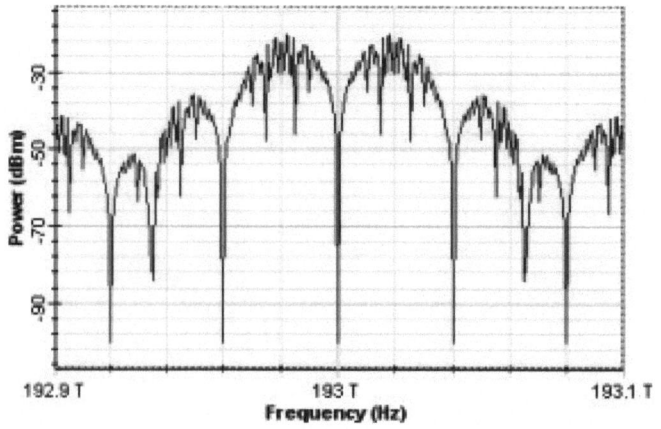

Fig. 7. MDRZ simulation diagram

3.1   Research on Transmission Performance of High-Speed DWDM 40 GB/s System

Since the dispersion causes an increase in the bit error rate and becomes a major limiting factor for high-speed transmission, the management of dispersion is important for high-speed transmission of 40 GB/s. In the 40 GB/s transmission system, the pure link is very critical, and the transmission distance is generally in the range of 50 km to 150 km [6]. First, the SMF fiber length in the simulation system should be set to 50 km, and the sensitivity of the receiving terminal PIN photodiode is 1 A/W, dark current is 0.1 nA, filtered by Bessel, the cutoff frequency is 50 GHz, and the depth is 100 dB. In this paper, the performance of the simulation system is measured by the Q factor, mainly in three different modulation modes [7]. When the simulated fiber input power is −4 dBm, 0 dBm, 2 dBm, 8 dBm, the following is a simulation diagram of the transmission performance of CSRZ, DRZ and MDRZ three modulation modes in 32-channel 40 Gbit/s system (Figs. 8, 9, 10 and 11):

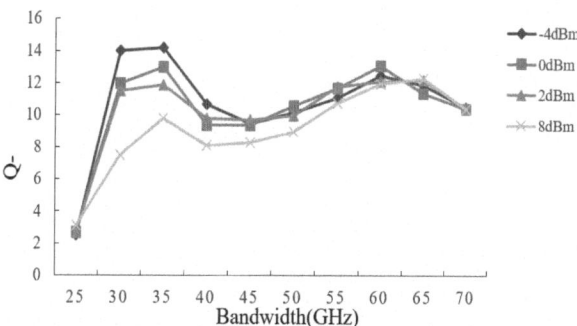

Fig. 8. MDRZ improved dual binary modulation (receive bandwidth is 25 GHZ–70 GHZ)

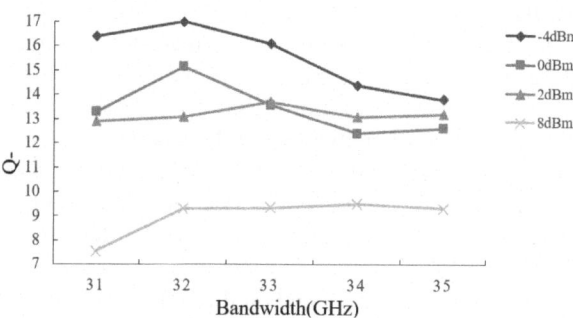

Fig. 9. MDRZ improved dual binary modulation (receiver bandwidth is 31 GHZ–35 GHZ)

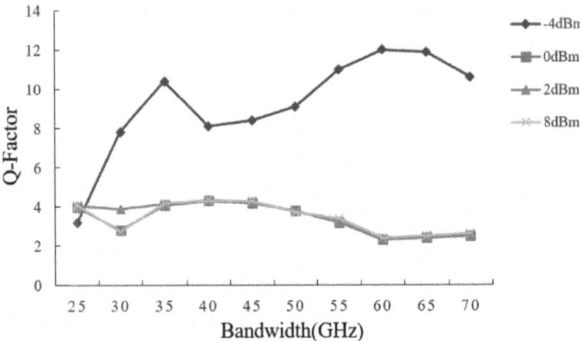

Fig. 10. DRZ dual binary modulation (receive bandwidth is 25 GHZ–70 GHZ)

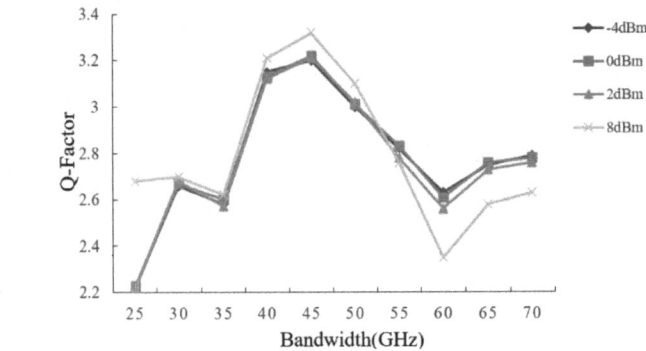

Fig. 11. CSRZ carrier suppression modulation (accepting bandwidth is 25 GHZ–70 GHZ)

As can be seen from the above figure, this is any of the three modulation methods. For the case of constant signal power, there is just an optimum value for the Q value. Whether the accepted bandwidth is greater or less than this value, the Q value of the entire system will be worse. This is explained by the fact that the bandwidth of the receiver affects the waveform of the input signal after passing through the filter [8]. Therefore, the wider the receiver bandwidth and the smaller the distortion effect of the waveform, the clearer the information of the original signal will be transmitted. However, if this optimal value is exceeded, the receiving bandwidth will be larger, and the noise entering the receiver will be larger, which will reduce the ability to transmit the original signal information. Therefore, in order to reduce the noise, it is necessary to find the optimal value of the receiving bandwidth, which is called the optimal optical receiving bandwidth [9].

It can be seen from the figure that the optimal Q value of the MDRZ modulation mode is between 30–35 GHz, and the Q value decreases with the increase of the channel power, which is greater than 6, but for the Q value of the bandwidth of 32 GHz, They are relatively high and relatively stable. For the DRZ modulated signal, the reception effect is best only when the input power of each channel is −4 dBm/ch, and when it is greater than −4 dBm/ch, the Q value is substantially unchanged, and less than 5 are basically impossible to use [10]. Therefore, it can be seen that in a system with high density and high rate, this modulation method cannot be used. For the CSRZ modulation method, regardless of the incident power, the Q value is always low, and below 3.5, it cannot to use.

4 Summary

In this paper, a DWDM model with a single channel transmission rate of 40 Gb/s is established. The transmission performance of three different modulation modes, MDRZ, DRZ and CSRZ, under in 32 channel conditions is compared and analyzed. Through the simulation platform, we can roughly see that the most suitable modulation method for high-speed DWDM campus LAN is MDRZ type, which has the best Q value.

References

1. Zhu, Y., Lee, W., et al.: A.40 Gbit/s-based long-span WDM transmission technologie. IEIC Trans. Commun. **E85-B**(2), 386–391 (2002)
2. Ying, S., Chen, M., et al.: Chromatic dispersion monitoring technique employing SOA spectral shift in 40 Gbit/s system. Opt. Commun. **249**(131), 79–84 (2005)
3. Marsan, M.A., Bianco, A., et al.: All-optical WDM multi-rings with differentiated QoS. IEEE Commun. Mag. **37**(2), 58–66 (2005)
4. Idler, W., Bigo, S.: Design of 40 Gbit/s-based multi-Terabit/s ultra-DWDM systems. IEICE Trans. Commun. **E85-B**(2), 394–399 (2002)
5. Madamopoulos, N., Vaughn, M.D., et al.: Metro network architecture scenarios, equipment requirements and implications for carriers. In: Optical Fiber Communication Conference & Exhibit (3), pp. WL2-1–WL2-3 (2001)
6. Chen, Y., Factehi, M.T., et al.: Metro optical networking. Bell Labs Tech. J. **4**(1), 163–181 (2003)
7. Tholey, V., Chawki, M.J., et al.: Demonstration of WDM survivable unidirectional ring network using tunable channel dropping receivers. Electron. Lett. **30**(16), 1323–1324 (2003)
8. Wada, N., Fujinuma, K., et al.: 40 Gbit/s packet bit error ratio and loss real-time measurement for ultrahigh-speed packet switched network. Opt. Switch. Netw. **4**(2), 201–208 (2005)
9. Modiano, E.: WDM-based packet networks. IEEE Commun. Mag. **3**, 130–135 (2006)
10. Kapil, V.S., Ian, M.W., et al.: HORNET a packet-over-WDM multiple access metropolitan area ring network. IEEE J. Sel. Areas Commun. **18**(10), 2004–2016 (2007)
11. Sheetal, A., et al.: Simulation of high capacity 40 Gb/s long haul DWDM system using different modulation formats and dispersion compensation schemes in the presence of Kerr's effect. Opt. Light Electron. **12**, 739–749 (2009)
12. Dahan, D., Eisenstein, G.: Numerical comparison between distributed and discrete amplification in a point-to-point 40 Gb/s 40-WDM-based transmission system with three different modulation formats. J. Lightwave Technol. **20**(3), 379–388 (2002)

Design of Intelligent Home Lighting Control System Based on Speech Recognition

Bao Liu[1], Xiaoyang He[1], Yuanqi Li[1], Yuxu Xiao[1], Xin Feng[1],
Lingping Chen[1], Jiayuan Lin[1], and Ling Yu[2(✉)]

[1] Research Institute of Photonics, Dalian Polytechnic University,
Dalian 116034, China
[2] Network Information Center, Dalian Polytechnic University,
Dalian 116034, China
yuling@dlpu.edu.cn

Abstract. Home lighting has always played a very important role in people's quality of life. How to make home lighting more humane is the trend of future development. This article designed a lighting control system that can be controlled by speech. The system receives the voice signal from the microphone, then uploads the voice signal to the server through the Raspberry Pi. The system uses the speech cloud service to identify and analyze the speech signal. The result of speech recognition is transmitted to the STM32 by the Raspberry Pi. STM32 controls single lamp or multiple lamps according to the recognition result. Since the speech cloud provides semantic analysis services, our speech instructions are less restrictive and more closer to everyday language. This system realizes the function of far-field identification and control linkage, while getting rid of the dependence on mobile phones, and the lighting control mode is more humanized.

Keywords: Speech recognition · Cloud computing · Lighting control · Raspberry Pi · STM32

1   Introduction

With the improvement of material levels, people pay more and more attention to high-quality life [1, 2], and smart homes gradually enter daily life. In 2014, the value of the global smart home market was US$20.38 billion, and it is expected to reach 58.68 billion yuan by 2020 [3, 4]. Most of the smart home products on the market now have a single structure, relatively complex control, and need to be operated at close range. The maneuverability and convenience cannot meet the requirements of people at present [5, 6], this article is intelligent. The intelligent control of lighting in the home and the convenience of handling are studied, breaking the limitation of the distance control in the past, and adding the speech recognition, which greatly improves the intelligence.

Supported by Science Foundation for Goldlamp Co., Ltd (2017-228195).

J. Jin et al. (Eds.): GreeNets 2019, LNICST 282, pp. 150–158, 2019.
https://doi.org/10.1007/978-3-030-21730-3_17

2   Principle of Speech Recognition Technology

Speech recognition process mainly includes speech signal preprocessing, feature extraction, training, pattern matching, and identify the output [7, 8]. The training is usually done offline, and the signal processing and feature extraction of the massive voice and language databases collected in advance are obtained. The "acoustic model" and "language model" required for the speech recognition system are obtained and stored as a template library. The recognition phase is usually completed online. The user's real-time voice signal through the same channel to get the voice characteristics of the parameters, generate test templates, and match with the reference templates. And the highest similarity of the reference template is the recognition result [9–11]. The basic block diagram of the speech recognition process is shown in Fig. 1.

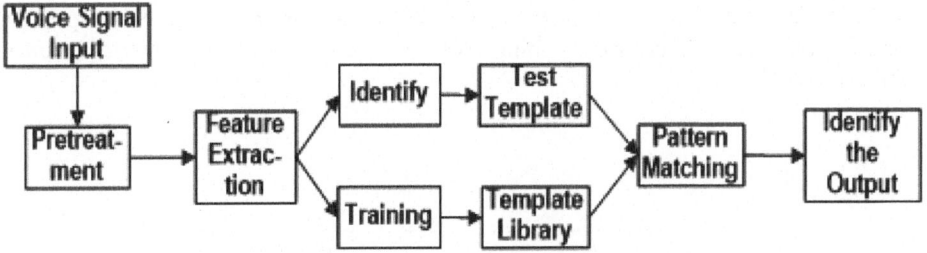

Fig. 1. The speech recognition process

3   System Architecture

The research content of this subject is to realize the intelligent control of the lighting in the home by means of voice. The system block diagram is shown in Fig. 2. The voice is collected through the microphone, and the collected signal is sent to the Raspberry Pi. The Raspberry Pi generates the wav audio file to upload to the cloud server. After the cloud server performs voice recognition, the recognized result is transmitted to the STM32 through the Raspberry Pi, and the STM32 is based on the voice command.

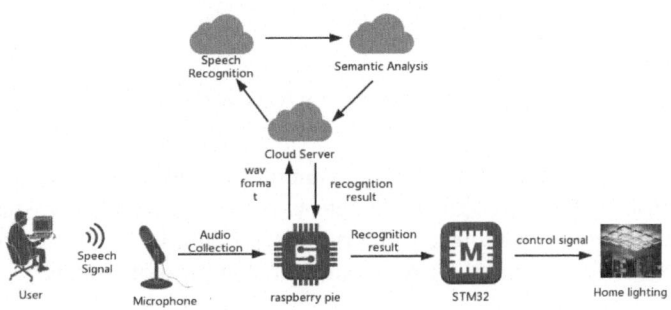

Fig. 2. The block diagram of system

Achieve control of the corresponding luminaire. The areas in the home that need illumination are living room, kitchen, bedroom, bathroom, study, etc. By coding and dividing the lamps in these areas, it is possible to realize the linkage control of multiple lamps with a single lamp.

4 Hardware Selection

The hardware part mainly consists of microphone, raspberry pie, STM32 and LED driver.

4.1 Raspberry Pi

Raspberry pie is an open source microcontroller with very small volume. It can support running Linux and Windows systems. The CPU is an ARM system. It is a popular microcontroller in the Internet of Things. Its minimum system schematic diagram is shown in Fig. 3.

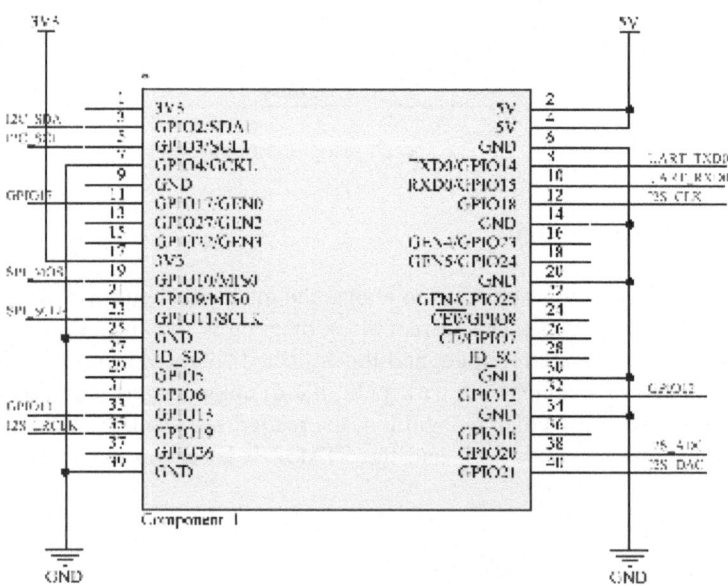

Fig. 3. The minimum system schematic diagram of RPI

Table 1 shows the performance comparison of different types of raspberry pies. As can be seen from Table 1, Raspberry Pi zero w has the advantages of small size, low power consumption and sufficient memory, and its built-in WiFi can solve the networking problem well without inserting wires, making it more independent.

Table 1. Performance comparison of different types of raspberry pie

Content	Type A	Type B	Type B+	Zero w
Soc	BCM 2835			
CPU	ARM11 700 MHz	4 core 900 MHz	1 core 1 GHz	
GPU	Broadcom			
RAM	256 M	512 M	1 G	512 M
USB2.0	1	2	4	1
Video output	Support PAL and NTSC, support HDMI (1.3 and 1.4), Resolution is 640 × 350 ~ 1920 × 1200.			
Audio output	3.5 mm Socket, HDMI Interface			
Borad stage	Standard SD interface			
Net interface	None	RJ45	RJ46, built-in WiFi	built-in WiFi
GPIO port	8	26	40	40
Power	5 V			
Power consumption	Low	High	High	Low
Size	65 × 56 × 10 mm	85 × 56 × 17 mm		65 × 30 × 5 mm

4.2   STM32

STM32 is a high-performance 32-bit microcontroller, a low-cost, high-performance, low-power microcontroller that uses the ARM Cortex-M3 core architecture. The following Figure (Fig. 4) is the minimum system schematic diagram of STM32. STM32 processing speed is 36 M, the power consumption of this MCU is very low, only 36 mA, which is the lowest power consumption of 32-bit MCU products. The product is only quite 0.5 microamps per megahertz. The most noteworthy is that the internal bus of the MCU adopts the Harvard structure, and its execution instructions are quite fast, which can reach 1.25 DMIPS/MHz. This chip is used as their main controller in more and more occasions.

4.3   Microphone

The voice acquisition module uses ReSpeaker 2-Mics Pi HAT. ReSpeaker 2-Mics Pi HAT is a Raspberry Pi dual microphone expansion board designed for AI and voice applications. This module can be applied to many versions of raspberry pie and has good compatibility. The board is a low power stereo codec based on WM8960. There are two microphones on both sides of the circuit board to collect sound, which can realize the function of far-field recognition, and has a longer recognition distance than ordinary microphones. The module provides three APA102 RGB LEDs, one user button and two on-board Grove interfaces for extending applications.

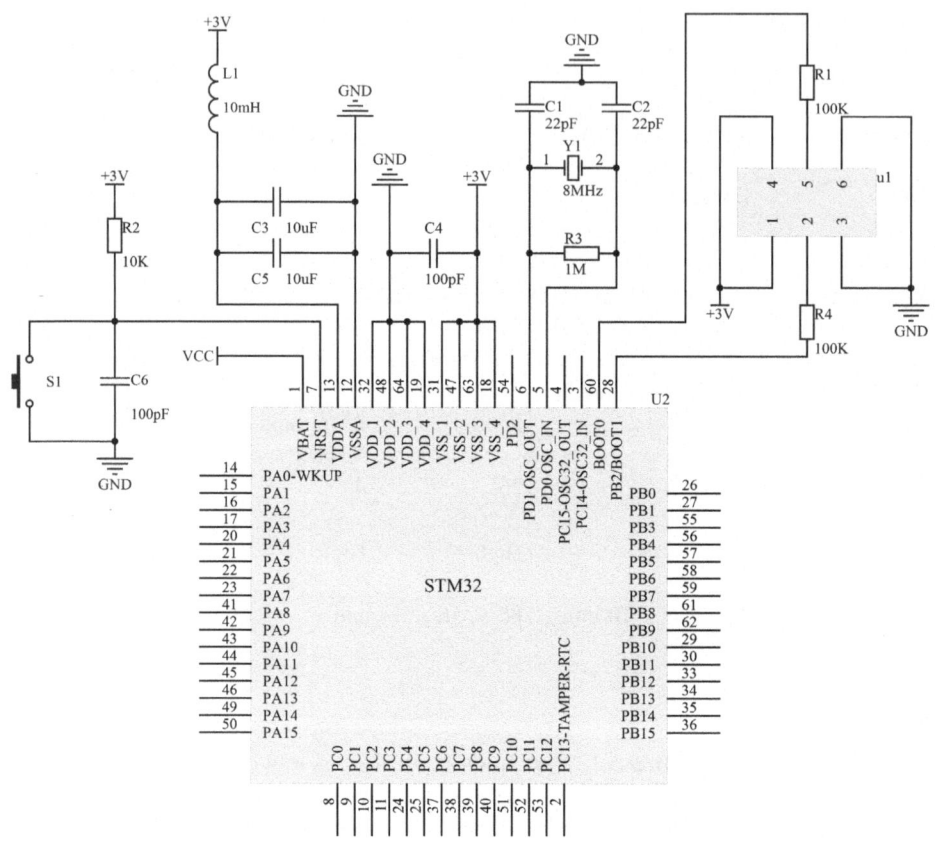

Fig. 4. The minimum system schematic diagram of STM32

5   System Software Design

5.1   Development Environment Configuration

Prepare a 16G SD card and burn the Debian system into raspberry pie using SD_CardFormatter and Win32 diskimager software. Then, we configure WIFI in Linux system and create a new blank document SSH in boot directory to facilitate remote login. After successful WIFI connection, open cmd, login remotely through PUTTY tool, and input user name and password to further configure the system.

5.2   Development Environment Configuration

First, enter the command sudo Su into super user mode to enhance privileges. Enter sudo nano/etc./apt/sources.list to switch the source to Tsinghua. Then, download and install the sound card driver in the raspberry pie. Enter arecord-f cd-Dhw:1 | aplay-Dhw:1 command for recording and playback test, and use the alsamixer command to enter the graphical interface to adjust the volume (Fig. 5).

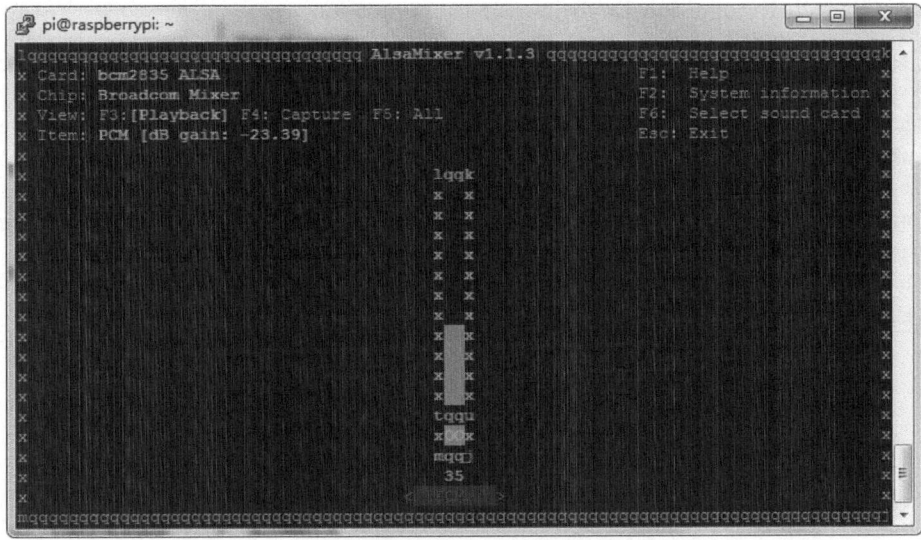

Fig. 5. Volume adjustment interface

5.3 Speech Recognition Environment Configuration

After adjusting the dual array microphone, Python 2 virtual environment can be installed in raspberry pie by downloading and installing commands. The virtual environment is named Env and placed in the ～ directory. Then, configure the Voice engine by executing the following commands in turn.

Enter the kws_doa.py file and modify lines 14–21, 2-Mics, as follows:

```
cd ~/4mics_hat
sudo apt install libatlas-base-dev    #install snowboy dependencies
sudo apt install python-pyaudio      #install pyaudio
pip install ./snowboy*.whl      # install snowboy
pip install ./webrtc*.whl       # install webrtc
cd ~/
git clone https://github.com/voice-engine/voice-engine  #write by seeed
cd voice-engine/
python setup.py install
cd examples
nano kws_doa.py
```

```
from voice_engine.doa_respeaker_4mic_array import DOA
def main( ):
    src = Source(rate=16000, channels=2)
    ch1 = ChannelPicker(channels=2, pick=1)
    kws = KWS()
    doa = DOA(rate=16000)
```

Then, run Python kws_doa.py in a virtual environment. Use snowboy to wake up.

5.4   Speech Recognition Environment Configuration

The flow chart of the system is shown in the Fig. 6. After the system is powered on, the system is initialized, the raspberry pie is connected to the Internet, and the array microphone is in working state. Then, it enters the state of voice detection. When the wake-up words are detected, the user's voice is recorded and the WAV format audio file is produced. The raspberry pie uploaded the audio file after the voice input was completed. When the recognition result is read, the recognition result is matched. If the match is passed, the recognition result is transmitted to STM32 through I2C communication protocol, and the corresponding control instructions are executed. Otherwise, play the audio file "Sorry, I didn't understand, please say it again."

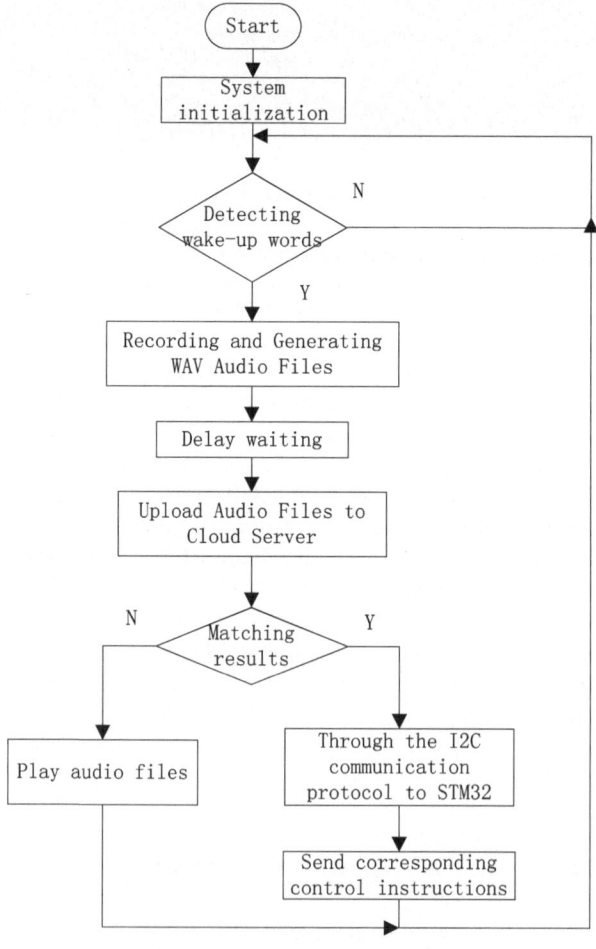

Fig. 6. The flow chart of system

6 Test

In order to test the recognition and practicability of the system, we tested the recognition rate of voice commands at different distances to different sexes. The test results are shown in Table 2.

From Table 2, we can see that within 2 m, the recognition rate of the system is very high, and within the range of 2–3 m, the speech recognition rate is higher than 95%. It has the ability of far-field recognition, and can meet the actual needs of use. The recognition rate decreases with the increase of distance more than 3 m. The main reason is that the effective recognition distance of microphone is limited, and different gender voices have no effect on the recognition rate of the system.

Table 2. Speech recognition rate test results

Distance L/m	Gender	Recognition rate
L < 1	Male	99/100
	Female	99/100
2 < L < 3	Male	97/100
	Female	95/100
L > 3	Male	82/100
	Female	79/100

7 Conclusion

The main content of this project is to achieve the precise control of home lighting through voice. The project uses voice cloud service, array microphone, raspberry pie and STM32 to complete this function. After testing, the system can realize the far-field recognition function and has the actual promotion ability. Unlike the traditional speech recognition system, this system not only realizes the function of voice interaction, but also realizes the linkage control of lighting with embedded technology. The project uses voice cloud service, electret microphone, raspberry pie and STM32 to complete this function. The voice cloud belongs to leasing service, but it needs to be integrated with our system to promote as a whole. In addition, STM32 has very powerful functions, and only part of its functions are used here. Therefore, the system also has a good expansion ability, which is conducive to the further development.

References

1. Wang, H., Bian, H.N., Zhang, H.X., Zhang, F.: The research and design of smart home system based on MQX. In: 2015 International Conference on Computer Science and Applications, pp. 188–190 (2015)
2. Rashid, M.A., Han, X.: Gesture control of ZigBee connected smart home Internet of Things. In: International Conference on Informatics, pp. 667–670 (2016)

3. Petnik, J., Vanus, J.: Design of smart home implementation within IoT with natural language interface. IFAC PapersOnLine **51**(6), 174–179 (2018)
4. Vanus, J., Stratil, T., Martinek, R., Bilik, P., Zidek, J.: The possibility of using VLC data transfer in the smart home. IFAC PapersOnLine **49**(25), 176–181 (2016)
5. Vanus, J., Novak, T., Koziorek, J., Konecny, J., Hrbac, R.: The proposal model of energy savings of lighting systems in the smart home care. IFAC Proc. Volumes **46**(28), 411–415 (2013)
6. Vanus, J., Stratil, T., Martinek, R., Bilik, P., Zidek, J.: The possibility of using VLC data transfer in the smart home. IFAC PapersOnLine **49**(25), 76–181 (2016)
7. Qian, Y., Chang, X., Yu, D.: Single-channel multi-talker speech recognition with permutation invariant training. Speech Commun. **104**, 1–11 (2018)
8. Song, J., Iverson, P.: Listening effort during speech perception enhances auditory and lexical processing for non-native listeners and accents. Cognition **179**, 163–170 (2018)
9. Errattahi, R., El Hannani, A., Ouahmane, H.: Automatic speech recognition errors detection and correction: a review. Procedia Comput. Sci. **128**, 32–37 (2018)
10. Marwan, M., Kartit, A., Ouahmane, H.: A cloud based solution for collaborative and secure sharing of medical data. Int. J. Enterp. Inf. Syst. (IJEIS) **14**(3), 128–145 (2018)
11. Ogawa, A., Hori, T.: Error detection and accuracy estimation in automatic speech recognition using deep bidirectional recurrent neural networks. Speech Commun. **89**, 70–83 (2017)

Energy-Efficient Networking

Dynamics and Synchronization Analysis of Chaotic Characteristic Interconnected Electrical Power System

Run Hao and Xuming Ma[✉]

State Grid Gansu Electric Power Company Linxia Power Supply Company,
Linxia 731100, China
13909300931@139.com

Abstract. In this paper, the chaos characteristics of interconnected electrical power system under different cycles load disturbance are analyzed by the phase diagram, bifurcation diagram and Lyapunov exponent spectrum. Then synchronization characteristics of the interconnected electrical power system are analyzed by coupling synchronization algorithm. The analysis results shown that the system under different cycle load disturbance, the system have more complexity state of motion, such as, appear periodic state, chaos oscillation, when system with different coupling coefficient of shock, the system arrives at the synchronization time is different. The analysis results have certain guiding significance to maintain the safe to operation of power system.

Keywords: Interconnected electric power system · Chaos characteristics · Synchronization characteristics

1 Introduction

Chaos is a deterministic nonlinear dynamics system, which are sensitive to initial values and system parameters. It is a complex state of motion that occurs in deterministic systems, and a natural phenomenon that exists extensively in nature and human society [1, 2].

With the development of chaotic systems, the idea of chaotic control comes into being. At present, chaos control has taken a breakthrough result. An important research direction of chaotic control is chaotic synchronization. Chaotic synchronization refers to two chaotic systems, which, over time, tend to converge in some way [3]. Since 1990 Pecora and Carroll [4] proposed a drive-response synchronization method, which the synchronization of chaotic systems becomes a hot research field. Then a variety of chaotic synchronization methods are proposed, for example, time-delay feedback method, adaptive control method [5, 6], and observer method [7].

Due to the rapid development of science and technology, the scale of power system has undergone great changes, especially, the transformation of power system to power grid interconnection. Power system is also a kind of nonlinear system with dynamic behavior, when the system parameters change, the system will show complex nonlinear dynamic characteristics. The interconnected power system is a typical nonlinear power

J. Jin et al. (Eds.): GreeNets 2019, LNICST 282, pp. 161–169, 2019.
https://doi.org/10.1007/978-3-030-21730-3_18

system, and the system has complex dynamic characteristics, such as, low frequency oscillation state, synchronous harmonic vibration state behavior, chaotic state behavior [8]. If there is a non-periodic load disturbance in the power system, when the load disturbance reaches a certain condition, the system will produce chaotic oscillation, so that the normal operation of the power grid is affected. If the chaotic oscillation is serious, it will cause the interconnected power system to crack directly, thus blocking the normal transmission of electricity [9]. Therefore, it is of special significance to study the chaotic phenomenon of power system to maintain the safe operation of power system.

The abnormal operation of the power grid is mainly caused by the chaotic oscillation in the power system, and the chaotic oscillation cannot make the power grid run properly by adding damping stabilizer to the system. Since the 20th century, many scholars have begun in-depth research on the causes of chaotic phenomena in power systems. Subsequently, unprecedented achievements have been made in the chaotic characteristics of power systems and the control of chaos in power systems [10–17]. However, so far, there is not a lot of expansion of the synchronous research of power system. Therefore, this paper will use the coupling synchronization algorithm to analyze the chaotic synchronization characteristics of interconnected power system, and use phase diagram, bifurcation diagram, Lyapunov spectrum and complexity to analyze the chaotic dynamics of the system.

In this paper, the chaotic characteristics and synchronization characteristics of interconnected power system are analyzed. The structure of the rest of article as follows, in Sect. 2, the mathematical state equation of the interconnected power system is established. The chaotic characteristics of interconnected power system are analyzed in Sect. 3. In Sect. 4, the coupling synchronization algorithm is detail described, and the synchronization characteristics of the interconnected power system are analyzed. Some conclusions are summarized in Sect. 5.

2 Model of Interconnected Electrical Power System

The structural model of the interconnected electrical power system is shown in Fig. 1. From the Fig. 1, we can see that the system model including system I, system II, connecting line and 7 elements. Where, the components 1, 3, 5 and 6 are equivalent generators, main transformers, loads and circuit breakers, respectively in system I. The components 2, 4, 5, 6 are the equivalent generators, main transformers, loads and circuit breakers in system II.

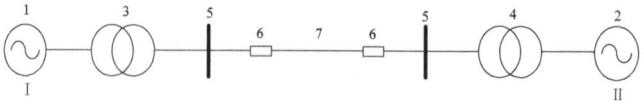

Fig. 1. Model of interconnected electrical power system

The dynamic mathematical model of a simple interconnection system containing two sets of generators is as follows:

$$\begin{cases} \frac{d\delta}{dt} = w \\ \frac{dw}{dt} = -\frac{1}{H}P_s \sin \delta - \frac{D}{H}w + \frac{1}{H}P_m + \frac{1}{H}P_e \cos \alpha t \end{cases}, \tag{1}$$

where, δ represent the relative angle between the equivalent generator potential of two power systems, the unit is rad. w means that the relative angular velocity, the unit is rad/s. h represent the moment of inertia, the unit is kg.m^2. D means that the damping coefficient, the unit is N.m.s/rad. P_m represent the equivalent generator of the system I mechanical power, the unit is W. P_s means that the maximum electromagnetic power value transmitted by system I to System II, the unit W. P_e is the load disturbance power amplitude, the unit is W. α represent the load disturbance frequency, the unit is Hz.

Set $x_1 = \delta$, $x_2 = w$, $x_3 = \cos(\alpha t)$, $x_4 = \sin(\alpha t)$, Eq. (1) can be written in the following form:

$$\begin{cases} \dot{x}_1 = x_2 \\ \dot{x}_2 = bx_2 + dx_3 + c - a \sin x_1 \\ \dot{x}_3 = -\alpha x_4 \\ \dot{x}_4 = \alpha x_3 \end{cases}, \tag{2}$$

where, $a = P_s/H$, $b = -D/H$, $c = P_m/H$, $d = P_e/H$.

The a, b, c, d, α represent the system parameter, x_1, x_2, x_3, x_4 means that the state variable of the system. Makes the system parameter $a = 1$, $b = -0.4$, $c = 0.2$, $d = 0.755$, $\alpha = 0.8$, the initial value $x_1 = 0.5$, $x_2 = 0.5$, $x_3 = 1$, $x_4 = 0$, and gets the chaotic attraction phase diagrams of system (2) in x_1–x_2 plane, x_1–x_3 plane, and x_1–x_4 plane are shown in Fig. 2. The Lyapunov exponents $LE_1 = 0.0255$, $LE_2 = -0.4255$, $LE_3 = 0$, $LE_4 = 0$, and Lyapunov exponent dimension $D_L = 3.0560$ are obtained by calculated. It is obvious that the system has a positive Lyapunov exponent and the sum of all Lyapunov exponents less than zero, so the system is chaotic.

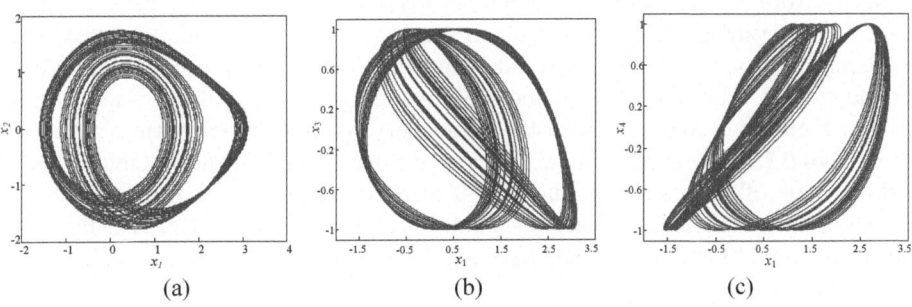

(a)   (b)   (c)

Fig. 2. Plane attractor diagram, (a) x_1–x_2 plane, (b) x_1–x_3 plane, (c) x_1–x_4 plane

3   Chaos Characteristics Analysis of Interconnected Electrical Power System

Keeping the above initial value and parameters values, when the parameter $d \in$ [0.5, 0.755]. We can get the corresponding bifurcation diagram, Lyapunov exponent spectrum, SE complexity and C0 complexity are shown in Fig. 3.

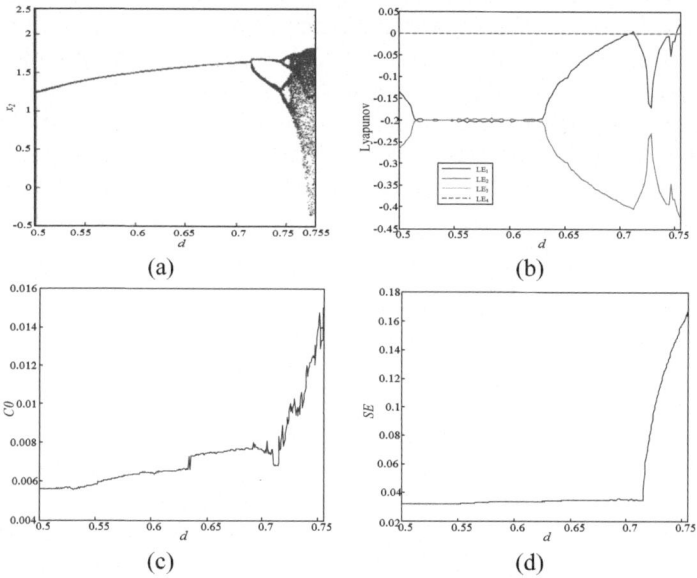

Fig. 3. (a) Bifurcation diagram, (b) Lyapunov exponent spectrum, (c) C0 complexity, (d) SE complexity

As can be seen from Fig. 3(a) and (b), when the system parameter d increases gradually from 0.5 to 0.755, the Lyapunov exponents spectrum and bifurcation diagram of the system can be visualized to see the change of the motion state of the interconnected power system. The interconnected electrical power system is transformed from a series of times periodic bifurcation process to chaotic state transformation. Figure 3(c) and (d), when the parameters d of the system increase gradually from 0.5 to 0.755, the complexity of the system is increasing, and the complexity of the periodic state of the system is much small than the chaotic states. Because the complexity of the system is the greatest in chaotic state, the complexity can visually see the transformation of the interconnected electrical power system from the periodic state to the chaotic state.

For the general nonlinear system, the change of the system parameters determines the state of the system, and the state transformation of the system can not only be displayed intuitively through bifurcation diagram, Lyapunov exponents spectrum and complexity, but also through the visual display of the phase diagram. The influence of the parameter change of the interconnected electrical power system on the system, and the parameters $a = 1$, $b = -0.4$, $c = 0.2$, $\alpha = 0.8$, changes the amplitude of the parameter load disturbance, let the $d = 0.5$, $d = 0.715$, $d = 0.745$ and $d = 0.755$. We get the limit ring of period 1, 2 and 4, and the chaotic attraction phase diagrams are shown in Fig. 4.

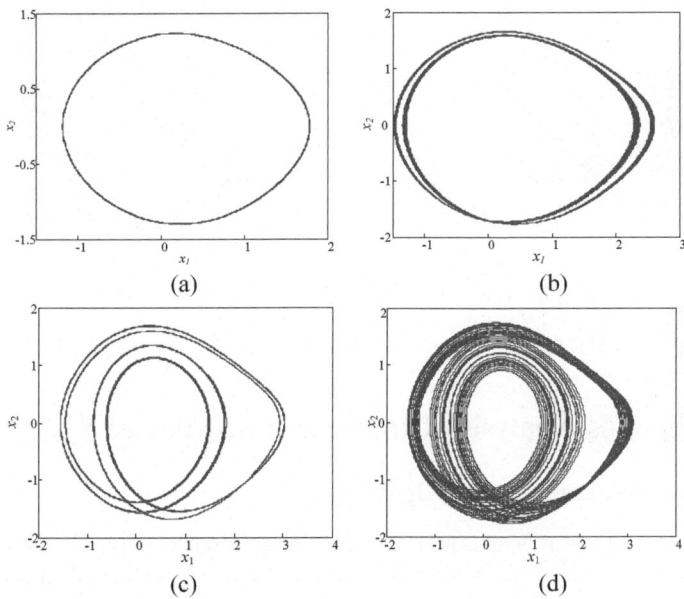

Fig. 4. Phase diagram, (a) $d = 0.5$, (b) $d = 0.715$, (c) $d = 0.745$, (d) $d = 0.755$

The influence of parameter load disturbance frequency change on system in interconnected electrical power system. The parameters $a = 1$, $b = -0.4$, $c = 0.2$, $d = 0.755$, change the parameter α. When $\alpha = 0.9$, $\alpha = 0.82$, $\alpha = 0.806$ and $\alpha = 0.8$, and the corresponding limit ring cycles 1, 2, 4 and chaotic attraction phase diagram are shown in Fig. 5.

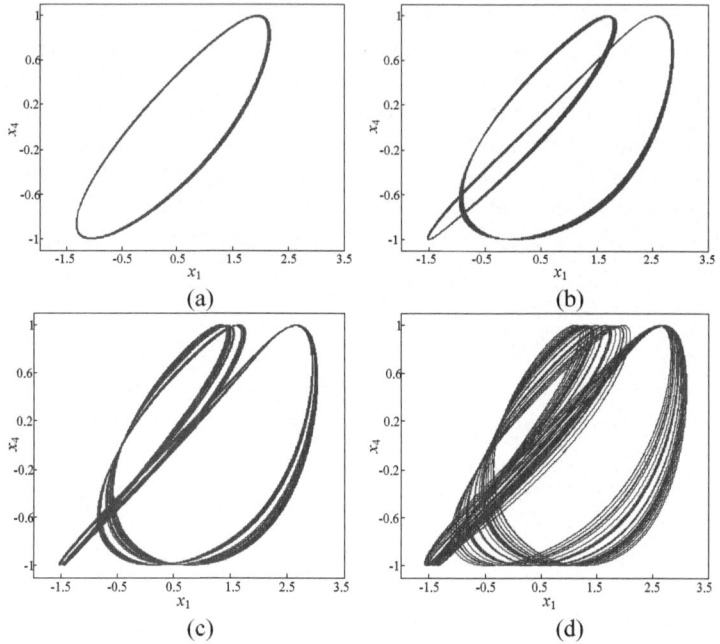

Fig. 5. Phase diagram, (a) $\alpha = 0.9$, (b) $\alpha = 0.82$, (c) $\alpha = 0.806$, (d) $\alpha = 0.8$

4   Synchronous Analysis of Interconnected Power System

4.1   Coupled Synchronization Algorithm

Coupled synchronization is all coupling variables or some variables in the drive system into the response system, so that the response system is synchronized with the drive system after coupling. A chaotic system is

$$\dot{X} = AX + f(X), \tag{3}$$

where, state vector $X \in R^n$, the constant matrix $A \in R^{n \times n}$, $f(X)$ is a continuous non-linear function of the linear part of the system. For the system with the different initial value and the same system parameters, they are synchronized by coupled synchronization algorithm. The drive-response synchronization equation is

$$\dot{X} = AX + f(X), \tag{4}$$

$$\dot{X'} = AX' + f(X') + K(X - X') \tag{5}$$

where, K is the coupling matrix.

The error vector is

$$E = X - X' \tag{6}$$

$$f(X) - f(X') = M_{X,X'}(X - X') \tag{7}$$

The error system is composed of drive system and response system by

$$\dot{E} = (A + M_{X,X'} - 2K)E \tag{8}$$

When the system error is zero, the system is in equilibrium state, that is, select the appropriate coupling coefficient matrix, make the system balance point is gradually stable, two chaotic systems to reach synchronization. In general, there are two kinds of coupling of similar variables between chaotic systems, single coupling and bidirectional coupling. Some chaotic systems can be synchronized by single-variable coupling, while some chaotic systems require two or even multiple variable coupling to achieve synchronization. Among them, the more coupled the number of variables, the stronger the synchronization ability. If it is a global variable coupling, as long as the number of coupling is large enough, the chaotic system can be coupled.

4.2 Coupling Synchronization Analysis of Interconnected Electrical Power Systems

The drive system is Eq. (2), the response system is obtained by the coupling synchronization algorithm as Eq. (9), and the error system is Eq. (10).

$$\begin{cases} \dot{x}_5 = x_6 + k_1(x_1 - x_5) \\ \dot{x}_6 = bx_6 + dx_7 + c - a\sin x_5 + k_2(x_2 - x_6) \\ \dot{x}_7 = -\alpha x_8 + k_3(x_3 - x_7) \\ \dot{x}_8 = \alpha x_7 + k_4(x_4 - x_8) \end{cases} \tag{9}$$

$$\begin{cases} e_1 = x_5 - x_1 \\ e_2 = x_6 - x_2 \\ e_3 = x_7 - x_3 \\ e_4 = x_8 - x_4 \end{cases} \tag{10}$$

where, k_1, k_2, k_3, k_4 represent the couple coefficients, x_5, x_6, x_7, x_8 means that state variable of response system.

When the drive system the same as the response system parameter $a = 1$, $b = -0.4$, $c = 0.2$, $d = 0.755$, $\alpha = 0.8$, the initial value of the drive system is $(0.5, 0.5, 1, 0)$, the initial value of the response system is $(1, 1, 1, 0.5)$, and the coupling coefficient $k_1 = k_2 = k_3 = k_4 = 3$. Obtain the system synchronization error curve as shown in Fig. 6(a). As can be seen from Fig. 6(a), after 2.5 s error variable e_1, e_2, e_3, e_4 all tend to 0, which indicates that in the 2.5 s time, the system parameters are the same, the initial values are different of two connected electrical power systems have reached the synchronization.

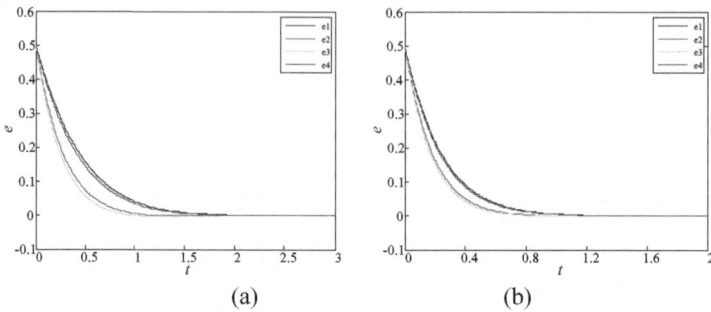

Fig. 6. Synchronization error curve, (a) $k = 3$, (b) $k = 5$

If the parameters and initial values of the response system and the drive system are unchanged, and the values of the coupling coefficients are changed, we get the synchronization error curves are shown in Fig. 6(b) when the coupling coefficients are $k_1 = k_2 = k_3 = k_4 = 5$. Through the comparison of Fig. 6(a) and (b), it can be clearly seen that with the increase of coupling coefficient, the time of synchronization of the system is decreasing. In the practical application process, it is sometimes necessary a long time for the two systems to reach synchronization, sometimes it takes a short time to make the two systems synchronized, and the coupling synchronization algorithm realizes the synchronization time by controlling the coupling coefficient for the two systems applied in practice, which is one of the advantages of the coupling synchronization algorithm.

5   Conclusions

In this paper, the chaotic characteristics of interconnected power systems are analyzed by using phase diagrams, bifurcation diagrams, Lyapunov exponent spectrum and complexity. The synchronous characteristics of interconnected power systems are analyzed by coupling synchronization algorithm. The analysis results show that there is no chaotic oscillation when the periodic load disturbance of the system is small, and when the perturbation amplitude increases gradually, the system has the phenomenon of double periodic bifurcation to chaos. By changing the amplitude of load disturbance and the frequency of load disturbance, different chaotic attractor phase diagrams are obtained, and the transformation of interconnected power system between periodic state and chaotic state under different disturbance loads can be clearly seen. The time of the interconnected power system reaches synchronization is different, when the coupling synchronization coefficient of interconnection power system with different values. If the coupling coefficient of the interconnected power system is controlled to a certain range, the system can control the synchronization time in the actual application, which will provide some ideas and methods for the safe operation of the power system. Next, we will continue to study the chaotic characteristics and synchronous control of interconnected power systems.

References

1. Lei, S., Sun, C., Zhou, Q., et al.: The research on short-term load forecasting method based on improving adding-weight one-rank load forecasting model. Electr. Measur. Instrum. **43**(5), 5–8 (2006)
2. Wen, J., Zhai, C., Chen, D., et al.: Nonlinear phenomena analysis in boost PFC converter with average-current-mode control. Electr. Measur. Instrum. **48**(12), 1–4 (2011)
3. Zhang, F.C., Shu, Y.L., Yao, X.Z.: The dynamical analysis of a disk dynamo system and its application in chaos synchronization. Diabetes Care **36**(2), 1360–1366 (2013)
4. Pecora, L.M., Carroll, T.L.: Synchronization is chaotic system. Phys. Rev. Lett. **64**, 821–824 (1990)
5. Zhou, X., Wu, Y., Li, Y., et al.: Adaptive control and synchronization of a novel hyperchaotic power system. Appl. Math. Comput. **20**(3), 80–85 (2008)
6. Jian, J., Wang, B., Guo, C.: Adaptive chaotic system synchronization for a class of power system with unknown parameters. Complex Syst. Appl.-Model., Control Simul. **14**, 575–579 (2007)
7. Morgul, Q., Solak, E.: On the synchronization of chaotic systems by using state observers. Int. J. Brifurcation, Chaos **7**(6), 1307–1322 (1997)
8. Song, D., Yang, X., Ding, Q., et al.: A survey on analysis on low frequency oscillation in large - scale interconnected power grid and its control measures. Power Syst. Technol. **35**(10), 22–28 (2011)
9. Yu, Y.N.: Electric Power System Dynamics. Academic Press, New York (1983)
10. Carreras, B.A., Lynch, V.E., Dobsob, I., et al.: Critical points and transitions in an electric power transmission model for cascading failure blackouts. Chaos **12**, 985–994 (2002)
11. Ohta, H., Ueda, Y.: Blue sky bifurcations caused by unstable limit cycle leading to voltage collapse in an electric power system. Chaos, Solitons Fractals **14**, 1227–1237 (2002)
12. Xiao, S.Y., Qing, D.L., Shi, J.C.: Horseshoe chaos and topological entropy estimate in a simple power system. Appl. Math. Comput. **211**(2), 467–473 (2009)
13. Liu, M.J., Piao, Z.L.: Study on chaos control for nonlinear power system. In: Intelligent Systems and Applications, pp. 1–4 (2009)
14. Deepak, K.L., Swarup, K.S.: Modeling and simulation of chaotic phenomena in electrical power systems. Applied Soft Computing, In Press, Corrected Proof (2009). https://doi.org/10.1016/j.asoc.11.001. Accessed 18 Nov2009
15. Lee, B., Ajjarapu, V.: Period- doubling route to chaos in an electrical power system. IEEE Proc. Gener. Transm. Distrib. **140**(6), 490–496 (1993)
16. Tetsuya, M., Takashi, N., Naohik, I.: Chaotic attractor with a characteristic of torus. IEEE Trans. Circ. Syst. I Fundam. Theory Appl. **47**(6), 944–948 (2000)
17. Ye, X.L., Mou, J., Luo, C.F., et al.: Dynamics analysis of Wien-bridge hyperchaotic memristive circuit system. Nonlinear Dyn. **92**(3), 923–933 (2018)

Dynamical Analysis of Nose-Hoover Continuous Chaotic System Based on Gingerbreadman Discrete Chaotic Sequence

Run Hao and Xuming Ma$^{(\boxtimes)}$

State Grid Gansu Electric Power Company Linxia Power Supply Company,
Linxia 731100, China
13909300931@139.com

Abstract. Apply the discrete chaotic sequence of Gingerbreadman System to the only one control parameter of Nose-Hoover continuous chaotic system, can get completely different simulation results. Namely, extracting a part of sequence of Gingerbreadman discrete system randomly, and take this sequence to control Nose-Hoover continuous chaotic system, then make analysis of this new system. Dynamic analysis of the new system, which is based on Nose-Hoover continuous chaotic system under the control of the discrete chaotic sequence of Gingerbreadman system. Compared with the original system carefully, find that phase diagram arising from new system produce obvious changes. We also calculate Lyapunov exponents, compared with the Lyapunov exponents computed from original system, find it also changed. It proved that our new system has chaotic characteristics, provide new method for the chaotic system which are used in the fields of cryptography, secure communication and information security etc.

Keywords: Gingerbreadman discrete chaotic sequence ·
Nose-Hoover chaotic system · Phase diagram · Lyapunov expontents

1 Introduction

In recent years, chaos theory has been widely applied in the fields of cryptography, secure communication and information security. It is reported that chaos coding technology and decoding technology have entered the U.S. defense department [1]. Chaotic systems can be divided into continuous and discrete systems, and continuous systems used for encryption often need to be discretized. Information security was studied in the early 1990s [2].

Habutsu [3] firstly used the discrete chaotic dynamic system to construct the encryption algorithm in 1991. Bianco [4, 5] used logistic map to generate a floating-point sequence in 1991 and 1994, then converted it into binary sequence which is Exclusive OR [XOR] with plain text. In 1991, Deffeyes [6] described a method to generate a two-dimensional N-by-M region from a one-dimensional password, which is similar to the generalized two-dimensional back-mapping in the long distance and

© ICST Institute for Computer Sciences, Social Informatics and Telecommunications Engineering 2019
Published by Springer Nature Switzerland AG 2019. All Rights Reserved
J. Jin et al. (Eds.): GreeNets 2019, LNICST 282, pp. 170–180, 2019.
https://doi.org/10.1007/978-3-030-21730-3_19

mainly relies on geometry. and also the chaotic encryption methods based on synchronization proposed by Caroll and Pecora [7–13], Cuomo and Oppenheim [14, 15], Murali [16], Koearev [17], KHZ [18], Papadimitriou [19] et al. Bernstein and Lieberman [20] established a pseudo-random sequence generator with chaos circuit in 1991, and Gutowicz [21, 22] described an encryption scheme based on one-dimensional cellular automata. Firstly in 1994 and 1995, Pichler and Scharinger [23] introduced the encryption method with two-dimensional discrete chaotic systems. In 1997, Götz et al. proposed a new one-dimensional iterative method [24], and Kotulski proposed the inverse iterative algorithm [25]. Study of continuous chaotic system is a hot topic in recent years scientists to explore, from 1963 the American scientists Lorenz found chaos, 1975 the Chinese scholars Tien-Yien Li and the American mathematician Yorke published the famous article "period three implies chaos" [26] in "America Mathematics" magazine, to now, there is no need to repeat because it is too familiar to us.

Due to the defects of the encryption algorithm itself or the insufficient security of the inherent characteristics of the discrete chaotic system, the cryptographic system is actually a process of reversible transformation from plaintext space to ciphertext space determined by the key [27]. In recent years, people have stayed on the study of chaotic attractors generated by a single continuous system with parameter changes, and further analyzed on the basis of a system that has proved to be chaotic. Such as the research of Wang Fanzhen et al. [28]. based on a four-wing attractor of Qi et al. [29], or fine-tuning the original equation, increasing or decreasing the dimension to find new chaotic phenomena, In the field of chaotic circuit engineering, many techniques have used non-smooth nonlinear terms to generate multi-volume chaotic attractors [30–34]. Based on the above considerations, the key question discussed in this paper is: Can a chaotic sequence generated by a discrete system be used to control a certain parameter of a continuous system, so that it can change with discrete sequences, and whether new chaotic phenomena can be generated under such conditions? This paper gives a certain dynamic analysis through calculation and simulation, and gives certain conclusions at the end of the article.

The main method of time series chaos determination [35] analyzes the dynamic characteristics of chaotic characteristics from different angles. This paper analyzes the Nose-Hoover system controlled by the sequence generated by the discrete system from the aspects of Lyapunov exponent analysis and direct observation of phase diagram trajectory, and compares it with the simulation results of the original Nose-Hoover system to analyze the phase diagram. The formation of the trajectory is used to determine the effect of the sequence on the Nose-Hoover system.

So far, only a few literatures have studied and illustrated the phase diagram of the Gingerbreadman discrete chaotic system. This paper adds a study on the variation of the Lyapunov exponent with parameters. Discrete systems are analyzed on the basis of logistic map, and one-dimensional chaotic maps are the most studied. The chaotic behavior of logistic mapping was first proposed by American mathematical biologist R. May. In 1976, he published a review article in the American magazine Nature [36]. This article will not describe the basic principles.

Nowadays, many theorems and inferences have been proposed for the prediction of chaotic attractors [37, 38]. The method of this paper provides a new idea for judging the existence of chaos and analyzing the formation of chaotic attractors, and this assumption is proved by calculation and simulation.

2   Dynamic Analysis of Discrete and Continuous Chaotic Systems

2.1   Dynamic Analysis of Gingerbreadman Discrete System

The mathematical model of system Gingerbreadman is:

$$\begin{cases} X_{n+1} = 1 + |X_n| - aY_n \\ Y_{n+1} = X_n \end{cases} \tag{1}$$

When the initial value of the system is $X_0 = 0.5$, $Y_0 = 3.7$, and $a = 1$, Gingerbreadman's attractor phase diagram on the x-y plane is shown in Fig. 1(a), The Lyapunov exponent of the system is $LE_1 = 0.09054$ and $LE_2 = -0.09054$, the system is in a chaotic state. It can be seen from Fig. 1(a) that the value of phase diagram parameter x is within the interval $(-4, 8]$. In this paper, the discrete sequence generated by Xn is shown in Table 1.1 for simulation of Nose-Hoover system under the control of discrete sequences in 2.1 and 2.2. the relationship curve of Lyapunov exponent of Gingerbreadman discrete system with parameter a, as shown in Fig. 1(b). When the value of parameter a is between [0.95, 5.5], the maximum Lyapunov exponent of the system is always greater than 0, indicating that the system is in a chaotic state within this interval.

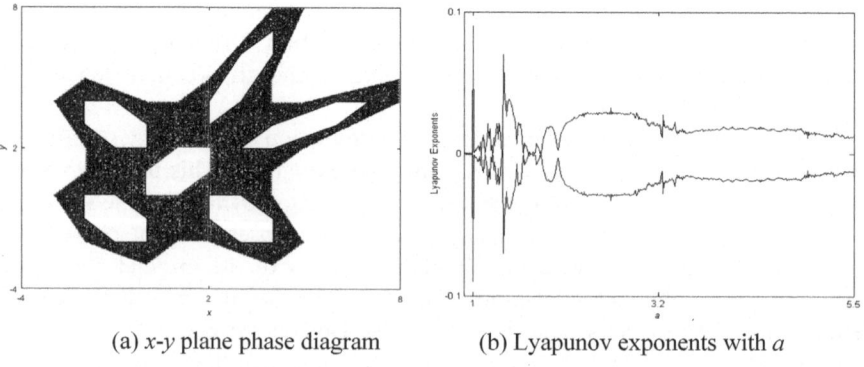

(a) x-y plane phase diagram   (b) Lyapunov exponents with a

Fig. 1. Gingerbreadman system simulation

2.2   Dynamic Analysis of Nose-Hoover Continuous System

The modeling process and feature principle of the Nose-Hoover system can be found in the specific literature [39].

The mathematical model of system Nose-Hoover is:

$$\begin{cases} \dot{x} = y \\ \dot{y} = -x + yz \\ \dot{z} = c - y^2 \end{cases} \tag{2}$$

When the initial value of the system is $x_0 = 0$, $y_0 = 5$, $z_0 = 0$, $c = 0.99$, and the simulation time step is 0.05 s, the attractor phase diagram on the x-y plane is shown in Fig. 2(a). The Lyapunov exponent of the system is $LE_1 = 0.0218$, $LE_2 = 0$, and $LE_3 = -0.0466$, so the Lyaounov dimension can be calculated as 2.4678. As shown in Fig. 2(b), you can see how the Lyapunov exponent of nose-hoover system changes with parameter c. When parameter c is within the interval [0, 15], the Lyapunov exponent always has a part greater than 0, which indicates that nose-hoover system within this interval is in a chaotic state. It can be seen from this that system Gingerbreadman's discrete sequence is in the range where parameter c can make the system have chaotic characteristics. In order to more accurately analyze the chaotic feature of Nose-Hoover continuous system, a bifurcation diagram of the continuous system can be made. The bifurcation diagram of Nose-Hoover system varying with parameter c is shown in Fig. 2(c). By comparing the curve of Lyapunov exponent of the system changing with parameter c with the bifurcation diagram of the system changing with parameter c, it can be seen that when $c = 8.5$ and $c = 12.13$, the system has a periodic window, and the system in the range of these two values is in a periodic state when c is in the interval (0,6.05], the whole Nose-Hoover system is in the period doubling bifurcation state. When $c > 6.05$, it enters the first bifurcation of the system, generates three periodic states, and again appears the more obvious periodic window at $c = 9$, and the second period-doubling bifurcation of the system at $c = 11.28$. In Fig. 2(b) and (c) shows that the system's Lyapunov exponent and bifurcation diagram is consistent, further contrast C0 complexity and SE complexity of x vary with parameters c, as shown in Fig. 2(d) and (e). Parameter c, for example, in the interval [7.852, 10.07], when $c > 7.852$, with the increase of c value, the SE and C0 complexity of system as the rising trend. When $c > 10.07$, with the increase of c value, the SE and C0 complexity of system as the declining trend. When c is in the interval [10.07, 13.19], the system enters into the anti-period-doubling-bifurcation state, which is consistent with the results verified by the corresponding Lyapunov exponents and the bifurcation diagram of the system. The stability of chaos dynamics of Nose-Hoover system can be explained, which further proves that this continuous system can be used as the control carrier of Gingerbreadman discrete sequence.

When analyzing Nose-Hoover system, Wolf algorithm [40] was used to calculate Lyapunov exponents, draw the spectrum graph of Lyapunov exponents changing with system parameters, make bifurcation diagram, and analyze the complexity of the system changing with parameter c. Through the above basic dynamics analysis, chaos characteristics of Nose-Hoover system can be explained. The preliminary proof is given for analyzing the control of discrete sequence based on this method.

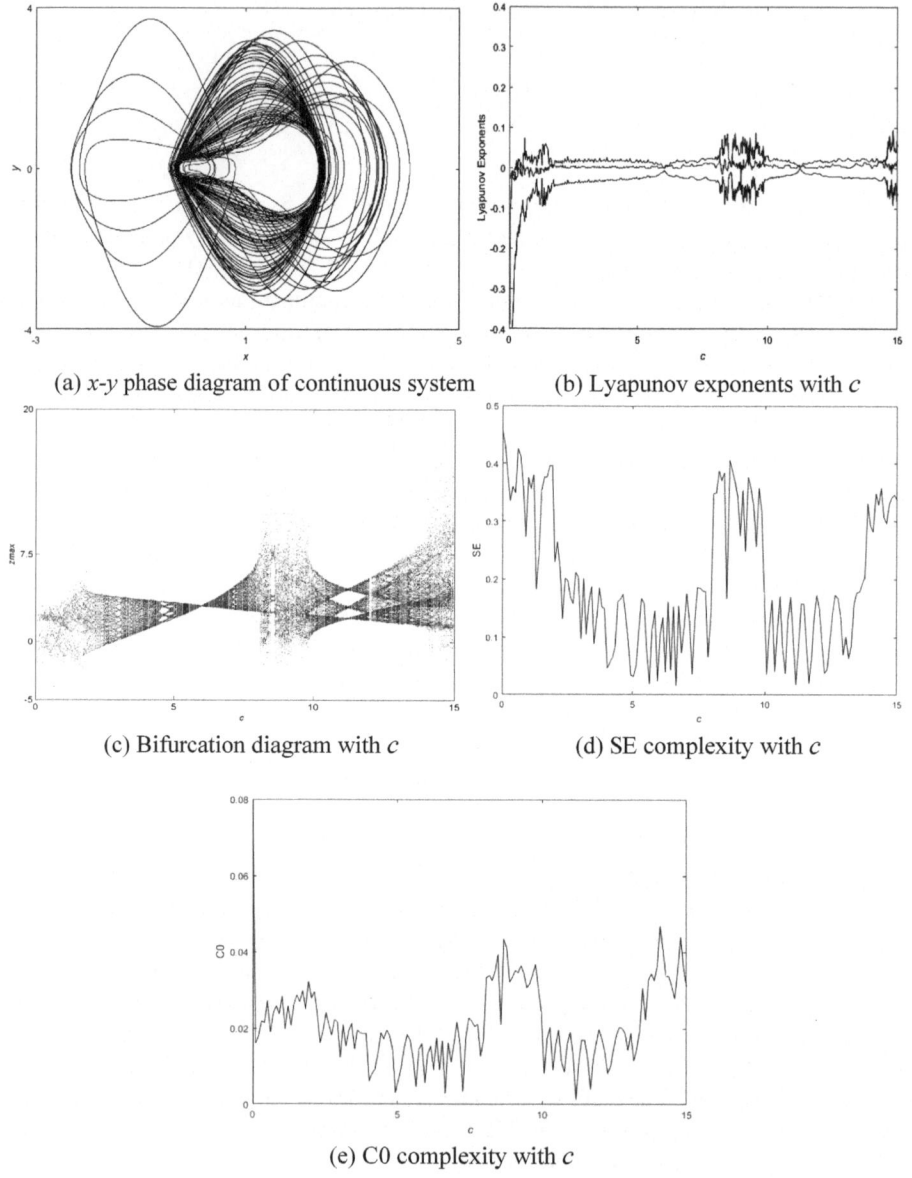

(a) *x-y* phase diagram of continuous system   (b) Lyapunov exponents with *c*

(c) Bifurcation diagram with *c*   (d) SE complexity with *c*

(e) C0 complexity with *c*

Fig. 2. Simulation diagram of Nose-Hoover

3 The Nose-Hoover Continuous System Under the Control of Discrete Sequence of Gingerbreadman System

3.1 Dynamical Analysis

In this paper, the basic mathematical model of nose-hoover system under Gingerbreadman discrete sequence control parameters is shown in Eq. (3).

$$\begin{cases} \dot{x} = y \\ \dot{y} = -x + bxy \\ \dot{z} = c - y^2 \end{cases} \tag{3}$$

As can be seen from Eq. (3), a parameter b is introduced in the second line and the second item of the original equation. If b is equal to 1, it is not fundamentally different from the mathematical model of nose-hoover system. However, this part of this paper also considers the influence of system parameter b. This article will illustrate the advantages and disadvantages of the new system through the following introduction. Gingerbreadman discrete system was numerically simulated to obtain a series of Xn discrete sequences, some of which are shown in Table 1. When the time interval $t = 0.5$ s is taken, the Lyapunov exponents of the system can be obtained by calculating that $LE_1 = 0.1295$, $LE_2 = 0$, and $LE_3 = -0.1411$. The Lyapunov dimension of nose-hoover system under the control of discrete sequence is further calculated to be 2.9179, and the parameter c under the control of discrete sequence is finally shown to be 7.7. In the experimental simulation, it was found that when the time-varying parameter c in the system was moved to the numerical solution algorithm of nose-hoover equation, the parameter c did not change finally, but it affected the simulation results, indicating that the stability of the chaotic system was affected by many factors. Figure 3(a) shows the curve of Lyapunov exponents changing with parameter b, by comparing Fig. 2(b) of the original Nose-Hoover system, it is found that the peak value of Lyapunov exponents shown in Fig. 3(a) increases with parameter b, and Lyapunov exponent value is always greater than 0, indicating that the Nose-Hoover system found in this paper under the control of Gingerbreadman discrete system has better chaotic characteristics. In addition, it can be seen that, in the same region [0, 15], the exponential waveform of Lyapunov exponents in the range of [1.025, 8.15] as shown in Fig. 3(a) is roughly the same as the waveform in the range of [0, 11.28] as shown in Fig. 2(b). The exponential curve of the former is half as compressed as that of the latter, and the entire change period is twice as long as that of the original system. By referring to the bifurcation diagram of the system changing with parameter b, as shown in Fig. 3(b), the time step is still 0.5 s. However, by comparing Figs. 3(b) and Fig. 2 (c), it is found that the chaotic characteristics of the system are different even under the control of changing parameters. In order to study how this graph is formed, and under two conditions (control parameters before numerical solution and control parameters after numerical solution), the number of plot points is about $300 \sim 500$, which can be simulated in Fig. 3(b), and the trajectory shown, it can be seen that even if the same parameter c, the value is located before or after the solution of the system numerical value, it will affect the trajectory of the system, and finally the overall phase diagram of the drawing will be different. We can see that the shape of the whole system has changed, which is an attractor with two diamond-shaped torus, and from the basic observation of chaotic attractors, it can be judged that the system still has chaotic characteristics [41, 42].

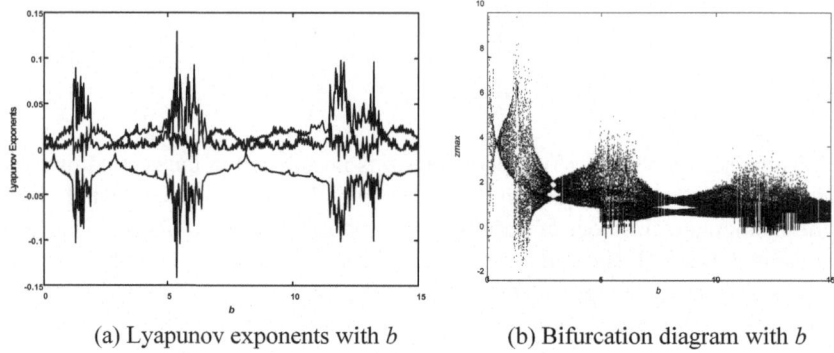

(a) Lyapunov exponents with b (b) Bifurcation diagram with b

Fig. 3. Analysis of Nose-Hoover system under discrete sequence control

Table 1. The Xn sequence generated by the discrete system corresponds to the value of the continuous system parameter C_i.

$Xn(n = 1, 2, 3……)$	Continuous system corresponding parameter Ci ($i = 1, 2, 3……$)	
0.5	C1	0.5
−2.2	C2	−2,2
2.7	C3	2.7
5.9	C4	5.9
4.2	C5	4.2
−0.7	C6	−0.7
−2.5	C7	−2.5
4.2	C8	4.2
7.7	C9	7.7
……	……	

3.2   Comparative Analysis of the Nose-Hoover System Under the Condition of Parameter c in Two Cases

It can be seen from the above analysis that the phase diagram of the Nose-Hoover system has different chaotic characteristics under different conditions. The original hypothesis can be proved: The Nose-Hoover continuous system under the discrete sequence control of the discrete system Gingerbreadman has chaos characteristic.

Comparing phase diagram Fig. 2(a) with Fig. 3(a), it is found that the Nose-Hoover system under discrete sequence control is more convergent. In order to further analyze the trajectory changes of the Nose-Hoover system, the trajectories formed by the Nose-Hoover system at different stages are successively simulated. The trajectory phase diagrams drawn by different points in the simulation can be clearly understood and formed as shown in the Fig. 2(a). Of cause the process of the attractor shown in Fig. 2 (a) can be judged based on the periodic orbital theory of chaotic attractors [42, 43]. When analyzing the formation of the phase diagram of the Nose-Hoover system, as shown in Fig. 2(a), the trajectory first forms two cycles from the middle part (the number of drawing points is around 300–500), and then enters a cycle of the right half (The number of drawing points is around 300–800), then the middle part is carried out for five cycles, and then enters the left half (the number of drawing points is around 300–1300). After completing four cycles (the number of drawing points is around 300–1900), it starts to enter the three periods of the middle part (the number of drawing points is around 300–2400), and then enters the period of the right half (the number of drawing points is around 300–2600), then enter the middle part of the three cycles (the number of drawing points is around 300–3150), then enter a cycle of the right half, then enter the three cycles of the middle part, and then enter the middle part, which can be repeated and a complete attractor phase diagram of the Nose-Hoover system as shown in Fig. 2(a) is obtained. When the plotting points number of this system is about 300 ~ 500, 300 ~ 800, 300 ~ 1500, 300 ~ 1900, the trajectory of Nose-Hoover is shown in Fig. 4(a), (b), (c), (d) respectively.

Comparing the trajectories of the Nose-Hoover system under discrete sequence control Fig. 3(b) and the trajectory of the Nose-Hoover system Fig. 4(a), (b), (c), (d), found by discrete system, it is found that the trajectory of Nose-Hoover system under the control of sequence generated by discrete system is simpler, the graph is more convergent, and the shape is more stable.

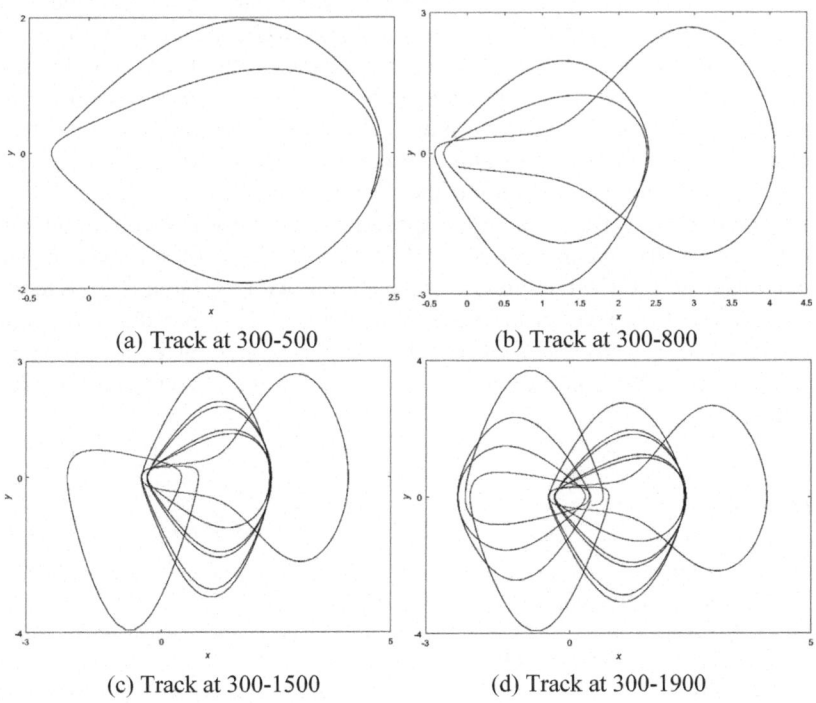

(a) Track at 300-500   (b) Track at 300-800

(c) Track at 300-1500   (d) Track at 300-1900

Fig. 4. Trajectory map of the formation process of Nose-Hoover system in each cycle

4   Conclusion

When studying the chaotic characteristics of a certain system, it can be studied by comparing the Lyapunov exponent, bifurcation diagram, complexity and other methods of the system. It can also be directly observed and compared with the original ones that have proved chaotic, and the formation process of the chaotic system can be understood. Many mathematicians and scientists have specific research on the formation control analysis of specific chaotic phenomena. For example, the literature [39] is the discovery of the Nose-Hoover system and the preliminary analysis process. Based on the original chaotic system, this paper makes further research and discovery by using new methods and new developments in chaotic systems in recent years. The proof process for specific mathematical models will not be described here.

The steady state value of the Lyapunov exponent of the Nose-Hoover system mentioned in this paper is larger under the condition of discrete sequence control, and the specific shape of the phase diagram also changes in macroscopic observation. An idea can be put forward: in the process of a series of changes in parameters, the Nose-Hoover system converges toward the periodic trajectory of the middle part of the Nose-Hoover system in Fig. 4.

The above experimental simulations show that the chaotic characteristics of the Nose-Hoover system change under the control parameters of the discrete sequence generated by the discrete system Gingerbreadman, and a chaotic attractor phase diagram different from the previous one is found in this sequence. The figure is in the shape of two side by side diamonds. It is found that the Nose-Hoover system under the control of Gingerbreadman discrete sequence has more stable chaotic characteristics. and has some chaotic characteristics of Gingerbreadman discrete system and Nose-Hoover continuous system as a whole. For example, it has the symmetry of the Gingerbreadman discrete system to some extent. The Lyapunov exponent of the Nose-Hoover continuous system changes with the parameters, the bifurcation diagram of the system with the parameter changes, and the complexity of the system with the parameter changes have certain similarity. However, in the detailed analysis, it is found that the continuous system controlled by discrete sequence has larger Lyapunov exponent value and better complexity under some discrete sequences, and the chaotic characteristics are more stable.

References

1. Hall, D., Proudfoot, L.: Memory and identity among irish migrants in nineteenth-century stawell. Comput. Eng. Appl. **44**(3), 47–49 (2008)
2. Masuda, N., Aihara, K.: Cryptosystems with discretized chaotic maps. IEEE Trans. Circ. Syst. I Fundam. Theory Appl. **49**(1), 28–40 (2002)
3. Habutsu, T., Nishio, Y., Sasase, I., Mori, S.: A secret key cryptosystem by iterating a chaotic map. In: Davies, D.W. (ed.) EUROCRYPT 1991. LNCS, vol. 547, pp. 127–140. Springer, Heidelberg (1991). https://doi.org/10.1007/3-540-46416-6_11
4. Bianco M E, Reed D A. Encryption system based on chaos theory: US, US5048086[P] (1991)

5. Bianco, M.E., Mayhew, G.L.: High speed encryption system and method: US, US 5365588 A[P] (1994)
6. Deffeyes, K.S.: Encryption system and method. US (1991)
7. Pecora, L.M., Carroll, T.L.: Paper 9–synchronization in chaotic systems. Phys. Rev. Lett. **64**(8), 821–824 (1990)
8. Pecora, L.M., Carroll, T.L.: Driving systems with chaotic signals. Phys. Rev. A **44**(4), 2374 (1991)
9. Carroll, T.L., Pecora, L.M.: A circuit for studying the synchronization of chaotic systems. Int. J. Bifurcat. Chaos **2**(3), 659–667 (2011)
10. Carroll, T.L., Pecora, L.M.: Cascading synchronized chaotic systems. Phys. D Nonlinear Phenom. **67**(1–3), 126–140 (1993)
11. Pecora, L.M., Carroll, T.L.: System for producing synchronized signals, US5245660[P] (1993)
12. Pecora, L.M., Carroll, T.L.: Cascading synchronized chaotic systems: US, US5379346[P] (1995)
13. Carroll, T.L., Pecora, L.M., Heagy, J.F.: Synchronization of nonautonomous chaotic systems: Patent Application Department of the Navy, Washington, DC. US5473694[P] (1995)
14. Cuomo, K.M., Oppenheim, A.V.: Communication using synchronized chaotic systems: US, US5291555[P] (1994)
15. Cuomo, K.M., Oppenheim, A.V.: Circuit implementation of synchronized chaos with applications to communications. Controlling Chaos **71**(1), 153–156 (1996)
16. Murali, K., Lakshmanan, M.: Transmission of signals by synchronization in a chaotic Van der Pol-Duffing oscillator. Phys. Rev. E Stat. Phys. Plasmas Fluids Relat. Interdisc. Topics **48**(3), R1624–R1626 (1993)
17. Kocarev, L., Halle, K.S., Eckert, K., et al.: Experimental demonstration of secure communications via chaotic synchronization. Int. J. Bifurcat. Chaos **2**(03), 709–713 (1992)
18. Parlitz, U., Chua, L.O., Kocarev, Lj., et al.: Transmission of digital signals by chaotic synchronization. Int. J. Bifurcat. Chaos **2**(2), 973–977 (2011)
19. Papadimitriou, S., Bezerianos, A., Bountis, T.: Secure communication with chaotic systems of difference equations. IEEE Trans. Comput. **46**(1), 27–38 (1997)
20. Bernstein, G.M., Lieberman, M.A.: Method and apparatus for generating secure random numbers using chaos: US, US5007087[P] (1991)
21. Gutowitz, H.: Cryptography with dynamical systems. In: Boccara, N., Goles, E., Martinez, S., Picco, P. (eds.) Cellular Automata and Cooperative Systems. NATO ASI Series (Series C: Mathematical and Physical Sciences), pp. 237–274. Springer, Dordrecht (1993). https://doi.org/10.1007/978-94-011-1691-6_21
22. Gutowitz, H.A.: Method and apparatus for encryption, decryption and authentication using dynamical systems: US, US5365589[P] (1994)
23. Pichler, F., Scharinger, J.: Ciphering by Bernoulli-shifts in finite abelian groups
24. Götz, M., Kelber, K., Schwarz, W.: Discrete-time chaotic encryption systems. I. Statistical design approach. IEEE Trans. Circ. Syst. I Fundam. Theory Appl. **44**(10), 963–970 (1997)
25. Kotulski, Z., Szczepański, J., et al.: Application of discrete chaotic dynamical systems in cryptography—DCC method. Int. J. Bifurcat. Chaos **9**(06), 1121–1135 (2011)
26. Li, T.Y., Yorke, J.A.: Period three implies chaos. Am. Math. Mon. **82**(82), 985 (1975)
27. Da, L.H., Guo, F.D.: Composite nonlinare descrete chaotic dynamical systems and stream cipher systems. Acta Electronica Sin. **31**(8), 1209–1212 (2003)
28. Fanzhen, W., Guoyuan, Q., Zengqiang, C., et al.: On a four-winged chaotic attractor. Acta Phys. Sin. **56**(6), 3137–3144 (2007)

29. Qi, G., Chen, G., Wyk, M.A.V., et al.: A four-wing chaotic attractor generated from a new 3-D quadratic autonomous system. Chaos, Solitons Fractals **38**(3), 705–721 (2008)
30. Chua, L.O., Roska, T.: The CNN paradigm. IEEE Trans. Circ. Syst. I Fundam. Theory Appl. **40**(3), 147–156 (1993)
31. Suykens, J.A.K., Vandewalle, J.: Generation of n-double scrolls (n = 1, 2, 3, 4...). IEEE Trans. Circ. Syst. I Fundam. Theory Appl. **40**(11), 861–867 (1993)
32. Jinhu, H.F., Yu, X., et al.: Generating 3-D multi-scroll chaotic attractors: a hysteresis series switching method. Automatica **40**(10), 1677–1687 (2004)
33. Lu, J., Yu, X., Chen, G.: Generating chaotic attractors with multiple merged basins of attraction: a switching piecewise-linear control approach. IEEE Trans. Circ. Syst. I Fundam. Theory Appl. **50**(2), 198–207 (2003)
34. Qi, G., Du, S., Chen, G., et al.: On a four-dimensional chaotic system. Chaos, Solitons Fractals **23**(5), 1671–1682 (2005)
35. Li, Y.J., Wen, W.Q.: Research of Judging the Chaotic Characteristics with the Lyapunov Exponents. J. Wuhan Univ. Technol. (2004)
36. May, R.M.: Simple mathematical models with very complicated dynamics. Nature **261** (5560), 459 (1976)
37. Huang, Y., Zhang, P., Zhao, W.: Novel grid multiwing butterfly chaotic attractors and their circuit design. IEEE Trans. Circ. Syst. II Express Briefs **62**(5), 496–500 (2017)
38. Ye, X., Mou, J., Luo, C., et al.: Dynamics analysis of Wien-bridge hyperchaotic memristive circuit system. Nonlinear Dyn. **92**(3), 923–933 (2018)
39. Holian, B.L., Hoover, W.G.: Numerical test of the Liouville equation. Phys. Rev. **34**(5), 4229–4237 (1986)
40. Wolf, A., Swift, J.B., Swinney, H.L., et al.: Determining Lyapounov exponents from a time series. Phys. D Nonlinear Phenom. **16**(3), 285–317 (1985)
41. Shui-Sheng, Q.: Study on periodic orbit theory of chaotic attractors (I). J. Circ. Syst. (2003)
42. Shui-Sheng, Q.: Study on periodic orbit theory of chaotic attractors (II). J. Circ. Syst. (2004)
43. Qiu, S.S.: A cell model of chaotic attractor. In: IEEE International Symposium on Circuits and Systems. IEEE Xplore, 1997:1033-1036, vol. 2 (2002)

Dynamical Analysis of the Fractional-Order Memristive Band Pass Filter Chaotic Circuit

Chenguang Ma[1,2], Xiaoqiang Yu[1,2], Feifei Yang[1,2], and Jun Mou[1,2(✉)]

[1] School of Information Science and Engineering,
Dalian Polytechnic University, Dalian 116034, China
[2] School of Physics and Electronics, Central South University,
Changsha 410083, China
moujun@csu.edu.cn

Abstract. In this paper, a memristive band pass filter chaotic circuit system was designed based on a band pass filter circuit. The system numerical solutions were calculated by using the Adomian decomposition (ADM) algorithm. On this basis, the dynamical characteristics of the system were analyzed by means of bifurcation diagram, Lyapunov exponent spectrum, phase diagram of chaotic attractor, Poincaré section, SE (spectral entropy) and C_0 complexity algorithm. The results of analysis show that the fractional-order memristive chaotic system has richer dynamical behaviors compared with the integer order system. This paper provides a theoretical basis for the application of fractional-order memristor chaotic circuits in the fields of secure communication and information security.

Keywords: ADM algorithm · Fractional-order system ·
Dynamic characteristic · Memristor chaotic circuit

1 Introduction

Memristor is the fourth basic electrical element besides resistance, capacitance and inductance. The chaotic circuit constructed by memrisor can be widely used in the fields of physics, biomedicine, secure communication and information security [1–3], so the construction of well-performing memristor chaotic circuits has attracted extensive attention of scholars [4–6]. Memristor is a device that describes the relationship between charge and magnetic flux, which is generally divided into charge-controlled memristor and magnetic-controlled memristor. The main difference is the difference in the dominant quantity, the dominant quantity of the charge-controlled memristor is the charge, and the magnetic-control memristor plays the dominant volume is the magnetic flux [7, 8]. At present, although commercial memristor has not yet begun to be applied, the study of equivalent circuit to achieve the function of memristor has been vigorously carried out. So far, many chaotic circuits based on memristor have been proposed. Among them, Ye et al. designed a hyperchaotic system based on the Venn-bridge self-oscillating circuit, and analyzed the dynamic characteristics of the system by using SE and C_0 complexity algorithms [9]. A hyperchaotic memristor circuit based on Lorentz

© ICST Institute for Computer Sciences, Social Informatics and Telecommunications Engineering 2019
Published by Springer Nature Switzerland AG 2019. All Rights Reserved
J. Jin et al. (Eds.): GreeNets 2019, LNICST 282, pp. 181–192, 2019.
https://doi.org/10.1007/978-3-030-21730-3_20

system was constructed by Ruan et al. and its dynamical characteristics was analyzed [10]. Compared with integer order memristor chaotic system, fractional-order memristor chaotic system often has more complex dynamic characteristics. In recent years, the research on fractional-order memristor chaotic systems has become a hot topic. The definition of fractional calculus mainly includes Riemann-Liouville and Caputo. Up to now, there are three main methods to solve fractional-order chaotic systems, namely frequency-domain analysis [11], predictive correction [12] (ABM) and Adomian [13] algorithm (ADM). Among them, ADM algorithm has the superiority like high accuracy, fast convergence, does not need discrete processing, and occupies less computer memory. So ADM algorithm is widely used in the analysis of fractional-order chaotic systems. Sun et al. made a detailed analysis of the dynamic characteristics of fractional-order simplified unified chaotic system by means of direct observation of phase diagram, calculation of power spectrum and other methods [14]. Numerical solution of the fractional-order diffusionless Lorentz system was analyzed by He and others using ADM algorithm. [15]. Xu et al. used ADM algorithm to analyze the dynamic characteristics of simplified unified fractional-order chaotic system [14]. These studies show that fractional-order chaotic systems usually have more complex dynamic characteristic than integer-order chaotic systems. And the SE and C_0 complexity algorithms can be used to evaluate the randomness of the system [15, 16]. Bao et al. designed a simple third-order memristor chaotic circuit and analyzed its chaotic characteristics in detail [17], but the fractional-order system is not analyzed. Therefore, based on this circuit, a new fractional-order memristor band-pass filter chaotic circuit system is designed and its dynamic characteristics are analyzed in detail in this paper.

In this paper, the dynamic characteristics of fractional-order memristor band pass filter chaotic circuits are analyzed. In the first part, a fractional-order memristor chaotic circuit is defined based on the third-order memristor band pass filter chaotic circuit. The second part describes the ADM algorithm in detail, and analyzes the parameter iterative relation of fractional-order memristor chaotic circuit, as well as the numerical accurate solution of the system. In the third part, the dynamic characteristics of the fractional-order system are analyzed. The fourth part is the conclusion.

2   Memristive BPF Chaotic Circuit System

An improved charge-controlled memristor equivalent circuit is shown in Fig. 1, which is composed of a capacitor, two multipliers, three resistors and two op-amplifiers. V and I represent the voltage and current at the input port, respectively. V_0 represents the voltage across the integral capacitor C_0, and g is the proportional coefficient between the multipliers. The memristor can be expressed as:

$$\begin{cases} i = W(V_0)v = \frac{1}{R_c}\left(1 - gV_0^2\right)v \\ \frac{dV_0}{dt} = f(V_0, v) = -\frac{1}{R_bC_0}V_0 - \frac{1}{R_aC_0}v \end{cases} \tag{1}$$

Figure 2(a) shows a band-pass filter circuit consisting of 4 resistors, 2 capacitors and an op-amplifier. The filter circuit is similar to a typical Venn oscillating circuit, but

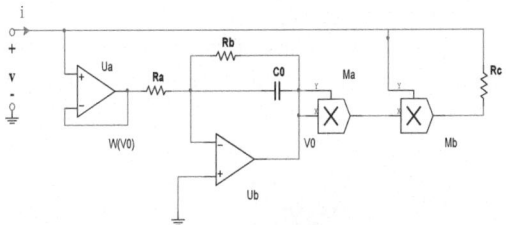

Fig. 1. Improved charge-controlled memristor

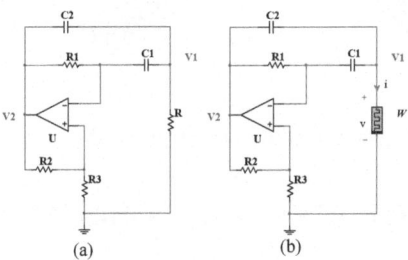

Fig. 2. BPF chaotic circuit and memristive BPF chaotic circuit

the topological structure is different. Replace the resistor R in Fig. 2(a) with the improved charge-controlled memristor W shown in Fig. 1, the chaotic circuit of memristive band-pass filter as shown in Fig. 2(b) will obtained. The third-order memristor chaotic circuit consists of 6 resistors, 3 op-amplifiers, 3 capacitors and 2 multipliers.

According to the model of memristor and the memristor circuit, based on Kirchhoff's law and ohm's law, the circuit equation of the system can be obtained as:

$$\begin{cases} \frac{dV_0}{dt} = -\frac{1}{R_b C_0} V_0 - \frac{1}{R_a C_0} V_1 \\ \frac{dV_1}{dt} = \frac{1-gV_0^2}{(k-1)R_c C_2} V_1 - \frac{1}{R_1}\left(\frac{1}{C_1} + \frac{1}{kC_2}\right)V_2 , \\ \frac{dV_2}{dt} = \frac{k(1-gV_0^2)}{(k-1)R_c C_2} V_1 - \frac{1}{R_1}\left(\frac{1}{C_1} + \frac{1}{C_2}\right)V_2 \end{cases} \tag{2}$$

Where, $k = 1 + R_2/R_3$, V_0, V_1, V_2 are the potentials of the three nodes in the circuit, let $x = V_0$, $y = V_1$, $z = V_2$, $u = du/d\tau$ ($u \equiv x, y, z$), $C_1 = C_2 = C$, $\tau = t/R_1 C$, $a = R_1 C/R_b C_0$, $b = R_1 C/R_a C_0$, $c = R_1/R_c$. By substituting them into Eq. (2) and doing dimensionless processing of the circuit parameters, the dimensionless system equation can be obtained as:

$$\begin{cases} \dot{x} = -ax - by \\ \dot{y} = c(1 - gx^2)y/(k-1) - (k+1)z/k . \\ \dot{z} = kc(1 - gx^2)y/(k-1) - 2z \end{cases} \tag{3}$$

Let $a = 8$, $b = 80$, $c = 500/3$, $g = 0.1$, $k = 21$. The attractor phase diagram is shown in Fig. 3. The Lyapunov exponents of the system is (1.0893, 0, −6.2240), while the Lyapunov dimension $D_L = 2.175$, which indicates that the system is in chaotic state.

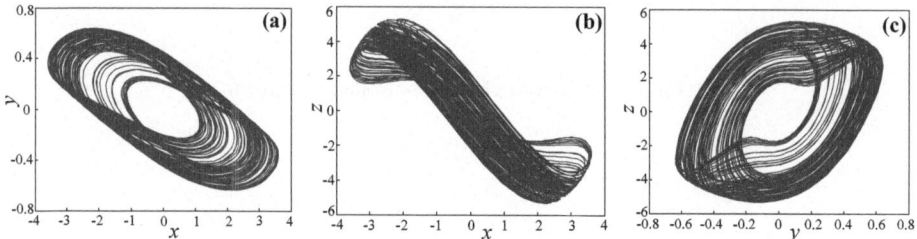

Fig. 3. Attractor phase diagram (a) x-y plane, (b) x-z plane, (c) y-z plane

3   Numerical Analysis of Fractional-Order Memristor Chaotic Circuit

3.1   Adomian Decomposition Algorithm

For a certain fractional-order chaotic system $*D_{to}^q x(t) = f(x(t)) + g(t)$. where, $x(t) = [x_1(t), x_2(t), \ldots, x_n(t)]^T$ is the system state variable. For a autonomous systems, $g(t) = [g_1(t), g_2(t), \ldots, g_n(t)]^T$ is a constant. $f(x(t))$ contains linear part and nonlinear part. Then, the system equation can be decomposed into:

$$\begin{cases} {}^*D_{t_0}^q x(t) = Lx(t) + Nx(t) + g(x(t)) \\ x^{(k)}(t_0^+) = b_k, k = 0, 1, 2 \cdots m-1, \\ m \in N, m-1 < q \le m \end{cases} \quad (4)$$

Where, $^*D_{to}^q$ is a q-order Caputo differential operator, and L and N are the linear and nonlinear parts of the system respectively. The b_k is the initial value. The solutions of equations as follows can be obtained after applying Riemann-Liouville fractional integral operator J_{to}^q on both sides of the equations.

$$x = J_{t_0}^q Lx + J_{t_0}^q Nx + J_{t_0}^q g + \sum_{k=0}^{m-1} \frac{(t-t_0)^k}{k!}. \quad (5)$$

According to the principle of Adomian decomposition method, the nonlinear part can be decomposed into:

$$A_j^i = \frac{1}{i!} \left[\frac{d^i}{d\lambda^i} N\left(\sum_{k=0}^i (\lambda)^k x_j^k \right) \right]_{\lambda=0}, \quad (6)$$

Where, $i = 0, 1, \ldots, j = 0, 1, \ldots n$. Thus, the nonlinear term can be expressed as:

$$Nx = \sum_{i=0}^{\infty} A^i(x^0, x^1, x^2, \ldots, x^i), \qquad (7)$$

Therefore, the solution of Eq. (4) is:

$$x = \sum_{i=0}^{\infty} x^i = J_{t_0}^q L \sum_{i=0}^{\infty} x^i + J_{t_0}^q \sum_{i=0}^{\infty} A^i + J_{t_0}^q g + \sum_{k=0}^{m-1} \frac{(t-t_0)^k}{k!}. \qquad (8)$$

And its operation relation is:

$$\begin{cases} x^0 = J_{t_0}^q g + \sum_{k=0}^{m-1} \frac{(t-t_0)^k}{k!} \\ x^1 = J_{t_0}^q L x^0 + J_{t_0}^q A^0(x^0) \\ x^2 = J_{t_0}^q L x^1 + J_{t_0}^q A^1(x^0, x^1) \\ \ldots \\ x^i = J_{t_0}^q L x^{i-1} + J_{t_0}^q A^{i-1}(x^0, x^1, \ldots, x^{i-1}) \end{cases} \qquad (9)$$

3.2 Numerical Solutions to the System Equations

From the system (3), the system equation of the fractional-order memristor chaotic circuit can be obtained by

$$\begin{cases} {}^*D_{t_0}^q x_1 = -ax_1 - bx_2 \\ {}^*D_{t_0}^q x_2 = c(1 - gx_1^2)x_2/(k-1) - (k+1)x_3/k, \\ {}^*D_{t_0}^q x_3 = kc(1 - gx_1^2)x_2/(k-1) - 2x_3 \end{cases} \qquad (10)$$

Where, q is the order of the system, x, y and z represent the state variable of the system. Based on the Adomian algorithm, the linear and nonlinear parts of the system can be decomposed as:

$$\begin{bmatrix} Lx_1 \\ Lx_2 \\ Lx_3 \end{bmatrix} = \begin{bmatrix} -ax_1 - bx_2 \\ cx_2/(k-1) - (k+1)x_3/k \\ kcx_2/(k-1) - 2x_3 \end{bmatrix}, \quad \begin{bmatrix} Nx_1 \\ Nx_2 \\ Nx_3 \end{bmatrix} = \begin{bmatrix} 0 \\ -dx_1^2 x_2 \\ -kdx_1^2 x_2 \end{bmatrix},$$

$$\begin{bmatrix} g_1 \\ g_2 \\ g_3 \end{bmatrix} = \begin{bmatrix} 0 \\ 0 \\ 0 \end{bmatrix} \qquad (11)$$

Where, $d = cg/(k-1)$. Therefore:

$$A_2 = -dx_1^2 x_2, A_3 = -kdx_1^2 x_2 \tag{12}$$

The nonlinear term $x_1^2 x_2$ is decomposed according to the Eq. (6), and the first 5 items are intercepted on the premise of ensuring the calculation accuracy, which can be expressed as:

$$\begin{cases}
A_2^0 = -x_2^0(x_1^0)^2, \\
A_2^1 = -x_2^1(x_1^0)^2 - 2x_2^0 x_1^1 x_1^0, \\
A_2^2 = -x_2^2(x_1^0)^2 - 2x_2^1 x_1^1 x_1^0 - 2x_2^0 x_1^2 x_1^0 - x_2^0(x_1^1)^2, \\
A_2^3 = -x_2^3(x_1^0)^2 - 2x_2^2 x_1^1 x_1^0 - x_2^1(x_1^1)^2 - 2x_2^1 x_1^2 x_1^0 - 2x_2^0 x_1^3 x_1^0 - 2x_2^0 x_1^2 x_1^1, \\
A_2^4 = -x_2^4(x_1^0)^2 - 2x_2^3 x_1^1 x_1^0 - x_2^2(x_1^1)^2 - 2x_2^2 x_1^2 x_1^0 - 2x_2^1 x_1^2 x_1^1 - 2x_2^1 x_1^3 x_1^0 - 2x_2^0 x_1^4 x_1^0 - 2x_2^0 x_1^3 x_1^1 - x_2^0(x_1^2)^2
\end{cases} \tag{13}$$

$$\begin{cases}
A_3^0 = -x_2^0(x_1^0)^2, \\
A_3^1 = -x_2^1(x_1^0)^2 - 2x_2^0 x_1^1 x_1^0, \\
A_3^2 = -x_2^2(x_1^0)^2 - 2x_2^1 x_1^1 x_1^0 - 2x_2^0 x_1^2 x_1^0 - x_2^0(x_1^1)^2, \\
A_3^3 = -x_2^3(x_1^0)^2 - 2x_2^2 x_1^1 x_1^0 - x_2^1(x_1^1)^2 - 2x_2^1 x_1^2 x_1^0 - 2x_2^0 x_1^3 x_1^0 - 2x_2^0 x_1^3 x_3^3, \\
A_3^4 = -x_2^4(x_1^0)^2 - 2x_2^3 x_1^1 x_1^0 - x_2^2(x_1^1)^2 - 2x_2^2 x_1^2 x_1^0 - 2x_2^1 x_1^2 x_1^1 - 2x_2^1 x_1^3 x_1^0 - 2x_2^0 x_1^4 x_1^0 - 2x_2^0 x_1^3 x_1^1 - x_2^0(x_1^2)^2.
\end{cases} \tag{14}$$

$$\begin{cases}
x_1^1 = (-ax_1^0 - bx_2^0)\frac{(t-t_0)^q}{\Gamma(q+1)} \\
x_2^1 = [c(1 - g(x_1^0)^2)x_2^0/(k-1) - (k+1)x_3^0/k]\frac{(t-t_0)^q}{\Gamma(q+1)} \\
x_3^1 = [kc(1 - g(x_1^0)^2)x_2^0/(k-1) - 2x_3^0]\frac{(t-t_0)^q}{\Gamma(q+1)}
\end{cases} \tag{15}$$

Equation (17) is obtained from the initial conditions, where $x_j^0 (j = 1, 2, 3)$ is the initial value of the system (4) and $h = t - t_0$. Similarly, the remaining three terms can be obtained, so the numerical solution of the system is

$$\tilde{x}_j(t) = x_j^0 + x_j^1 + x_j^2 + x_j^3 + x_j^4 \tag{16}$$

Let

$$\begin{cases}
c_1^0 = x_1^0 \\
c_2^0 = x_2^0 \\
c_3^0 = x_3^0
\end{cases} \tag{17}$$

$$\begin{cases}
c_1^1 = -ac_1^0 - bc_2^0, \\
c_2^1 = cc_2^0/(k-1) - (k+1)c_3^0/k - dc_2^0(c_1^0)^2 \\
c_3^1 = kcc_2^0/(k-1) - 2c_3^0 - kdc_2^0(c_1^0)^2
\end{cases} \tag{18}$$

$$\begin{cases} c_1^2 = -ac_1^1 - bc_2^1 \\ c_2^2 = cc_2^1/(k-1) - (k+1)c_3^1/k - d[c_2^1(c_1^0)^2 - 2c_2^0c_1^1c_1^0] \\ c_3^2 = kcc_2^1/(k-1) - 2c_3^1 - kd[c_2^1(c_1^0)^2 - 2c_2^0c_1^1c_1^0] \end{cases} \quad (19)$$

$$\begin{cases} c_1^3 = -ac_1^2 - bc_2^2, \\ c_2^3 = cc_2^2/(k-1) - (k+1)c_3^2/k - dc_2^2(c_1^0)^2 - d[(2c_2^1c_1^1c_1^0 + c_2^0(c_1^1)^2)\frac{\Gamma(2q+1)}{\Gamma^2(q+1)} + 2c_2^0c_1^2c_1^0] \\ c_3^3 = kcc_2^2/(k-1) - 2c_3^2 - kdc_2^2(c_1^0)^2 - kd[(2c_2^1c_1^1c_1^0 + c_2^0(c_1^1)^2)\frac{\Gamma(2q+1)}{\Gamma^2(q+1)} + 2c_2^0c_1^2c_1^0] \end{cases}$$
$$(20)$$

$$\begin{cases} c_1^4 = -ac_1^3 - bc_2^3 \\ c_2^4 = cc_2^3/(k-1) - (k+1)c_3^3/k - d[c_2^3(c_1^0)^2 + 2c_2^0c_1^3c_1^0 + c_2^1(c_1^1)^2\frac{\Gamma(3q+1)}{\Gamma^3(q+1)}] \\ \quad + (2c_2^2c_1^1c_1^0 + 2c_2^1c_1^2c_1^0 + 2c_2^0c_1^1c_1^2)\frac{\Gamma(3q+1)}{\Gamma(2q+1)\Gamma(q+1)} \\ c_3^4 = kcc_2^3/(k-1) - 2c_3^3 - kd[c_2^3(c_1^0)^2 + 2c_2^0c_1^3c_1^0 + c_2^1(c_1^1)^2\frac{\Gamma(3q+1)}{\Gamma^3(q+1)}] \\ \quad + (2c_2^2c_1^1c_1^0 + 2c_2^1c_1^2c_1^0 + 2c_2^0c_1^1c_1^2)\frac{\Gamma(3q+1)}{\Gamma(2q+1)\Gamma(q+1)} \end{cases} \quad (21)$$

Therefore, the Eq. (16) is same as Eq. (22) as follow:

$$\tilde{x}_j(t) = c_j^0 + c_j^1\frac{(t-t_0)^q}{\Gamma(q+1)} + c_j^2\frac{(t-t_0)^{2q}}{\Gamma(2q+1)} + c_j^3\frac{(t-t_0)^{3q}}{\Gamma(3q+1)} + c_j^4\frac{(t-t_0)^{4q}}{\Gamma(4q+1)} \quad (22)$$

In the process of solving, the integral interval needs to be divided into small sections (t_k, t_{k+1}), and the result obtained will be the initial value of the next section (t_{k+1}, t_{k+2}). Let $h = (t_k - t_{k-1})$, a total of $(t_{k+1} - t_k)/(h-1)$ iterations is required.

4 Dynamic Analysis of Fractional-Order Memristor Chaotic Circuits

4.1 The Influence of Parameter a on the Dynamic Characteristics of the System

Let $q = 0.9$, and initial value $x_0 = [0, 0.000006, 0]$, $h = 0.001$, the phase diagram of the system is shown in Fig. 4. In this point the Lyapunov exponent is (1.8255, 0, −12.9251), with the Lyapunov dimension $D_L = 2.14$. The system is in a chaotic state at this time, due to a positive Lyapunov exponent. And the maximum Lyapunov exponent is larger than the maximum Lyapunov exponent of integer order. So the system has more complex chaotic characteristics.

If $q = 0.9$, the bifurcation diagram of the system when a changes from 7 to 11 is shown in Fig. 5(a). It can be seen from the bifurcation diagram that, when the parameters $a \in (7, 7.172)$ and $a \in (8.925, 11)$, the system is in a periodic state. However, when $a \in (7.172, 8.925)$, the system is in a chaotic state.

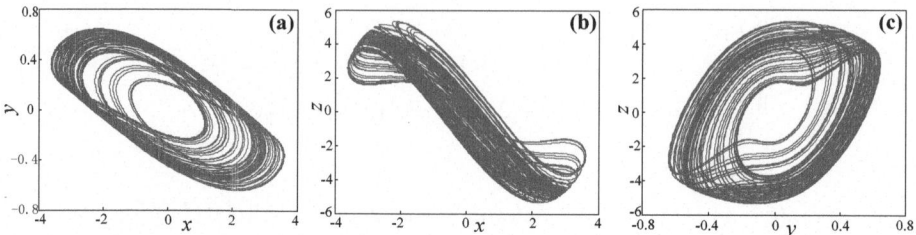

Fig. 4. Attractor phase diagram of system with $a = 8$ and $q = 0.9$ (a) x-y plane, (b) x-z plane, (c) y-z plane

Based on the ADM algorithm, QR decomposition method is used to calculate the Lyapunov exponent spectrum of the system varying with parameter a, as shown in Fig. 5(b). It can be seen from the figure that when $a \in (7.172, 8.925)$, the Lyapunov exponent of the system is positive and the system is in a chaotic state, which is corresponding to the bifurcation diagram. In particular, when $7.809 < a < 7.875$, the Lyapunov exponent of the system is small and the randomness of chaotic sequence is weak. The maximum Lyapunov exponent of the fractional order is greater than 2, while the maximum Lyapunov exponent of the integer order is less than 2. Therefore, the dynamic characteristics of the fractional order chaotic system are better than that of the corresponding integer order chaotic system.

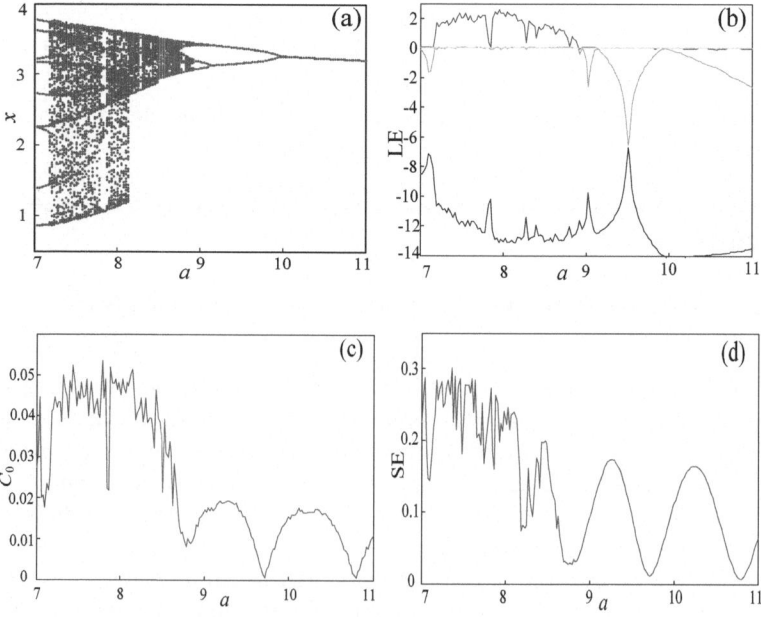

Fig. 5. The system varies with parameter a (a) Bifurcation diagram, (b) Lyapunov exponent spectrum, (c) C_0 complexity, (d) SE complexity

In order to further characterize the dynamic characteristics of the chaotic system, SE and C_0 complexity algorithms were used to obtain the complexity of the system varying with parameter a, as shown in Fig. 5(c) and (d). When $a \in (7.172, 8.9)$, system is periodic state, both SE and C_0 values are small. And when the system enters chaotic state, the complexity of the system increases and the fluctuation amplitude is large. The system enters the periodic state again when a in the $(8.9, 11)$. In this time SE and C_0 both change gently and gradually approach 0, which indicate the complexity of system' sequence decreases, that is, the randomness of chaotic sequence decreases.

4.2 Dynamic Characteristics of the System Varying with Order q

Set $a = 8$, q varying from 0.5 to 1, and keep other parameter values unchanged, the bifurcation diagram of the system is shown in Fig. 6(a). As can be seen from Fig. 6(a), when $q > 0.709$, the system enters a chaotic state through period-doubling bifurcation. Figure 6(b) shows the Lyapunov exponent spectrum of the system changing with the order q. Chaos characteristics of the system are mainly affected by the maximum Lyapunov exponent, so in order to show clarity, the minimum Lyapunov exponent curve is omitted from Fig. 6(b). It can also be seen from the Fig. 6(b) that the Lyapunov exponent increases with the increase of order q, and the minimum order of chaos generation is 0.709, which is completely corresponding to the bifurcation diagram.

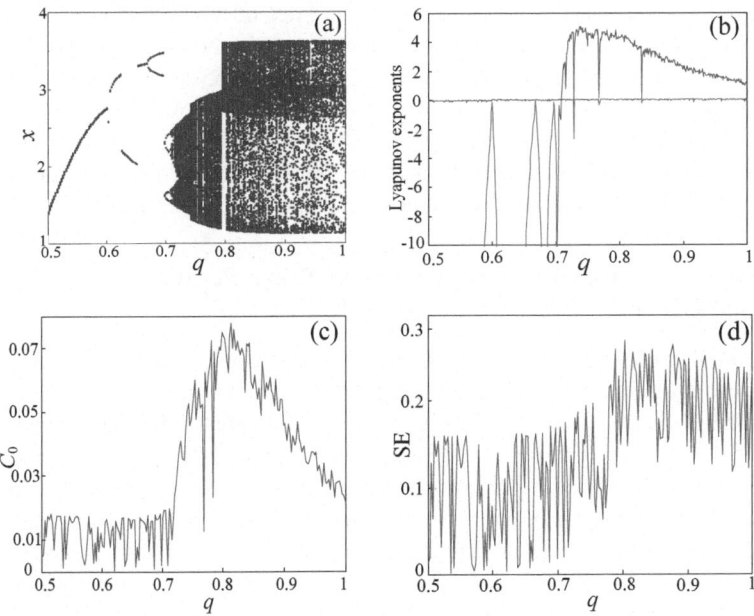

Fig. 6. The system varies with parameter q (a) Bifurcation diagram, (b) Lyapunov exponent spectra (c) C_0 complexity, (d) SE complexity

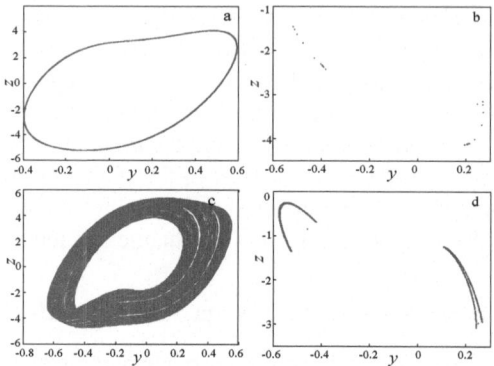

Fig. 7. Phase diagram and Poincaré section of the system in the y-z plane (a) Phase diagram of system on the y-z plane when $a = 8$, $q = 0.65$; (b) Poincaré section on the y-z plane when $a = 8$, $q = 0.65$; (c) Phase diagram of system on the y-z plane when $a = 8$, $q = 0.8$; (d) Poincaré section on the y-z plane when $a = 8$, $q = 0.65$

To further analyze the dynamic characteristics of the system, the C_0 and SE complexity of the system when the order q changes is analyzed, as shown in Fig. 6(c) and (d). It can be seen from the figure that when $0.5 < q < 0.709$, the system complexity is low, and when $q > 0.709$, the system enters the chaotic state system and the complexity increases, and the dynamic characteristics of the system are more complex.

The Fig. 7 shows the phase diagram of the system in the y-z plane and the Poincaré section of the y-z in the plane $x = 1$ when $a = 8$, $q = 0.65$ and $a = 8$, $q = 0.8$. When $a = 8$ and $q = 0.65$, the phase diagram of the system shows a limit cycle and the Poincaré section shows limit discrete point. When $a = 8$ and $q = 0.8$, chaotic attractors appear in the system. Poincaré section is the dense point of fractal structure, which corresponds to the bifurcation graph and Lyapunov exponent spectrum.

4.3 Dynamic Characteristics of the System When Parameters a and Order q Change Simultaneously

Let the initial value be $x_0 = [0, 0.000006, 0]$, $h = 0.001$, and keep other parameter values unchanged. Based on SE and C_0 algorithms, 2D SE and C_0 complexity contour lines can be obtained, as shown in Fig. 8(a) and (b). This figure represents the complexity of the system with different parameter a and q, and provides a reference for selecting appropriate system parameters and order numbers for better application. In Fig. 8, different colors indicate different complexity. The darker the color represents the higher the complexity and the higher the randomness of chaotic sequences. The maximum complexity of SE is 0.3712, corresponding $a = 7$, $q = 0.8243$, and the maximum Lyapunov exponent is 3.419. The maximum complexity of C_0 is 0.1113, $a = 7$, $q = 0.7207$, and the maximum Lyapunov exponent is 6.3243. It should be pointed out that when $a = 7$, $0.7207 < q < 0.8$, C_0 complexity is small, and in practical

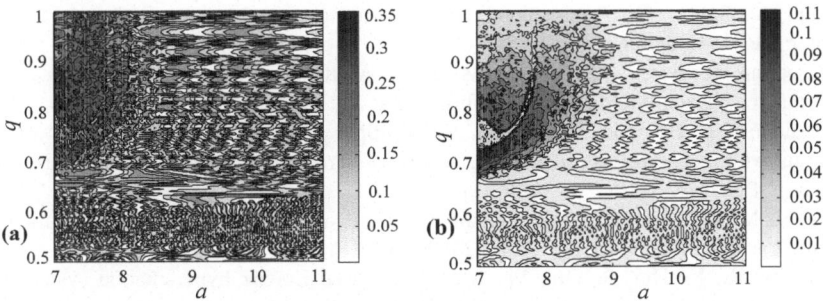

Fig. 8. Complexity of the system varying with parameters a and order q (a) 2D SE complexity, (b) 2D C_0 complexity

applications should avoid taking values in this range. In general, when $a = 7$, $0.8 < q < 0.9$, chaos sequences within the range of this region should be selected as far as possible because the system has a good stochastic performance.

5   Conclusion

In this paper, a novel memristor band pass chaotic filter circuit is constructed and the numerical solution of fractional-order memristor chaotic circuit is calculated based on Adomian algorithm. The dynamic characteristics of the system are analyzed by means of phase diagram, Poincaré section, bifurcation diagram, Lyapunov exponent spectrum, SE and C_0 complexity algorithms. The results show that the dynamical characteristics of fractional-order memristor band pass chaotic circuit system are more complex than its corresponding integer order system and more suitable for the application of secure communication and other fields. When $a = 7$, $0.8 < q < 0.9$, the system chaotic sequence has the best randomness and the highest security. The research results of this paper provide a theoretical basis for the application of memristor band pass filter chaotic circuit in secure communication and other fields and have high theoretical and application value.

References

1. Joglekar, Y.N., Wolf, S.J.: The elusive memristor: signatures in basic electrical circuits (2008)
2. Mou, J., Li, P., Wang, J., et al.: Synchronization study of chaotic system and study in the security communication. ICIC Express Lett. **6**(9), 2325–2330 (2012)
3. Yang, S., Li, C., Huang, T.: Impulsive control and synchronization of memristor-based chaotic circuits. Int. J. Bifurc. Chaos **24**(12), 1450162 (2014)
4. Bao, B., Ma, Z., Jianping, X., et al.: A simple memristor chaotic circuit with complex dynamics. Int. J. Bifurc. Chaos **21**(09), 1102999 (2011)
5. Wang, W., Wang, G., Tan, D.: A new memristor based chaotic circuit. In: International Workshop on Chaos-Fractals Theories and Applications (2011)

6. Saini, S., Saini, J.S.: Secure communication using memristor based chaotic circuit. In: International Conference on Parallel (2015)

7. Buscarino, A., Fortuna, L., Frasca, M., et al.: A chaotic circuit based on Hewlett-Packard memristor. Chaos Interdiscip. J. Nonlinear Sci. 22(2), 80–83 (2012)

8. Chandia, K.J., Bologna, M., Tellini, B.: Multiple scale approach to dynamics of an LC circuit with a charge-controlled memristor. IEEE Trans. Circ. Syst. II Express Briefs 65(1), 120–124 (2017)

9. Ye, X., Mou, J., Luo, C., et al.: Dynamics analysis of Wien-bridge hyperchaotic memristive circuit system. Nonlinear Dyn. 92, 923–933 (2018)

10. Jing-Ya, R., Ke-Hui, S., Jun, M.: Memristor-based Lorenz hyper-chaotic system and its circuit implementation. Acta Phys. Sin. 65, 190502 (2016)

11. Charef, A., Sun, H.H., Tsao, Y.Y., et al.: Fractal system as represented by singularity function. IEEE Trans. Autom. Control 37(9), 1465–1470 (2002)

12. Sun, H., Abdelwahab, A., Onaral, B.: Linear approximation of transfer function with a pole of fractional power. IEEE Trans. Autom. Control 29(5), 441–444 (1984)

13. He, S., Sun, K., Wang, H.: Dynamics of the fractional-order Lorenz system based on Adomian decomposition method and its DSP implementation. IEEE/CAA J. Autom. Sin. 1–6 (2017)

14. Xu, Y., Sun, K., He, S., et al.: Dynamics of a fractional-order simplified unified system based on the Adomian decomposition method. Eur. Phys. J. Plus 131(6), 1–12 (2016)

15. He, S., Sun, K., Banerjee, S.: Dynamical properties and complexity in fractional-order diffusionless Lorenz system. Eur. Phys. J. Plus 131(8), 254 (2016)

16. He, S., Sun, K., Wang, H.: Complexity analysis and DSP implementation of the fractional-order Lorenz hyperchaotic system. Entropy 17(12), 8299–8311 (2015)

17. Bao, B., Wang, N., Xu, Q., et al.: A simple third-order memristive band pass filter chaotic circuit. IEEE Trans. Circuits Syst. II Express Briefs 64(8), 977–979 (2017)

A New Pseudo-random Sequence Generator Based on a Discrete Hyperchaotic System

Xujiong Ma, Jiawu Yu[✉], and Yinghong Cao

School of Information Science and Engineering, Dalian Polytechnic University,
Dalian 116034, China
yujiawu_dlpu@sina.com

Abstract. In this paper, the dynamic characteristics of four-dimensional discrete hyperchaotic mapping are analyzed by phase diagram, bifurcation diagram, Lyapunov exponential spectrum and permutation entropy complexity. On this basis, a new hyperchaotic pseudo-random sequence generator is designed by using the four-dimensional discrete hyperchaotic sequence and multi-quantization algorithm. The performance of the hyperchaotic pseudo-random sequence generator is tested by NIST SP800-22 and sequence correlation. The test results can indicate whether the sequence generated by the chaotic pseudo-random sequence generator has good randomness and correlation. The research results in this paper will provide theoretical basis and experimental basis for the application of chaotic pseudo-random sequences in information security fields such as secure communication.

Keywords: Hyperchaotic system · Pseudo-random sequence ·
Dynamical characteristic · NIST test

1 Introduction

Pseudo-random sequences are deterministic sequences with some random characteristics. Due to their excellent randomness and statistical properties close to white noise, pseudo-random sequences are widely used in many scientific and engineering fields in modern science. For example, it can be applied to satellites, spacecraft orbits, radar technology, secure communications, digital information processing systems, and spread spectrum communications [1–3]. The use of computer systems can not produce random sequences in the true sense, only pseudo-random sequences can be produced [3–5]. The commonly used pseudo-random sequence generated by traditional pseudo-random sequence generation methods such as m-sequence [6, 7] and Gold-sequence [8, 9] based on linear congruence theory has low complexity and has hidden dangers in information security. At the same time, the speed of password generation in cryptography design is also limited [10]. In order to design a pseudo-random sequence with excellent performance, it is a research hotspot to find a new pseudo-random sequence production method.

Chaos is a seemingly random but deterministic dynamic behavior. It is a unique nonlinear dynamic phenomenon. Its extreme sensitivity to initial values and parameters and long-term unpredictability of orbits enable chaotic systems to generate

© ICST Institute for Computer Sciences, Social Informatics and Telecommunications Engineering 2019
Published by Springer Nature Switzerland AG 2019. All Rights Reserved
J. Jin et al. (Eds.): GreeNets 2019, LNICST 282, pp. 193–203, 2019.
https://doi.org/10.1007/978-3-030-21730-3_21

pseudo-random sequence that seemingly unpredictable, so the study of pseudo-random sequence generator based on chaotic system is a hot topic in the research of pseudo-random sequence generation scheme [11–21].

Chaotic systems are divided into continuous chaotic systems and discrete chaotic systems. The dynamic behaviors of different kinds of chaotic systems are not the same, so the randomness of chaotic pseudo-random sequences generated by them is also different. Therefore, the choice of chaotic systems is very important for the generation of pseudo-random sequences [22]. For continuous chaotic systems, many pseudo-random sequences based on chaotic systems have proved that they have good statistical properties, however, the fixed-step integration method often used in continuous chaotic systems to solve differential equations can easily lead chaotic dynamic behavior to degradation, and the complexity of the sequence will not change much because of the increase in the number of scrolls in the attractor [23]. For discrete chaotic systems, it is a common method to generate pseudo-random sequences by using low-dimensional chaotic systems or low-dimensional chaotic systems based on them. The advantage of this method is that the time is short and the form is simple, and the dynamical property of the chaotic system will not degrade when solving. The disadvantage is that the complexity is not high and the difficulty of deciphering is small. Hyperchaotic systems have two or more positive Lyapunov exponents [24–29], usually its sequence randomness is better than the general low-dimensional chaotic system. Therefore, one of the effective ways to solve these problems is to use a hyperchaotic system to generate pseudo-random sequences, which can effectively improve the security of pseudo-random sequences. For the above reasons, the best way to design a pseudo-random sequence generator is to use a high-dimensional discrete hyperchaotic system.

This paper intends to use a four-dimensional discrete hyperchaotic mapping system based on the modified Marotto theorem. Firstly, by analyzing the dynamic characteristics of the system, the appropriate system parameters are selected, so that the chaotic pseudo-random sequence generated by the pseudo-random sequence generator has the best random performance in theory. Secondly, a pseudo-random sequence generator is designed by using a quantization algorithm; Finally, the performance of the generated pseudo-random sequence is tested.

2   Four-Dimensional Discrete Hyperchaotic Mapping System and Its Dynamics Analysis

2.1   Four-Dimensional Discrete Hyperchaotic Mapping System

The mathematical model of the four-dimensional discrete hyperchaotic mapping system is:

$$
\begin{cases}
x_{n+1} = \sin(x_n)\sin(y_n) - a\sin(w_n) \\
y_{n+1} = b\sin(x_n)\cos(y_n) - x_n \\
z_{n+1} = cy_n + t\sin(z_n) \\
w_{n+1} = dy_n
\end{cases}
\tag{1}
$$

Take $a = 4$, $b = 4$, $c = 3.5$, $d = 2$, $t = 4$, the initial value of the system [x_0, y_0, z_0, w_0] = [0.7, 0.8, 1.5, 0.8], the simulation step size is 0.0001. At this time, the Lyapunov exponents of the system are [0.8665, 0.6941, 0.6248, 0.1993], so the system is hyperchaotic. The corresponding chaotic attractor phase diagram is shown in Fig. 1.

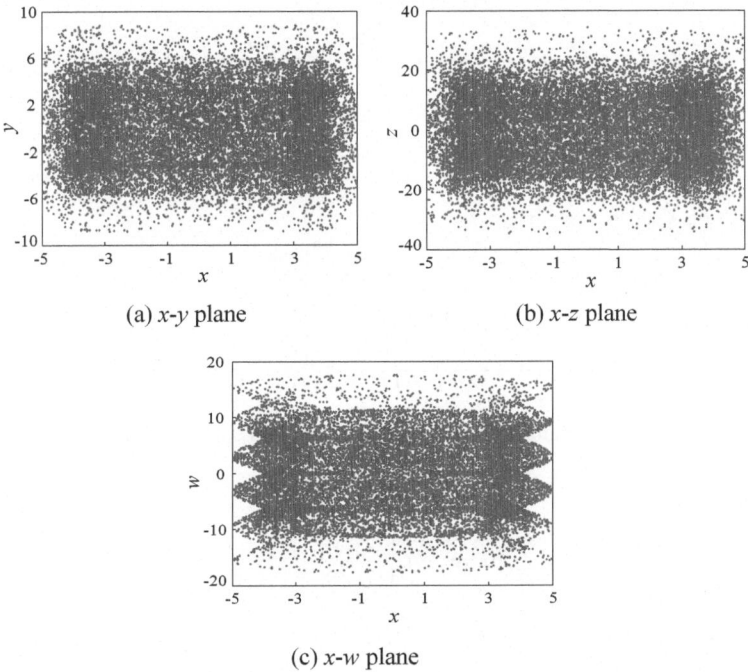

(a) x-y plane   (b) x-z plane

(c) x-w plane

Fig. 1. Phase diagram of four-dimensional discrete hyperchaotic system

2.2   Analysis of Dynamic Characteristics

2.2.1   Bifurcation Diagram and Lyapunov Exponent Spectrum

When the parameter $b \in [0, 5]$, let $a = 4$, $c = 3.5$, $d = 2$, $t = 4$, the initial value of the system [x_0, y_0, z_0, w_0] = [0.7, 0.8, 1.5, 0.8], At this time, the Lyapunov exponent spectrum and the bifurcation diagram of the system are shown in Fig. 2. It can be seen from Fig. 2 that the bifurcation diagram and the Lyapunov exponent spectrum agree well. When $0 \leqslant b \leqslant 0.88$, $1.75 \leqslant b \leqslant 2.19$ $2.47 \leqslant b \leqslant 5$, there are four positive Lyapunov exponents in the system, and the system is in hyperchaotic state. However, when $b \in [1.248, 1.252]$, $b \in [1.556, 1.573]$, there are two obvious periodic windows in the system, so when selecting parameter b, the value of the period window should be avoided.

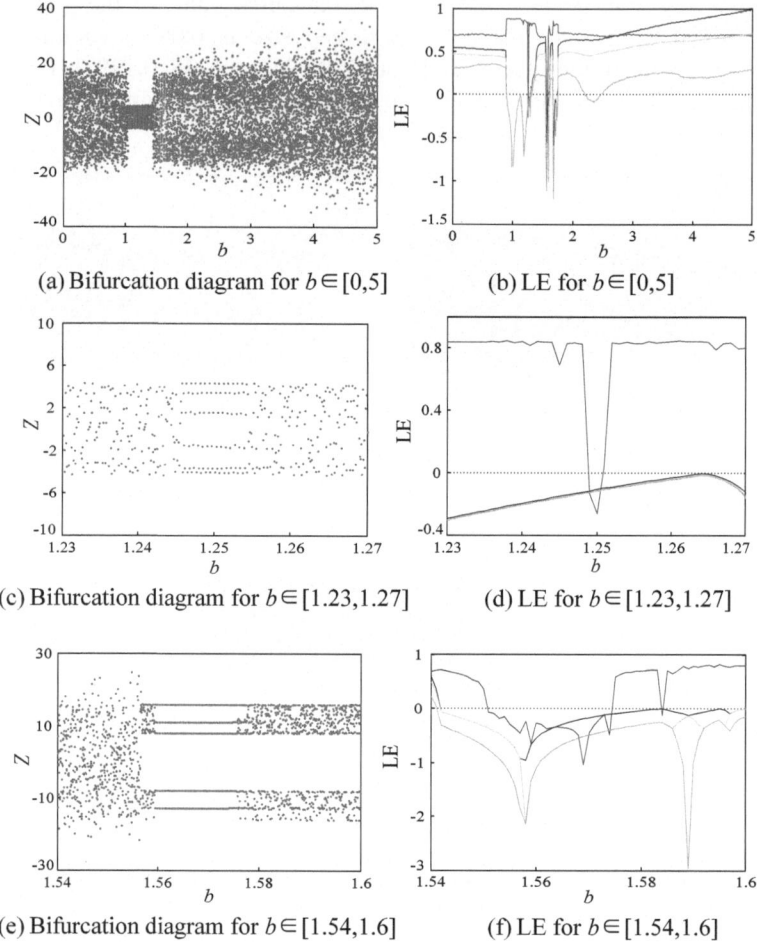

Fig. 2. Bifurcation diagram and Lyapunov exponent spectrum of the system as b changes

When the parameter $d \in [0, 2.5]$, the remaining system parameters remain unchanged, and the Lyapunov exponent spectrum and the bifurcation diagram of the system are shown in Fig. 3. It can be seen from Fig. 3 that the results of the bifurcation diagram and the Lyapunov exponent spectrum also agree. When $1.19 \leqslant d \leqslant 1.38$ and $1.53 \leqslant d \leqslant 5$, the four Lyapunov exponents of the system are positive values, indicating that the system state is hyperchaotic too, but the system obviously has a periodic window when $d \in [0.586, 0.594]$. Therefore, the selection of the parameter d should avoid selecting the value of the period of the periodic window.

When designing a pseudo-random sequence generator using hyperchaotic maps, appropriate parameters can be chosen to ensure that the system has two or more positive Lyapunov exponents. After analyzing the dynamic characteristics of the system, the parameters $a = 4$, $b = 4$, $c = 3.5$, $d = 2$, $t = 4$ are selected to ensure that the system has four positive Lyapunov exponents to design hyperchaotic pseudo-random sequence generator.

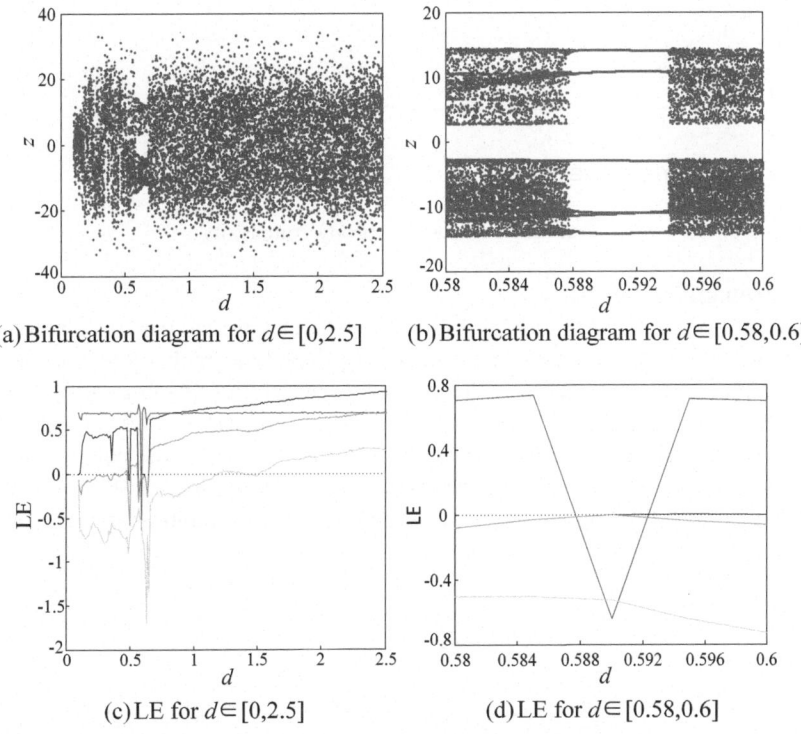

(a) Bifurcation diagram for $d \in [0, 2.5]$ (b) Bifurcation diagram for $d \in [0.58, 0.6]$

(c) LE for $d \in [0, 2.5]$ (d) LE for $d \in [0.58, 0.6]$

Fig. 3. Bifurcation diagram and Lyapunov exponent spectrum of the system as d changes

2.2.2 Permutation Entropy Complexity Analysis

In order to measure and calculate the complexity of time series, this paper uses the permutation entropy complexity algorithm for analysis. Compared with other algorithms, the algorithm is simple to calculate, the image is clear and easier to implement. In this analysis, let the dimension $p = 5$, the sequence length is 10000, and other system parameters are unchanged. When the parameters $b \in [0, 5]$ and $d \in [0, 2.5]$, the permutation entropy complexity of the chaotic sequence is obtained as shown in Fig. 4. As can be seen from Fig. 4, when the parameter b and the parameter d change, the trend of the dynamic characteristics of the system is consistent with the bifurcation diagram and the Lyapunov exponents spectrum.

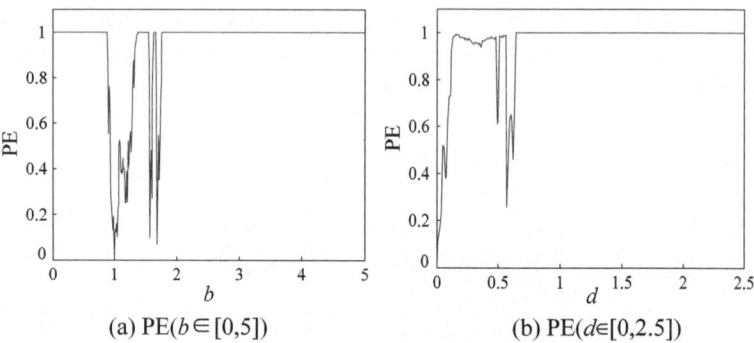

(a) PE($b \in [0,5]$)   (b) PE($d \in [0,2.5]$)

Fig. 4. Permutation entropy complexity

2.2.3   Probability Density

For example, the probability density function of the chaotic sequence generated by the classical Logistic map approximates the Chebyshev type with more ends and less middle, which is not conducive to the efficiency and ability of search [30].

The probability density of four discrete sequences X_n, Y_n, Z_n and W_n generated by the four-dimensional discrete hyperchaotic mapping system in this paper is shown in Fig. 5, which are similar to the Chebyshev type distribution, and shows that the probability density distribution meets the demand, and the chaotic sequence generated by it has good randomness.

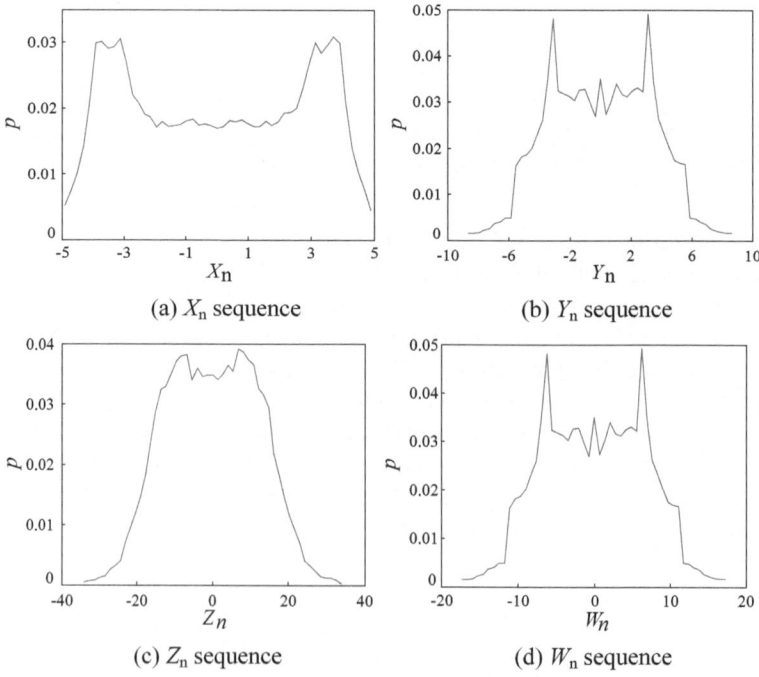

(a) X_n sequence   (b) Y_n sequence

(c) Z_n sequence   (d) W_n sequence

Fig. 5. Probability density test

3 Design of Pseudo-random Sequence Generator

The chaotic pseudo-random sequence is a binary sequence obtained by quantizing the sequence generated by the chaotic system. This binary sequence can reflect the randomness of the chaotic system. In the process of generating pseudo-random sequences, quantization is the most important link. The choice of quantization algorithm will directly affect the randomness, complexity and security of the generated pseudo-random sequence [31]. Therefore, in order to ensure the performance of the pseudo-random sequence generator, an appropriate quantization method must be selected. In this paper, the system parameters are taken as $a = 4$, $b = 4$, $c = 3.5$, $d = 2$, $t = 4$, and the initial value of the system $[x_0, y_0, z_0, w_0] = [0.7, 0.8, 1.5, 0.8]$. The four chaotic sequences generated by the system are quantized by the following quantization algorithm. The specific steps are as follows:

Step 1. After setting the system parameters and initial values, iterate N times to eliminate the transient effect and ensure that the system enters the chaotic state. Continue to iterate the hyperchaotic system to obtain four real values x_n, y_n, z_n, w_n, and obtain four new real values x_n', y_n', z_n', w_n' by Eq. (2).

$$k' = \pi \log k, k = x_n, y_n, z_n, w_n. \tag{2}$$

Step 2. The integer part of the four real values of x_n', y_n', z_n', and w_n' is removed by the Eq. (3), and the fractional part $A = (A_x, A_y, A_z, A_w)$ of the real value is obtained.

$$A = abs\left(k'\right) - floor\left(abs\left(k'\right)\right). \tag{3}$$

Step 3. The rounding method is used to represent the decimal A in binary:

$$A' = a_1 a_2 \cdots a_m. \tag{4}$$

Where $A' = \left(A_x', A_y', A_z', A_w'\right)$, $a_m = 0$ or 1, m is computer precision.

Step 4. XOR the obtained four binary sequences according to Eq. (5) to obtain a new sequence S:

$$S = A_x' \oplus A_y' \oplus A_z' \oplus A_w'. \tag{5}$$

Step 5. Continue to iterate the hyperchaotic system and repeat the above four steps until a hyperchaotic pseudo-random sequence of the desired length is obtained.

In the above algorithm, the sequence x_0, y_0, z_0, w_0 generated by the initial value of the hyperchaotic system, and the number of iterations N can be used as a key. If the precision of the computer is 16, the key space of the algorithm is 10^{64}, so the algorithm has a large key space and is sufficiently resistant to general exhaustive attacks.

4 Performance Analysis of Pseudo-random Sequences

4.1 NIST SP800-22 Test

There are many standards for detecting pseudo-random number performance, such as the Federal Information Processing Standard FIPS 140-2, the Diehard Battery test by Marsaglia, and the random sequence test standard SP 800-22 developed by the National Institute of Standards and Technology (NIST). This paper adopts the most widely used and authoritative NIST SP 800-22 standard in the world. The standard has a total of 15 test indicators, using the ideal random sequence as a reference, and testing the pseudo-random from different angles in statistical characteristics. The degree of deviation of the sequence is generally considered to be good pseudo-random performance by the sequence that can be detected. Each test of the SP 800-20 standard provides two criteria for determining the pass rate and the uniformity of the P-value distribution. All the tests took a significant level of $\alpha = 0.01$, and test sequence has β groups, the confidence interval for defining the pass rate was:

$$\left(1 - \alpha - 3\sqrt{\frac{\alpha(1 - \alpha)}{\beta}}, 1 + \alpha - 3\sqrt{\frac{\alpha(1 - \alpha)}{\beta}}\right). \tag{6}$$

When the pass rate falls within this confidence interval, it indicates that the sequence passes the test, and if P-value > 0.0001, it indicates that the P-value of the measured sequence is evenly distributed, and the sequence is random.

The test conditions used herein are: significant level $\alpha = 0.01$, test sequence $\beta = 100$ groups, each group is 1000000 bit in length, and the confidence interval is [0.96, 1]. The results obtained after the test are shown in Table 1. It can be seen from the results in Table 1 that the pseudo-random sequence generated by the pseudo-random sequence generator designed in this paper has passed the NIST SP 800-20 test, and compared with the NIST test results of the chaotic pseudo-random sequence generated by the pseudo-random sequence generator designed by Chung-Yi Li based on Logistic chaotic mapping system and Afshin Akhshani using three-dimensional discrete hyperchaotic mapping system, the NIST test results of the chaotic pseudo-random sequence generated by the pseudo-random sequence generator based on the high-dimensional discrete chaotic system designed in this paper have the P-value of 12 indicators larger than the results in the literature [32], and there are 11 indicators of P-value are larger than the result in literature [33]. Therefore, this pseudo-random sequence is more random and more secure and reliable in the field of information security such as secure communication.

Table 1. Test results of NIST SP 800-22

Number	Test name	P-value	Pass rate	Times	Result
1	Frequency	0.997 823	1	1	Pass
2	Block frequency	0.383 827	1	1	Pass
3	Cumulative sums[a]	0.534 146	1	2	Pass
4	Runs	0.401 199	0.99	1	Pass
5	Longest run	0.437 274	0.99	1	Pass

(*continued*)

Table 1. (*continued*)

Number	Test name	*P*-value	Pass rate	Times	Result
6	Rank	0.224 821	0.96	1	Pass
7	FFT	0.816 537	0.98	1	Pass
8	Non-overlapping template[a]	0.935 716	0.96	148	Pass
9	Overlapping template	0.816 537	1	1	Pass
10	Universal	0.304 126	0.98	1	Pass
11	Approximate entropy	0.657 933	1	1	Pass
12	Random excursions[a]	0.232 760	0.96	8	Pass
13	Random excursions variant[a]	0.028 181	0.97	18	Pass
14	Serial[a]	0.616 305	0.99	2	Pass
15	Linear complexity	0.834 308	1	1	Pass

Note: [a]Test contains multiple tests, listed as worst case

4.2 Correlation Analysis

Correlation is an important indicator for testing pseudo-random sequences. Good correlation is an important guarantee for the system to operate reliably. Correlation includes autocorrelation and cross-correlation. The ideal random sequence has an autocorrelation function close to the δ function and its cross-correlation function is close to 0. The δ function is defined as

$$\delta(t) = \begin{cases} \infty & t = 0 \\ 0 & t \neq 0 \end{cases}. \tag{7}$$

Let the system parameters $a = 4$, $b = 4$, $c = 3.5$, $d = 2$, $t = 4$, the initial value of the system $[x_0, y_0, z_0, w_0] = [0.7, 0.8, 1.5, 0.8]$, and 60000 values from the A' sequence are selected randomly. Then get the corresponding autocorrelation and cross-correlation results are shown in Fig. 6. The Fig. 6 shows that the autocorrelation of the binary sequences generated by the pseudo-random sequence generator is satisfied with δ function and the cross-correlation is closed to 0. Therefore, the sequence has superior correlation.

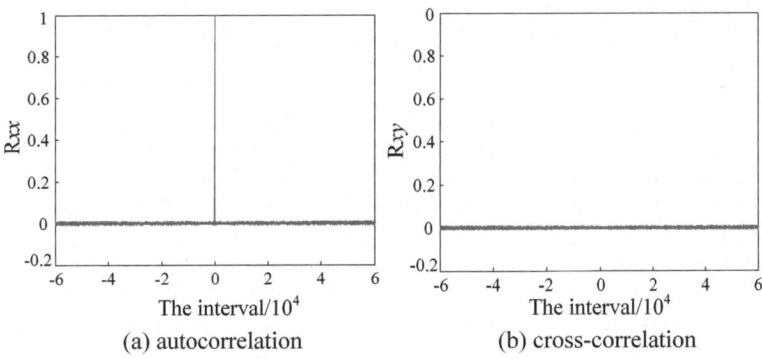

(a) autocorrelation   (b) cross-correlation

Fig. 6. Correlation analysis

5 Conclusion

By analyzing the dynamic characteristics of the four-dimensional discrete hyperchaotic mapping system based on the modified Marotto theorem, the parameter range of the system in hyperchaotic state is determined, which provides a theoretical basis for the implementation of pseudo-random sequence generator. Secondly, the pseudo-random sequence generator is designed by combining multiple quantization algorithms. The simulation results show that the pseudo-random sequence generator can quantize the sequence generated by the hyperchaotic system into a hyperchaotic pseudo-random sequence. Then, the quantized hyperchaotic pseudo-random sequence is tested by NIST SP 800-20 test. The test results show that the sequence generated by the designed pseudo-random sequence generator has good randomness. Finally, the autocorrelation and cross-correlation of hyperchaotic pseudo-random sequences are analyzed. The analysis results show that the sequence generated by this generator has an autocorrelation close to the δ function and a cross-correlation close to zero. Therefore, the sequence generated by the chaotic pseudo-random sequence generator can be applied to information security fields such as secure communication.

Acknowledgments. This work supported by Scientific Research Projects in General of Liaoning Province (Grant no. L2015043), and Doctoral Research Startup Fund Guidance Program of Liaoning Province (Grant no. 201601280).

References

1. Tisa, S., Villa, F., Giudice, A.: High-speed quantum random number generation using CMOS photon counting detectors. IEEE J. Sel. Top. Quantum Electron. **21**(3), 1–7 (2015)
2. Sánchez, S., Criado, R., Vega, C.: A generator of pseudo-random numbers sequences with a very long period. IEEE J. Sel. Top. Quantum Electron. **42**(7), 809–816 (2005)
3. Zheng, F., Tian, X., Song, J.: Pseudo-random sequence generator based on the generalized Henon map. J. China Univ. Posts Telecommun. **15**(3), 64–68 (2008)
4. Behnia, S., Akhavan, A., Akhshani, A., et al.: A novel dynamic model of pseudo random number generator[J]. J. Comput. Appl. Math. **235**(12), 3455–3463 (2011)
5. Luo, Q.B.: A new approach to generate chaotic pseudo-random sequence. J. Electron. Inf. Technol. **28**, 1262–1265 (2006)
6. Wang, H., Li, B.: Design and Realize of m-sequence generator. J. Beijing Electron. Sci. Technol. Inst. (2007)
7. Xianyong, W., Zhou, X.: A kind of generating method of m-sequence pseudo-code generator. Meas. Control. Technol. **22**(9), 56–58 (2003)
8. Xinyu, Z.X.Z.: Analysis of m-sequence and Gold-sequence in CDMA system. In: IEEE International Conference on Communication Software and Networks. IEEE (2011)
9. Wang, F., Huang, Z., Zhou, Y.: A new method for m-sequence and Gold-sequence generator polynomial estimation. In: International Symposium on Microwave
10. Kotulski, Z., Szczepański, J., et al.: Application of discrete chaotic dynamical systems in cryptography — DCC method. Int. J. Bifurc. Chaos **9**(06), 1121–1135 (2011)
11. Da, L.H., Guo, F.D.: Composite nonlinare descrete chaotic dynamical systems and stream cipher systems. Acta Electron. Sin. **31**(8), 1209–1212 (2003)

12. Cai, J.P., Li, Z., Song, W.T.: Analysis on the chaotic pseudo-random sequence complexity. Acta Phys. Sin. **52**(8), 1871–1876 (2003)
13. Huang, Y., Zhang, P., Zhao, W.: Novel grid multiwing butterfly chaotic attractors and their circuit design. IEEE Trans. Circuits & Syst. Express Briefs **62**(5), 496–500 (2017)
14. Wang, X.Y., Yang, L.: Design of pseudo-random bit generator based on chaotic maps. Int. J. Mod. Phys. B **26**(32), 1250208 (2012)
15. François, M., Grosges, T., Barchiesi, D., et al.: Pseudo-random number generator based on mixing of three chaotic maps. Commun. Nonlinear Sci. Numer. Simul. **19**(4), 887–895 (2014)
16. Xiang, F., Qiu, S.S.: Analysis on stability of binary chaotic pseudorandom sequence. IEEE Commun. Lett. **12**(5), 337–339 (2008)
17. Hu, H.P., Liu, L.F., Ding, N.D.: Pseudorandom sequence generator based on the Chen chaotic system. Comput. Phys. Commun. **184**(3), 765–768 (2013)
18. Suneel, M.: Cryptographic pseudo-random sequences from the chaotic Hénon map. Sadhana **34**(5), 689–701 (2006)
19. Pellicer-Lostao, C., López-Ruiz, R.: Pseudo-random bit generation based on 2D chaotic maps of logistic type and its applications in chaotic cryptography. In: Gervasi, O., Murgante, B., Laganà, A., Taniar, D., Mun, Y., Gavrilova, M.L. (eds.) ICCSA 2008. LNCS, vol. 5073, pp. 784–796. Springer, Heidelberg (2008). https://doi.org/10.1007/978-3-540-69848-7_62
20. Zelinka, I.: Behaviour of pseudo-random and chaotic sources of stochasticity in nature-inspired optimization methods. Soft. Comput. **18**(4), 619–629 (2014)
21. Li, X., Li, C., Lee, I.K.: Chaotic image encryption using pseudo-random masks and pixel mapping. Signal Process. **125**(C), 48–63 (2016)
22. Dabal, P., Pelka, R.: A study on fast pipelined pseudo-random number generator based on chaotic logistic map. In: International Symposium on Design and Diagnostics of Electronic Circuits and Systems (2014)
23. Qi, W.U., Tan, Z.W., Wan, C.X.: Harmonically coupled chaotic system for a pseudo-random bit generator. J. Chin. Comput. Syst. **32**(4), 639–643 (2011)
24. Chen, C.-H., Sheu, L.J., et al.: A new hyper-chaotic system and its synchronization. Nonlinear Anal. Real World Appl. **10**(4), 2088–2096 (2009)
25. University N, Tianjin: Generation and circuit implementation of a large range hyper-chaotic system. Acta Phys. Sin. **58**(7), 4469–4476 (2009)
26. Liu, H., Wang, X., Kadir, A.: Color image encryption using Choquet fuzzy integral and hyper chaotic system. Opt. Int. J. Light. Electron Opt. **124**(18), 3527–3533 (2013)
27. Kadir, A., Hamdulla, A., Guo, W.Q.: Color image encryption using skew tent map and hyper chaotic system of 6th-order CNN. Opt. Int. J. Light. Electron Opt. **125**(5), 1671–1675 (2014)
28. Carroll, T.L., Pecora, L.M.: Cascading synchronized chaotic systems. Phys. D Nonlinear Phenom. **67**(1–3), 126–140 (1993)
29. Min, F.H.: Dislocated projective synchronization of Qi hyper-chaotic system and its application to secure communication. Acta Phys. Sin. **59**(11), 509–518 (2010)
30. Flores-Franulič, A., Román-Flores, H.: A Chebyshev type inequality for fuzzy integrals. Inf. Sci. **190**(2), 1178–1184 (2007)
31. Chiang, Y.T., Wang, H.S., Wang, Y.N.: A chaotic-based pseudo-random bit generator for navigation applications. Appl. Mech. Mater. **311**, 99–104 (2013)
32. Li, C.Y., Chen, Y.H., Chang, T.Y., et al.: Period extension and randomness enhancement using high-throughput reseeding-mixing PRNG. IEEE Trans. Very Large Scale Integr. (VLSI) Syst. **20**(2), 385–389 (2012)
33. Akhshani, A., Akhavan, A., Mobaraki, A., et al.: Pseudo random number generator based on quantum chaotic map. Commun. Nonlinear Sci. Numer. Simul. **19**(1), 101–111 (2014)

A Trademark Graphic Encryption Algorithm Based on Discrete Chaotic System and Its Performance Analysis

Ji Xu[1], Bo Sun[2(✉)], Xujiong Ma[1], Peng Li[1], and Jun Mou[1]

[1] School of Food Science and Technology, Dalian Polytechnic University,
Dalian 116034, China
[2] School of Management, Dalian Polytechnic University, Dalian 116034, China
sunbo_0709@126.com

Abstract. Based on chaos system and DNA encryption algorithm, a novel encryption scheme for enterprise trademark image has been proposed. Firstly, chaotic sequence generate by chaotic map is employed for disrupt the value of each pixel point in the encrypted trademark, In next stage, image matrix are encode into DNA sequence and through DNA calculation operation to diffusing the image matrix, Finally obtain cipher image. Experimental simulation results show that the algorithm can effectively encrypt the trademark image, and the correlation with the original image is very low, and it has a large key space can resist conventional attack and convenient for practical application. The trademark encryption algorithm based on chaotic system and DNA sequence operation proposed in this paper has a good application value in the protection of enterprise intellectual property rights.

Keywords: DNA sequence · 3D discrete chaotic model · Dynamic analysis · Image encryption algorithm

1 Introduction

With the rapid development of computer science and communication, data protection has become increasingly serious issue to internet industries. Because of the registered trademark include many sensitive information, they have special value to enterprise. As turn out, They may be more easily to be the target of attacker [1]. Based on traditional data encryption algorithms such as DES and AES can effectively protect sensitive data of enterprises from attacker [2, 3]. However, considering the characteristics of strong correlation between adjacent pixels and large amount of data in the image data of trademarks, and with the constant change of data attack mode, the technical details of the above algorithm can no longer competent the requirements of data encryption. As a result, design new encryption algorithm on the basis of high-randomness sequence with more better performance and randomness drawn more and more attention.

Chaotic maps have advantages are shown in complexity, good ergodicity in the phase space and sensitivity to initial parameters, which is suitable infiltrated into information security [4, 5]. Therefore, in accordance with chaotic maps, a variety of

J. Jin et al. (Eds.): GreeNets 2019, LNICST 282, pp. 204–217, 2019.
https://doi.org/10.1007/978-3-030-21730-3_22

image encryption algorithm has been widely used in image processing field [6–26, 30]. For instance, the encryption algorithm on based of HD discrete chaotic map [4, 17], it has good encryption features, including have larger information entropy space, good Pixels Change Rate (Number of Pixels Change Rate, NCPR) and the Unified Average Changing Intensity (UACI) reduce the correlation between the encrypted image and the plaintext image.

In this paper, a novel encryption algorithm based on HD discrete chaotic map and DNA encode operation of trademark image has proposed. The rest part of this paper structure as follow. In Sect. 2, dynamics analysis of the chaotic system is carried out, show the corresponding analysis results. In Sect. 3, the genetic coding law of DNA is briefly explained. In Sect. 4, describe the encryption algorithm and decryption algorithm workflow respectively, and shows the encryption and decryption image. In Sect. 5, according to the obtained images, the security performance of the algorithm has analyzed, and the results of relevant technical performance indexes are presented. In Sect. 6, obtain important conclusion.

2 Characteristic Analysis of 3D Discrete Chaotic System

2.1 Chaos Dynamics Analysis of 3D Discrete Chaos Model

As discussed in Sect. 1, In this research, a new 3D discrete chaotic map based on Sine and ICMIC map has accepted. The chaotic map is defined as Eq. (1).

$$\begin{cases} x_{i+1} = a \sin(bz_i) \sin(\frac{c}{x_i}) \\ y_{i+1} = a \sin(bx_{i+1}) \sin(\frac{c}{y_i}) \\ z_{i+1} = a \sin(by_{i+1}) \sin(\frac{c}{z_i}) \end{cases} \quad (1)$$

Set system parameters $a = 1$, $b = 2\pi$, $c = 11.5$, initial value $(x_0, y_0, z_0) = [0.3, 0.5, 0.6]$. At this point, the system phase diagram is shown in Fig. 1.

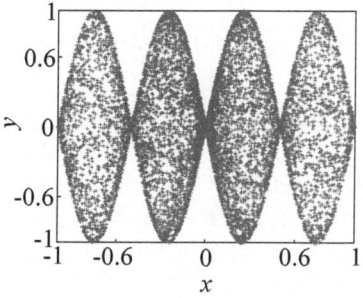

Fig. 1. Chaotic attractor phase diagram in the x-y plane

As show in Fig. 1, On the one view point, the attractor phase diagram occupies most of the region in the x-y plane, indicating that the system has a large key space., On another advantage point, The phase diagram is symmetric about the X-axis and Y-axis in the x-y plane. Because of the ergodicity of the chaotic system and sensitivity to initial conditions, the state of the system at the next moment is unpredictable. Therefore, it is more advantageous to use this system to generate pseudo-random sequences.

2.2   Influence of Parameters on System Performance

Keep the initial value of the system $(x_0, y_0, z_0) = [0.3, 0.5, 0.6]$, change the parameters and use Lyapunov exponent spectrum and bifurcation diagram to evaluate system performance. The Fig. 2 shown the LEs and BDs of 3D-SIMM.

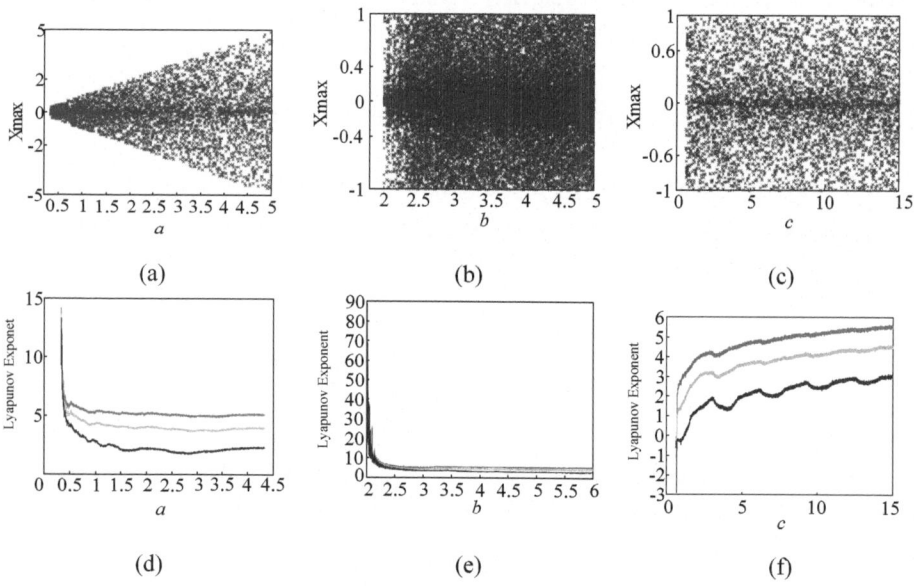

Fig. 2. Lyapunov exponent spectrum and bifurcation diagram

When parameters $a = 1$, $b = 2\pi$, $c = 11.5$, the Lyapunov exponent of the system are obtained as $(\lambda_1, \lambda_2, \lambda_3) = (5.2325, 4.2972, 2.7538)$. on the basic of Lyapunov exponent, the system is hyper-chaotic.

When parameters had changed, As shown in Figs. 2(a) and (d), 3D-SIMM is hyper-chaotic when $a \in [0.33, 5]$, As shown in Figs. 2(b) and (c), When $b \in [2, 8]$, the system is hyper-chaotic. As shown in Figs. 2(c) and (f), When $c \in [0.62, 15]$, the system is hyper-chaotic.

2.3 Entropy Complexity of Permutation

The randomness of the system can be expressed by permutation entropy. The higher of permutation entropy number show good randomness of the system. Set $d = 5$ for the embedded dimension and time delay is 1. The entropy results of system arrangement are shown in Fig. 3.

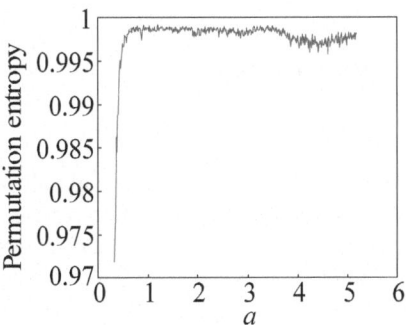

Fig. 3. Permutation entropy complexity

When the system parameter a $\in$ (0.33, 5), the entropy of system is 0.997, which is close to the theoretical value 1. It can proved the system has good randomness and generate more complex chaotic sequences.

3 DNA Coding Rules

The basic unit of deoxyribonucleic acid (DNA) is the deoxynucleotide. In the process of encryption, algorithm is subject to the principle of base complementary pairing. The specific content as follows: Adenine (A) is associated with Thymine (T). Cytosine (C) pairs with Guanine (G). According to the principle of base complementary pairing, the number of elements in DNA sequence follows the Eq. (2).

$$\begin{cases} x_i \neq L(x_i) \neq L(L(x_i)) \neq L(L(L(x_i))) \\ x_i = L(L(L(L(x_i)))) \end{cases} \tag{2}$$

The law of correspondence between DNA and binary number and the law of addition and subtraction of the four basic elements of DNA are shown in the following Tables 1 and 2.

Table 1. The law of encoding

Rule	1	2	3	4	5	6	7	8
00	A	A	T	T	G	G	C	C
01	C	G	C	G	T	A	T	A
10	G	C	G	C	A	T	A	T
11	T	T	A	A	C	C	G	G

Table 2. Addition and subtraction rules

+	A	C	G	T	–	A	C	G	T
A	A	C	G	T	A	A	T	G	C
C	C	G	T	A	C	C	A	T	G
G	G	T	A	C	G	G	C	A	T
T	T	A	C	G	T	T	G	C	A

4 Encryption Algorithm Design

4.1 Key Format

Set (a, b, c) are system parameters, (x_0, y_0, z_0) are initial values, m and n as the number of iterations required by the system to generate pseudo random sequences. On the other side, the initial deoxynucleotide code was c_0, the code of DNA coding and decoding rules was expressed as $\alpha(\alpha \in [1, 8])$ and $\beta(\beta \in [1, 6])$, respectively, and the code of base complementary pairing rules was $L_i(L \in [1, 6], i = 1, 2..., 8)$. The key format composition involved in the algorithm designed in this paper are shown in Table 3.

Table 3. Key format

a	b	c	x_0	y_0	z_0	m	n	c_0	α	β	L_i

4.2 Encryption Algorithm Flow

In this paper, The encryption algorithm designed includes image matrix scrambling and pixel number diffusion. In the scrambling part, at the begin, a pseudo-random sequence generated and transformed by 3D-SIMM, the image matrix of the encrypted object is scrambled by this sequence. In the pixel diffusion part, the scrambled image matrix and pseudo-random sequence are encoded into DNA sequence, and then the image pixel points are diffused. Finally, the algorithm will obtain the final pixel value matrix and output the encrypted image. The specific encryption process is shown in Fig. 4.

The detailed steps of the encryption algorithm are as follows:

Step 1: Input the image and convert it into the pixel value matrix. According to the Eqs. (3) and (4), use initial value and system parameters of the chaotic map to obtain the new system variable values of the chaotic map.

$$S = \frac{\sum_{i=1}^{H} \sum_{j=1}^{W} I(i,j)}{10^{10}} \tag{3}$$

$$\begin{cases} x_0' = x_0 + S \\ y_0' = y_0 + S \\ z_0' = z_0 + S \end{cases} \tag{4}$$

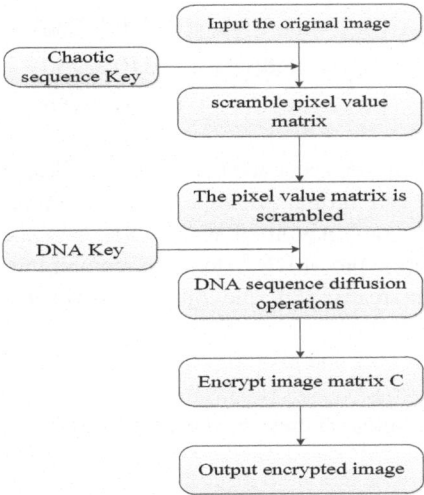

Fig. 4. The flow chart of algorithm

Step 2: Set $N = MAX(H, W)$, change the initial value of the chaotic system, and defer to Eq. (1), repeat iterative calculation $(m + N)$ times get the chaotic sequence. For good randomness of the chaotic sequence and the sensitivity of the initial value of the chaotic system, the data generated by the first m times of calculation is abandoned. Moreover, the times of row and column scrambling of image matrix in the scrambling part is determined by Eq. (5).

$$\begin{cases} Br = \mathrm{mod}((\lfloor |x_i| \rfloor) \times 10^{16}, \dfrac{W}{2}) \\ Bc = \mathrm{mod}((\lfloor |y_i| \rfloor) \times 10^{16}, \dfrac{H}{2}) \end{cases} \tag{5}$$

Step 3: The image matrix is introduced into the algorithm program, and the row and column of the matrix are scrambled respectively. First, the element of pixel matrix is shifted to the left, and the new row scrambling vector TK2 is obtained.

Step 4: Reconstruct the TK2 pixel value matrix with the size of $H \times M$ and start the column scrambling calculation. The detail as follow, the element of TK2 is move up, and get new column scrambling vector TK3. After reconstructing TK3, the scrambled image matrix TK is obtained.

Step 5: The scrambled image matrix is changed into binary numbers matrix, and the matrix size is $H \times 8 \times W$. On the ground of DNA coding rules, the numerical matrix is converted to form the DNA sequence matrix S1, which is $H \times 4 \times W$ in size.

Step 6: According to the initial value and system parameters of the chaotic system, a set of pseudo-random sequence numbers are generated after $(n + H \times W)$ calculation. The generation of the sequence follows the Eq. (6).

$$\begin{cases} k_1 = \mathrm{mod}((\lfloor |x_i| \rfloor) \times 10^{16}, 256) \\ k_2 = \mathrm{mod}((\lfloor |y_i| \rfloor) \times 10^{16}, 256) \\ k_3 = \mathrm{mod}((\lfloor |z_i| \rfloor) \times 10^{16}, 256) \end{cases} \tag{6}$$

Step 7: Use random number sequence matrix K1 to diffusion pixel value matrix S1. The specific process is basic on the principle of base complementary pairing, scrambling the original DNA combination of matrix S1, generate new DNA sequences. Then, according to the principle of DNA addition, combining the new DNA sequence and pseudo-random data matrix K1 and obtain the pixel value matrix C1 of the encrypted image.

Step 8: Recover matrix C1 and restore it to the pixel value matrix C represented by decimal number.

Step 9: Output the results. Therefore, the encrypted image is obtained. Complete the encryption process.

4.3 Decryption Algorithm Flow

In this paper, the decryption algorithm is the inverse process of the encryption algorithm. Firstly, in the decryption part, the receiver get the encrypted image, encodes the image matrix into DNA sequence, and use the 3D-SIMM discrete chaotic system to generate decode sequence. Use this sequence to reconstruct trademark image. In the process of scrambled restoration part, the undecrypted image matrix will be restored, and the original decrypted image matrix is restored to the decimal number pixel value matrix. The algorithm will obtain the final decrypted image. The specific decryption process is shown in Fig. 5.

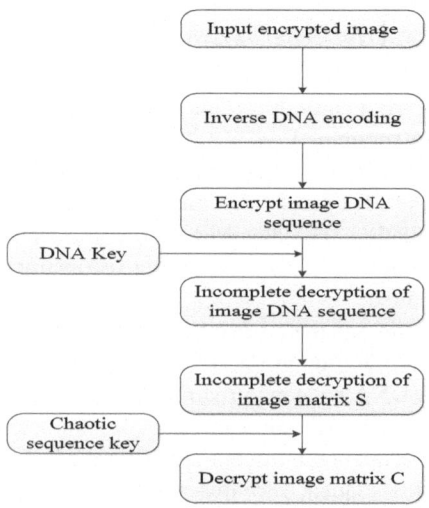

Fig. 5. The flow chart of algorithm

Step 1: Input the encrypted image, generate the image matrix of $H \times W$, and inversely encode the image matrix to generate the DNA sequence C1, the size of which is $H \times 4 \times W$.

Step 2: Generate pseudo random sequence as decryption key according to Eq. (1), and restore the DNA sequence of the encrypted image. In the process of reduction, get a new pixel diffusion sequence, and the new pixel diffusion sequence is combine with the decrypted pseudo random sequence according to the principle of base complementation and pairing. The incomplete DNA sequence S1 is obtained.

Step 3: Transform S1 into an $H \times M$ matrix and compile it into a binary image matrix TK. Then, the chaotic sequence generated by Eq. (1) can scramble TK.

Step 4: Scramble the rows and columns of TK separately. The procedure is to move elements in TK down to generate the column scrambling vector TK3.

Step 5: Reconstruct TK3 into an $H \times M$ image matrix and start the row scrambling calculation. The process is to move a member of TK3 to the right and get a new row scrambling vector TK3. After reconstruction of TK3, the decrypted image matrix TK5 is obtained.

Step 6: Convert the decrypted image matrix to a decimal number image matrix and output the decrypted result. Complete the decryption process.

4.4 Simulation Results of the Algorithm

This paper takes the sea cucumber trademark of a certain brand in China as the encryption object, and the target image size is 512×512 pixels. in the key format, when $a = 1$, $b = 2\pi$, $c = 11.5$, $[x_0, y_0, z_0] = [0.3, 0.5, 0.6]$, $c_0 = C$, $\alpha = 1$, $\beta = 3$. The encryption and decryption results are shown in Fig. 6.

(a)original image   (b)Encryption image   (c)Decryption image

Fig. 6. Simulation test results

5 Encryption Performance Analysis

5.1 Key Space Analysis

The key space involved in this algorithm should be large enough for resist brute force attack. When the computer computational accuracy is 10^{-15}, the key space size formed by a, b, c and x_0, y_0, z_0 is 10^{90}, conversion to 2^{299}. Beside, c_0 represents four deoxynucleotides, α, β respectively represent six base pairs calculation rules, and L_i represents eight DNA coding rules used by the algorithm. The key space constituted by this part is $2^2 \times 2^6 \times 2^{20} = 2^{28}$. As a result, the key space of this algorithm can reach 2^{327}, with a large key space, as shown in Table 4, compared to other algorithm, the algorithm proposed in this study can effectively resist violence attack.

Scheme	Proposed	Ref. [21]	Ref. [19]	Ref. [20]
Key space	2^{327}	2^{319}	2^{90}	2^{78}

5.2 Key Sensitivity Analysis

In order to test the sensitivity of the algorithm to keys, the initial value will be change of 10^{-16}, and use new secret key to decrypted the encrypted image. The decryption results are shown in Fig. 7.

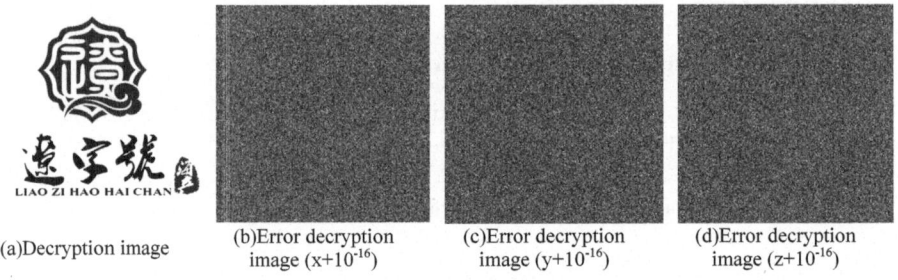

(a)Decryption image   (b)Error decryption image $(x+10^{-16})$ (c)Error decryption image $(y+10^{-16})$ (d)Error decryption image $(z+10^{-16})$

Fig. 7. Initial value sensitivity analysis

The results show that when the secret key is change, the algorithm cannot get the correct decrypted image. Hence, the algorithm has good sensitivity to initial value.

5.3 Statistical Performance Analysis

The statistical performance of the encrypted image is analyzed to measure the degree of confidentiality of the trademark image information of the algorithm designed in this paper.

5.3.1 Histogram Analysis

Histogram reflects the distribution of pixel values in the image, the abscissa reflects the gray value of the pixel, and the ordinate reflects the distribution of the pixel value in the image. According this, the histogram analysis results of pixel value distribution of trademark image and encrypted image are shown in Fig. 8.

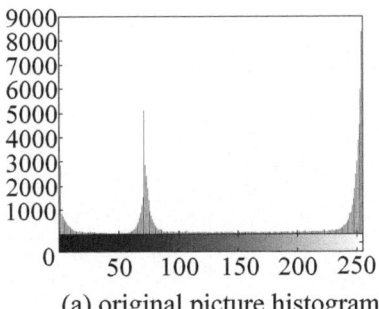

(a) original picture histogram

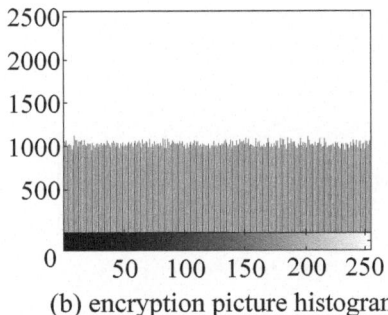

(b) encryption picture histogram

Fig. 8. Histogram analysis results

As shown in Fig. 8(b), the histogram of the encrypted image is a smooth histogram image, with pixel points distributed in different pixel value intervals, while as shown in Fig. 8(a), pixel values are relatively concentrated in different regions. Through comparison, it can be seen that the correlation between the encrypted image and the original image has been reduced, so that the encrypted image can effectively resist the histogram attack.

5.3.2 Image Correlation Coefficient Analysis

The image correlation coefficient is used to measure the correlation between adjacent pixels in different directions, and compare correlation coefficient between plaintext image and cipher image to prove algorithm has good security performance, The result obtained as following.

$$r_{xy} = \frac{\text{cov}(x, y)}{\sqrt{D(X)D(Y)}} \tag{7}$$

$$\text{cov}(x, y) = E\{[x - E(x)][y - E(y)]\} \tag{8}$$

$$E(x) = \frac{1}{N}\sum_{i=1}^{N} x_i \tag{9}$$

$$D(x) = \frac{1}{N}\sum_{i=1}^{N} [x_i - E(x)]^2 \tag{10}$$

Theoretically, due to the strong correlation between adjacent pixels, the cipher image correlation should be reduced than trademark picture and correlation coefficient of cipher image should close to 0. After simulation experiment, the correlation coefficient between the trademark image and the encrypted image are shown in Fig. 9.

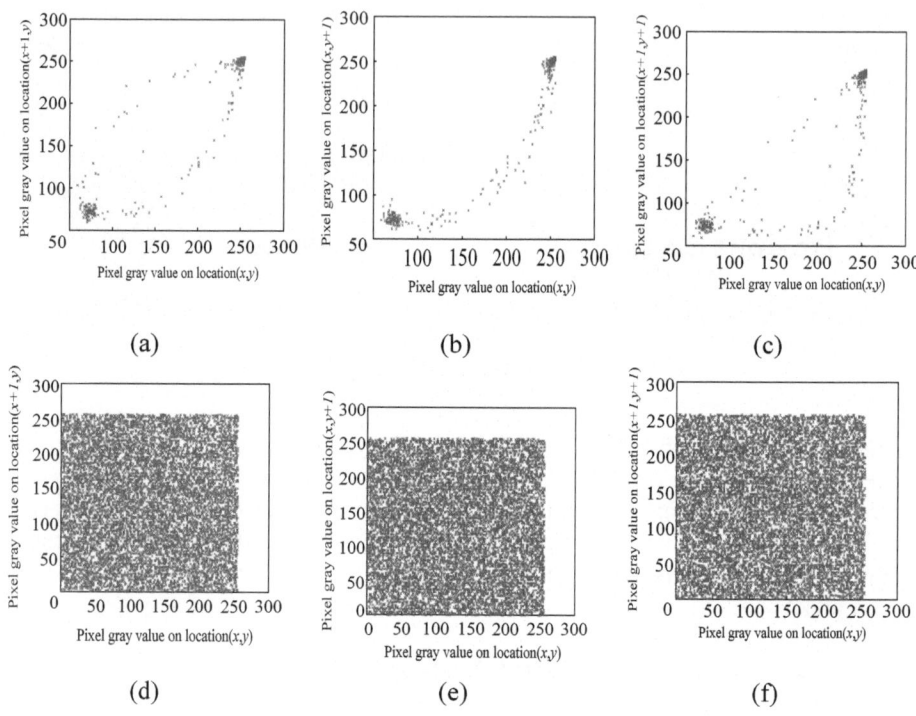

Fig. 9. The correlation coefficient analysis results

Table 5. Table of correlation coefficient

Direction	Original image	Encryption image
Horizontal	0.9653	−0.0051
Vertical	0.9602	−0.0030
Diagonal	0.9331	0.0004

As can be seen from Table 5, The correlation coefficient results show that in adjacent position, the original image has strong correlation and the distributed of pixel point is intensive, the encryption image has low correlation, almost close to 0 and the pixel point distribute all pixel area. As shown in Table 6, compared to other algorithm, the algorithm proposed in this research can effectively reduce the correlation with the original image. Therefore, the proposed scheme has good security performance.

Table 6. Table of correlation comparison

Scheme	Horizontal	Vertical	Diagonal
Proposed	−0.0051	−0.0030	0.0004
Ref. [22]	0.0036	0.0023	0.0039
Ref. [23]	−0.0048	−0.0112	−0.0045
Ref. [26]	−0.0066	−0.0089	0.0424

5.4   Information Entropy Analysis

Information entropy reflects the uncertainty of image information. Theoretically, the higher value of the entropy, the more uncertain the information and less visible the information. The calculation of information entropy is shown below.

For gray image L = 256, the theoretical value of information entropy is 8. Through calculation, the information entropy of the encrypted image is 7.9993, which is close to the theoretical value. As shown in Table 7 compared to other algorithm, the proposed algorithm can make the information in the encrypted image have great uncertainty.

Table 7. Table of information entropy

Scheme	Proposed	Ref. [7]	Ref. [22]	Ref. [23]
Entropy number	7.9993	7.9993	7.9980	7.9963

5.5   Differential Attack Analysis

NCPR and UACI were used to measure the performance of the algorithm to test the performance of the algorithm. The specific calculation method is shown as follows.

$$NPCR = \frac{\sum\limits_{i,j} D(i,j)}{L} \times 100\% \tag{11}$$

$$UACI = \frac{1}{L}\sum\limits_{i,j} \frac{|C(i,j) - C_1(i,j)|}{256} \times 100\% \tag{12}$$

In this algorithm, the mean value of NCPR and UACI was calculated by repeated calculation for 10 times in the test of tolerance analysis performance. After calculation, the NCPR value was 99.63% and the UACI value was 33.41%. The technical index of this algorithm is close to the theoretical value. As shown in Table 8, between other algorithm, the proposed encryption can resist differential attack.

Table 8. Table of information entropy

Scheme	Proposed	Ref. [21]	Ref. [26]	Ref. [7]
NCPR	99.63%	99.62%	99.61%	99.60%
UACI	33.41%	33.06%	33.63%	33.47%

6   Conclusion

In this paper, an algorithm to encrypt the trademark image basic on 3D discrete chaotic map had designed. On the basic of 3D-SIMM map has good chaotic dynamic characteristics. Use this map to generate chaotic sequences have good randomness, and the encrypted image cannot be decrypted without a correct key. The performance analysis shows that the encrypted image has a large entropy space and sensitivity to the initial value of the key. In conclude, this algorithm has good encryption characteristics, can effectively resist common attacks and protect the image information of trademarks, and is convenient for implementation and large-scale application. It provides effective guarantee for preventing trademark misappropriation and protecting the rights and interests of trademark owners.

References

1. Davison, M.: The legitimacy of plain packaging under international intellectual property law: why there is no right to use a trademark under either the paris convention or the trips agreement, pp. 81–108. Social Science Electronic Publishing (2012)
2. Biryukov, A., De Cannière, C.: Data Encryption Standard (DES). In: van Tilborg, H.C.A., Jajodia, S. (eds.) Encyclopedia of Cryptography and Security, vol. 28(2), pp. 295–301. Springer, Boston (2011). https://doi.org/10.1007/978-1-4419-5906-5
3. Singh, A., Marwaha, M., Singh, B., et al.: Comparative study of DES, 3DES, AES and RSA. Int. J. Comput. Technol. **9**(3), 97–102 (2013)
4. Ye, X.L., Mou, J., Luo, C.F., et al.: Dynamics analysis of Wien-bridge hyperchaotic memristive circuit system. Nonlinear Dyn. **92**(3), 923–933 (2018)
5. Ye, X.L., Wang, X.Y., Mou, J., et al.: Characteristic analysis of the fractional-order hyperchaotic memristive circuit based on the Wien bridge oscillator. Eur. Phys. J. Plus **133**(12), 516 (2018)
6. Liu, W., Sun, K., He, S.: SF-SIMM high-dimensional hyperchaotic map and its performance analysis. Nonlinear Dyn. **89**(4), 2521–2532 (2017)
7. Chai, X., Gan, Z., Lu, Y., et al.: A novel image encryption algorithm based on the chaotic system and DNA computing. Int. J. Mod. Phys. C **28**(05), 1 (2017)
8. Chen, J.X., Zhu, Z.L., Fu, C., et al.: A fast chaos-based image encryption scheme with a dynamic state variables selection mechanism. Commun. Nonlinear Sci. Numer. Simul. **20**(3), 846–860 (2015)
9. Chai, X., Chen, Y., Broyde, L.: A novel chaos-based image encryption algorithm using DNA sequence operations. Opt. Lasers Eng. **88**(Complete), 197–213 (2017)
10. Norouzi, B., Seyedzadeh, S.M., Mirzakuchaki, S., et al.: A novel image encryption based on row-column, masking and main diffusion processes with hyper chaos. Multimed. Tools Appl. **74**(3), 781–811 (2015)
11. Luo, Y., Du, M., Liu, J.: A symmetrical image encryption scheme in wavelet and time domain. Commun. Nonlinear Sci. Numer. Simul. **20**(2), 447–460 (2015)
12. Aqeel-ur-Rehman, Liao, X., Hahsmi, M.A., et al.: An efficient mixed inter-intra pixels substitution at 2bits-level for image encryption technique using DNA and Chaos. Opt. Int. J. Light. Electron Opt. S0030402617311695 (2017)
13. Wei, X., Zhang, Q., Liu, L.: Improved algorithm for image encryption based on DNA encoding and multi-chaotic maps. AEUE Int. J. Electron. Commun. **68**(3), 186–192 (2014)
14. Wang, X.Y., Gu, S.X., Zhang, Y.Q.: Novel image encryption algorithm based on cycle shift and chaotic system. Opt. Lasers Eng. **68**, 126–134 (2015)
15. Zhang, Y.: The image encryption algorithm based on chaos and DNA computing. Multimedia Tools Appl. **77**, 21589–21615 (2018)
16. Liu, W., Sun, K., He, Y., et al.: Color image encryption using three-dimensional sine ICMIC modulation map and DNA sequence operations. Int. J. Bifurc. Chaos **27**(11), 120511–121743 (2017)

17. Liu, W., Sun, K., Zhu, C.: A fast image encryption algorithm based on chaotic map. Opt. Lasers Eng. **84**, 26–36 (2016)
18. Huang, R., Rhee, K.H., Uchida, S.: A parallel image encryption method based on compressive sensing. Multimedia Tools Appl. **72**(1), 71–93 (2014)
19. George, S.N., Augustine, N., Pattathil, D.P.: Audio security through compressive sampling and cellular automata. Multimedia Tools Appl. **74**(23), 10393–10417 (2015)
20. George, S.N., Pattathil, D.P.: A secure LFSR based random measurement matrix for compressive sensing. Sens. Imaging **15**(1), 1–29 (2014)
21. Jain, A., Rajpal, N.: A robust image encryption algorithm resistant to attacks using DNA and chaotic logistic maps. Multimedia Tools Appl. **75**(10), 5455–5472 (2016)
22. Zhang, Q., Guo, L., Wei, X.: Image encryption using DNA addition combining with chaotic maps. Math. Comput. Model. **52**(11–12), 2028–2035 (2010)
23. Belazi, A., El-Latif, A.A.A., Belghith, S.: A novel image encryption scheme based on substitution-permutation network and chaos. Signal Process. **128**, 155–170 (2016)
24. Wang, X., Wang, Q., Zhang, Y.: A fast image algorithm based on rows and columns switch. Nonlinear Dyn. **79**(2), 1141–1149 (2015)
25. Xingyuan, W.A.N.G., Teng, L.I.N., Qin, X.U.E.: A novel colour image encryption algorithm based on chaos. Signal Process. **92**(4), 1101–1108 (2012)
26. Zhongyun, H.U.A., et al.: 2D Sine Logistic modulation map for image encryption. Inf. Sci. **297**, 80–94 (2015)

Lighting Measurements and Evaluation

Research on the Emotional Response Level of Museum Visitors Based on Lighting Design Methods and Parameters

Jiahui Liu[1], Zhisheng Wang[1,2(✉)], Yukari Nagai[2], and Nianyu Zou[1]

[1] Research Institute of Photonics, Dalian Polytechnic University, Dalian, China
wangzs@dlpu.edu.cn
[2] School of Knowledge Science, Japan Advanced Institute
of Science and Technology, Nomi, Japan

Abstract. This study is based on the survey data of Zhongshan Art Museum in Dalian. To investigate changes in the emotional response of visitors to various lighting conditions. The museum is divided into two areas: display space and non-display space. The optical parameters of each space and space are measured. Data analysis was used to evaluate the impact of museum interior lighting on visitors' mood in different lighting environments. It is pointed out that the light intensity and the contrast of CCT, environment are the main viewpoints of the evaluation index. The degree of comfort of visitors in each space was discussed according to the scores of 11 emotional indicators. At the same time, the influence of illumination parameters on the mood of visitors was analyzed by investigating the illumination and color temperature in different scene modes, visual psychology of observer evaluation and so on. The range of illumination and color temperature that is most suitable for visitors is obtained.

Keywords: Emotional response level · Lighting design · Visual factors

1 Introduction

Lighting is one of the essential life elements in nature. The reason why human eyes can see this colorful world is also because of light. It can be said that all human activities are inseparable from light. The natural sunlight irradiation has provided the condition for people's normal life, but now more and more artificial light source has brought more colorful world to people. In the present exhibition activities, how to make better use of light effect has become one of the most important issues for designers. Whether it is a museum or an exhibition, the light effect directly determines the effect of the exhibition. Today's society advocates environmental protection and energy saving, so more and more new energy saving lamps and lanterns have been used in the exhibition.

The lighting in the museum not only meets the visual requirements of tourists, but also makes tourists feel comfortable and enjoy during the visit of the museum. The environmental condition of the museum is a key factor in creating an appropriate

J. Jin et al. (Eds.): GreeNets 2019, LNICST 282, pp. 221–239, 2019.
https://doi.org/10.1007/978-3-030-21730-3_23

exhibition space for tourists and museums. Lighting design plays an important role in museum design, and it is even more important in exhibition hall. Different kinds of museums should have different display themes, which also means different lighting techniques [1].

Light is arguably one of the greatest causes of deterioration in museum collections, on one hand it can be destructive and thus conflicts with the museum's role in preserving our heritage; on the other it is essential to vision, the principal means of communicating the information held within and around the objects in the museum's collection [2].

The environmental space of the museum is divided into two types of Spaces, the main spaces of the museum are defined as the display space, and the secondary space is defined as the non-display space. The lighting modes of different Spaces are divided into environmental lighting and booth lighting. According to the lamps and lanterns of lighting the way of the bottom of the top lighting, lighting, side lighting and mixed lighting, test types and power LED lamps and lanterns, lighting design and layout of space is analyzed. The display space and the non-display space have their own evaluation indexes, and for different emotional response evaluation indexes.

This research refers to the data analysis during the investigation of Zhongshan museum of art, and discusses various factors affecting visitors' emotional response in two aspects of objective experimental data and subjective evaluation. The objective experimental data is mainly to analyze when the display area detects the illumination of its exhibits, it also tests the illumination of the surrounding environment space and calculates the ambient contrast with its illumination. The colour temperature, colour rendering and colour tolerance parameters of the lamps in the display area are tested, and the parameters are classified and analyzed. Display the ambient temperature and temperature test to ensure that the temperature of the exhibit and the ambient temperature meet the requirements of the exhibition while not damaging the exhibit [3]. Compare and analyze the ambient temperature and display temperature to ensure that the physical properties of the exhibit are not damaged while providing more suitable lighting conditions. The subjective evaluation is carried out by inviting the audience to fill in the questionnaire, which is convenient for statistics. A total of 240 groups of data were collected from over 40 people. The exhibition area includes calligraphy works, painting works and sculpture exhibits [4].

In this article, we studied the main types of museum lighting design and the technical indicators used by the led light source in museum lighting environment. Through the analysis of psychophysical experiments and questionnaire survey data, we discussed what kind of lighting design and lighting can create the most suitable light environment for the audience to visit. The research project aims to explore the influence of lighting methods on visitors' emotional response level. Analysis of Zhongshan art museum's investigation through objective measurement results and subjective evaluation results. As shown in Fig. 1.

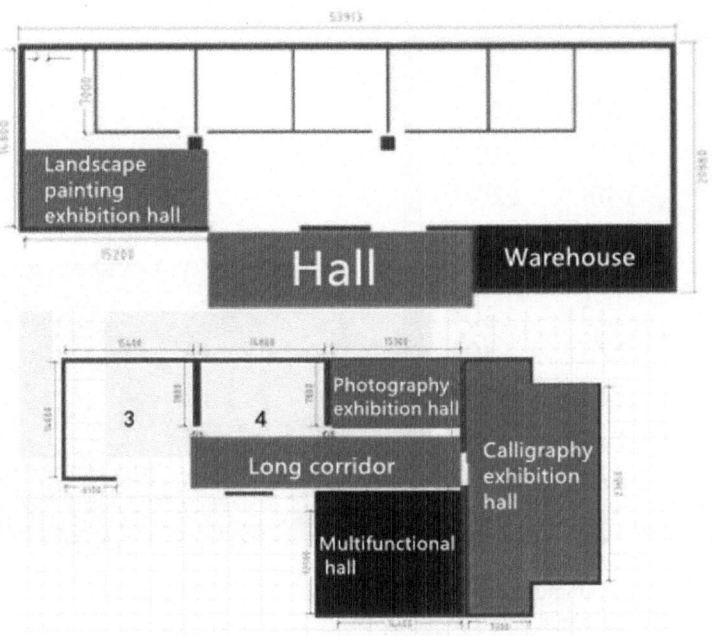

Fig. 1. Floor 1 and floor 2 plan of Dalian Zhongshan art museum

2 Environmental Space

2.1 Display Space

The display space includes calligraphy work area, photography work area, painting work area and three-dimensional exhibit area.

The purpose of exhibit lighting is to make the exhibit attractive and can be fully appreciated and studied by people. In order to achieve this truth, the lighting design should enable the exhibits to fully display their shapes, colours and textures [5].

The illuminance measurement is performed on each partial area to obtain an illuminance distribution map.

An objective measurement of a calligraphy work in the exhibition hall was carried out. The average value of the reflectance is 71.1%, and the ground uniformity and light colour test are taken by the central point method to take the point 3 * 12, and the average value is taken (Eq. 1). As shown in Fig. 2. The objective measurement of the photographic works in the exhibition hall was carried out. The average value of the reflectivity was 62.5%. The ground uniformity and light colour test were taken by the central point method to take 2 * 10 and averaged. As shown in Fig. 4. An objective measurement of a painting in the exhibition hall was carried out. The reflectance takes the average of 3 points as 62.3%. The ground uniformity and light colour test use the central point method to take the point 2 * 6 and take the average value. As shown in Fig. 6. An objective measurement of a three-dimensional exhibit in the exhibition hall

580cm

240+	230 +	210 +
260+	180 +	200 +
280+	160 +	130 +
240+	140 +	120 +
180+	130 +	110 +
160+	120 +	110 +
200+	130+	130+
230+	120+	130+
280+	140+	150+
280+	130+	150+
300+	170+	180+
320+	210+	210+

2400cm

Entrance

Fig. 2. Local ground illuminance Distribution map of calligraphy exhibition hall (Eav 185.0 lx, Uniformity 0.595)

Fig. 3. Calligraphy exhibition hall

was carried out. Ground uniformity and light colour test using the central point method to take the point 1 * 4, take the average. As shown in Fig. 8. The illuminance uniformity of each group was calculated respectively (Eq. 2) (Figs. 3, 5, 7 and 9).

$$Eav = \frac{1}{M \bullet N} \sum Ei \qquad (1)$$

Formula:

Eav—Average illumination, The unit is lx;
Ei—Illuminance at point I, The unit is lx;
M—Longitudinal measuring points;
N—Lateral measuring points.

$$U0 = Emin/Eav \qquad (2)$$

What kind of lighting source is used in the museum is a major problem for lighting designers to adopt lighting methods. Different types of light emitting sources should be given enough attention in terms of luminous ability, and the appreciation of the displayed objects should be reflected in appropriate lighting conditions. The illuminance spectrum of each region was analyzed, and the results are shown in Fig. 10 below.

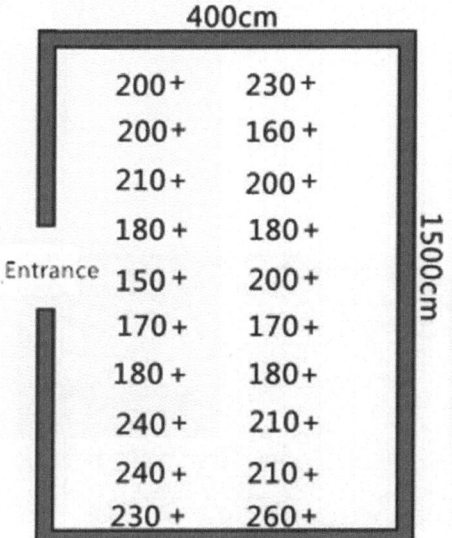

Fig. 4. Ground illuminance distribution hall in exhibition hall of photographic works (Eav 200.0 lx, Uniformity 0.80)

Fig. 5. Photography exhibition hall

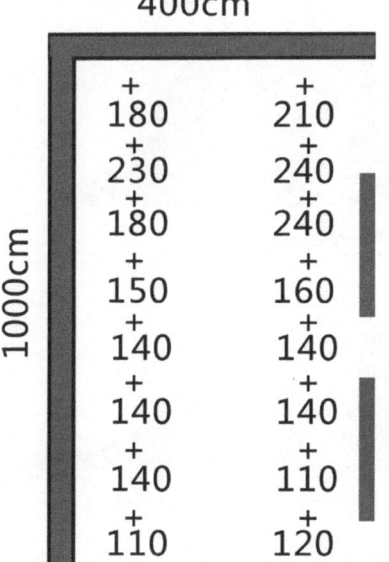

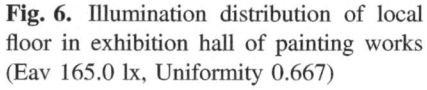

Fig. 6. Illumination distribution of local floor in exhibition hall of painting works (Eav 165.0 lx, Uniformity 0.667)

Fig. 7. Painting exhibition hall

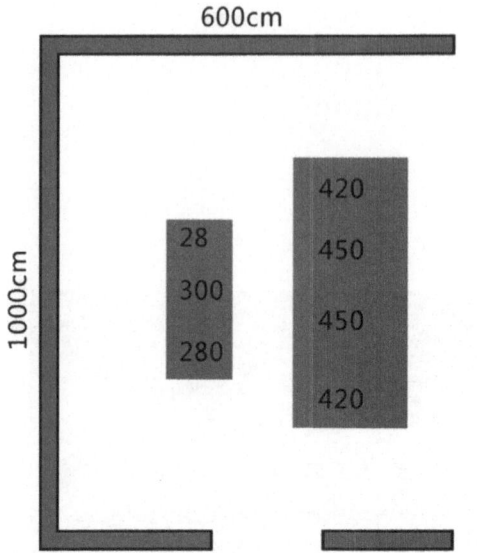

Fig. 8. Illumination distribution of local working face in exhibition hall of three-dimensional exhibits (Eav 317.43 lx, Uniformity 0.759)

Fig. 9. Three - dimensional exhibition hall

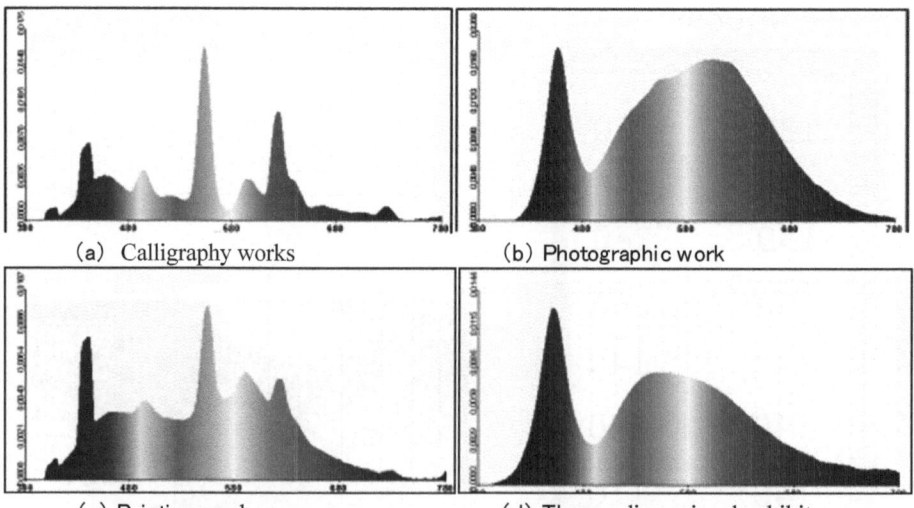

(a) Calligraphy works

(b) Photographic work

(c) Painting work

(d) Three - dimensional exhibit

Fig. 10. Shows the spatial illuminance spectrum

2.2   Non-display Space

For the non-display space, the illumination, brightness distribution and spectral distribution of the lobby area and corridor are mainly targeted. Some areas of the lobby rely on natural light for illumination, and the glass wall is designed so that sunlight can penetrate through the glass and enter the stadium. The roof of the shed is equipped with downlights as auxiliary lighting for night visits. The hall (Fig. 12) uniformity and light colour test uses the central cloth method to take the average value of 4 * 4 points.

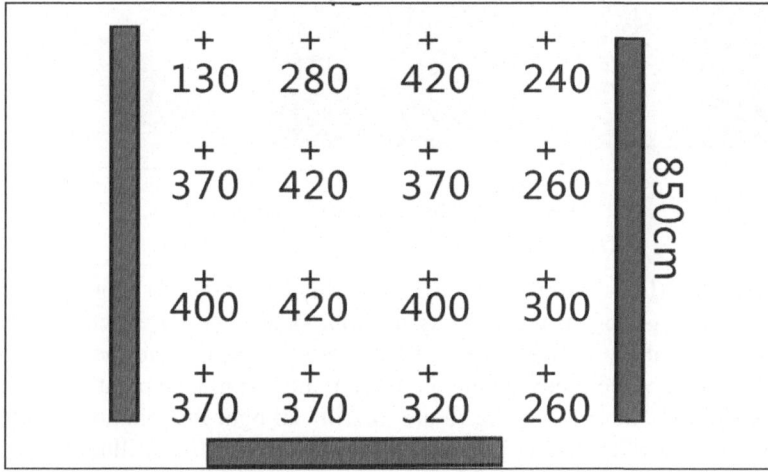

Fig. 11. Illuminance distribution in lobby (Eav 333.13 lx, Uniformity 0.390)

Fig. 12. Dalian Zhongshan art museum lobby

The colour temperature of artificial lighting in the lobby is 5406 k, the average horizontal illuminance is 333.13 LX, and the uniformity of horizontal illuminance is 0.390. As shown in Figs. 11 and 13.

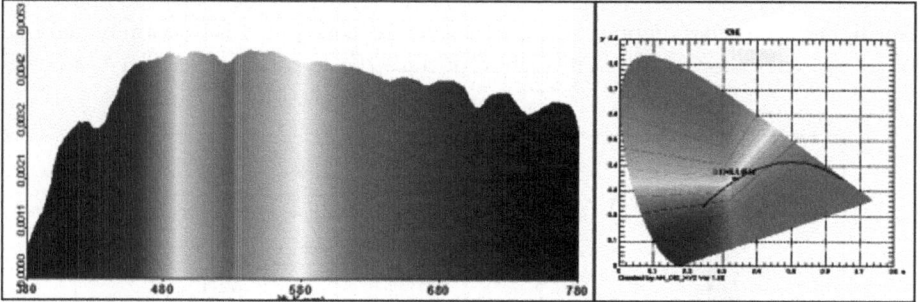

Fig. 13. Lobby illuminance spectrum

The corridor (Fig. 15) relies on led guideway spotlights to illuminate the light reflected by the lighting of the exhibits on both sides. The reflectivity of each wall surface is 62.5% of the average value of the sampling points, and the uniformity and light colour test uses the central point distribution method to take point 1 * 17 and take the average value. The colour temperature of artificial light illumination is 3862 k, the horizontal average illumination is 161.77 LX, and the horizontal illumination uniformity is 0.68. As shown in Figs. 14 and 16.

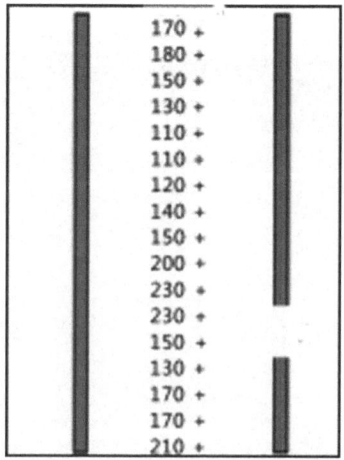

Fig. 14. Illuminance distribution in illuminance corridor (Eav 161.77 lx, Uniformity 0.68)

Fig. 15. Dalian Zhongshan art museum corridor

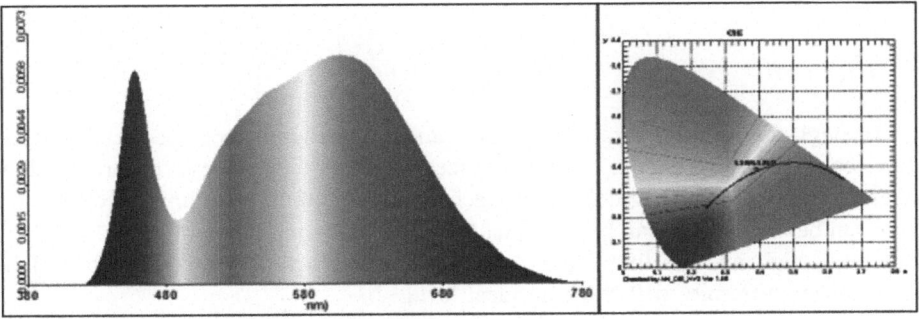

Fig. 16. Corridor illuminance spectrum

2.3 Summary

No matter where the light source is in the spectrum, it is an energy. And energy will drive the chemicals on the object, causing the object to fade and damage [6]. From the two parts of the environment space, the display space and the non-display space, it can be seen that white led lamps are the most suitable choice of lamps and lanterns. Illuminance values, colour rendering index, brightness uniformity and data deviation are measured on different artworks or historical relics. For this kind of situation, it is suggested to solve the problem of visitors' experience based on the standard of adapting to tourists' light level. Through this investigation, we understand the distribution of lighting sources, the types of light sources and the optical parameters of the light sources for the museum lighting, and analyze its exhibition lighting and working lighting. Judging from the light effect alone, led is the main light source, which is easy to adjust. Compared with the original heat radiation light, it is more protective to the exhibits and reduces the exposure. However, due to the uneven selection of led, some exhibits' lighting performance will not be robbed. In addition, there are some halogen lamps. According to the optical parameters of each exhibit, we can know that the infrared radiation of halogen lamps is very strong, so the amount of infrared radiation will be relatively increased, especially the lighting of display cabinets [7]. The Table 1 below for Summary of objective measurement results.

Table 1. Summary of objective measurement results.

Type	Surface temperature/°C	Ra	Colour tolerance adjustment	Brightness/cd/m^2	Brightness uniformity	Illuminance/lx	Illuminance uniformity
Calligraphy exhibition hall	5.4	93.5	9.4	27.34	0.732	933.33	0.857
Photography exhibition hall	5.8	83.4	0.7	15.5	0.839	855	0.866
Painting exhibition hall	10.0	76.2	9.1	36.5	0.767	536.3	0.836
Exhibition hall for three-dimensional works	20.0	83.3	4.0	—	—	1623.33	0.431
Lobby	—	98.6	5.1	—	—	333.13	0.390
Corridor	—	82.7	4.6	—	—	161.77	0.68

Through the use of the measuring instrument, the illuminance spectrum, temperature, color rendering index, color tolerance, brightness, brightness uniformity, illuminance and illuminance uniformity of each space area of the museum reflected in the table can be obtained. It can be seen that the color rendering index of each area of the museum is high, and the illuminance in the display area will be relatively high, and the illuminance uniformity will reach an ideal level.

3 Emotional Response Level

3.1 Subjective Evaluation Survey

The subjective evaluation is carried out by inviting the audience to scan the QR code on site to fill in the questionnaire, which is convenient, efficient and convenient for statistics. A total of 113 sets of data were collected for more than 40 people. The display areas are photographic work areas, oil painting areas and oil painting areas, while the non-display areas are lobby, corridor and leisure areas. The questionnaire is shown in Table 2. The subjective evaluation is carried out by inviting the audience to scan the QR code on site to fill in the questionnaire, which is convenient, efficient and convenient for statistics. A total of 113 sets of data were collected for more than 40 people. The display areas are photographic work areas, oil painting areas and oil painting areas, while the non-display areas are lobby, corridor and leisure areas. The questionnaire is shown in Table 2 [8].

Table 2. Emotional response levels evaluate.

Index/Score	Excellent		Good		Normal	
	6	5	4	3	2	1
Pleasant	11	8	9	12	0	0
Comfortable	10	8	10	12	0	0
Bright	13	7	13	7	0	0
Colourful	15	6	7	1	1	0
Clear	9	13	10	7	1	0
Natural	12	12	11	4	1	0
Active	14	8	7	8	3	0
Relaxing	12	9	9	10	0	0
Soft	8	14	8	9	1	0
Classical	16	8	14	2	0	0
Warm	8	14	12	5	1	0

The emotional index were find into 11 items index, will each index go to rated, construct different illumination environment experimental conditions. Though to change the parameters of illumination, environmental luminance contrast, colour temperature and colour rendering index [9].

The goal of this study was to define the relationships among visual perceptions for different combinations of CCTs at various illuminances. The uncertainty of the experimental rating data was examined with the root mean square (RMS) value on emotional scales by means of intra- and inter-observer variability. The intra-observer variability indicates how well an observer's responses can be repeated under the same evaluation conditions. The inter-observer variability indicates how well the observers' responses agree with the mean within the group. 19 In addition, the RMS value could determine how well the two data sets agree with each other (Eq. 3). Smaller RMS value shows more agreement between two data sets. Higher RMS value means poorer intra- or inter-observer agreement. The variation of RMS depends upon the scale range of the data sets.

$$RMS = \sqrt{\frac{\sum_{i1}^{n}(y_i - x)^2}{n}} \qquad (3)$$

For intra-observer variability, x_i and y_i represent the first score and the second score of the individual observer for the ith stimulus, respectively. For inter-observer

Table 3. Root-mean-square (RMS) values of inter- and intra-observer variability.

Emotional scale	Inter-observer variability	Intra-observer variability
Pleasant	0.92	0.38
Comfortable	0.92	0.37
Bright	0.89	0.38
Colourful	0.92	0.36
Clear	0.88	0.33
Natural	0.96	0.38
Active	0.92	0.36
Relaxing	0.90	0.37
Soft	0.83	0.34
Classical	0.85	0.35
Warm	0.84	0.35
Mean value	0.89	0.36

Table 4. Conversion relation table of grading grades.

Rating scale	Excellent		Good		Normal	
Score grade	A^+	A^-	B^+	B^-	C^+	C^-
Corresponding score	6	5	4	3	2	1

variability, y_i is the individual observer's score for the ith stimulus; x_i is the mean score of all observers for the ith stimulus; and n is the total number of stimuli [10]. The grading scale is shown in the Table 4.

The specific calculation is as follows Table 3:

In the survey questionnaire, for the testees, the psychological and visual acceptance of cultural relic - grade calligraphy and painting exhibits after lowering the illuminance, the change of light and shade in the light environment, the adaptation in visual perception, the coordination of the overall space light and shade and space colour of the art gallery exhibition hall, the psychological feeling, the visual fatigue after the visit, the absence of comfortable shadows on the floor and wall surfaces of the exhibition space, and the feeling of shadows that are too strong to be compared. In terms of artistic expression of light, evaluating whether the overall artistic effect of lighting and the wonderful lighting performance effect have achieved a sense of comfort to the tested person, and whether they have achieved a unified and coordinated overall with the exhibition content by using light forms, which can convey good effects and have deep-level performance, contrast and deduction effects on the exhibition site [11].

3.2 Emotional Response

Emotion is an experience of subjective consciousness, which is a kind of emotional or emotional feeling different from cognition or will. The human eye will automatically adjust the amount of light in order to adapt to the angle level of the scene, and the brightness of the scene will also affect the brightness adaptation level of the person. Generally speaking, it is related to the illuminance on site. The illuminance in different parts of the museum will deviate from the average illuminance to varying degrees, which may make it difficult for visitors' eyes to adapt to the difference in illuminance. Glare sources will often be formed in places where illuminance is too high, making visitors unable to see the exhibits clearly. Uneven illumination distribution on the exhibits and even uncomfortable dark areas or spots will affect the mood of the visitors. The difference in colour temperature of the light source can enhance the display effect. It is usually hoped that the difference in colour temperature is neither large nor small so as not to distract the visitors from the exhibit. The final result of lighting is to create a good visual environment for the audience, so that visitors can feel the cultural relics and painting breath while also keeping a comfortable and comfortable atmosphere in their hearts under the current lighting environment [12].

4 Main Observation Review

Subjective evaluations are all evaluated by means of inviting viewers to scan the QR code to fill out the questionnaire, which is convenient, efficient and convenient for statistics. A total of 121 sets of data were collected from about 20 people. The exhibition area is the calligraphy work area, the photography work area, the painting work area, and the three-dimensional exhibit area. The non-display area is the lobby and the corridor.

Calculate the weight: mean * weight, used to evaluate the lighting design of its venue.

According to the data in Table 5 and the on-site research report, the subjective evaluation results of each display space are obtained. Then calculate the score of each

Table 5. Subjective evaluation index system.

Secondary indicators	Weights	Examination points
Exhibit color realism	20%	(a) Meet the daily testers' true judgment on the color of the exhibits
Light source color preference	5%	(a) The tester can recognize the choice of the cold-warm color of the light source (b) The color of the light source is highly compatible with the psychological expectation of the evaluator
Exhibit detail expression	10%	(a) The light environment clearly shows the details of the exhibit (b) The light environment is accurate and satisfactory for the exhibits
Three-dimensional expressive power	5%	(a) The three-dimensional effect of the exhibits is obvious, and the contrast of light and color is just right (b) The three-dimensional effect of the exhibits is rich in expression, which can improve the aesthetic effect of the art

(continued)

Table 5. (*continued*)

Secondary indicators	Weights	Examination points
Exhibit texture clarity	5%	(a) The details of the material of the exhibits are clearly expressed (b) The material of the exhibits is rich in texture and landscaping
Exhibit outline	5%	(a) Whether the overall outline of the exhibit can be clearly seen (b) Whether the performance of the exhibit outline is easy to identify
Bright acceptance of exhibits	5%	(a) After the cultural relics and paintings and exhibits reduced the illumination, the subjects were highly psychologically and visually accepted (b) The light environment meets the requirements for the protection of exhibit lighting and has a rich artistic appeal
Visual adaptability	5%	(a) The tester changes the light environment in a light and dark manner, and adapts to the visual perception of the project (b) The tester has a psychologically effective scoring project for the light and dark changes in the light environment
Visual comfort (subjective)	5%	(a) The degree of psychological feeling in the overall spatial light and shadow of the exhibition hall and the coordination of spatial color matching (b) The degree of visual fatigue of the tester after the visit
Psychological pleasure	5%	(a) It is uncomfortable for the presence or absence of the brightness distribution in the field of view in the evaluated space, or the presence of extreme brightness contrast (b) A scoring item for the presence or absence of uncomfortable shadows on the floor and walls of the display space, as well as visual effects that are too strong for contrasting shadows or for reducing the ability to observe details or targets
The preference of using light art	20%	(a) The overall artistic effect of the lighting is outstanding, and the tester has high visual comfort (b) There are wonderful lighting effects, which are fascinating and memorable (c) The use of light design to add color to the entire building environment has become a classic case
Infective preference	10%	(a) It conforms to the positioning and collection features of the museum itself (b) The light form of the exhibition is closely related to the theme, forming a unified and coordinated whole with the exhibition content, and it can convey good effects in the form of light (c) The exhibition has deep performance, dedication and interpretation

Table 6. Basic display subjective evaluation results.

Project/Sample number	A+: 10	A−: 8	B+: 7	B−: 6	C+: 5	C−: 4	D+: 3	D−: 0	Mean value	Secondary weight	Weighting × 10
Exhibit color realism	9	12	0	1	3	0	0	0	8.3	20%	16.6
Light source color preference	10	5	6	2	2	0	0	0	8.2	5%	4.1
Exhibit detail expression	10	7	4	3	1	0	0	0	8.3	10%	8.3
Three-dimensional expressive power	9	6	7	1	2	0	0	0	8.1	5%	4.1
Exhibit texture clarity	9	11	3	1	1	0	0	0	8.4	5%	4.2
Exhibit outline	9	9	4	2	1	0	0	0	8.3	5%	4.2
Bright acceptance of exhibits	10	7	5	2	1	0	0	0	8.3	5%	4.2
Visual adaptability	9	9	4	2	1	0	0	0	8.3	5%	4.2
Visual comfort (subjective)	9	10	4	1	1	0	0	0	8.4	5%	4.2
Psychological pleasure	10	4	7	3	0	1	0	0	8.1	5%	4.1
The preference of using light art	9	10	2	2	0	1	1	0	8.1	20%	16.2
Infective preference	11	6	5	2	0	0	1	0	8.3	10%	8.3
Total										100%	82.7

space, basic displays are shown in Table 6, temporary exhibitions in Table 7, halls in Table 8, corridors in Table 9, and auxiliary spaces in Table 10.

According to each evaluation, the corresponding score is 80 points or more, 70 points or more, 60 points or more, and 60 points or less. Divided into 4 levels, excellent, good, average, and poor. From the above four tables, we can see that the basic display, temporary exhibition, and the scores of the three areas of the hall are all above 80, which is a good grade, and the score of the corridor is above 70, which belongs to the general level.

According to the evaluation index system of art museum, the weight of basic display space is 40%, that of temporary exhibition area is 20%, that of lobby is 20%, and that of corridor and auxiliary space is 10%. The final score for the summary is shown in Table 11 below.

It can be seen from the above table that the total score reached 81 points and above 80 points, which was considered as excellent lighting quality for the environmental experience of visitors.

Table 7. Temporary exhibition subjective evaluation results.

Project/Sample number	A+: 10	A−: 8	B+: 7	B−: 6	C+: 5	C−: 4	D+: 3	D−: 0	Mean value	Secondary weight	Weighting × 10
Exhibit color realism	7	10	3	1	0	1	0	0	81	20%	16.6
Light source color preference	7	5	8	2	0	0	1	0	7.9	5%	4
Exhibit detail expression	7	8	5	1	1	0	0	1	7.8	10%	7.8
Three-dimensional expressive power	7	7	6	6	3	0	0	0	8.1	5%	4.1
Exhibit texture clarity	7	4	9	1	2	0	0	0	7.9	5%	4
Exhibit outline	7	8	4	4	0	0	0	0	8.1	5%	4.1
Bright acceptance of exhibits	7	9	3	3	1	0	0	0	8.1	5%	4.1
Visual adaptability	6	8	6	2	1	0	0	0	8	5%	4
Visual comfort (subjective)	7	10	3	1	2	0	0	0	8.1	5%	4.1
Psychological pleasure	7	9	4	2	1	0	0	0	8.1	5%	4.1
The preference of using light art	7	9	4	2	1	0	0	0	8.1	20%	16.2
Infective preference	7	5	8	2	1	0	0	0	8	10%	8
Total										100%	80.7

Table 8. Hall subjective evaluation results.

Project/Sample number	A+: 10	A−: 8	B+: 7	B−: 6	C+: 5	C−: 4	D+: 3	D−: 0	Mean value	Secondary weight	Weighting × 10
Bright acceptance of exhibits	8	9	5	3	0	0	0	0	8.2	10%	8.2
Visual adaptability	8	4	13	0	0	0	0	0	8.1	10%	8.1
Visual comfort (subjective)	9	9	5	1	1	0	0	0	8.3	10%	8.3
Psychological pleasure	7	6	9	3	0	0	0	0	8	10%	8
The preference of using light art	8	8	5	3	1	0	0	0	8.1	40%	32.4
Infective preference	7	10	3	3	2	0	0	0	8	20%	16
Total										100%	81

Table 9. Corridor subjective evaluation results.

Project/Sample number	A+: 10	A−: 8	B+: 7	B−: 6	C+: 5	C−: 4	D+: 3	D−: 0	Mean value	Secondary weight	Weighting × 10
Bright acceptance of exhibits	8	5	7	3	0	0	0	0	8.1	10%	8.1
Visual adaptability	7	6	8	2	0	0	0	0	8.1	10%	8.1
Visual comfort (subjective)	8	7	5	3	0	0	0	0	8.2	10%	8.2
Psychological pleasure	7	6	7	2	1	0	0	0	8	10%	8
The preference of using light art	7	6	6	2	2	0	0	0	7.9	40%	31.6
Infective preference	7	5	5	3	3	0	0	0	7.7	20%	15.4
Total										100%	79.4

Table 10. Auxiliary space evaluation results.

Project/Sample number	A+: 10	A−: 8	B+: 7	B−: 6	C+: 5	C−: 4	D+: 3	D−: 0	Mean value	Secondary weight	Weighting × 10
Bright acceptance of exhibits	8	6	7	4	0	0	0	0	8	10%	8
Visual adaptability	6	7	8	2	2	0	0	0	7.8	10%	7.8
Visual comfort (subjective)	8	7	4	3	3	0	0	0	7.9	10%	7.9
Psychological pleasure	7	6	8	2	1	0	0	0	7.6	10%	7.6
The preference of using light art	8	6	7	2	2	0	0	0	8	40%	32
Infective preference	7	5	5	1	2	1	0	0	7.7	20%	13.2
Total										100%	76.5

Table 11. Summary of subjective evaluation results

	Space category	Sample size	Score	Weight	Final score	Total points
Display space	Basic display	25	82.7	40	33.1	81
	Temporary exhibition	23	80.7	20	16.1	
Non-display space	Hall	25	81	20	16.2	
	Corridor	23	79.4	10	7.9	
	Auxiliary space	25	76.5	10	7.7	

5   Conclusion

Through a series of investigations and data analysis of Dalian Zhongshan art museum, we can see the influence of environmental contrast on visitors' emotional response level. Data analysis method was used to evaluate the lighting design of museum interior space under different ambient lighting.

In today's society, museum lighting can no longer be considered alone, respecting the specifications of some lighting quality and lighting parameters. Neither a single architectural configuration nor a single lighting technology can well achieve the final lighting effect. The design must follow the principles conducive to viewing and protecting exhibits, and strive to better apply modern new technologies and new concepts to museum lighting design, and integrate lighting technology, exhibition theme, artistic effect and visitors' psychology into a comprehensive design.

The choice of lighting parameters and light sources should be carefully designed and strictly controlled so as to protect sensitive exhibits and provide comfortable exhibition conditions for tourists. Led technology seems to have completed most of the required tasks. Proper temperature and humidity can preserve the comfort level in the museum, but there are still suggestions to exist in some museums. In the lighting design method, white led lamps with minimal damage to cultural relics are preferred. At the same time, considering the comfort level of visitors, the illuminance selection is about 300 LX, while the colour temperature range is about 3500 K. The influence of visitors' emotional response needs to be studied and discussed by the professional knowledge of various professionals with "museum experience" so as to further explore and discuss.

Similar to the concept of the Kruithof's pleasing zone, perception zone maps for museum indoor lighting were established. The analytical results indicated that the pleasant zone found in this study partially agreed with Kruithof's rule. These new experiments will be performed again to examine higher illuminances and a wider CCT range in future work.

References

1. Rui, D., Mingyu, Z., Gang, L., et al.: Investigation and study on Chen lighting of museum exhibition based on cultural relic protection. China Illum. Eng. J. **24**(3), 18–23 (2013)
2. Rui, D., Jie, L., Gang, L., et al.: Protective lighting source for light colour painting in China based on colour difference analysis. J. Lumin., 723–728 (2018)
3. Zhai, Q.Y., Luo, M.R., Liu, X.Y.: The impact of LED lighting parameters on viewing fine art paintings. Lighting Research and Technology. https://doi.org/10.1177/477153515578468. Accessed 1 Apr 2015
4. Ajmat, R., Sandoval, J., Arana Sema, F., O'Donell, B., Gor, S., Alonso, H.: Lighting design in museums:exhibition vs. Preservation. WIT Transactions on The Built Environment, vol 118 © 2011 WIT Press
5. Kruithof, A.A.: Tubular luminance lamps for general illumination. Philips Tech. Rev. **6**, 65–96 (1941)
6. Scuello, M., Abramov, I., Gordon, J., Weintraub, S.: Museum lighting: optimizing the illuminant. Colour Res. Appl. **29**, 121–127 (2004)

7. Pinto, P.D., Linhares, J.M., Nascimento, S.M.: Correlated colour temperature preferred by observers for illumination of artistic paintings. J. Opt. Soc. Am. A **25**, 623–630 (2008)
8. Masuda, O., Nascimento, S.M.C.: Best lighting for naturalness and preference. J. Vis. **13**, 1–14 (2013)
9. Zhai, Q.Y., Luo, M.R., Liu, X.Y.: The impact of illuminance and colour temperature on viewing fine art paintings under LED lighting. Lighting Research and Technology. https://doi.org/10.1177/1477153514541832. Accessed 9 July 2014
10. Commission Internationale de l'Eclairage. CIE Publication 177:2007. Colour Rendering of White LED Light Sources. CIE, Vienna (2007)
11. Arana Sema, F., Ceron Palma, E., Rizzi, M.: Evaluation of visual adaptation to illumination levels, Universitat Politécnica de Catalunya (2009). Author, F.: Article title. Journal **2**(5), 99–110 (2016)
12. Author, F., Author, S.: Title of a proceedings paper. In: Editor, F., Editor, S. (eds.) CONFERENCE 2016, LNCS, vol. 9999, pp. 1–13. Springer, Heidelberg (2016)

Design and Implementation of Intelligent Car for Light Environment Detection Based on Data Analysis

Xiangfeng Li[1], Li Shao[2], Yuxu Xiao[1], Ling Yu[3], Bao Liu[1], Xue Yan[1], Jiabao Zou[1], Ya-nan Yang[1], and Xiaoyang He[1(✉)]

[1] Research Institutes of Photonics, Dalian Polytechnic University, Dalian, China
hexy@dlpu.edu.cn
[2] Computer Basic Teaching and Research Department,
Dalian Polytechnic University, Dalian, China
[3] Network Information Center, Dalian Polytechnic University,
Dalian 116034, China

Abstract. With the wide application of LED lighting products in road lighting, there are more and more requirements for illumination measurement. Traditional road illumination measurement uses full manual method, which takes a long time, but the amount of data collected is small, which easily leads to inadequate measurement accuracy, and the full manual measurement method cannot guarantee the personal safety of the surveyors. Therefore, the development and design of an intelligent car can accurately and quickly detect the illumination of street lamp and road surface. The design of this intelligent car is based on cloud server. The hardware core is composed of Raspberry pie and Arduino. Through Arduino management and scheduling illuminance measurement module, GPS positioning module and wireless remote control module, the measured data are packaged and sent to the cloud server through Raspberry pie for data storage and analysis in real time. Finally, the data are stored and analyzed through the visual window. The test results were displayed. Compared with the traditional road lighting detection method, the illumination detection method based on intelligent car can improve the detection efficiency, increase the data accuracy and ensure the safety of the inspectors.

Keywords: Intelligent car · Illumination measurement ·
Wireless remote control · Cloud server

1 Introduction

Road lighting detection technology is an important means to evaluate and test the lighting quality of road lighting products. It is of great significance for accurate and fast detection of illumination parameters of street lamps and pavement. The North American Institute of Lighting Engineering has made a thorough study on road lighting

Supported by Science Foundation for Goldlamp Co., Ltd (2017-228195).

J. Jin et al. (Eds.): GreeNets 2019, LNICST 282, pp. 240–248, 2019.
https://doi.org/10.1007/978-3-030-21730-3_24

standards [1]. Illumination and brightness are the main test parameters required by the National Lighting Standards of the United States for road lighting. The measurement methods, operating instruments and the distribution of monitoring points are standardized, and began to try to use cars for mobile testing. In our country, the light environment detection only stipulates the lighting detection indicators or design requirements, and most of them directly apply the relevant foreign standards. At present, the basis of detecting and evaluating road illumination quality is mainly composed of two evaluation indexes: road illumination parameters (road illumination, average illumination, illumination uniformity) and power consumption. For the measurement method of illumination, the center distribution method and the four corners distribution method are mainly adopted [2]. The on-site detection steps of road illumination parameters are as follows:

(1) Enclosing the detection lane before detection, measuring the distance between the two street lights and determining the spacing of the distribution points;
(2) After locating the points according to the standard method, the inspectors use the illuminometer to test and record points by points.
(3) Using the same steps to measure the adjacent lanes.

The whole process of this testing method is manual testing (30–40 min per test) low detection efficiency, low level of automation, difficult to guarantee the accuracy and consistency of measurement results, personnel working in semi-closed traffic, which is easy to cause greater security risks. It fails to meet the requirement of shortening test period and reducing test times. Therefore, the detection method of road illumination is in urgent need of improvement. Currently, vehicle-based detection equipment has appeared in China [3, 4]. But this kind of car is not very perfect in function, neither can realize intelligent remote control, nor can the data collected for storage and analysis. The intelligent light environment detection car based on data analysis designed in this paper has the function of automatic detection of road illumination. It can continuously pick up points in the test range and form large data storage. It is helpful to shorten the detection period and ensure the safety of the inspectors.

2   System Overall Design

This design is based on cloud server. The hardware core is composed of Raspberry pie and Arduino. The overall design, hardware selection and software compilation of illumination measurement system are carried out. Intelligent car drives DC motor by double H bridge chip to control the car's driving; GY-616 axis gyroscope attitude sensor is used to measure the car's motion state, adjust the car's driving direction and speed; GPS module is used to locate the car's longitude and latitude in real time; BH1750FVI illumination module is used to measure illumination and pass through. Through I2C protocol, the data will be transferred to Arduino, and then through serial communication, the data measured by the module will be transmitted to Raspberry pie. The Raspberry pie will pack the data and send it to the cloud server. After receiving the data packet, the cloud server will analyses and store the data in real time. Finally, the collected data will be presented through the visual window. The system block diagram is shown in Fig. 1:

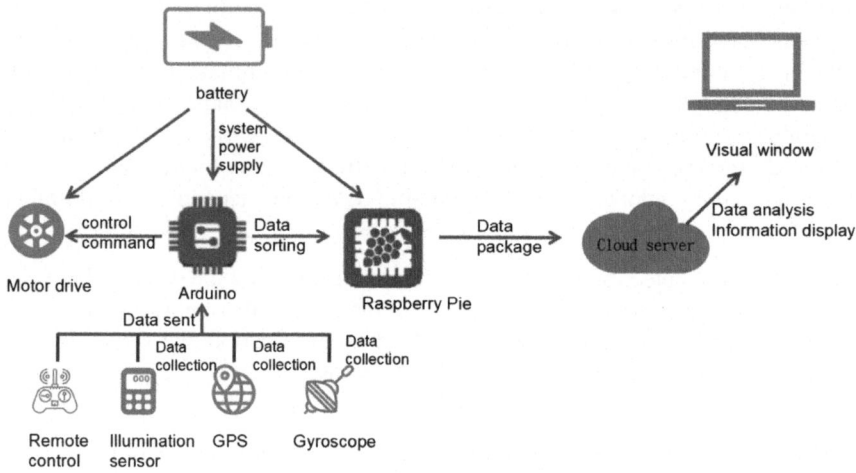

Fig. 1. System block diagram

3   Hardware Design

The intelligent light environment detection vehicle based on large data analysis includes GY-30 digital light sensor BH1750FVI module, 2.4G remote controller, DC motor drive, ATMEGA328P, 12 V lithium battery, Raspberry Pie 3 generation B+type, GY-616 axis gyroscope attitude sensor, GPS module, flash memory card, metal frame and other components.

3.1   Main Control System

The main control system includes body, extended version, Arduino board and Raspberry pie. Arduino controls the motor's forward and backward rotation and speed by controlling the dual H bridge L298 driver chip, thus realizing the control of the car's Omni-directional driving; adding GY-616 axis gyroscope attitude sensor to detect the car's motion information can realize the functions of automatic speed regulation and direction adjustment; in addition, Arduino receives the pulse width modulation from the remote controller. Signal, remote control can be realized (Fig. 2).

3.2   Sensor System

The sensor system consists of three parts: GY-30 digital light intensity illumination sensor, GY-616 axis gyroscope attitude sensor and GPS module. Among them, GY-30 digital light intensity illumination sensor collects illumination information, GY-616

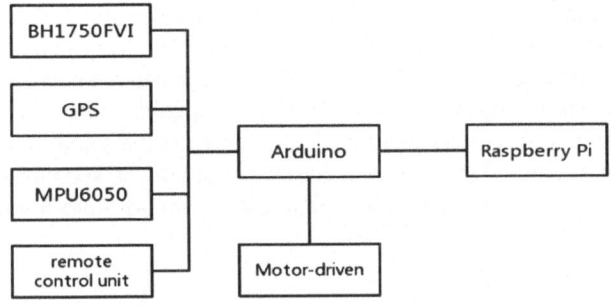

Fig. 2. Hardware block diagram

axis gyroscope attitude sensor detects the motion state of the car, and GPS module is used for positioning. All sensors and Arduino communicate with each other through I2C mode to transmit data. The measured data are analyzed and real-time adjusted to the direction and speed of the car, illumination and other information.

1: GY-30 Digital Light Intensity Sensor
    BH1750FVI, a digital ambient light intensity sensor without distinguishing light sources, is an integrated circuit with two-wire serial bus interface [5]. It has the advantages of high measurement accuracy and convenient data acquisition. BH1750FVI can monitor the environment according to the collected light intensity data. Its high resolution can detect a wide range of light intensity changes. It has a high resolution of 0-65535Lx and can support a wide range of light intensity changes. Among them, ADDR is the port to control the address of BH1750; DVI is the reference voltage port of I2C bus and the asynchronous reset port of chip; SCL is the clock signal terminal of I2C bus to produce high and low level changes and control data transmission; SDA is the data terminal of I2C bus for data transmission.

2: GY-616 Axis Gyroscope Attitude Sensor
    Y-616 Axis Gyroscope Attitude Sensor is a high precision, high stability, small volume attitude measurement module. It integrates three-axis acceleration, three-axis gyroscope output, and combines Kalman filter technology; the measurement results are more accurate. In addition, it has an automatic zero offset detection and calibration algorithm, which can automatically identify the motion state of the module and automatically calibrate the gyro's zero offset when the module is still. The power input is 5 V/3.3 V. XDA/XCL is used to connect other IIC interface sensors. SCL and SDA are used as clock signal ports and data terminals of I2C bus. INT generates interrupt signals and connects them to Arduino.

3: GPS module
    GPS module is an integrated circuit which integrates RF chip, baseband chip and core CPU, together with related peripheral circuits. With up to 50 parallel channels, fast start searching ability, accurate positioning effect, compact size and excellent performance, it is very suitable for applications with high performance and low power consumption. The module has amplifier circuit, which is helpful for passive

ceramic antenna to search satellites quickly. It can set various parameters through serial port, and can be saved in EEEPROM. It is also very convenient to use. In addition, the module also has SMA interface, which can connect all kinds of active antennas. It has strong adaptability and is compatible with 3.3/5 V level. It is convenient to connect all kinds of MCU systems. At the same time, it has its own rechargeable backup battery, which has the function of keeping ephemeris data when power is off. GPS module communicates with Arduino through I2C bus.

3.3 Power Supply System

The power supply system consists of rechargeable 12 V lithium batteries and LM2596S DC-DC DC adjustable step-down regulated power supply module. The 12 V lithium battery not only provides driving voltage for JGA25-371 deceleration motor, but also provides 5 V DC regulated power supply for the whole system through LM2596S power supply module [6] (Fig. 3).

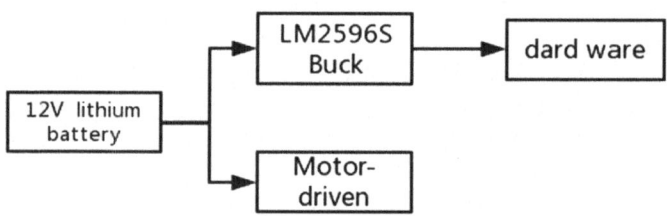

Fig. 3. Power supply system diagram

4 Software Design

4.1 Illuminance Measurement Function

The photometric data measured by photosensitive diode (PD) is amplified by integrated operational amplifier (AMP) and then transferred to analog-to-digital converter (ADC), converted into digital signal, and then into illumination calculator for calculation. The illumination data is transmitted back to Arduino through IC communication. Arduino sends the data to Raspberry pie after sorting, and then uses the principle of message-driven mechanism to pack and upload the data to the cloud server according to the message format. The local visual window obtains the data from the message queue of the cloud server and displays it. Figure 4 shows the data processing flow of illumination measurement.

On the Arduino to Raspberry pie in the process of data processing [7], SendMsg function is responsible for data processing according to the planned format, including the related parameters of software version number, message serial number, UTC time for data collection, the precision of the collected data, collected data of GPS data, temperature, humidity, the current device's MAC address, data specification and checking information and intensity of illumination, which also have reserved fields, convenient later to expand the content of the message data. When the collected data are

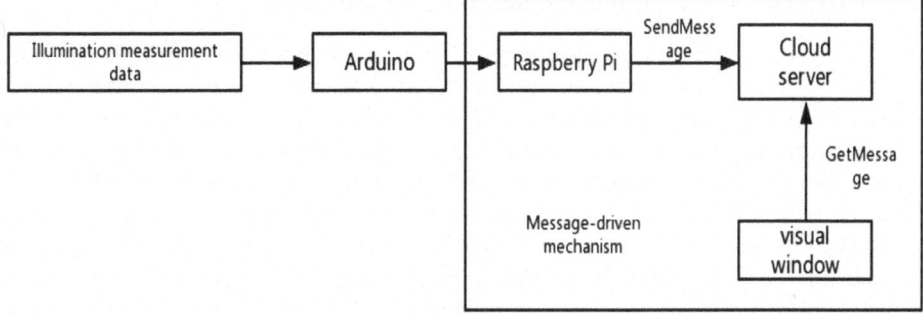

Fig. 4. Illuminance measurement data processing

sorted out, the socket is used to communicate with the cloud server and the data is uploaded to the cloud server for storage and analysis.

4.2 Intelligent Car Attitude Detection Function

GY-61 6 Axis Gyroscope Attitude Sensor module measures the attitude of the car, calculates the motion information of the car, converts the measured analog quantity into the output digital quantity through three 16-bit ADCs on the module, and finally transmits the measured data back to the Arduino board through SDA interface. After receiving the data, the Arduino board runs the algorithm stored in the Arduino board to control the running of the car, thus changing the driving state of the car [8] (Fig. 5).

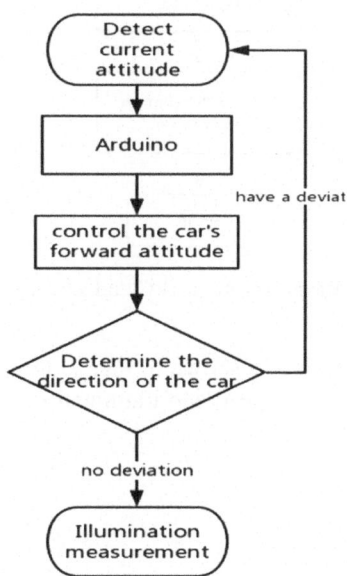

Fig. 5. Flow chart of intelligent car attitude detection

4.3   Network Data Transmission and Data Visualization

The intelligent car server designed in this paper selects the DataV data visualization service of Aliyun [9]. Compared with the traditional chart and data dashboard, this service can provide a more friendly and vivid form. The system collates the data collected from the Raspberry pie according to time periods and packages them into packets. When the network communication is good, the packet will be sent directly to the cloud server. If the signal is not good, the packet will be delayed to prevent data loss. After receiving the data packet, the cloud server will dismantle the data and store the data in the cloud MySQL database. Finally, the data required by the user is displayed in real time on a visual screen created with DataV. The interaction process between Raspberry pie and Cloud server is shown in Fig. 6:

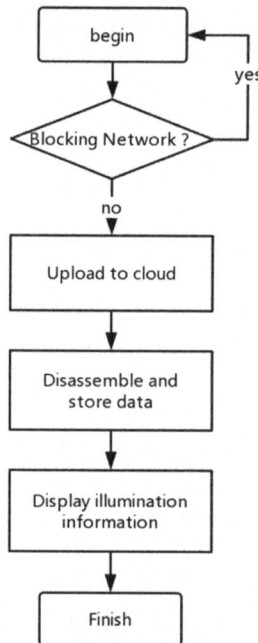

Fig. 6. Raspberry pie and Cloud server processes

The data visualization window is shown in Fig. 7. In the visualization window, the map information, current running speed and illumination curve of the smart car can be displayed in real time.

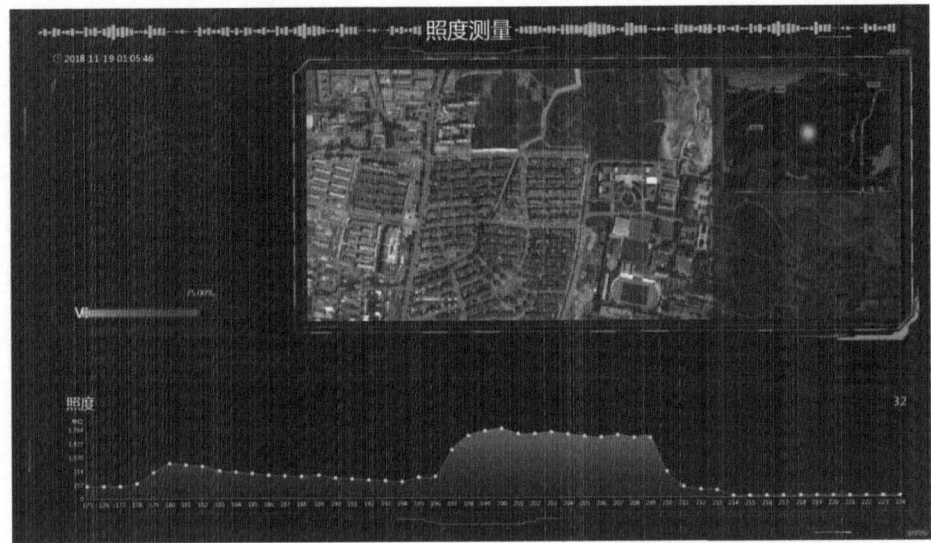

Fig. 7. Visualization window

5   Concluding Remarks

This paper designs an intelligent car for light environment detection based on data analysis, which has the functions of road illumination automatic measurement, GPS positioning and wireless remote control. At the same time, the data storage and analysis function can be realized by connecting the cloud server with the wireless network. This design not only has the advantages of fast measurement speed, low labor intensity, convenient data processing and more intuitive display results, but also greatly reduces the danger of manual measurement and guarantees the safety of the surveyors. The use of car measurement also eliminates the difference of light shielding, reflection and height of the measuring points caused by the surveyors in the field. Due to the interference of other factors, more measurement data and less calculation error are obtained, which effectively improves the accuracy of measurement and data acquisition.

With the increasing application of domestic LED lighting products in the field of public lighting and lighting energy-saving transformation, the intelligent car will realize the level of information and automation of detection technology, further optimize the standard system, and promote the healthy development of the lighting industry, which has important research and development value and practical significance.

References

1. ANSI/IESNA RP-8-00:2005 American National Standard Practice for Roadway Lighting
2. GB/T 5700 Lighting measurement method. Standards Press of China (2008)
3. Xu, J.: Design and application of vehicular road lighting detector. Light Light. **42**(4), 23–25 (2018)

4. Kuicai, S.: Design and application of vehicle-borne road lighting detection system based on AT89S52 single chip microcomputer. Lamps Light. (2), 16–18 (2018)
5. Liu, B.: Design of light intensity data acquisition system based on BH1750. J. Henan Sci. Technol. (13), 27–28 2016
6. Wu, B., Kong, J., Wang, X.: Design and implementation of intelligent car based on Arduino and Raspberry Pi. Electron. Des. Eng. **25**(15), 58–61 (2017)
7. Princy, S.E., Nigel, K.G.J.: Implementation of cloud server for real time data storage using Raspberry Pi. In: 2015 Online International Conference on Green Engineering and Technologies (IC-GET) (2015)
8. Gu, M., Jiao, Z., Wang, W., Hou, J., Jiang, W.: Design of multifunctional navigation intelligent car. Microcomput. Appl. **36**(12), 33–35 (2017)
9. Zhang, G., Guo, W., Sun, Y.: Design of warp workshop data acquisition and monitoring system. Autom. Instrum. **33**(9), 54–58, 103 (2018)

LED Floodlight Optical System Design

Xinpeng Zhang, Yijing Wei, Xue Yan, and Yuncui Zhang[✉]

School of Information and Engineering, Dalian Polytechnic University,
Dalian 116034, China
Zhang_yc@dlpu.edu.cn

Abstract. According to the requirements of this design, a new type of lens was designed. The uniformity of illumination on the two walls was 0.83 and 0.64 respectively, which solved the problem that one wall surface was basically no light when the traditional wall washer illuminates the two walls. The light source is selected from the CREE XM-L2 type lamp bead with a power of 10 W. In this paper, the cutting method is used as the design idea of the free-form optical system, and the secondary optical design of the LED floodlight optical system is carried out.

Keywords: Uniformity of illumination · Cutting method · LED flood light

1 Introduction

With the development of science and technology, LED lighting fixtures are increasingly used by people. In order to get better lighting effects, it is indispensable for the optical components to re-adjust the light. In order to get better lighting effects, the researchers immediately proposed the concept of free-form surface illumination, in order to solve the problems that traditional lighting optical systems can't solve. The free-form surfaces themselves do not have specific mathematical expressions, each of which is derived independently, so it can be considered that many surface patches are constructed under conditions that satisfy a certain continuity. Thanks to its good local operability, it is easy to optimize the design of the system later. As a result, the design freedom of the free-form surface is extremely high, and the distribution of light energy can be flexibly controlled to meet different lighting requirements. Replacing conventional surfaces with free-form surfaces as optical systems can accelerate the development of new lighting applications. At present, the mainstream methods for optical system design include cutting method, partial differential equation solving method, synchronous multi-surface solving method and mesh dividing method. This paper designs and analyzes the lens design process for the cutting method [1].

2 Design Principle

The lens busbars designed in this paper are designed for one plane and become a lens model through multiple iterations. Therefore, the design of the three-dimensional angle problem of the lens can be simplified to the two-dimensional angle problem of the lens.

© ICST Institute for Computer Sciences, Social Informatics and Telecommunications Engineering 2019
Published by Springer Nature Switzerland AG 2019. All Rights Reserved
J. Jin et al. (Eds.): GreeNets 2019, LNICST 282, pp. 249–257, 2019.
https://doi.org/10.1007/978-3-030-21730-3_25

The initial coordinate point (x0, y0) of the curve and the normal vector N0 and the tangent (unit) vector T0 are obtained from the actually required lens aperture size. The angle between the light emitted by the light source and the coordinate axis y axis is θ1, and the light is considered to intersect the tangent vector T0 at (x1, y1) as the second discrete point on the free curve bus. The normal vector N1 and the tangent vector T1 of the intersection are determined by Huygens' theorem. Considering the light from the light source and the angle θ2 of the coordinate axis y2, the third discrete point coordinate (x2, y2) and the normal vector N2 and the tangent vector T2 can be obtained by the above principle. The analogy can obtain the discrete point data set {(xi, yi)} of the optical system, the set of normal and tangent vectors {Ni, Ti}, and the obtained discrete points are successively connected to obtain the target lens bus [2] (Fig. 1).

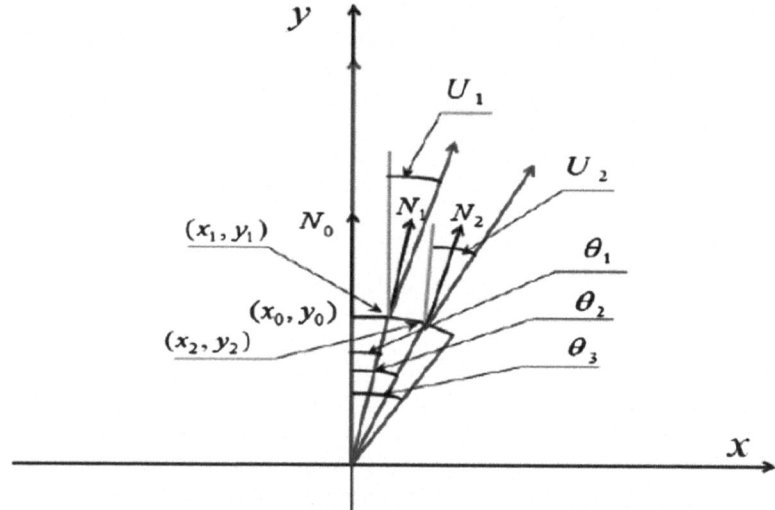

Fig. 1. Schematic diagram of the cutting method

The above design ideas exist in the recursive relationship of the optical system discrete point data set {(xi, yi)}, the normal and the tangent vector set {Ni, Ti}; the refraction surface recursive relationship of the lens optical system can be derived from the Huygens theorem vector form inferred.

3 Design Goals

With the increasing progress of LEDs, traditional optical systems can not meet the lighting effects of LED lamps, so the design of free-form optical systems is increasingly needed. LED floodlights are widely used in exterior lighting of buildings. Because the light distribution design of ordinary light-transmitting lamps can not meet the requirements of uniformity of illumination of special walls, this design combines

(a) Lamp placement position bottom view

(b) Lamp placement position top view

Fig. 2. Luminaire placed real scene

specific examples to analyze multiple floodlights simultaneously. In the process of use, the influence of illumination is optimized to obtain a half-cut LED floodlight optical system [3] (Fig. 2).

Among them, the technical requirements are shown in Table 1.

Table 1. Technical requirements

Request detail	Parameter value
Type of lamp	LED flood light
Lighting fixtures for each floor	2
Lamp manufacturer	CREE
Rated voltage	AC220V
Protection level	IP67
Average illumination	90lx
Illumination uniformity	≥ 0.6
Single light flux	3000l m
Floodlight mounting bracket length	1 m
Irradiation range	4.5 m * 2.4 m
Lamp and wall distance	1.5 m
Power	10 W

The lighting area of the luminaire is shown in Fig. 3. Figure 3(a) is a plan view of the building, and the B side of the A side is an area requiring illumination. Figure 3(b) shows the area that the DIAlux software simulates that the building needs to be illuminated. At the same time, the wall of the n layer will not only be affected by the wall washer, but also by the wall washers of the n − 1 layer and the n + 1 layer. So this analysis simulates 3 floors and takes the middle floor as the test area [4].

According to the illumination area division of Fig. 3, it can be understood that the luminaire needs to uniformly illuminate the wall of 4.5 m * 2.4 m at a distance of 1.5 m from the wall of the B wall. Therefore, the light emitted by the LED chip needs to be re-adjusted by the lens [5].

4   Designing Process

For the wall lighting requirements, find the appropriate light source XM-L2 on CREE's official website. The light source can output a luminous flux of 1052 lm. The following is a suitable light distribution curve for the luminaire found on the market [6]. The size chart of the lamp is shown in Fig. 4.

In summary, the luminaire needs to uniformly illuminate a wall of 4.5 m * 2.4 m at a distance of 1.5 m from the wall of the B wall, and the luminaire is on one side of the wall. The target light distribution curve is shown in Fig. 7. It is necessary to reduce the illumination by the corner of the wall and increase the illumination angle not by the corner of the wall so that it can illuminate farther [7].

The XYZ coordinate axis is established with the LED as the origin of the coordinate axis. As shown in Fig. 5, the hemisphere in the figure is a lens to be designed. The illumination angles in the x-axis direction are not the same, and the illumination angles in the y-axis direction are the same but are small [8].

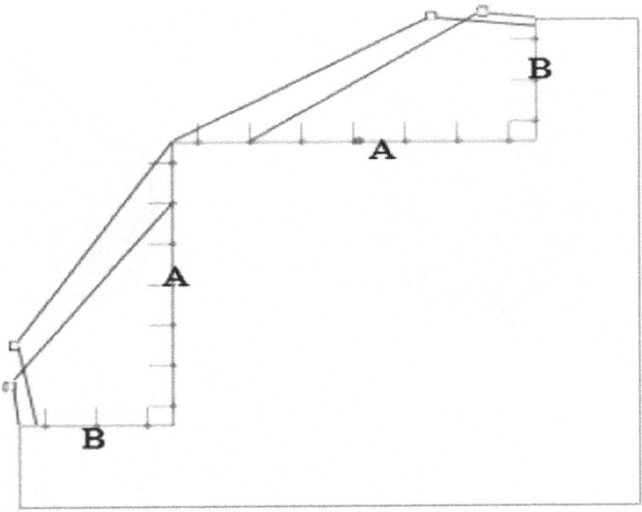

(a) Lighting range of lamps

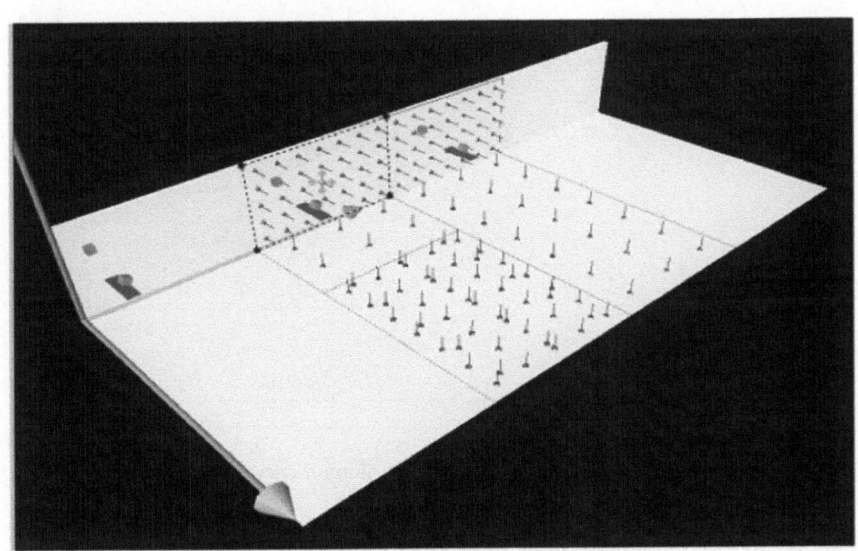

(b) Lighting simulation of building

Fig. 3. Simulated building

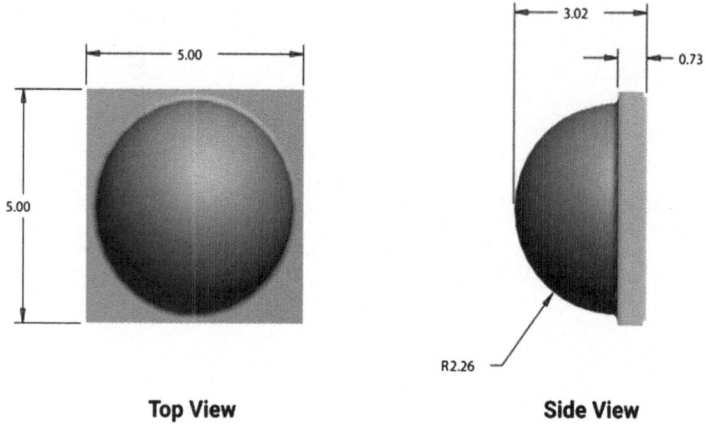

Top View   **Side View**

Fig. 4. XM-L2 size chart

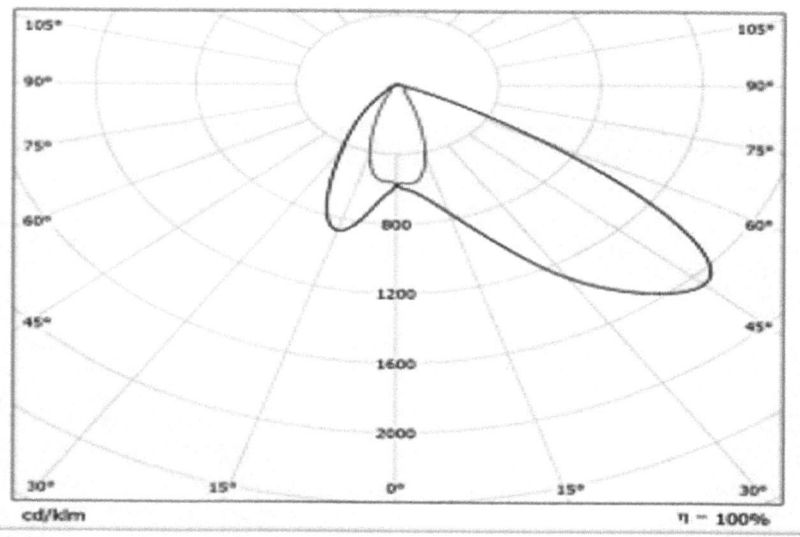

Fig. 5. Target light distribution curve

Finally, the maximum illumination angles in the four directions are ranked 60°, 23°, 30°, and 23° in a clockwise direction. The lens model is shown in Fig. 6 [9].

After the use, the simulated scene situation in DIAlux.

Among them, the yellow line in Fig. 7 represents the light distribution curve of the luminaire, and the blue area represents the test area.

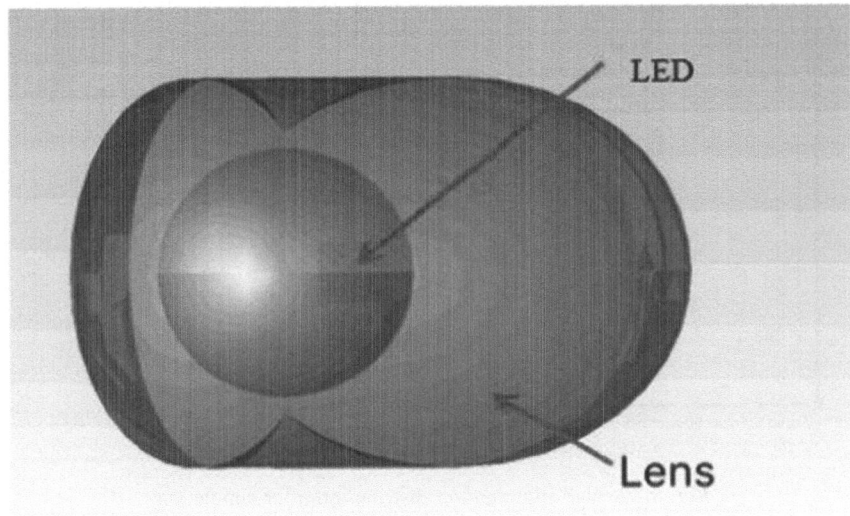

Fig. 6. Positional relationship between lens and COB

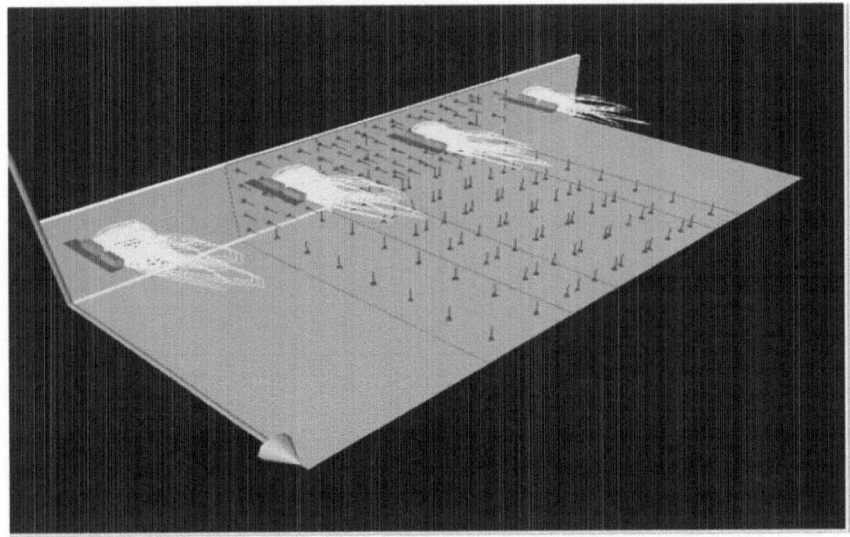

Fig. 7. Graphic design after simulation

5   Design Effect and Analysis

The luminaire with the added lens eliminates the need for the worker to adjust the angle in the horizontal direction during installation. The angle between the outer lamp and the horizontal line is 70°, and the angle between the inner lamp and the horizontal line

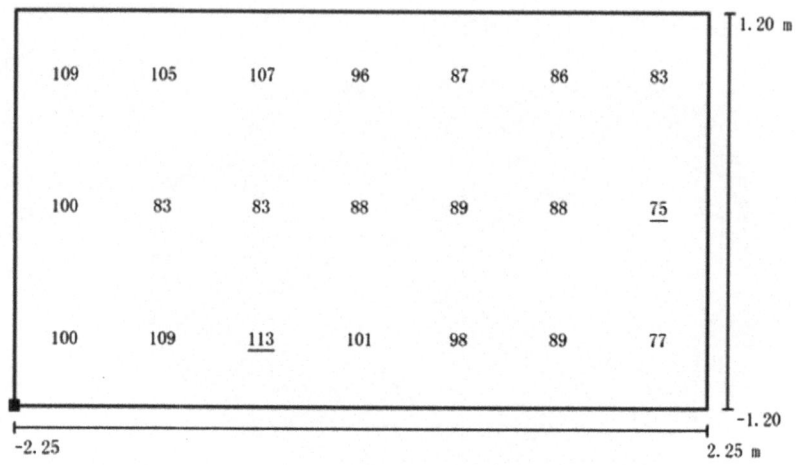

Fig. 8. A wall illumination distribution after simulation

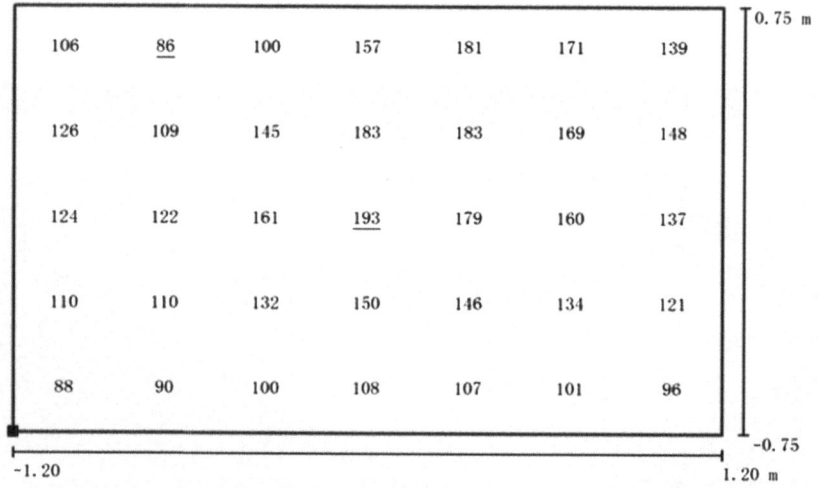

Fig. 9. B wall illumination distribution after simulation

is 80° [10]. The illuminance uniformity of the A wall and the B wall are 0.83 and 0.64, respectively, and the average illuminance is 94 lx and 133 lx, respectively, and the difference is 39 lx (Figs. 8 and 9).

The comparison shows that the illuminance uniformity of the new lens on the A wall surface and the B wall surface is 0.83 and 0.64, which are in line with the project requirements. Generally, the wall washer optical system can only uniformly level the A wall illumination to 0.7, and the B wall surface is basically dull [10]. When the AB wall is illuminated by the street light optical system, the illumination uniformity is 0.5 or less, and the B wall surface is extremely bright. Therefore, the comprehensive comparison shows that the new lens is more suitable for use in this project [11].

6 Conclusion

In this paper, the secondary optical design of the optical system of the LED floodlight is carried out by using the cutting method as the design idea of the free-form optical system. Taking the half-cut lens as the design object, the required lens light distribution curve is analyzed, and the free-form optical system is designed to make the optical system finally achieve the required lighting effect.

References

1. Jin, X., Wang, C., Wang, Z.: Road light distribution design for LED extended light source. Photoelectron·Laser **25**(5), 857–863 (2014)
2. Liu, Z., Sun, Y., Lin, Y.: Design of rectangular illumination free-form surface reflector based on differential geometry. J. Opt. **32**(10), 1–5 (2012)
3. Shi, Y., Mai, D., Ning, L.: A survey of LED free-form surface lens design methods for uniform lighting of roads. J. Light. Eng. 05 (2010)
4. Su, D.: LED application and optical design case analysis in aircraft navigation lights. Appl. Optics 06 (2014)
5. Liu, X., Xue, S., Huang, D.: White LED status and problems. Light Source Light. (3) (2003)
6. Chen, J.-J.: Freeform surface design for a light-emitting. Opt. Eng. **49**(9), 1–8 (2010)
7. Liu, P.: Optimized design of LED freeform lens for uniform circular illumination. Zhejiang Univ-Sci. C **13**(12), 929–936 (2012)
8. Zhen, Y.: The optimal design of TIR lens for improving LED illumination uniformity and efficiency. In: Proceedings of SPIE, vol. 6834, pp. 1–8 (2007)
9. Spencer, D.E.: Design of reflector contours to satisfy photometric criteria using physically realizable light sources. In: Nonimaging Optics: Maximum Efficiency Light Transfer VI (2011)
10. Zhang, Z., Wang, K., Deng, J., Hai, Y.: A method for pulsed scannerless laser imaging using focal plane array. In: International Symposium on Photoelectronic Detection and Imaging 2011: Laser Sensing and Imaging; and Biological and Medical Applications of Photonics Sensing and Imaging (2011)
11. Fournier, G.R., Bonnier, D., Forand, J.L., Pace, P.W.: LUCIE ROV-mounted laser imaging system. In: Ocean Optics XI (1992)

Emotional Feedback Lighting Control System Based on Face Recognition

Xiangfeng Li, Ling Yu, Yini Zhang, Zeyuan Shao, Linyu Huang,
Chaoyang Zhang, and Xiaoyang He[(⊠)]

Dalian Polytechnic University, Dalin 116000, China
hexy@dlpu.edu.cn

Abstract. In order to solve the vicious circle of negative emotions caused by stress spreading in the family. This paper designs a lighting control system that reflects the user's emotions in real time to assist users in managing emotions. The system establishes an emotion-color conversion model based on color psychology. Based on the Face++ face recognition cloud platform, the Raspberry Pi and Arduino form the hardware core for the overall design, hardware selection and software programming of the lighting control system. The system collects the user's facial image and uploads the image to the cloud platform, and then the cloud platform performs face recognition on the image. The recognized face parameters are returned to the system. Then according to the emotion-color conversion model, the face parameters are converted into light parameters. Finally, the system transforms the light according to the light parameters, so that it realizes the effect of transforming the light color according to the facial expression of the user, and plays a role in supporting the management of emotions.

Keywords: Face recognition · Emotions · Lighting system

1 Introduction

Nowadays, people generally need to face the pressure problems brought by modern fast-paced life. Negative emotions caused by stress are infectious and diffuse [1]. This negative emotion is bring to the family easily, and causes family disharmony. Eventually it will lead to a vicious circle of stress accumulation. This vicious circle will keep people in a sub-health state for a long time [2]. To solve such this vicious circle, we need to pay attention to managing emotions and avoid putting work pressure on the family.

This paper designed a lighting control system. The system uses the expression recognition technology in face recognition to develop a lighting control system that reflects the user's real-time emotions. The system captures the user's expression through the built-in camera, and uploads the captured expression to the server for analysis and processing. The expression is converted into a light color parameter,

Supported by Science Foundation for Goldlamp Co., Ltd (2017-228195).

J. Jin et al. (Eds.): GreeNets 2019, LNICST 282, pp. 258–266, 2019.
https://doi.org/10.1007/978-3-030-21730-3_26

which controls the user's the current expression state through the change of the color of the light, so as to achieve the effect of supporting the management of emotions.

2 Face Recognition Technology

After more than 60 years of development, artificial intelligence has made break-throughs in algorithm and data accumulation. In recent years, artificial intelligence has triggered new scenes in many industries, inspiring unprecedented value and triggering investment from the world [3]. As an important field of artificial intelligence, face recognition constantly breaks through the research bottleneck, and it has greatly improved in various aspects such as recognition speed and accuracy. Therefore, its application value is gradually reflected [4–7].

The main process of the traditional face recognition system is shown in Fig. 1.

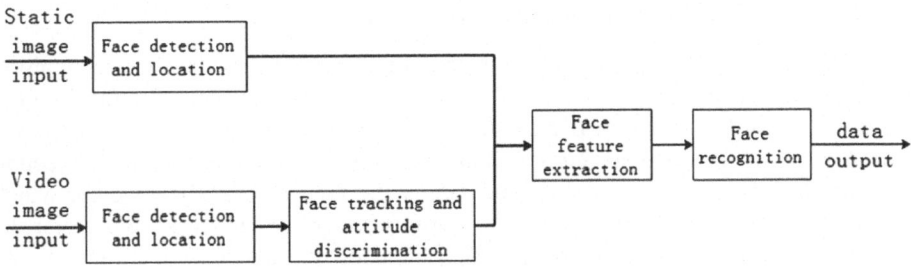

Fig. 1. Flow diagram of face recognition system

First, check if there is a human face in the image, determine its position in the image and separate it from the image. Secondly, extracting the facial features. Finally, identifying the processed image. The purpose is to match the recognized image with the pre-stored face image in the database and output the matching result [8–10].

3 Description of the System

3.1 Description of System Flow

The system uses a combination of Raspberry Pi and Arduino as the control system. The face image is captured by the camera. The face image is processed by the Raspberry Pi and uploaded to the Face++ artificial intelligence cloud platform. After the face image is processed by the Raspberry Pi, it will be uploaded to the Face++ artificial intelligence cloud platform.

Cloud platform analyzes face images, and then obtain feature data. After receiving the feature data, the Raspberry Pi processes it and outputs the corresponding control parameters. Arduino implements the corresponding light changes based on the received control parameters. The system flow is shown in Fig. 2.

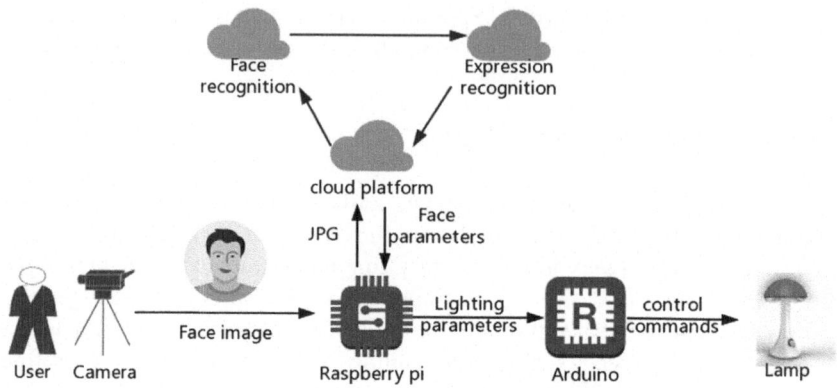

Fig. 2. Flow diagram of system

3.2 Description of the System Structure

The system uses Face++ artificial intelligence open platform as the face recognition platform, and the Raspberry Pi and Arduino as the hardware core for the lighting control system software and hardware design. The system is divided into three parts: the first part is the image acquisition module, which includes the functions of collecting and uploading face images; the second part is the face recognition module, which includes collecting and recognizing face features and returning face parameters; the third part is the light control module, which includes the functions of receiving face parameters and controlling light changes.

Functional architecture is shown in Fig. 3:

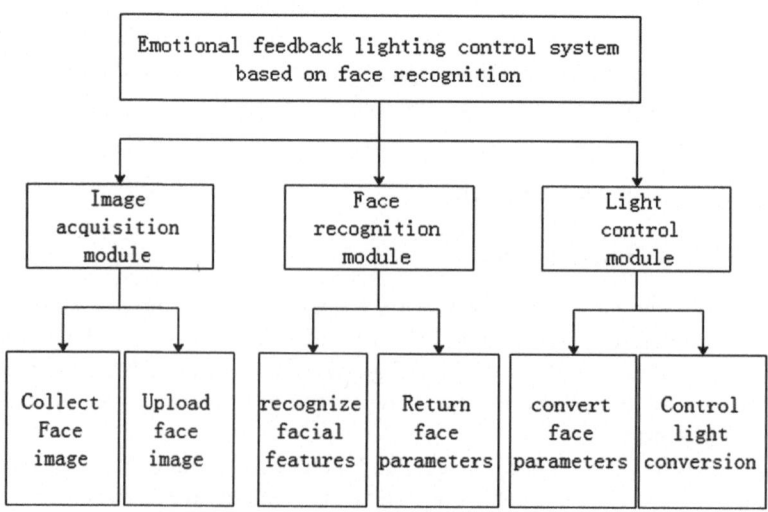

Fig. 3. System function diagram

(1) Collect face image: collect face image from the camera on the Raspberry Pi.
(2) Upload face image: the captured image is preprocessed and uploaded to the Face+ + face recognition cloud platform.
(3) Recognize facial features: cloud platform uses face recognition technology to identify current images.
(4) Return face parameters: the cloud platform sends the recognized face parameters to the Raspberry Pi.
(5) Convert face parameters: the Raspberry Pi converts the face parameters into light parameters according to the preset formula and sends them to the Arduino through serial communication.
(6) Control light conversion: Arduino further processes the received light parameters to achieve the light transformation.

3.3 Description of System Functions

The system establishes an emotion-color mapping relationship, as shown in Fig. 4. According to color psychology, based on red, green and blue light colors, dividing the color circle into three areas of equal area, each representing an emotion. Its mathematical model is established as follows: extract the light colors corresponding to the three emotions of happiness, surprise, and sadness. They are orange, purple, and cyan. Then take the complementary colors of these three colors, which are blue, green, and red. This gives an inverse relationship between light and color: When the proportion of "happiness" is increased, the blue component of the light color will decrease and the light will be more yellow; When the proportion of "surprise" is increased, the green component of the light color will decrease and the light will be more purple; When the proportion of "sadness" is increased, the red component of the light color will decrease and the light will be more cyan. Through this emotional color mapping, the user can know the current expression state from the light color.

Fig. 4. Emotion-color mapping diagram (Color figure online)

4   System Software and Hardware Design

4.1   System Hardware Design

The system hardware structure is shown in Fig. 5. This system consists of host computer and slave computer two levels system: Raspberry Pi as the host computer, Arduino as the slave computer. They are connected to the camera and the controlled light sources. Power supply to the Raspberry Pi, Arduino, and controlled light sources.

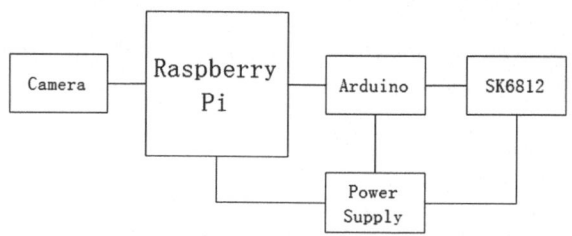

Fig. 5. Hardware structure diagram

As the host computer, the Raspberry Pi mainly undertakes the functions of data uploading, data receiving and data conversion of the system. As a slave computer, Arduino has a powerful expansion capability to make up for the shortcomings of the expansion of the Raspberry Pi. This makes the system more perfect.

Raspberry Pi and Arduino use the serial communication between them to exchange parameters. The connection method is shown in Fig. 6.

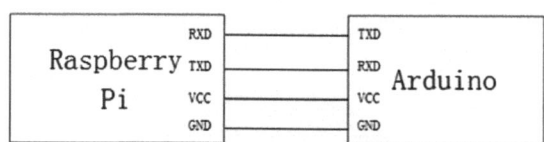

Fig. 6. Connection diagram of Raspberry Pi and Arduino

In the latest hardware upgrade of Raspberry Pi 0 W, the camera interface has been added, which enables the system to directly use the Raspberry Pi to achieve image acquisition. The camera interface category is CMOS Sensor Interface (CSI), so the system uses the matching CSI camera to achieve image acquisition. In terms of light source, the system uses RGB full color lamp bead SK6812. Its driving circuit and RGB chip are integrated in a 5050 package component to form a complete external control pixel point, which enables the system to achieve precise dimming effect.

The SK6812's data protocol uses a single-pole return to MA communication mode. The connection method is shown in Fig. 7.

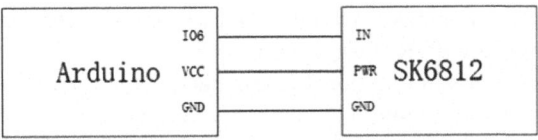

Fig. 7. Connection diagram of Arduino and SK6812

4.2 System Software Design

The system software part mainly includes the Raspberry Pi program and the Arduino program. Designed mainly according to the system flow chart of Fig. 8.

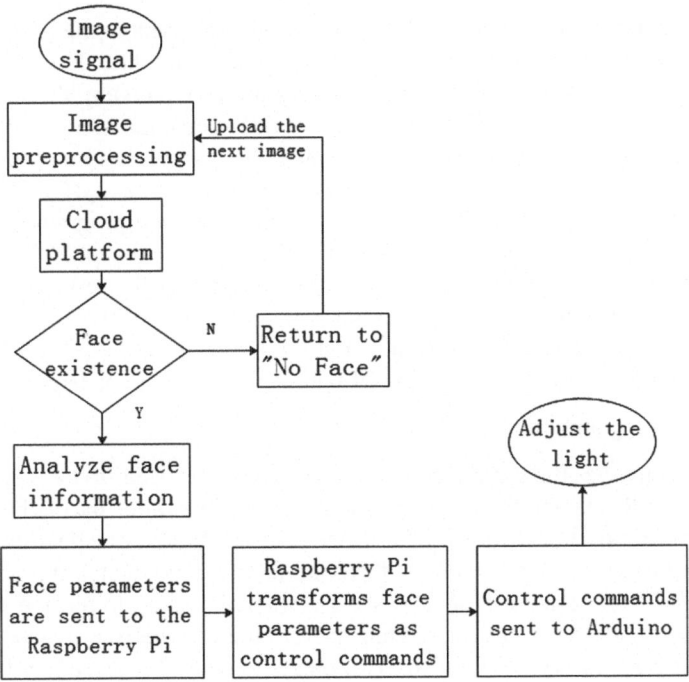

Fig. 8. System flow chart

(1) Raspberry Pi programming

As the host computer, the Raspberry Pi needs to complete the five functions of acquiring images, uploading images, receiving face parameters, transforming face parameters, and sending control commands.

First, call PiCamera to capture the image and save the image data captured by the camera. Then call the image upload function to upload the image to the face recognition cloud platform via the API provided by face++. Analytic data from the cloud platform will return to the Raspberry Pi. If there is a face in the image, it will get 4 emotional parameters: happiness, neutral, sadness, surprise. If there is no face in the image, it will prompt "ERROR: face_capture".

After obtaining 4 kinds of emotional parameters, the Raspberry Pi needs to convert the emotional parameters into light parameters. The system selects RGB lamp beads as the light source, so, selecting "sadness, surprise, happiness" three kinds of emotion parameter corresponding conversion in the program.

b = int(255 − 255*data['happiness']/100), When the proportion of "happiness" is increased, the blue component of the light color will decrease and the light will be more yellow; g = int(255 − 255*data['surprise']/100), When the proportion of "surprise" is increased, the green component of the light color will decrease and the light will be more purple; r = int(255 − 255*data['sadness']/100), When the proportion of "sadness" is increased, the red component of the light color will decrease and the light will be more cyan.

After the conversion is completed, the data needs to be sent to the Arduino through the serial communication. It is necessary to install and configure the pyserial module before using the Raspberry Pi serial communication. Configure the serial port to automatically recognize the serial port number mode. The baud rate is set to 9600 and the time of connection timeout is 0.1 s. Because the Raspberry Pi's own serial communication command interferes with the data transmission of this system. For example, its end command is "0", etc. Therefore, you need to use the program to rewrite the system commands. So, it is necessary to rewrite the system commands. Set 251–255 as the system verification command, 255 to verify the status of the serial port ready, 254 to verify the status of the data termination transmission, 129–250 to reserve the instruction set for the cmd command, 1–127 is the data. Use "X-X/2 + 1" and "X/2 + 1" to achieve split transmission of data and avoid the appearance of "0".

(2) Arduino programming

Arduino is used as the slave computer in this system. It needs to be written with the host computer (Raspberry Pi) in programming. Therefore, after the Arduino receives the split data sent by the Raspberry Pi, it needs to synthesize two data into one data.

First need to set the serial port, set the baud rate to 9600, match the raspberry pie, rial.begin(9600). After the serial port is set up, use Serial.read() to receive the data sent by the Raspberry Pi. Since the data obtained from the Raspberry Pi has been split and zeroed out, it is necessary to synthesize two pieces of data after receiving the data, data [i] = data_buffer[2*i] + data_buffer[2*i + 1] − 2.

After the setup is completed, the data is received and processed by the serial communication, and the Adafruit_NeoPixel-master of Arduino is called to control the SK6812. The complete RGB parameters are loaded into pixels.Color() to control the RGB light source.

5   Implementation Case

After the system circuit is completed, testing system functions.

The face image is collected by the Raspberry Pi camera, uploaded to the cloud platform for face recognition, and the returned face parameters are converted by the

Raspberry Pi to obtain the light parameters. After receiving the light parameters, the Arduino performs dimming control on the light source.

The test results are: happy corresponding to yellow light, sad corresponding to blue light, surprised corresponding to purple light (Figs. 9, 10 and 11).

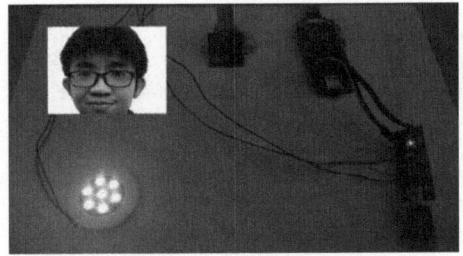 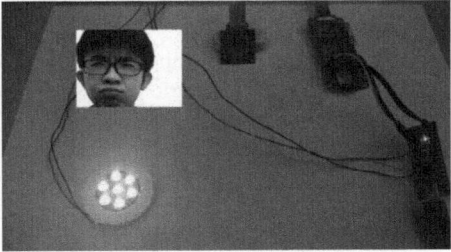

Fig. 9. Happy state (Color figure online)   **Fig. 10.** Sad state (Color figure online)

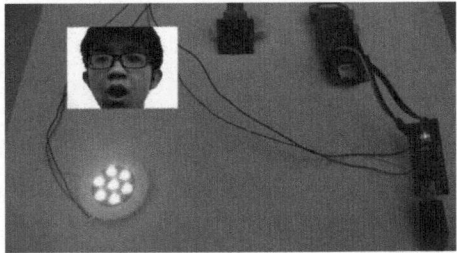

Fig. 11. Surprised state (Color figure online)

6 Summary

The system completes the user's emotions through expression recognition technology and converts them into lights for output. Remind the user's current expression status by changing the color of the light to help the user manage the emotions.

The system collects facial images through a camera and analyzes facial attributes using face++ face recognition cloud platform. After receiving the face parameters, the Raspberry Pi converts according to the emotion-color correspondence and outputs the light parameters through the serial port. After receiving the parameters, Arduino outputs control commands to control the lights. When the user is happy, the light will turn red; when sad, it will turn blue; when surprised, it will turn purple.

Advantages and features: Using face recognition technology to achieve luminaire control, this control method is closer to the concept of "smart" than traditional panel or remote control. Among the key links, face recognition is realized through the cloud platform interface, which is a popular practice in product development, and can guarantee its implementation effect and stability. The Raspberry Pi 0 and Arduino NANO selected by this system are the smallest controllers in the same type of products, which are easy to embed and low in cost.

References

1. Goldin, P.R., Mcrae, K., Ramel, W., et al.: The neural bases of emotion regulation: reappraisal and suppression of negative emotion. Biol. Psychiat. **63**(6), 577–586 (2008)
2. Nicolaou: Electronic performance monitoring: the crossover between self-discipline and emotion management (2015)
3. Sheth, S., Ajmera, A., Sharma, A., et al.: Design and development of intelligent AGV using computer vision and artificial intelligence (2018)
4. Ahonen, T., Hadid, A., Pietikinen, M.: Face description with local binary patterns: application to face recognition. IEEE Trans. Pattern Anal. Mach. Intell. **28**(12), 2037–2041 (2006)
5. Georghiades, A.S., Belhumeur, P.N., Kriegman, D.J.: From few to many: illumination cone models for face recognition under variable lighting and pose. IEEE Trans. Pattern Anal. Mach. Intell. **23**(6), 643–660 (2001)
6. Belhumeur, P.N., Kriegman, D.J.: What is the set of images of an object under all possible illumination conditions?. Kluwer Academic Publishers, Hingham (1998)
7. Brunelli, R., Poggio, T.: Face recognition: features versus templates. IEEE Trans. Pattern Anal. Mach. Intell. **15**(10), 1042–1052 (1993)
8. Samaria, Ferdinando, Young, Steve: HMM-based architecture for face identification. Image Vis. Comput. **12**(8), 537–543 (1994)
9. Lee, D.D., Seung, H.S.: Algorithms for non-negative matrix factorization. In: NIPS, pp. 556–562 (2000)
10. Turk, M., Pentland, A.: Eigenfaces for recognition. J. Cogn. Neurosci. **3**(1), 71–86 (1991)

Mapping Research on 1931 Chromaticity Diagram and Fengshui Five Elements Theory

Yini Zhang, Ling Yu, Xiangfeng Li, Yiyu Wu, Yan Liu,
Peiming Zeng, and Xiaoyang He[✉]

Dalian Polytechnic University, Dalin 116000, China
hexy@dlpu.edu.cn

Abstract. The combination of Feng shui and lighting can create a yin and yang balanced light space, which will become the trend of lighting design in the new era. The suitable lighting environment is beneficial to the physical and mental health of the occupants. By collating and analyzing the theoretical system of Feng Shui, this paper maps the 1931 chromaticity diagram and the five elements, and then selects the appropriate light source to adjust the energy of the human body and the surrounding environment. The combination of traditional Chinese martial arts and modern lighting is a new kind of interdisciplinary research, which is of great significance for the harmonious between human and light.

Keywords: Fengshui · 1931 chromaticity diagram · Five elements theory · Lighting environment · Mapping model

1 Introduction

With the rapid development of science and technology in the 21st century, the needs to life are arisen, which manifested in various fields such as clothing, food, housing, and transportation [1]. The lighting affects the comfort of the living to a certain extent. To make the lighting and people better integrate is an eternal topic, and it is a complicated and long-term work [2]. Feng Shui is a theory that studies the microscopic substances (air, water and soil) and the macro environment (the universe) [1]. The core purpose is to live in harmony with nature [3]. This study explores the corresponding relationship between Feng Shui and colorimetry, deduces and analyzes the model, and extends it to indoor and outdoor light environments. This is a new application direction that realizes the integration of human and light.

Supported by Science Foundation for Goldlamp Co., Ltd (2017-228195).

J. Jin et al. (Eds.): GreeNets 2019, LNICST 282, pp. 267–275, 2019.
https://doi.org/10.1007/978-3-030-21730-3_27

2 Research Assumption

The functional expression v = f(u) of the Planckian locus represented in Chromatic coordinates as a chromaticity diagram [4]. In the chromaticity diagram, each color occupies a certain position, and the coordinates of the color are composed of the proportional coefficients R, G, and B, and the X-axis chromaticity coordinates in the chromaticity coordinates are equivalent to the ratio of the red primary color. The Y-axis chromaticity coordinate corresponds to the ratio of the green base color, and the Z coordinate axis can be calculated by X + Y + Z = 1 [5].

The study used the 1931 chromaticity diagram of 2 degree field of view angle (as shown in Fig. 1). In the trajectory and surrounding of the Planckian locus, CIE artificially defined the A, B, C, D, E five characteristic points which representing five standard light sources. In these five points, the E point is a coordinate point of the white light spot, is a mixture of three primary colors of light and the same stimulating light energy, the corresponding color temperature is 5400 K, and point A is the chromaticity coordinate point of the standard illuminator A, the CCT (color temperature) is 2856 K; point B, which next to the Planckian locus, is the chromaticity coordinate point of the standard illuminator B, the CCT is 4874 K; which is similar to the noon sunshine; the point C that belows the Planckian locus is the chromaticity coordinate of standard illuminator C, the light color is similar to the daylight of the cloudy sky, CCT = 6774 K; and D is the chromaticity coordinate point of the standard illuminator D65, called recombination daylight, the CCT is 6504 K [6].

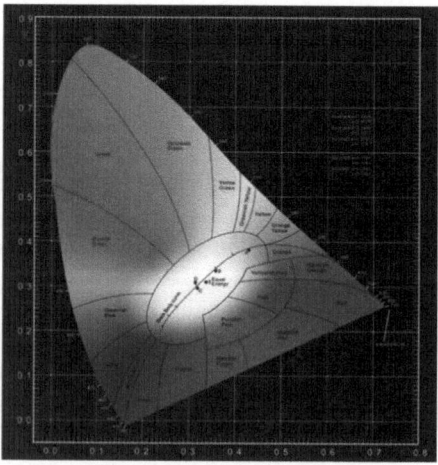

Fig. 1. CIE1931 chromaticity diagram

3 Set up the Mapping Model

In terms of the connection between Colorimetry and Feng Shui, the ancients established a five-color system as early as 2500 years ago, which is the earliest color system in the history of the world. The system is earlier than the Western in that age. In the Han Dynasty, the yin and yang five elements of the theory was prevailed. The theory showed that the color also has the attributes of yin and yang, black and blue belong to water, cyan and green belong to wood, red and purple belong to fire, yellow and brown belong to earth [7]. So, water represent black, metal represent white, fire represent red, wood represent green, earth represent yellow. In Feng Shui, metal, wood, water, fire, and earth are five components of the Five Elements. In the process of seeking the same point between lighting and Feng Shui, color and five elements are used as point of penetration for research.

In the process of searching the center point of the chromaticity map, the standard points A, B, C, D and E are respectively selected to establish the coordinate origin. Firstly, the CIE chromaticity map is established by MATLAB. By inputting the coordinates of 380–780 nm which form the edge of the tongue graph of the chromaticity map, then set up the coordinates on MATLAB. The MATLAB programming are used to select the suitable points in chromaticity diagram for the construction of coordinate system. For example, the point with wavelength 450 nm is set as M point, and the slope k_1, k_2, k_3, k_4, k_5 of the point with standard point A, B, C, D and E are calculated respectively. Secondly, $1/k$ can be used to calculate the corresponding vertical line. Then determine whether the line that M point located and the line perpendicular to it are located at the demarcation point of the color in chromaticity diagram. If so, keep it. If not, discard the result. The keep calculating until the most suitable point is found. The calculation results show that if the point with 492 nm wavelength is set as S point (0.0454, 0.2950) [8], and the slope of the line connecting S point with equal energy white light E point (0.333, 0.333) is k1, then the slope of the line SE (k1) is −0.314; and the point with wavelength of 565 nm is set as P point (0.4087, 0.5896), the slope of the connection between point P and point E, which is the equivalent mixing of white light, is k_2, and the slope of the line PE (k_2) is 3.390; multiplying k_1 and k_2, k_1 multiplying k_2 is −1.06, which means that the two lines nearly vertically, and the most important is that these two lines also located on the color boundary, so that the line segment connecting 490 nm and point E and the line segment connecting 565 nm to point E were set as a new coordinate system, as shown in Fig. 2.

After consulting plenty of literature and analyzing the relevant data, 560 nm is the dividing line between yellow-green and yellow, and 492 nm is the dividing line between blue and blue-green, which is the boundary between water and wood. Therefore, as shown in Fig. 2, the and point S and point P are the boundary points of these two colors, and the point at the 610 nm where the SE extension line intersects the chromaticity diagram, is the boundary line of orange and red, which is the dividing line of earth and fire.

After finding the corresponding wavelength that divide the chromaticity and white with the five rows of wood, water, fire, earth and metal, and place the metal in the central part of the chromaticity diagram, and the chromaticity diagram is based on the

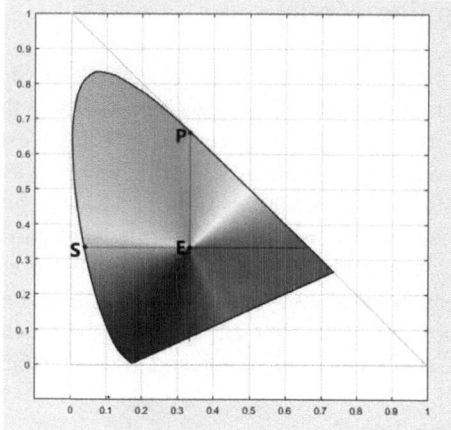

Fig. 2. New coordinate system established on the chromaticity diagram (Color figure online)

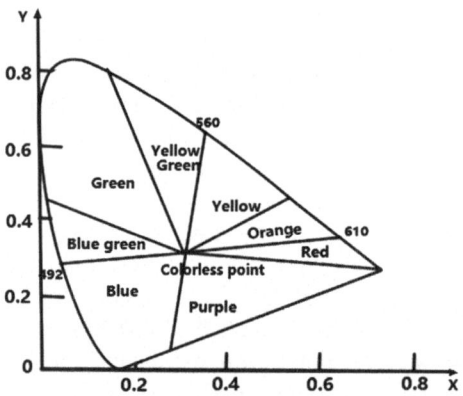

Fig. 3. Chromaticity diagram color block diagram

chromaticity coordinate of point E, and the color is broadly divided into five regions, as shown in Fig. 3, Dividing the chromaticity diagram into five color regions by coloring the same color in the human eye, which are green, blue, red, yellow, and white. It is found that the five elements and five colors can be matched on the chromaticity diagram. It is to say, each color area in the chromaticity diagram has its corresponding five element attribute, and not only the relationship between the five element but also the corresponding colors can also be used. There is a principle of mutual phase, and this theory is intuitively organized into a model map, that is a mapping model of Feng Shui five elements and chromaticity diagram, as shown in Fig. 4.

By analyzing this theory in a more intuitive way, The chromaticity diagram is expanded into a number of all the spectral colors with the same abscissa from 380 nm to 780 nm, and the properties of each wavelength range are marked on the number axis, as shown in Fig. 5.

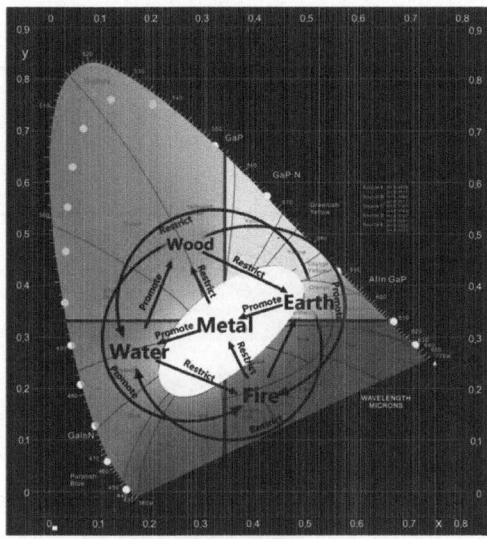

Fig. 4. Mapping model of five lines and chromaticity diagram (Color figure online)

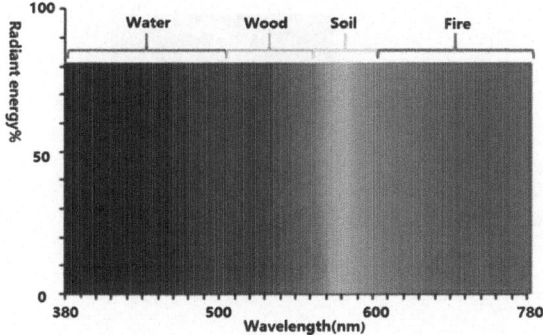

Fig. 5. Corresponding map between the visible bands and the five elements (Color figure online)

4 Set up the Mapping Model

The speculations on the principles of light Feng shui can be applied to indoor and outdoor houses to compensate for the housing owner's fortune or compensate for the lack of a certain line. For example, if a house lacks wood, then we can use the principle of water promote wood [9], to make up for the vacancy of wood energy by increasing the energy of the water in the house. We can choose lamps with higher wavelengths in the spectrum from 450 nm to 500 nm, such as LED lights and so on. Through placing a lamp that can increase energy in a suitable position in the room to compensate for the defects and maintain the balance of the energy field in the room [10], as shown in Table 1.

Table 1. Correspondence table of five elements

Five Elements attribute	Color	Wavelength range	Spectral type	light source
Metal	White	380-780nm		Sun light, D65 light source
Wood	Green	492-554nm		Fluorescent lamp
Water	Blue	380-491nm		LED lamps with a color temperature of 4000k
Fire	Red	611-770nm		Low color temperature LED light
Earth	Yellow	555-610nm		Sodium lamp

5   Example Description

Because the orientation, location, furniture placement and other factors of the house that may have certain impact on the energy field, which due to the lack of energy in a certain space, the energy should be investigated conscientiously. Taking a living room that lack water energy in a house as an example, we create an indoor model and use the light to supplement the energy field. The model of Fig. 6 is based on the lighting design software Dialux Evo.

It is very important to consider the energy of living room, because it is one of the most significant place in our daily life. It is also an important place to meet guests and friends. The feng shui of the living room is related to the fortune of the family. Due to the lack of water energy of this case and according to the correspondence of five elements in Table 1, by using the lamps with higher water energy, the energy field can

Fig. 6. Day view of the living room

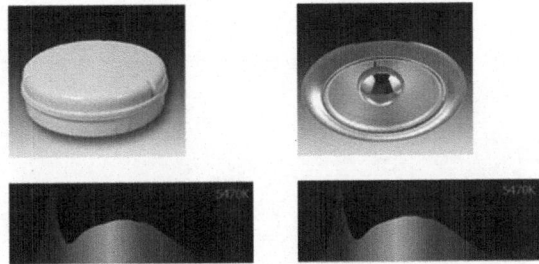

Fig. 7. Selection of room lamps

be adjusted. Therefore, in terms of lamps, select the LED light that spectral peak between 400 and 450 nm can supplement the energy field, as shown in Fig. 7.

The lighting simulation is based on the Dialux evo. Figure 8 shows the simulated night view of the living room. In Dialux evo, the pseudo-color map can also be exported, as shown in Fig. 9.

In the case above, by simulate a space which lack of some energy, in order to reflect the practical application of the mapping model of the five elements and the chromaticity diagram. The corresponding light source is used to supplement the missing energy field of the environment. However, is also need to be adjust according to actual condition.

Fig. 8. Night view of the living room

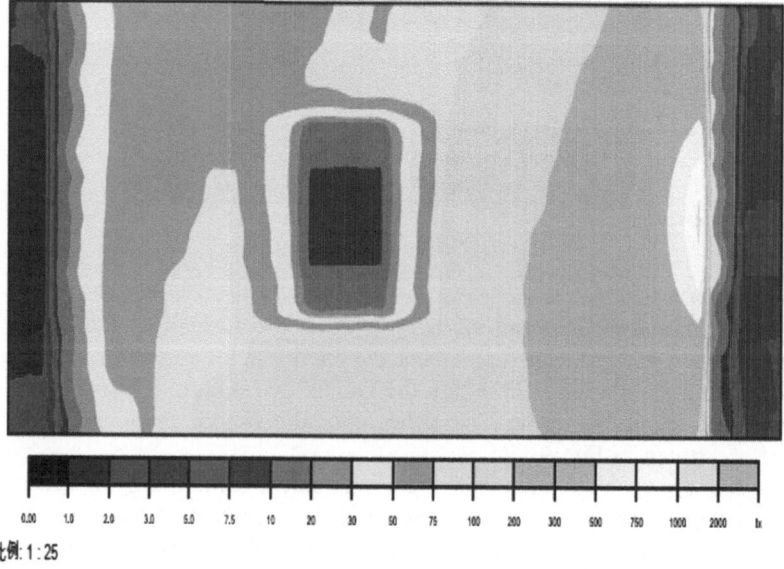

比例: 1 : 25

Fig. 9. Pseudo-color map of meeting room (Color figure online)

6   Conclusion

This study combines the five elements of Fengshui with modern chromaticity diagram theory. By searching for the relationship between these two subject, the five attributes of metal, wood, water, fire and earth and five colors of white, green, blue, red and yellow are mapped. In combination, a mapping model of five elements and chromaticity diagrams can be obtained. This model can be extended to the luminaire products, and the energy of the source spectrum itself can be used to adjust the energy field of indoor and outdoor houses, which is beneficial to the harmony of people and lighting. It is a potential and new application direction. This research is aimed at the exploration between two different subject areas. Therefore, there are still some limitations in mapping analysis and model building, and will continue to expand and improve in the future work.

References

1. Zhang, T.T., Ma, J.W.: Application of Feng Shui in bar environment design. J. Yangtze Univ. (Social Science Edition), **37**(02) (2014). (in Chinese)
2. Hubalek, S., Brink, M., Schierz, C.: Office workers' daily exposure to light and its influence on sleep quality and mood. Lighting Res. Technol. **42**(1), 33–50 (2010)
3. Kim, G., Lim, H.S., Kim, J.T., Kim, T.: Sustainable lighting performance of refurbished glazed walls for old residential buildings. Energy Buildings **91**, 163–169 (2015)
4. Yangv, H.: Lighting and Feng Shui. Lighting Des. **2**, 81–83 (2015). (in Chinese)
5. Li, N.: Color Analysis and Research of Qingdao Architecture (1897∼1914). Shandong University (2008). (in Chinese)
6. Liu, H.W.: Application of Chinese Traditional Feng Shui Culture in Modern Home Interior Design. Hunan Normal University (2009). (in Chinese)
7. Field, S.: The Culture of Fengshui in Korea: an exploration of East Asian geomancy. J. Asian Stud. **67**(1), 333–334 (2008). Available from: Academic Search Premier, Ipswich, MA. Accessed June 2, 2018
8. Li, S.H., Chen, G.: Improving the color temperature of light source by curve fitting formula. Electron. Device, (S1), 106–111 (1995). (in Chinese)
9. Qi, J.H., Zheng, T., Huang J., et al.: Discussion on the new model of Wuxingshengke. Chin. J. Tradit. Chin. Med. (8), 1998–2003 (2012). (in Chinese)
10. Amara, M., Mandorlo, F., Couderc, R., Gerenton, F., Lemiti, M.: Temperature and color management of silicon solar cells for building integrated photovoltaic. EPJ Photovoltaics 1 (2018)

Author Index